School of the Word

CHRISTIANITY AND THE AFRICAN IMAGINATION

STUDIES OF RELIGION
IN AFRICA

SUPPLEMENTS TO THE JOURNAL OF RELIGION IN AFRICA

EDITED BY

ADRIAN HASTINGS (University of Leeds)
PAUL GIFFORD (Society of Oriental and African Studies, London)
MARC R. SPINDLER (University of Leiden)

CHRISTIANITY
AND THE
AFRICAN IMAGINATION

Essays in Honour of Adrian Hastings

EDITED BY

DAVID MAXWELL with INGRID LAWRIE

BRILL

LEIDEN · BOSTON · KÖLN

2002

This book is printed on acid-free paper.

Die Deutsche Bibliothek - CIP-Einheitsaufnahme

Christianity and the African imagination : essays in honour of Adrian Hastings /
ed. by David Maxwell with Ingrid Lawrie. – Leiden ; Boston ; Köln : Brill, 2001
(Studies of religion in Africa ; Vol. 23)
ISBN 90–04–11668–0

Library of Congress Cataloging-in-Publication Data

Library of Congress Cataloging-in-Publication Data is also available

ISSN   0169-9814
ISBN   90 04 11668 0

PRINTED IN THE NETHERLANDS

Adrian Hastings in retirement, November 2000

CONTENTS

ACKNOWLEDGEMENTS

This book grew from a special issue of the *Journal of Religion in Africa*, which marked Adrian Hastings's retirement as Editor. The issue was presented to him at a memorable dinner in Leiden, hosted by Brill Academic Publishers in honour of his fifteen years of work on the *Journal* and in celebration of his seventieth birthday. It was on that occasion that the idea was first mooted of extending the original set of four essays into a larger edited collection. From the outset, two people have been enthusiastic supporters of the project, Anniek Meinders-Durksz at Brill, and Paul Gifford, the new Editor of their *Studies of Religion in Africa* series. We are grateful to Paul for his encouragement and to Anniek for her advice and patience in seeing the book through to completion.

With regard to the production of the book, we owe a large debt of gratitude to Kevin Ward, whose input into several of the essays has been most valuable. The burden of copy-editing has been carried willingly and with unerring attention to detail by Cecily Bennett. Andrew Lawrence at Keele University helped to produce many of the splendid maps and charts, at short notice, and Jeff Dubberley in Leeds gave much-needed technical assistance. Alistair Mason solved bibliographic problems with enthusiasm. We offer our thanks to them all, and to the Department of Theology and Religious Studies at the University of Leeds for a grant towards additional production costs.

We have both learnt an enormous amount about editing from Adrian Hastings and we offer this book to him with gratitude and affection.

*   *   *

Adrian Hastings died on 30 May, 2001. He was aware from the beginning of the plans for this book, and learned with great pleasure, in the last weeks of his illness, that the manuscript had been submitted to the publishers. The editors have decided not to alter the text to take account of his death, and in particular present tenses have been retained in the biographical chapter, 'The Shaping of a Prophet'.

CONTRIBUTORS

Richard Gray is Emeritus Professor of History at the School of Oriental and African Studies, University of London. He has written extensively on African Christianity and has been an editor of the *Journal of African History*. Among his most notable publications is *Black Christians, White Missionaries* (1990).

Samuel Gyanfosu is a Lecturer in Religious Studies at the University of Cape Coast, Ghana. He received his BA at Cape Coast, his MA from the University of Nsukka, Nigeria, and his Ph.D. from Leeds in 1995, under the supervision of Adrian Hastings, on Christian-related independent religious movements in Ghana.

Ingrid Lawrie is Editorial Assistant and Reviews Editor of the *Journal of Religion in Africa*. As Adrian Hastings's secretary in Leeds, she worked on almost all his publications from 1985, and was an Assistant Editor for *A World History of Christianity* (1999), and *The Oxford Companion to Christian Thought* (2000). She is currently writing a biography of Adrian Hastings.

John Lonsdale is a Fellow of Trinity College, Cambridge University and a Reader in African History. He has written widely on Kenya and the Kikuyu, and is the author, with Bruce Berman, of the two-volume history, *Unhappy Valley: Conflict in Kenya and Africa* (1992).

Donald Mackay completed his Aberdeen Ph.D. on Simon Kimbangu (1985), and has published major articles on Kimbanguism in the *Journal of Religion in Africa*. He has been a lecturer in the University of Zimbabwe, a British Academy Research Fellow in the University of Leeds, and he now teaches and writes in Caithness, Scotland.

David Maxwell is a Senior Lecturer in International History at Keele University and teaches widely in the fields of African and Imperial History. He is the Senior Editor of the *Journal of Religion in Africa* and has written *Christians and Chiefs in Zimbabwe: A Social History of the Hwesa People c. 1870s–1990s* (1999). He is currently writing a monograph entitled *African Gifts of the Spirit: Pentecostalism and the Rise of a Zimbabwean Transnational Religious Movement.*

J.D.Y. Peel is Professor of Anthropology and Sociology at the School of Oriental and African Studies, University of London. He is the author of *Aladura: A Religious Movement among the Yoruba* (1968), *Ijeshas and Nigerians: The Incorporation of a Yoruba Kingdom, 1890–1970* (1983) and *Religious Encounter and the Making of the Yoruba* (2000).

Terence Ranger is Emeritus Professor of Race Relations in the University of Oxford. His numerous books include *Peasant Consciousness and Guerrilla War in Zimbabwe* (1985), *Are We Not Also Men? The Samkange Family and African Politics in Zimbabwe 1920–1964* (1995), and *Voices from the Rocks: Nature, Culture and History in the Matopos Hills of Zimbabwe* (1999).

Matthew Schoffeleers is Emeritus Professor of Anthropology at the University of Utrecht, Netherlands. Among his publications are *Guardians of the Land: Essays on Central African Territorial Cults* (edited, 1978), *River of Blood: The Genesis of the Martyr Cult in Southern Malawi, ca. A.D. 1600* (1992), and *In Search of Truth and Justice: Confrontations between Church and State in Malawi 1960–1994* (1999).

John Waliggo gained his Ph.D. in Cambridge in 1976 for a thesis on the Catholic Church in Buddu. He has served on the Uganda Constitutional Commission and the Catholic Justice and Peace Commission. He is currently Professor of History at Uganda Martyrs University as well as being a Uganda Human Rights Commissioner. His books include *A History of African Priests: Katigondo Major Seminary 1911–1986* (1988) and *A Man of Vision: Life and Legacy of Archbishop Joseph Kiwanuka (1899–1966)* (1992). He is a regular contributor to edited collections and journals.

Andrew Walls has lectured in the Universities of Sierra Leone, Nigeria, Aberdeen and Edinburgh, as well as Princeton Theological Seminary and Yale University. He was the founding editor of the *Journal of Religion in Africa* in 1967 and first director of the Centre for the Study of Christianity in the Non-Western World, now based at Edinburgh University. He has written extensively on the Church in Africa and has recently published *The Missionary Movement in Christian History* (1996) and *The Cross-Cultural Process in Christian History* (2001).

Kevin Ward taught for many years at Bishop Tucker Theological College, Uganda, and has been Lecturer in African Religious Studies at the University of Leeds since 1995. With Brian Stanley, he has edited *The Church Mission Society and World Christianity, 1799–1999* (2000). He is a Deputy Editor of the *Journal of Religion in Africa*.

INTRODUCTION

CHRISTIANITY AND THE AFRICAN IMAGINATION

David Maxwell

Adrian Hastings, in the concluding chapter of *A History of African Christianity 1950–1975*, threw down a challenge to scholars working in African Christian studies:

> The archbishops and theological colleges, the schools, the projects for development and ecumenism, the academic theology and international connections, the conferences and the policy statements, the conflicts with government and the co-operation: all these have their considerable importance, and the ecclesiastical historian, like the journalist, will only too willingly provide an account of them. The underlying social history of the church is less easy to write, yet it will still provide the heart of the matter and in its shifts and stresses, its sick areas and new sources of life, it is likely to control the superstructure rather more decisively than the latter can control it.[1]

These final sentences, and indeed the whole chapter itself, which was entitled, 'Between Politics and Prayer', were remarkable in that they were included in the book at all. The study was predominantly about church-state relations mediated by clerical and political elites in an era of decolonization. But Hastings intended the final chapter to act as a foil, a weighty reminder that prayer and not politics was the 'primary concern' of African churches. Moreover, it was at the local base rather than in the ecclesiastic superstructure that the dynamo and real significance of African Christianity lay:

> Its vast amorphous mass of devotion, cult, belief, superstition, new bonds of fellowship so often structured in ways that hardly accord with the rules of Rome, Geneva or Canterbury, may prove the most enduring ecclesiastical legacy of this quarter century. As the effective control of the western churches declines, one has the strong impression that the model of historic Ethiopia increasingly prevails: village Christianity with very little superstructure had been there all along together with much symbolic ritual now making its way right across the continent.[2]

---

[1] Hastings, 1979, p. 274.
[2] Ibid.

In essence Hastings was arguing that 'the heart of the matter' was popular Christianity: the religion of 'people who have little contact with institutional churches, little religious training, and who get their religious information through informal channels'.[3] It is highly syncretic, combining folk beliefs and practices with orthodox Christianity, and lacks intellectual cohesion, but it helps ordinary practitioners come to terms with existential passions and empowers them, through faith, to deal with material concerns for health, wealth and protection against evil. For Hastings, the crucible of African popular Christianity was the village and its agents were the Independent Church prophet, the Protestant evangelist and the Catholic catechist. But whoever the founders, given the pressure from below:

> The result might not be so different in the three cases—a religion combining a strong sense of the one God of judgement and mercy, some personal attachment to Christ, a deep belief in the value of baptism, the use of the Bible as a source of guidance, a sharing in the Christian tradition of prayer and ritual, all combined with a continuing acceptance of much traditional social and religious practice. Village Christianity may tolerantly co-exist with traditional beliefs in spirits and witchcraft or it may desperately challenge the behaviour which follows from them but it lives either way within the world of such things, as mission Christianity does not; yet it tempers them too with another vision which has somehow to attain the mastery from within.[4]

Hastings's assertion of the centrality of village Christianity was not a new revelation for him. It was grounded in his own experience as Catholic priest in Masaka diocese, southern Uganda. 'Popular religion' had been the subject of his previous book, *African Christianity: An Essay in Interpretation*, with its consideration of 'prayer and fasting, ecstasies and angels . . . the power of God and Christ. To save, to heal'.[5] And it was a theme that recurred throughout his subsequent work. The village catechists (and the African Sister) were the heroes of his *African Catholicism*.[6] An intensely Africanist agenda provided both the framework and the content for his *Church in Africa 1450–1950*:

> We can chart the movement of Christianity into the interior of Africa rather easily with reference to European missionaries. We know their names, their backgrounds, the Churches and societies to which they

---

[3] Wilson, 1999, p. 100.
[4] Hastings, 1979, p. 273.
[5] Hastings, 1976, p. 56.
[6] Hastings, 1989.

belonged. . . . We have their journals, their letters home. But the reality of the young Churches was a largely different one and far less easy to chart or to describe. The Christian advance was a black advance or it was nothing. It was one in which ever so many more people were involved but very few of whom we can even name . . . in general the black advance was far more low-key and often entirely unplanned and haphazard.[7]

The desire to chart the black Christian advance in Africa is shared by the contributors to this collection. Their interests are too numerous and varied to constitute a school. But as colleagues, friends, supervisors and students, they have collaborated over the years through conferences, edited collections and research projects, in the reconstruction of the social history of African Christianity (see Lawrie, chapter 11). This volume is intended as part of that ongoing project, to which Hastings has been so central.

The essays revisit old themes and help establish new ones. They represent the shift in focus from institutions to movements at the grass roots, examining critical processes of African adaptation and indigenization of Christianity. They also engage with more recent concerns about the power of texts and narratives and their role in the construction of identities. From first to last, across diverse periods and contexts, they demonstrate how Christianity has captured the African imagination. Richard Gray tells the story of a Kongo princess and Kongo ambassadors, committed to an African Catholic identity, reaching out to Europe to secure its future, and shaping the missionary enterprise in the Kongo for centuries to come.[8] Andrew Walls draws on a rich body of sources to recount the little known episode of Samuel Crowther's encounter with Islam. Reconstructing his sensitive and imaginative dialogue with Muslim leaders, Walls shows how 'Crowther, the African leader of an African Mission . . . developed an African Christian approach to Islam in an African setting'. The first two chapters powerfully disengage Christianity from capitalist imperialism, locating it in an informal mercantile empire

---

[7] Hastings, 1994, pp. 437–438.
[8] Kongo Christianity was first and foremost the religion of the Royal Court. Moreover its elite practitioners were concerned with questions of orthodoxy, even authenticity. In this sense Kongo Christian religion would have fitted better into what James and Johnson describe as 'vernacular Christianity'. Nevertheless, Catholic religious practice did become popular. Gray notes that crowds of 30,000 turned out to greet the Statue of the Virgin Mary when it was brought to Mbanza Kongo. James and Johnson, 1988, pp. vi–viii and pp. 1–12.

where relations with African leaders were more finely balanced and
the triumph of the church was by no means inevitable. John Waliggo's
essay, taken from his much lauded unpublished Ph.D. thesis,[9] reconstructs the first great modern Catholic breakthrough into an African
society, in Buganda in the 1880s and 1890s, at the highpoint of new
imperialism. He examines this movement of mass conversion, explaining its appeal in terms both of its continuity with traditional religion
and of the challenge of something completely new.

The themes of old and new are repeated in chapters by Terence
Ranger, John Lonsdale and Matthew Schoffeleers. These scholars
offer us studies of regions that have been the focus of their research
throughout their lengthy careers. Using the whole range of their
archives, written and oral, they show the full chronological sequence
of religious change, exploring the way in which Christianity, as a
fluid medium, is sensitive to the varied and varying needs of youth,
women, old men and labour migrants, urban and rural dwellers.
Ranger returns to the now famous Makoni district, Manicaland, to
draw together his earlier work on popular forms of mission Christianity
and also to trace its dialectical relation with an emerging Christian
Independency in the 1930s. Lonsdale engages with contemporary
scholarly concern about the power of narrative to show how the
Kikuyu used biblical and theological ideas to help fashion their own
ethnic identity and history. Schoffeleers offers an updated version of
his influential study of religious interactions in Nsanje district in
Malawi's Shire Valley, examining how a sequence of Pentecostal
churches dating from the 1950s have redefined rural social relations
across gender, generation and class, with serious consequences for
all concerned. Peel's paper exhibits the same sensitivity to idiom and
context and the same deep knowledge of a single society, but his
purpose is the inverse of the three previous studies. While they focus
on the fine grain of religious change, Peel shows how Christian ideas
and images are woven into the fabric of Yoruba society. Such is the
extent of their cultural impact that Peel's close reading of the (post-
Christian) writer Wole Soyinka's *Ìsarà* reveals how the thematic of
nationalism was no less religious than it was political or economic.

David Maxwell and Sam Gyanfosu shift the focus from regions
to religious movements that transcend the boundaries of the nation
state. Maxwell describes the rise and evolution of Zimbabwe Assemblies

---

[9] Waliggo, 1976.

of God Africa (ZAOGA), as it expanded from its township base in colonial Salisbury, Southern Rhodesia, into neighbouring nations and beyond. He shows how ZAOGA draws both material and ideological resources from the American dominated global born-again movement, while still retaining local control. The theme of African religious autonomy and African authenticity was one of the objects of the Ghanaian-derived Afrikania movement founded by Vincent Damuah in 1982. Gyanfosu traces Damuah's religious and intellectual formation from his strong Catholic heritage to his rejection of a supposedly westernizing and deculturating Christianity. Damuah's short lived neo-traditionalist religious experiment suggests that he was wrong in his conclusions, but Gyanfosu's analysis of the Afrikania movement raises important questions about issues of inculturation and authenticity. Finally, Ward considers African Christianity as embodied in the life of one man, Archbishop Janani Luwum. Product of the East African revival and Uganda's rich Anglican traditions, Luwum matured into a remarkable Christian leader, murdered by General Idi Amin. While Luwum is widely recognized as a martyr by the church beyond Uganda, he is remembered within Uganda in a more ambiguous way, and Ward examines the reasons for this.

Many of the contributions are grounded in fieldwork, an intense and deeply personal interaction with the 'subjects' of research. Donald Mackay's poems wonderfully evoke the challenges and tensions, joys and moments of revelation that accompany such encounters.

The writers have attempted to link religious developments to wider social, economic and political change. Their search for a more total history, attentive to the religious base as well as the ecclesiastical superstructure, makes it easier for them than for more orthodox church historians to consider the real stuff of popular Christianity: pilgrimage and prayer, healing and exorcism, rain-making and miracle. It is Terence Ranger who has done most to conceptualize and classify the contents of African popular Christianity, and his schema is useful for drawing together the ideas in this collection.[10] His first criterion, the seizing hold of the landscape, is amply demonstrated in his essay: 'The Trappists erected Lourdes Grottoes; the American Methodists organised Revivals and Camp Meetings and thus triggered off the descent of the Holy Spirit on their African agents . . .

---

[10] Ranger, 1985(b), pp. 37–41.

the Anglicans baptized by immersion in Jordan rivers and "took hold
of the land" by turning Christian cemeteries into places of power
and pilgrimage'. All this was initiated by 'symbolically sensitive missionaries'. But his essay finishes at Mazowe hill where 'every September
thousands of Apostles flock to [the prophet's] grave'. Waliggo describes
a similar Catholic seizure of the landscape whereby Kyawangabi hill
in Buddu became the site of regular Marian feasts. But it is clear
that this seizure was initiated by African chiefs who consciously sought
to 'set up a geographical and ceremonial counterpart of the queen
mother at the capital'.

The second of Ranger's criteria is the reliance of missionaries on
African agents who healed, made rain and founded their own Christian
villages. These often unnamed heroes pervade the pages of this collection. They range from the desperately overworked catechists of
Waliggo's paper to the devout Catholic labour migrants and Anglican
teachers of Ranger's study to the 'hot' and irrepressible Pentecostal
labour migrants and evangelists of Schoffeleers's and Maxwell's essays.
Together these men and women convened regular local gatherings
in the absence of missionaries and worked out particularly localized
versions of the faith. And it was these agents who were often the
first to adopt Christian symbols and powers and Christian literacy
because they had 'practical utility in relating to the colonial economy': the third of Ranger's criteria. Thus Waliggo recounts the uses
made of rosaries and medals:

> They became medicine for headaches and fevers . . . weapons to ter-
> rify lions and leopards on the way to church . . . articles to ward off
> evil charms . . . Medals and rosaries, as well as blessed palms, were
> thrown into the courtyard or placed on the threshold to stop thun-
> derstorms, tempests and hailstones. They were also used to secure good
> harvest, for good luck in general and to help barren women conceive.

Likewise the Bible could be put to non-literary uses. Walls describes
how Christians in Sierra Leone used its pages as a prophylactic, a
protective charm, to ward off evil spirits. Christian ideas were also
important in class formation. Manyika American Methodism with its
strong emphasis on the 'gospel of the plough' helped make peasant
entrepreneurs. Similarly in Malawi's Shire Valley, Pentecostalism
helped young men break away from the demands of traditional commensality and set themselves apart as accumulators.

However, African popular Christianity was by no means purely
instrumental. African Christians were motivated by a genuine pious
urge, a sincere desire to act decisively on their beliefs. Gray's essay
reveals how Kongo Christians responded with a spontaneous and
enduring enthusiasm to the Portuguese proclamation of the gospel,
which they strove to preserve for the next three centuries. It was
that same love of Catholic traditions that led the labour migrant
Patrick Kwesha to persevere within the Catholic Church in twentieth-
century Manicaland in very trying circumstances. Others were driven
by a strong desire to spread the gospel. It led Samuel Crowther into
patient dialogue with his Muslim interlocutors and pushed Johane
Masowe to break free from missionary control and found his own
movement with a message for 'ALL NATIONS'. Several decades
later Masowe's Pentecostal cousins in ZAOGA, fired by the Holy
Spirit and an 'Adventist zeal', journeyed far beyond the borders of
Zimbabwe, and subsequently beyond the continent, in 'relentless
proselytism'. In putting the Kingdom of God before the Kingdom
of Man, martyrs like Janani Luwum surely reach the height of religious devotion. It was prayer that gave Luwum 'the divine calm to
face Idi Amin',[11] and it is this type of confrontation that Hastings
reads as 'evidence of religion's quick crossing of the frontier, from
a European and imperial world to an independently African one'.[12]

While these examples of popular Christianity are syncretistic they
are not so in the pejorative sense of being a confused mixture of
Christian and traditional ideas and practices. They are syncretistic
in the sense that all traditions, religious or otherwise, are 'bastard',
formed out of the gamut of processes involved in culture contact.[13]
African Christian leaders and practitioners borrowed from traditional
culture and religion but their appropriations were re-coded when
located within a Christian system of ideas, and thus took on a new
form and significance which had great appeal.

The success of new forms of popular Christianity lay in both their
continuity and discontinuity with what had gone before. Waliggo
reveals how Marian devotion found force through its association with
the figure of the queen mother, while similar notions of royalty helped
the Baganda encounter God the Father. Moreover medals and rosaries

---

[11] Hastings, 1979, p. 266.
[12] Hastings, 1989, p. 8.
[13] Maxwell, 2001 and Shaw & Stewart, 1994.

proved so efficacious because they were Christian versions of traditional charms and other magical substances. Elsewhere the Holy Spirit could undercut ancestral cults in Zimbabwe or female possession cults in Malawi while standing in their trajectory.

But rupture, or what Lonsdale calls rebellion, was an equally important element in Christian conversion. Christianity brought many new and powerful ideas: sin and hell, judgement and redemption. It introduced Africans to Christ and Mary, who, as we have seen, demanded unwavering devotion. African cultures were open and plural and religious leaders did not order knowledge systems like European imperialists who were obsessed with notions of evolution and hierarchy. It was often the 'ideas men and women', the diviners, shrine priests and spirit mediums, who were first to embrace these new conceptions of the High God and sources of empowerment.[14] New 'personally compelling' ideas also often 'harnessed the energy of generational conflict' not only amongst Lonsdale's Kikuyu but also across the continent. Young men could object to their religious exclusion by elders from ancestor veneration, or their resentment might be more materially motivated: lack of access to women, the appropriation of their hard-earned wages in the migrant labour economy, their general low status. But, whatever their grievance, the language of conversion—'coming forward', 'setting yourself apart'— provided 'legitimate grounds for denying formerly legitimate obligations'.[15] Thus, Schoffeleers and Ranger also show young Christian men, and later women, turning their backs on the religious and social practices of male gerontocratic culture: ancestor veneration, beer and polygamy. But it is women whose central role in the church has been 'the most discontinuous in the relationship to the pattern of African society'. Female religious orders, with at least five times more members than their male counterparts, with an aspiration for celibacy and separation stretching back to Gray's unnamed Kongo princess, must surely be the epitome of that discontinuity.[16]

It is within this spectrum of popular Christianities that Christian Independency should be located. Here Ranger and Hastings have shared an important goal of narrowing the gap between so-called

---

[14] Elizabeth Isichei provides a fascinating example of a West African convert, a former traditional leader, whose life was profoundly affected by a sermon on Hell, 1995, p. 173.

[15] Fields, 1985, pp. 41 and 46.

[16] Hastings, 1989, p. 14.

African Independent movements and mission-derived churches by stressing the missionary roots of the former and the functional equivalence of the prophet, catechist and evangelist in the village melting pot.[17] Thus Ranger's essay demonstrates how in the Great Depression, when the missionary project contracted and the virtues of biomedicine and education became tarnished, the Independent Church prophet took on 'the missionary's task because it seemed so important'.

Christian Independency, particularly the Zionist or Spirit-type churches of Southern and West Africa, also fits well into the model of continuity and discontinuity. There is continuity in the material of 'religious culture' carried across from traditional religious practices: 'the type of melody, the hand-clapping, the ecstatic dancing, the appeal to visions, the interpretation of dreams'.[18] There is often (with some exceptions, such as the Kimbanguist Church) continuity in purity laws, food taboos, leadership styles, and polygamy.[19] But there is also radical discontinuity. Ancestor religion is forcefully rejected: 'Christ alone saves by the power of God'.[20] And African Christian prophets, like contemporary Pentecostals, are extremely intolerant of traditional religious practices 'and have at times adopted a more vigorously hostile line to "fetishes", shrines and "pagan" worship than missionaries themselves'.[21]

Such revelations about the disruptive nature of Independency are unwelcome to numerous African university theologians, who have tended to advance it as a model of authentic African Christianity. Theirs is a different project of the development of an African theology that seeks the 'authenticity of continuity', first and foremost the continuity of God.[22] While this theology has established the significance of pre-Christian African monotheism, the enduring and filial relationship with one's ancestors, and the ethic of community,[23] it is nevertheless somewhat a-historical.[24] It ignores the significance of the centuries-long process of African reception and adaptation of

---

[17] Hastings, 1976, chapters 3 and 4; 1979, chapter 5; 1994, chapter 11.
[18] Hastings, 1976, pp. 54–55.
[19] For a study of the external missionary influences acting on Independency see Maxwell 1999(b).
[20] Hastings, 1976, p. 55.
[21] Ibid., p. 9.
[22] Ibid., p. 52.
[23] Ibid.
[24] Hastings, 1989, p. 27.

missionary Christianity, asserting that it is still alien.[25] These 'cul-
ture-preoccupied' theologians need to be situated in a 'wider African
cultural renaissance, literary and historical, of the post-independence
years'.[26] The renaissance itself was rooted in the cultural nationalist
period which preceded it, which Peel describes as a time in which
'the values, symbols and idioms of traditional religion tended to be
revived in a nationalist discourse as the highest expression of the
soul of the people'. Like many of the latest generation of colonial
discourse theorists, the majority of contemporary Africa's most prominent theologians live in the west and remain obsessed with the affronts
of cultural imperialism rather than more weighty issues of class and
capital, and more pressing questions of material deprivation.[27]

This is the intellectual context in which Vincent Damuah's Afrikania
movement needs to be located. Damuah came of age during Ghana's
nationalist period but his education, like that of so many African
theologians, took place mainly in the USA. Thus his western intellectual formation was just as important as his African experience
in shaping the content of the Afrikania movement. Ideas from the
black power movement, eastern and ancient religions, the theology
of Vatican II, were combined with more local ideas from Ghanaian
religions to form the heavily constructed pastiche that became Afrikania. Like other neo-traditional inventions, such as the Association
of Concheros in Central Mexico, Damuah's new religion appealed
mostly to researchers and a few literate elites.[28] It made most sense
at international conferences on world religions and failed to appeal
to Ghanaian youth. The latter preferred the growing 'Christian Neo-
Pentecostalist or Charismatic Churches', doubtless because, to borrow Schoffeleers's analysis from the Malawian context, this type of
Christianity 'directs itself at problems which are of immediate relevance to the faithful, such as spirit afflictions amongst the women
and drunkenness amongst the men'. While Damuah condemned
Christianity as alien and alienating, most Ghanaians did not see it

---

[25] Hastings first made these criticisms of African theology in 1976 but repeated
them in 1989, arguing that African theology was stuck in a rut, continuously recy-
cling the work of Mbiti or Idowu, p. 31. Etherington came to similar conclusions
in his 1996 review.
[26] Hastings, 1989, p. 27.
[27] On colonial discourse theory see Washbrook, 1999, p. 608. On culture obses-
sion see Hastings, 1989, p. 31 and Isichei, 1995, p. 331.
[28] The Concheros fuse Catholicism with a blend of national religious traditions
from peoples such as the Aztecs and the Chichemecas. Rostas, 1993.

that way. For them, as for many of the African Christians in these essays, Christianity was 'popular'. It helped them encounter the divine, and understand and make the best of the world around them.

It is clear that the story of the encounter between Christianity and African traditional religion is often full of ironic twists. It is apparent from Ranger's essay that he prefers the older unreflexive and ethnocentric pioneering missionaries to the younger professionals of the 1930s. The former brought Lourdes Grottos, and outdoor baptisms wholesale from the west. But in a serendipitous way the strategies worked, as one imported rural localism merged with another, mediated by African agents. Ranger comments that these missionary initiatives did not look 'proper to later theorists of inculturation' but inculturationists have often got it wrong. Sometimes their 'top-down' programmes have met with indifference from the 'bottom-up'.[29] At others they have been met with resistance. As recent studies on Anglicanism and Catholicism in Tanzania have shown:

> The Christian traditions of the nineteenth century missionaries are now so deeply incorporated in the devotions of the faithful that many Anglicans, like many Catholics, strenuously object to pluralist measures imposed to indigenise and Africanise the liturgy; above all, the Mass. The introduced orthodoxy of the past has the appeal of popular religion of the present.[30]

In this context *indigenous* or *local* is not interpreted by the recipients of inculturation as a reflection of popular aspiration but as *marginality*. It has long been the aspiration of African Christians to belong to something bigger, to be part of something that counts. This desire led Catholics living in the sixteenth-century Kingdom of Kongo to reach out to Rome. The same longing draws millions of young Africans, disillusioned with fading nation-states, to join city mega-churches and become part of the global born-again movement. Maxwell's case-study shows that, while individual movements have their own particular agendas, their propensity to attach the label 'International' to their name or bedeck their conference centres with foreign flags points to the appeal of the global. Maxwell also highlights the final irony in the inculturation debate. Although academic social scientists have long dispensed with the notion of authenticity, religious and secular NGOs have adopted it as their new sacred cow.

---

[29] Maxwell, 1999(a), chapters 3 and 4.
[30] Werbner, 1997, p. 314, citing Clayton, 1993 and Green, 1992.

He shows how Pentecostal movements like ZAOGA with little concern to protect 'indigenous cultures' play up their authentic credentials in pursuit of resources from the West.

None of this should suggest, however, the demise of African traditional religion, which despite its problematic label[31] is just as dynamic
and plural as Christianity. The causes of Mau Mau are complex but
Lonsdale highlights how one of the reasons for its emergence was
the failure of missionary Christianity to deal with social inequality
and the occult power associated with it: 'Mau Mau oaths did not
so much oppose Christianity as supplement it in a magical field that
missionaries could not enter.' In the earlier 1985 version of his paper
Schoffeleers suggested Mbona was in its last days. But a decade or
two of inaction is too short a period to write off the poly-faceted
cult with a centuries long tradition of innovation. In this version of
his paper he is able to report that by 1997 the cult and the shrine
were once again functioning normally.[32] Even Pentecostal zealots are
not enough to see off Mbona. But where African traditional religion
often finds most force in contemporary Africa is as an 'expression
of communal and ethnic identity'[33] against some threatening 'other'.
Both Jerry Rawlings and Vincent Damuah had much to gain from
their alliance. While Damuah legitimated Rawlings's regime with the
rhetoric of African particularism and cultural renewal, he received
resources, significantly the media, in return. And it is clear that the
two leaders shared ideological goals. Damuah's notion of a mono-
lithic African culture and his search for a unitary religion reflect
the homogenizing and engrossing character of African nationalism.[34]
The Church of Ancestors in Malawi sought a similar symbiotic relationship with the Ruling Party, imitating its organizational structures
and adopting nationalist symbols and ideas. The movement achieved
a limited success because, unlike Afrikania, it *did* have a local leadership and a local constituency. Yet this success was the reason why
the Malawi Congress Party (MCP) paid it little heed. Restricted as
it was to illiterate peasants, who were often also aged men, it was
never going to challenge the state. Given Malawi's rich Christian

---

[31] While 'traditional' suggests a static and closed character the alternative labels—
'indigenous', 'local', 'African'—are more problematic, given that these essays show
that Christianity can be all of these things.
[32] Schoffeleers, fn. 88.
[33] Peel, 1994, p. 163.
[34] For another example see Moyo, 1985. For the critique see Ranger, 1985(a).

heritage the MCP was shrewd enough to ignore it. A decade and a half later Zambia's Kenneth Kaunda publicly dabbled in non-Christian religions to his peril.[35]

Indeed the significant extent of the Christianization of the African imagination means that, while African traditional religion remains, it is nevertheless transformed. Although antagonistic toward Christianity, it is striking how reliant the Afrikania movement was on Christian ideas and practices. Likewise, it is remarkable that although the Shire Valley ancestral group wanted to 'spit at Jesus' it still called itself a 'Church'. Moreover its anti-Christian rallies began with sermons taken from biblical texts. Yet this is not unexpected, given Schoffeleers's observation that 'The very fact that thousands had for a longer or shorter period been exposed to Bible and Catechism resulted in Christian ideas and symbols being directly or indirectly transmitted to practically the entire population, including those who had never gone to school or church'. The same is true elsewhere in Africa. Peel tells us that although the Nigerian Soyinka has 'personally left Christianity behind', the Bible nevertheless contributes to the pool of religious ideas that 'saturate' Ìsarà.

The Bible appears again and again in this collection as the pre-eminent African text. Amidst the cultural diversity of so many African states it provides what Schoffeleers describes as a 'major unifying symbol'. Mediated by priests, catechists and evangelists who were often seen to embody the spirit of modernity, or by hot young men and women, empowered by the Holy Spirit if not by learning, its authority was immense and its effects numerous and diverse. But Africa has received not one but many Bibles, in European languages and vernaculars, in both literate and non-literate societies. In West Africa, Muslims were already familiar with many of the Hebrew scriptures and Walls demonstrates Bishop Crowther's use of this 'common ground at the nexus of Qur'an and Bible' to stage a remarkable African Christian dialogue with Islam. In the late nineteenth century Crowther had already identified the emerging African Christianity as 'Biblicist in character'. Maxwell tells us how nearly a century later in 1963 the Zimbabwean born-again prophet Ezekiel Guti had the revelation that he should preach in English. The decision ensured the success of his transnational movement. His prophetic

---

[35] Gifford, 1998, chapter 5.

forerunner, Johane Masowe, had operated in the 'sacred language' of ChiShona,[36] but ZAOGA's use of English meant that it was able to establish connections well beyond its African neighbours and their diaspora. English scriptures helped Guti and his friends assert a bond of brotherhood and a shared sense of mission with North American and European Christians and, because of that, resources flowed into their Zimbabwean-based movement.

But the Bible was most potent in the vernacular. As Lonsdale observes 'it tells the same stories, with all their teleological possibilities, in all the main vernaculars. It shapes both popular and educated minds'. It fuelled the African imagination by providing that rich body of new ideas about Heaven and Hell, God and Judgement, Jesus and the Holy Spirit that so exercised the first generation of converts. It made available a rich corpus for the founders of Christian Independency. Ranger tells how, in Zimbabwe, the great Apostolic movements of Maranke and Masowe, characterized by their 'eschatological biblicism', grew in the fertile soil of popular Methodism with its strong emphasis on equipping the believer with the translated word.[37] Outside the sterile environment of the mission school, imaginative Zimbabwean prophets mined the Scriptures for legitimating charters for what were to become great transnational movements.[38] Likewise, in Kenya, the publication of the Gikuyu New Testament in 1926 spurred revival and later 'gave birth to a totally different Christianity, embodied in the earliest "praying" or *akurinu* church'.

For social and cultural historians the Bible has been attributed far more significance than as simply a source of revelation. It has come to be seen as crucial to the formation of ethnic identities, itself a theme of Hastings's recent study *The Construction of Nationhood: Ethnicity, Religion and Nationalism*.[39] Lonsdale explores how in Kenya scripture provided a massive ideological input into the 'discursive arena' of 'moral ethnicity' in which Kikuyu sought to understand and define themselves.[40] In particular he shows how the Kikuyu have read the Bible as 'an allegory of their own history—a story of servitude and salvation, exile and return'. Thus in the early stages of their strug-

---

[36] Dillon-Malone, 1978, p. 116.
[37] See also Ranger, 1995, chapter 1.
[38] Dillon-Malone, 1978, appendices.
[39] Hastings, 1997.
[40] Lonsdale, 1996, p. 18.

gle to forge an ethnic nationalist consciousness, on the eve of the
Mau Mau emergency, they embraced the Exodus story, likening themselves to the Children of Israel and the British to Pharaoh's Egyptians.
The force of such a comparison was grounded in the publication of
the Gikuyu Old Testament in 1951.

The appearance of the Gikuyu Old Testament should also alert
scholars to the issue of which *portion* of the Bible was translated and
when. Missionary biblical translations took a long time to complete
and sometimes were never finished. Certain books, Revelation for
example, were delayed and had a great impact when they were eventually completed.[41] Thus, in some regions, particularly Catholic ones
such as Hastings's own Masaka diocese in Buganda, where the vernacular Bible never arrived, attention must be paid to the content
and influence of the catechism.[42] It is a well-established fact that
where the Bible remained in English, in the hands of authoritarian
priests, the chances of Independency were far more limited.

Lonsdale's paper takes the discussion of the Bible one stage further, showing how scripture was used as a 'primer in communal
responsibility', influencing popular and elite discourses on Kenyan
politics. And here its effect has been as varied as the scriptural canon
itself. It turns members of conservative evangelical, mission-derived
and Independent churches into loyal supporters of the state, which
is 'a divinely sanctioned authority, as Paul reminded the Romans'.
Conversely more mainstream church leaders, such as Anglican
Archbishop David Gitari, draw from the Old Testament prophets
and the 'terminal tumult' of Revelation 'to authorize their critique
of state power'. And here Lonsdale offers valuable insight into why
the Bible can carry such enormous weight as moral reproof by
reminding us how much Africans were creatively involved in the
translation process: 'Kikuyu . . . have long quarried the Bible for comment on justice and peace, but it is important to remember that in
the creative task of Bible translation they first put their own images
into its word'.

If Christianity was central to the creation of tribes it was even
more complicit in the making of African nations, as Peel explains:
'it promoted the idea that ethno-linguistic units were natural or God-
given, polities in *posse*; through Bible translation it standardized the

---

[41] Ranger, 1999. See also West and Dube, 2000.
[42] Hastings, 1989, pp. 73 and 74 and chapter 7.

languages which gave them voice; through education it produced the
nationalists'. Yet the church often sat uneasily alongside the first generation of Independent Africa's leaders who were jealous of their
newly won powers. In the late 1970s Hastings already perceived the
importance of the mainline churches as 'the one recognisable alternative' to the growing authority of one-party and military states, and
the importance of church leaders such as Malula, Zoa and Luwum
in providing 'the only alternative personality with continuing national
significance to that of the current president'.[43] He also highlighted
the personal danger that faced such church figures and Ward's essay
reminds us of the cost of Luwum's opposition to Idi Amin.

The church's role as an important counter-balance to the African
state pre-figured its significant contribution to the 'Second African
Revolution' or democratization movement which flourished at the
end of the 1980s when a number of one-party states were swept
away to be replaced by multi-party democracies. Even though the
political reforms from this second revolution were often short lived,
most African politicians today would not be foolish enough to kill
an outspoken cleric. In the 1960s and 1970s the continent had not
yet experienced deep socio-economic malaise and African leaders
were more secure in their command of their state's resources (more
substantial in that era) and in their developmentalist goals. But at
the turn of the twenty-first century the African state needs the church
more than the church needs the state. And its politicians do not just
want the church for its body: that rich array of health and educational institutions.[44] In this post-socialist, post-nationalist period, what
they need most are sources of legitimation.[45] This explains why the
Kenyan President, Daniel arap Moi, has an intimate liaison with
evangelical churches, and the otherwise staunchly atheistic President
of Zimbabwe, Robert Mugabe, has aided ZAOGA's transnational
expansion and turned a blind eye to the previously restricted crusading activities of American born-agains.[46]

The mention of American born-agains highlights one of the most
noteworthy things about this collection: its revision of the missionary contribution to the dissemination of Christian ideas and practices.

[43] Hastings, 1979, p. 263.
[44] Gifford, 1998.
[45] Ranger, 1999.
[46] Maxwell, 2000.

All the contributors share Norman Etherington's recent observation that 'the most important mental transformations occurred far away from missionary eyes'.[47] Maxwell's contribution is admittedly about missionaries but they are African Pentecostals who are consciously 'taking on the missionary's task'. The shift in focus is powerfully illustrated in Peel's discussion of Soyinka's *Ìsarà*, where missionaries remain in the background as the significant other. Peel notes how missionaries are represented and contained within the images of the past that Africans on both sides of the divide continued to have but they are now one stage further removed from him as historian of the Yoruba. While few missionaries are mentioned by name in this collection, a humble but industrious Malawian labour migrant, J.P. Chitakata, appears in both Maxwell's narrative and Schoffeleers's footnotes. Scholarship has indeed moved a long way from Groves's *The Planting of Christianity in Africa* of forty and more years ago, which recorded the advance of the Christian faith in terms of institution-building by predominantly male missionaries.[48]

Perhaps the pendulum has swung too far in the opposite direction. African Christian studies do need more work on individual missionaries. Not more hagiographies of bold Christians fellows bringing the light of the gospel and civilization to the back of beyond; nor more academic studies of nineteenth-century pioneers, who generally failed in attempts at mass conversion, and twentieth-century liberals whose advocacy of African rights makes the history of imperialism a little more savoury than otherwise. What are needed are studies of run-of-the-mill, unreconstructed, twentieth-century missionaries whose lives coincided with the Christianization of the continent. The importance of these men and women does not lie in the work of conversion as was often assumed. Those missionaries whose 'service' coincided with movements of mass conversion, as in late nineteenth-century Buganda or early twentieth-century Manicaland, realized that they were privy to something remarkable, and their letters and missionary journals described these modern-day Acts of the Apostles with much animation. But, reading through their triumphalistic accounts of these moments of founding of popular Christianity, it is clear that they had little control over what was going on around

---

[47] Etherington, 1996, p. 217.
[48] Groves, 1948–58.

them.[49] Their significance lies in other, sometimes unintended, areas: in their work on translation, literacy and the creation of ethnicity; in their redefinition of gender relations and making of class through inculcating ideas of domesticity and respectability; in the formation of post-colonial elites through education, in healthcare; in popularizing Africa through tracts, journals, photography, poetry and painting.

However, before scholars assume that missionaries have had their day, both Maxwell and Lonsdale raise the spectre of a new impetus from American born-again missionaries. Lonsdale writes: 'In the 1990s Kenya had 1,300 of them, an astounding figure, twice as many as any other African country, and a second missionization none would have foretold in 1963'. Although this missionization is particularly pronounced in Kenya, doubtless because of its favourable climate and former status as a developed white-settler colony, the explosion of born-again Christianity, to which it is inextricably linked, has occurred with force in numerous other parts of the continent such as South Africa, Zambia, Ghana, Nigeria, and of course Zimbabwe. It is, in fact, a global movement which first broke in Latin America in the 1960s and then in Asia and Africa in the late 1970s and 1980s. Thus, as Maxwell's and Lonsdale's essays suggest, Africa's contemporary Christian landscape looks very different from the mainline missionary-dominated world of a century ago. And it barely resembles the ecclesiastical scene of only three decades ago when African Independent churches appeared to be in the ascendant.[50] Indeed, in states like Kenya and Zimbabwe born-agains are so numerous and their leaders so influential that they are just as mainstream or established as Anglicans or Catholics.

Although Lonsdale attributes Kenya's born-again explosion to a second wave of missionization, it could be argued that it is more simply the latest permutation of a century-long *third* wave of missionary activity and African response. The broad outlines of this third wave are suggested within a number of the papers but it is worth sketching its history in more detail. Its antecedents lay in the profusion of Holiness and Faith Missions, which entered Africa at the end of the

---

[49] Hastings, 1994, pp. 437–78.
[50] Hastings did not note the rise of the born-again movement in his 1976 and 1979 studies. He was doubtless too close to the event. He did, later, begin to grasp its significance through the undergraduate essays and projects submitted by his students when he was teaching at the University of Zimbabwe. Some of these projects are now in my possession. The movements he describes as a 'new independency' are in fact self-consciously 'born-again'. See 1989, p. 33.

nineteenth century, and whose strands, along with revivalist tendencies, came together in the first decade of the twentieth century
to create Pentecostalism. By the 1910s independent western Pentecostal
missionaries were at work in Africa driven on by the movement's
Adventist zeal. A decade later they were followed by missionaries from
the earliest denominations in America, Canada, Sweden, Norway and
Britain. This missionary Pentecostalism often combined with revivalist tendencies in mainline Christianity to stimulate the rise of Zionist
or spirit-type Independent churches, a symbiosis that created the
Maranke and Masowe movements in Zimbabwe. On the whole the
missionary-derived Pentecostal denominations of the Assemblies of
God type remained relatively small and were often carried forward
by labour migrants and semi-independent African evangelists as described by Maxwell and Schoffeleers. But new missionary Pentecostal
and evangelical movements continued to arrive, connecting with established African churches, to form that rich tapestry of Pentecostalism
which emerged in Malawi's Shire Valley and Zimbabwe's and Kenya's
major towns and cities between 1950 and 1980.

Lonsdale's and Maxwell's essays do suggest, however, a qualitative
difference within the predominantly urban strands of contemporary
born-again Christianity. It often casts itself as interdenominational
and global in character. It has a tendency to produce oligarchic governments and is sympathetic to authoritarian politicians. It has
embraced media technologies, particularly the electronic media and
religious broadcasting, with great zeal. It has adopted the faith gospel,
drawing from the teachings of Oral Roberts, T.L. Osborn, Kenneth
Hagin and Kenneth Copeland to argue that material success is a
sign of faith and of God's blessing. And its African leaders are particularly susceptible to the tools and values of modernity, especially
the values of liberal capitalism. Indeed it is this desire to be associated with modernity that causes many born-agains to play down
their very real historic links with Christian Independency, and this
raises the important question of whether Africa's born-again movement is a manifestation of American imperialism.

While the field of scholars working on contemporary African
Christianity still has to explore this matter, these essays offer an historical perspective on some of the issues involved. Pentecostalism
does have a great propensity to localize itself. In its reliance on lay
initiative it is no different from, for example, American Methodism
or village Catholicism. Yet its relatively shallow historical roots, its
lack of tradition, its scorn for formal theological education, and its

dominant emphasis on gifts of the Spirit make it particularly responsive to quotidian struggles.

Today the religious media are very different, the mobile video
parlour has replaced the magic lantern and the flannel-graph as a
most effective medium. Millions in Africa, and billions beyond, have
seen the Campus Crusade for Christ *Jesus* film, which is moving and
reasonably accurate, but sadly portrays a messiah who looks more
like a Swedish hippie than a first-century Jew.[51] In rural townships
(and Kenyan taxicabs) the radio is constantly on, pouring out gospel
music. Cash-strapped national broadcasting companies buy subsi-
dized American tele-evangelism, like the prolific 700 Club, beaming
it into front rooms in townships and suburbs where the television is
rarely switched off. Yet, as Maxwell's essay demonstrates, the electronic technologies involved could be put to very specific local uses
in identity construction.

With regard to models of authority and government, it is clear
from Maxwell's and Ranger's essays that religious movements evolve,
driven by internal and external motors, bringing often-dramatic
changes from one generation to another. Sometimes ageing can have
a detrimental effect. Accounting for the loss of the initial Christian
impetus in Manicaland, Ranger writes: 'By the 1930s the bright
young men—and women—who had been the makers of the first
Christian Movement had become elders and were seen as repressive
of their juniors'. Such elders often appropriate and reproduce patterns of gerontocracy present in wider society, thus dampening their
earlier egalitarian tendencies. Nevertheless, Christianity *has* changed
cultures and individuals in more positive ways. It can pick up democratic and progressive tendencies from society just as easily as authoritarian ones. Ward stresses the importance of the East African Revival
in Archbishop Luwum's formation. And Maxwell points to the influence of nationalism on ZAOGA's drive for autonomy.

Given the trajectories of Wesleyan Methodism, or for that matter
American Methodism, it is perhaps too early to draw conclusions about
the cultural and political impact of the born-again movement. Masowe-
style Independency already looks very different from its birth two
generations ago. Although it still cultivates an authentic persona to
appeal to western donors, it has nevertheless embraced 'development',

---

[51] The film is produced by Campus Crusade for Christ who record that approximately four billion people worldwide have seen the film. *WWW.jesusfilm.org/update/
statistics.html*.

theological education and western ecological concerns.[52] The virulent brand of Protestantism described by Lonsdale is still close to its North American sources. At present it may appear 'utterly foreign' but it might look more savoury in several decades' time, given the redeeming power of the Kikuyu imagination. Its current strong emphasis on 'gluttonous prosperity'[53] is very different again from the Mozambican brand described by Maxwell, whose informant survived the travails of Frelimo and RENAMO sustained by little more than the inspiration of the Psalms: a theology of hope, action and endurance. It is different again from the slick electronic religion of his Zimbabwean overlords.

Some more prosperous African born-agains in Kenya, Zimbabwe and elsewhere have embraced the tools and some of the values of modernity. But, for most, Pentecostalism helps them come to terms with their marginalization from it. Suburban, socially mobile African born-agains may be fixated with prosperity but most of their urban and rural brethren are more concerned with security. While the recent anthropological concern to locate religious manifestations in relation to modernity, or modernities, is illuminating the born-again explosion, like other prior expressions of Christianity it is about many other 'traditional' [sic] things: the usual existential passions for purity, healing, empowerment and meaning.[54]

As the born-again explosion reverberates throughout African societies it is tempered by a religious field so much more complex than a century ago. The historic churches remain enormously influential, still staffed by expatriate missionaries who work in tandem with and usually under the authority of African clerics. Their contribution to health and education is immense, though supplemented by the state sector. Added to these institutions is the huge range of NGOs, religious and secular, local and international, staffed by a floating cohort of development workers, African and Western. And at their disposal is a wealth of ideologies and knowledge systems: Marxism-Leninism, liberal capitalism, nationalism, and the range of Christian theologies. While the latest wave of US missionaries formulate their programmes of mass evangelism, evangelism by the African masses continues unabated. This is also more complex and more dynamic than ever. The range of locations has expanded to include the township and

---

[52] Daneel, 1989. On Independency more generally see Hastings, 1994, pp. 525–27.
[53] Isichei, 1995, p. 312.
[54] For a useful review of literature on religion and modernity see Englund and Leach, 2000.

the black middle-class suburb, alongside the village. And enhanced
communication and social mobility has swollen the ranks of the pros-
elytizers from labour migrants, catechists and evangelists to include
nurses and teachers and civil servants on placement, returning students, often accompanied by their Christian Union or Scripture
Union brethren, and urban churches on 'crusade' determined to
establish rural branches. Added to this low-level, face-to-face form
of evangelism is church planting by the enormous transnational traffic
in refugees across so many parts of the continent. And born-again
Americans are not the only new missionaries. An impetus arises from
the south. Brazilian Baptists are at work in Mozambique and the
contentious Universal Church of the Kingdom of God has established itself throughout Southern Africa. The African vision too has
extended beyond the continent. Highflying African born-again executives, like Ezekiel Guti, itinerate American and European preaching and healing circuits, often visiting 'international' branches of their
movements founded by their diaspora. And pastors and priests from
the historic churches participate in western mission through diocesan twinning programmes.

   Whatever the effects of the latest wave of missionization, and its
relation to American imperialism, it is clear that scholars have much
to learn from the debate about the relation between Christianity,
Capitalism and formal Empire, a theme that runs throughout these
essays. Again and again we see processes of localization, seizure and
manipulation at work, whether it be with sacred objects, liturgies,
the translation of the Bible or the wealth of ideas about evil, healing, authority and identity contained within it. African consciousness
was too resilient, too immediately engaged with the possibilities of a
new religion, to be crushed or colonized by colonial-missionary hegemony. To borrow Lonsdale's phrase the 'long international conversation' between missionaries and Africans was often on 'equal terms'.[55]
Together, these essays show that Christianity, partially established
before formal empire, rooted itself, spread and flourished across much
of sub-Saharan Africa in the colonial era. It escaped missionary hands
within a generation or two, and by the turn of the twenty-first century it had become the corner stone of African culture and society.

---

[55] The notion of a 'conversation' between missionaries and Africans derives from
the influential and important agenda set by Comaroff and Comaroff, 1991.

BIBLIOGRAPHY

Clayton, A., *Christianity and Islam in South-East Tanzania: A Study of Religious Appropriation among the Makonde*, Ph.D. thesis, University of Manchester, 1993.
Comaroff, J. and J., *Of Revelation and Revolution: Christianity, Colonialism and Consciousness in South Africa*, vol. 1, Chicago, University of Chicago Press, 1991.
Daneel, M.L., *Fambidzano: Ecumenical Movement of Zimbabwean Independent Churches*, Gweru, Mambo Press, 1989.
Dillon-Malone, C., *The Korsten Basketmakers: A Study of the Masowe Apostles, An Indigenous African Religious Movement*, Manchester, Manchester University Press, 1978.
Englund, Harri, and Leach, James, 'Ethnography and Meta-Narratives of Modernity', *Current Anthropology*, 41, 2, 2000.
Etherington, Norman, 'Recent Trends in the Historiography of Christianity in Southern Africa', *Journal of Southern African Studies*, 22, 2, 1996, pp. 201–219.
Fields, K., *Revival and Rebellion in Colonial Central Africa*, Princeton, Princeton University Press, 1985.
Gifford, Paul, *The New Crusaders: Christianity and the New Right in Southern Africa*, London, Pluto, 1991.
———, *African Christianity: Its Public Role*, London, Hurst, 1998.
Green, M., *The Construction of 'Religion' and the Perpetuation of 'Tradition' among Pogoro Catholics, Southern Tanzania*, Ph.D. thesis, London School of Economics, 1992.
Groves, C.P., *The Planting of Christianity in Africa*, 4 vols., London, Lutterworth, 1948–58.
Hastings, Adrian, *African Christianity: An Essay in Interpretation*, London, Geoffrey Chapman, 1976.
———, *A History of African Christianity 1950–1975*, Cambridge, Cambridge University Press, 1979.
———, *African Catholicism: Essays in Discovery*, London, SCM, 1989.
———, *The Church in Africa 1450–1950*, Oxford, Clarendon Press, 1994.
———, *The Construction of Nationhood: Ethnicity, Religion and Nationalism*, Cambridge, Cambridge University Press, 1997.
Isichei, Elizabeth, *A History of Christianity in Africa: From Antiquity to the Present*, London, SPCK, 1995.
James, Wendy, and Johnson, Douglas, 'Preface' and 'Introduction: On "Native" Christianity' in James and Johnson (eds.), *Vernacular Christianity: Essays in the Social Anthropology of Religion*, Oxford, JASO, 1988.
Lonsdale, John, '"Listen While I Read": The Orality of Christian Literacy in the Young Kenyatta's Making of the Kikuyu', in Louise de la Gorgendière and Kenneth King (eds.), *Ethnicity in Africa*, Edinburgh University, Centre of African Studies, 1996.
Maxwell, David, *Christians and Chiefs in Zimbabwe: A Social History of the Hwesa People c. 1870s–1990s*, Edinburgh University Press, Edinburgh, 1999(a).
———, 'Historizing Christian Independency: The Southern African Pentecostal Movement 1908–1950', *Journal of African History*, 40, pp. 234–264, 1999(b).
———, '"Catch the Cockerel Before Dawn": Pentecostalism and Politics in Post-Colonial Zimbabwe', *Africa*, 70. 2, 2000.
———, 'Religion: Culture Contact in Africa and Latin America' in N.J. Smelser and P.B. Baltes (eds.), *International Encyclopedia of the Social & Behavioral Sciences*, Oxford, Pergamon, 2001.
Moyo, A., 'Religion and Politics in Zimbabwe', in K. Holst-Peterson (ed.), *Religion, Development and African Identity*, Uppsala, Scandinavian Institute of African Studies, 1985.
Peel, J.D.Y., 'Historicity and Pluralism in Some Recent Studies of Yoruba Religion', *Africa*, 64, 1, pp. 150–164, 1994.

Ranger, T.O., 'Concluding Summary', in K. Holst-Peterson (ed.), *Religion, Development and African Identity*, Uppsala, Scandinavian Institute of African Studies, 1985(a).
———, 'Religion, Development and African Christian Identity' in K. Holst-Peterson (ed.), *Religion, Development and African Identity*, Uppsala, Scandinavian Institute of African Studies, 1985(b).
———, *Are We Not Also Men? The Samkange Family and African Politics in Zimbabwe 1920–1964*, London, James Currey, 1995.
———, 'Report of the Africa Region Workshop on Evangelical Christianity and Political Democracy', unpublished manuscript, Harare, Zimbabwe, 15–16 October, 1999.
Rostas, S., 'The Mexica's Reformulation of the Conchero's Dance: The Popular Use of Autochthonous Religion in Mexico City', in S. Rostas and A. Droogers (eds.), *The Popular Use of Popular Religion in Latin America*, Amsterdam, CEDLA, 1993.
Schoffeleers, M., *Pentecostalism and Neo-Traditionalism: The Religious Polarization of a Rural District in Southern Malawi*, Amsterdam, Free University, 1985.
Shaw, Rosalind, and Stewart, Charles, 'Introduction', in Shaw and Stewart (eds.), *Syncretism/Anti-Syncretism: The Politics of Religious Synthesis*, London, Routledge, 1994.
Waliggo, John, *The Catholic Church in the Buddu Province of Buganda, 1879–1925*, Ph.D. thesis, Cambridge University, 1976.
Washbrook, D., 'Orients and Occidents: Colonial Discourse Theory and the Historiography of the British Empire', in *The Oxford History of the British Empire*, vol. 5, *Historiography*, Oxford, Oxford University Press, 1999.
Werbner, R., 'The Suffering Body: Passion and Ritual Allegory in Christian Encounters', *Journal of Southern African Studies*, 23, 2, 1997.
West, G.O., and Dube, M., *The Bible in Africa: Transactions, Trajectories and Trends*, Leiden, Brill, 2000.
Wilson, B., *Christianity*, London, Routledge, 1999.

CHAPTER ONE

A KONGO PRINCESS, THE KONGO AMBASSADORS AND THE PAPACY[1]

Richard Gray

With one most significant exception, relatively little is known concerning Christian women in the ancient kingdom of Kongo, whose
importance for the history of African Christianity has been so notably
demonstrated in Adrian Hastings's great history (Hastings, 1994).
Much of the seventeenth-century history of the neighbouring kingdom of Matamba is dominated by the exploits of Queen Nzinga,
but, apart from the dramatic, tragic and much studied career of
Beatrice Kimpa Vita, very little attention has been given to women
in the study of Kongo's ancient history. Yet scattered across the documents from the sixteenth to the early nineteenth century are a number of indications that women played an important, and even at
times vital, role in the maintenance and development of Kongo
Catholicism. As early as the mid-sixteenth century, a Jesuit reported
that the king had decided that 'all the women should be gathered
into a church called Ambiro', and that it was there that the Jesuits
said Mass for them and 'taught them to know Our Lord' (Van Wing,
40–41). A century later, the recognition by the Capuchin missionaries of Garcia II as a Catholic monarch was seriously endangered
by his persecution of leading Christian ladies, who from the arrival
of the Capuchins were reported to have 'daily participated in all the
spiritual exercises setting a great example and edification to the court'
(Mateo de Anguiano, 365–9). At the end of the seventeenth century
and well into the eighteenth, when the unity of the Kongo kingdom
had been destroyed and its power dissipated among competing rulers,
royal women continued to maintain the faith and warmly welcome
Catholic missionaries. Hastings has recently drawn attention to the
role of a former queen, Ana Afonso de Leão, 'a woman of great

[1] I am grateful to the Leverhulme Foundation and to the British Academy for
assistance in undertaking research in the Vatican and Italian archives.

authority . . . politically responsible and devoutly Catholic' (Hastings, 1998, 151), and her importance, together with that of other Kongolese women, has been amply illustrated in John Thornton's recent, most valuable book (Thornton, 1998). In 1749 Bernardino Ignazio d'Asti reported how a royal widow had been recently visited by a Capuchin in 'one of the most remote parts of Kongo'. He had been over-whelmed there for almost a month, making four thousand baptisms and hearing the confessions of all the people 'who had been pre-pared for the sacraments by that worthy lady'.[2] So far as is known, however, the impact of all these notable Christian women was confined to Kongo itself. Yet in the late sixteenth century the fancy, perhaps fleeting, of a young Kongo princess, through the response which it evoked in Europe, played a minor yet significant part in the process which eventually persuaded the papacy to establish in 1622 the Sacred Congregation of Propaganda Fide, which later became the most powerful organization in Catholic mission history.

It is a strange story; church historians might even dare to call it providential. A series of fragile, brief, yet powerfully consequential encounters established a network of Christian contacts which stretched across two continents. Perhaps the most extraordinary was the first: the audience given in the Escorial by Philip II of Spain to Teresa of Avila, probably in December 1577. She herself described the meet-ing as follows:

> Imagine what this poor woman must have felt when she saw so great
> a King before her. I was terribly embarrassed. I began to address him;
> but, when I saw his penetrating gaze fixed on me—the kind of gaze
> that goes deep down to the very soul—it seemed to pierce me through
> and through; so I lowered my eyes and told him what I wanted as
> briefly as I could. When I had finished telling him about the matter
> I looked up at him again. His face seemed to have changed. His
> expression was gentler and more tranquil. He asked me if I wanted
> anything further. I answered that what I had asked for was a great
> deal. Then he said 'Go away in peace, for everything shall be arranged
> as you wish . . .' I knelt to thank him for his great favour. He bade
> me rise, and making this poor nun, his unworthy servant, the most
> charming bow I ever saw, held out his hand to me again, which I
> kissed' (Peers, 146).

---

[2] Archives of Propaganda Fide, Scritture rif. nei Congressi, Angola, V. fol. 180. Memorandum by Bernardino Ignazio d'Asti, 12 December 1749.

At that time the persecution of her reform was at its height, but within two years Philip recommended Rome to grant it recognition.

The next chain of events began with the death of King Sebastian of Portugal at the battle of Alcazar-el-Kabir, that total defeat in 1578 of the last attempt by European Christendom to reconquer North Africa by the force of crusading arms. Two years after this death, Philip II of Spain successfully asserted his rights to the Portuguese crown. With bullion from Spanish America already providing a major part of his finances, he was anxious to explore the potential mineral riches of his new African dominions. Additional forces were despatched to Mina to protect the export of West African gold, and the rumours of silver mines in the hinterland of Luanda attracted his attention. Together with these material interests, he was concerned to develop and deepen the *Padroado*, the ecclesiastical rights and responsibilities that the Portuguese crown had been granted by the papacy in the course of the fifteenth century. Philip was careful not to offend unnecessarily the susceptibilities of his new subjects, and Portuguese affairs in general continued to be administered separately. Yet, for a mission to West Africa and Kongo in particular, Philip turned not to one of the orders which had previously sent Portuguese missionaries to the area, but to the order reformed by Teresa of Avila, which was attracting some of the most ardent spirits of Spanish Catholicism.

Jerónimo Gracián, the young confidant of the aged saint, had just been elected Provincial, and was informed of the royal wish that the Discalced Carmelites should undertake this mission. By March 1582 five Spanish Carmelites were chosen and instructed by Gracián, while their leader received words of encouragement from Teresa herself (Bontinck, 116). Philip went down to the port in Lisbon to see them set sail in April. The ship was lost at sea and the priests drowned. The following year a second group of Carmelite missionaries were captured by English pirates, but Philip encouraged Gracián to persevere, and a third group set out from Lisbon in 1584. After eleven days of missionary work on the island of São Tomé, the missionaries joined another boat sailing with military reinforcements 'sent by our king', as they reported, 'to conquer a mountain of silver discovered' in the kingdom of Angola (Florencio, 13–35). The ship's passengers neatly illustrated Philip's parallel, and competing, concerns.

Directly after their arrival in Luanda, the Carmelite missionaries set out for Kongo. When they were near the royal capital, they

informed King Alvaro I (1568–87) that they were bringing with them
a statue of the Virgin Mary and that they should therefore enter
Mbanza Kongo in a solemn procession. Diego de la Encarnación,
one of the missionaries, reported that a large crowd watched their
entry. He estimated that more than thirty thousand people participated, including one hundred Portuguese merchants resident there.
Immediately, he claimed, 'a great devotion to the image of the Virgin'
developed (Brásio, IV, 395–7). An unnamed princess, one of the four
daughters of Alvaro and his canonical wife Dona Catalina, was swept
up in this devotion. Seeing the statue clothed in the habit of a
Carmelite nun, she asked the reason and was told that this was
because the Virgin was the patron of the Order of Mount Carmel,
and that the nuns were so clothed. Listening to the preaching of the
Carmelites, she developed a great desire to enter the Order as a
Carmelite nun. She therefore wrote to Mother María de San José,
prioress of the newly founded convent in Lisbon, who replied to her,
promising that she would try to find some way of meeting her wishes.

We know nothing more about this princess, but one of the people to whom Mother María spoke about her request was Jean de
Brétigny, a young man from Rouen, then the second most important town in France (Sérouet, 54). Jean belonged to one of the rich
merchant families of Spanish, and often Jewish, origin who dominated the maritime trade of Rouen. His family came from Burgos,
in northern Spain, and his relatives there continued to trade with
Flanders and France. Jean's grandfather went to Rouen in 1510 and
married into a family of Spanish origin, already well established in
France, one of its members being a secretary to the king. Jean's
father married into an old landed family and continued to prosper
in trade. Jean, his eldest son, was born in 1556, but at the age of
six he was sent to live with an uncle in Seville until 1570, probably to avoid the turmoil and violence of the religious wars in France.
As a young teenager he returned to Rouen, and in 1581 was asked
by his father to go back to Seville to undertake various business
affairs. By this time, however, Jean was more interested in religion
than in his family's business, and, with his father's consent, he first
accompanied a group of Flemish Franciscan nuns to Lisbon, helping them to find a refuge there. Reaching Seville in 1582, he was
introduced by a Spanish friend to Mother María de San José, then
prioress of the Carmelite convent. She sent him to Jerónimo Gracián,
and for several months Jean attended the novitiate exercises of the

Carmelites while also undertaking his father's business affairs. Under the influence of Gracián, María and their colleagues, Jean began to learn that the ultimate aim of the Discalced Carmelites was not the individual perfection of their members, but the furtherance of the kingdom of God. Gradually they encouraged Jean to devote his considerable financial resources to this end (Sérouet, 2–51).

In 1584 María was sent to establish the convent in Lisbon, and soon Jean was entrusted with organizing, financing and accompanying a caravan of reinforcements from Seville to Lisbon. While he was there in 1585, María must have informed him about the princess in Kongo, for Jean never forgot this plea. In 1585, however, there was little that either he or Mother María could do to respond to it immediately. By then St Teresa had died, and in May Gracián was succeeded as provincial by Nicholas Jesús-María Doria, who did not share Gracián's enthusiasm for overseas missions. The Carmelites in Kongo, left with no reply to their requests for support and reinforcements, decided to return to Europe (Sérouet, 54–7).

The next initiatives came from Kongo, and there is one small but intriguing piece of evidence which indicates that the princess's request may have been more than a fleeting fancy on the part of one individual. While Philip II had been encouraging the Carmelites to send a mission to western Africa, Alvaro I was instructing Duarte Lopez, a Portuguese trader who had been living at his court since 1578, to go as his envoy to Philip and also to the pope (Bal, 11). The instructions given to Lopez for his mission to Rome, signed by the king on 15 January 1583, reveal some of the motivations which led Alvaro to seek to enter into a closer relationship with the papacy.[3] Alvaro clearly recognized Rome as a major source of the spiritual power and strength with which he wished to surround his office and his people. His envoy was ordered 'in the first instance to inform His Holiness in detail concerning what happens and takes place in these my kingdoms, to tell him the need that exists for ministers for so many Christian souls, and to ask for relics, indulgences and blessed objects so that with greater courage and devotion we may make progress in the service of God'. In the case of many European embassies in the sixteenth century, such requests and petitions might

---

[3] The original instructions were in Portuguese, but they are known to us only through an Italian translation held in the Vatican archives. They have been published by Brásio, III, 234–5, and by Filesi (1968) with a facsimile, 143–5.

indicate little more than a customary mode of approaching the
papacy. In the case of Kongo, they represented an urgent and serious demand. In the continuous cosmological conflict with evil as
experienced in this African kingdom, such requests to a new source
of spiritual power had lost nothing of their validity and immediacy,
as is indicated by other details in the instructions.

Lopez was told to negotiate 'that matter which you have learnt
by heart from me in our discussions, in the hope that you will carry
this through with diligence worthy of the trust in which I hold you'.
In all probability the hidden agenda thus committed to Lopez concerned the possibility of liberating Kongo from the restrictions and
burdens of Portuguese patronal claims, particularly as exercised by
the Portuguese bishop of São Tomé. Alvaro and his predecessors
had come into conflict with the bishop and other Portuguese ecclesiastical emissaries, including the first Portuguese Jesuits in Kongo.
Tension had arisen especially over Kongo practices which contra-
vened canon law marriage. Alvaro clearly wished to have far greater
control over the nature and development of Kongo Christianity. He
also specifically raised the issue of indigenous religious orders. Lopez
was told to insist that Alvaro should be given permission 'to provide
in these kingdoms orders of monks and nuns' and that suitable people in Kongo should be allowed to enter these orders. Lopez should
also ask for papal Bulls for the principal churches and confraternities, and for 'an image of Our Lady, copied directly from one of
the four painted by St Luke' with the indulgences attached to it.
This request probably referred to the thirteenth-century painting,
popularly attributed to St Luke, in the Basilica of Santa Maria
Maggiore in Rome. We do not know who had told Alvaro about
it, but in 1569 Francis Borgia had sent a copy of it to Queen Caterina
in Portugal (Suau, 414), after whom Alvaro's canon law wife (the
mother of our anonymous princess) was named. His interest in this
painting, and especially his specific request for Kongolese nuns, provides a fascinating background to his daughter's desire to become a
Carmelite. It forcibly suggests that the idea of entering a religious
order was not a novelty for women attached to the royal court at
Mbanza Kongo.

When Lopez eventually reached Rome, the pope, Sixtus V, was
unwilling to respond actively to Alvaro's initiative. Beset by the dis-
astrous religious wars in France and many other problems, he was
reluctant to challenge Philip's patronal rights. Doubtless he was also

aware of the logistical difficulties of sending an independent mis-
sionary expedition to Kongo. The critical, on-going contact with
Rome was made by Alvaro II, who succeeded his father in 1587.
Seven years later, his close relative, Antonio Vieira, arrived in Lisbon,
charged with negotiating the creation of a separate diocese for Kongo.
He quickly established a close and friendly relationship with Fabio
Biondi, the papal representative in Lisbon. Vieira gave Biondi a
lively, detailed account of the practice of the faith in Mbanza Kongo
(Brásio, III, 502–3). Already the king and his notables were members of six lay confraternities, actively supporting and participating
in their activities, which included attendance at a weekly mass offered
in part for the souls of previous members.[4] Kongo respect and veneration for the ancestors was gradually becoming subsumed into
orthodox Catholic practice.

Above all, Biondi was deeply impressed by Vieira's Christian character and knowledge. An indication of the impact which the Kongolese
ambassador made on Biondi can be glimpsed in the letters of recommendation that the papal collector wrote on his behalf when
Vieira was setting out from Lisbon for a visit to Madrid. Biondi
informed the Archbishop of Evora that the ambassador merited a
warm welcome on account of his personal qualities and 'particularly
for his religious commitment'. He added that in view of the remote-
ness of Kongo, God should be praised that there were Christians
there 'of this quality'. To the nuncio in Madrid, he affirmed that
Vieira was 'a very good Christian and devoted to the Apostolic See'.
On a later occasion Biondi admitted to being astonished at the fact
that the ambassador was 'very well instructed in Christian doctrine
and in ecclesiastical history'.[5]

As a result of these contacts, in November 1595 Biondi despatched
a long and very optimistic report to Rome on the nature of Kongo
Christianity, warmly supporting the request for a diocese to be created separate from that of São Tomé (Cuvelier and Jadin, 194–207).
The Portuguese Mesa de Consciência in Lisbon also supported the

---

[4] I have stressed elsewhere (Gray, 1990, 45) the role of the confraternities in
strengthening Christian commitment in late seventeenth-century Soyo. Following
Cavazzi's account, I had wrongly assumed that these confraternities were an innovation introduced to Kongo by the Capuchins.

[5] Vatican archives, Fondo Confalonieri, 28, f. 401, Biondi to Archbp of Evora,
27.XI. 1595, and f. 566v. to nuncio, same date, and f. 678–678v. to Silvio Antoniano,
31.VIII.1596.

request, and recommended to Philip that the bishop of São Salvador, or Mbanza Kongo, should be given by the crown the same salary as the bishop of São Tomé (Brásio, III, 480–1). With this recommendation, the council maintained the assumption that Kongo, although an independent kingdom, fell within the Portuguese *Padroado*. Its members may well have thought that the presence of a Portuguese bishop, paid for by the crown, would not only strengthen the faith but also serve Portuguese interests, since Alvaro II, unlike his father, had already been involved in hostile exchanges with the Portuguese settlers in Angola.

Since Vieira's request was thus supported both by the papal representative and by Philip II, with the Portuguese crown meeting the expenses, the papacy had no hesitation in creating the new diocese of São Salvador, approved at the consistory held on 20 May 1596 (Brásio, III, 490). Already however Biondi's links with Kongo, and his admiration for its people, had been strengthened. A letter written by Alvaro II in the previous September had just reached him in Lisbon. In it Alvaro thanked the pope for 'the favours and honours' shown by the papal collector to his ambassador, and asked, as a result of a letter he had received from Biondi, for further assistance from the papacy (Brásio, III, 490–1). Biondi reported how the messengers carrying the letter had been seized by English 'pirates' and taken to England. Ill-treated, only with difficulty had they been able to save the letter from destruction. The whole story prompted Biondi to a further affirmation of his interest and affection for the people of Kongo. Forwarding it to Cardinal Aldobrandino, the pope's secretary of state, Biondi said that 'they were people of great commonsense' and the ambassador and 'those who come from that kingdom give a very good account of their faith, which for me is exceeding wonderful, having so great a lack of priests who can instruct them. One could well say that the harvest is plentiful but the labourers are few indeed'.[6] His admiration was about to launch the papacy on a confrontation with the *Padroado* rights which was gradually, yet inexorably, to grow in intensity.

Pope Clement VIII read Alvaro's letter to all the cardinals in consistory, warmly invited him to send ambassadors to Rome and also sent him a plenary indulgence (Brásio, III, 544). Vieira left Lisbon

---

[6] Vatican archives, Fondo Confalonieri 27, f. 178v–179, Biondi to Aldobrandino, II.V.1596.

in March 1597, taking with him the papal brief and a long letter
from Biondi to Alvaro II, congratulating the king on the fact that
the Bishop of São Tomé would no longer have occasion to trouble
him. Biondi warmly underlined the papal invitation to send an ambassador to Rome 'as do all Christian Kings'. This, wrote Biondi, would
result in Alvaro's 'great glory and elevation', and he assured the king
that the ambassador would be 'received and honoured by His Holiness with every honour and paternal affection'.[7] These phrases proved
to be no mere diplomatic niceties, for Biondi was to be highly instrumental in turning them into reality.

On his return to Kongo, Vieira discussed with Alvaro the possibility of sending an embassy to Rome. Alvaro accepted the proposal,
but during the preparations Vieira died, and it was not until June
1604 that another ambassador was finally given his formal instructions. Alvaro chose his cousin, Antonio Manuele Nsaku ne Vunda,
a man in his early thirties, who was to be described in Rome by
those who saw him as someone 'of noble manners and above all
pious and devout, also endowed with strength and prudence in diplomacy'.[8] The embassy arrived in Lisbon in November 1605, but then
encountered many delays. When the ambassador eventually reached
Madrid, he was confronted by the authorities with stern and vigorous attempts to dissuade him from proceeding to Rome. The situation facing the ambassador was becoming desperate in the extreme.
Alvaro was reported to have sent his embassy equipped with at least
twenty-five attendants, but it was supplied merely with shell currency.[9] Although this was very effective when conducting commercial transactions with the Portuguese in Luanda, as soon as the
embassy left the African coast it ran into financial difficulties. According to a petition, the embassy had left Lisbon with very considerable
debts to traders there, and as late as June 1607 the authorities in
Madrid still hoped that the ambassador could be persuaded to entrust
his mission to the Portuguese and Spanish envoys in Rome (Brásio
V, 261–3, 311). Antonio eventually found board and lodgings in
Madrid with the Mercedarians, an Order whose principal task was

---

[7] Vatican archives, Fondo Confalonieri 28, f. 495v, Biondi to Alvaro II, 18.IX.1596.
See Confalonieri 27, ff. 203, 213, 227, 238 for letters from Biondi to Aldobrandino
dated 31.VIII.1596 to 15.III.1597 concerning Vieira's plans and movements.
[8] Vatican Library, Vat.Lat. 12516, f. 43v, a report almost certainly drawing on
information from Biondi amongst others.
[9] Vatican Library Urb.Lat. 1076, f. 5v–6. Avvisi di Roma, 5.I.1608.

to redeem Christian captives taken by North African Muslim cor-
sairs. But besides being a pauper, he was now a very sick man,
suffering severely from gallstones. After Antonio had been in the
house for three months, the Mercedarian provincial reported that
his behaviour and way of life had given them all 'a very great example'. He only went out of the house 'to discuss the affairs of his
embassy with the king or with his ministers.' For the rest of the time
he stayed in his room, suffering greatly 'with very great patience
submitting himself to the Will of God'.[10]

At this critical juncture, the Discalced Carmelites intervened. Most
members of the reformed order in Spain were still extremely hostile to Gracián's overseas missionary interests; indeed Gracián himself had been expelled from the Order in 1592 by his successor
Nicholas de Jesús-María. In Rome, however, the situation was completely different. Here the leader of the Discalced Carmelites was in
the forefront of curial strategic planning. The menace of Ottoman
expansion in the Balkans, which threatened Austria, Bohemia and
Poland, and also the Turkish raids on the Italian coast, which caused
terror in Rome, powerfully influenced what papal interest there was
in sub-Saharan Africa at this time. Beyond Ottoman power, the kingdom of Prester John (Ethiopia), long enshrouded in medieval myth,
had emerged in the minds of missionary strategists as a potential
ally of very great significance. Towards the end of his life, St Ignatius
had spent a great deal of time and energy on sending to Ethiopia
the most extensive mission ever launched by the founder of the
Jesuits. Later, the first major attempt in Rome to establish a curial
congregation charged with supervising and organizing the propagation of the faith, under the able direction of the remarkable Cardinal
Santori, had been very largely concerned with strengthening the ties
between Rome and the Christian communities within or neighbouring
the Ottoman Empire. And Ethiopia had a position of prime importance among these Christians on the underbelly of the Ottomans;
already it was believed that control of the Nile waters by its Christian
emperor could be a key to the mastery of Egypt. After Santori's
death in 1602 the nascent curial congregation was allowed to wither,
but leadership of these papal and missionary strategies devolved upon
Pedro de la Madre de Dios, the gifted and outstanding Spanish

---

[10] Vatican Archives, Misc. Armadio I, 91, f. 241. Certificate signed by the provincial, 10.X.1607.

leader of the Italian province of Discalced Carmelites. Clearly involved in the decision to send a mission to Persia, whose ruler had defeated an Ottoman army in 1603, he was often called upon to advise Paul V on Middle Eastern questions. He took a leading part in directing the negotiations with the Coptic Church in Egypt, and in an undated memorandum to the pope he highlighted the importance of fostering relations with Ethiopia through the Ethiopian monks in Jerusalem.[11]

Together with some of Santori's former assistants, Pedro had become deeply interested in investigating the feasibility of developing a transcontinental route from Kongo to Ethiopia. From the early sixteenth century an exaggerated idea of the southward extension of Ethiopia to the equator had lent credence to the belief that the journey from Kongo to Ethiopia would be a relatively easy undertaking. As soon as Pedro learned of Antonio Manuele's arrival in Madrid, he wrote to Tomás de Jesús, a leading young Spanish Carmelite who was already a key figure in the conflict between contemplative and missionary vocations within the reformed Order. Tomás's primary objective had been to promote the eremitical way of life, but gradually the needs of the missions both in Europe and overseas were brought before him. Pedro told Paul V that he hoped Tomás would take charge of a projected mission to Kongo and from there 'open a route to Prester John'. At first Tomás remained firmly set against accepting this mission, even when informed of the pope's approval, but while saying Mass one day he became convinced that he should accept the challenge, and immediately he began to collect information concerning 'the lands and languages of Congo and the Abyssinians'.[12] Pedro also contacted Diego de la Encarnación, a member of the 1584 mission to Kongo, ordering him to assist the ambassador in his attempt to reach Rome. The papal nuncio, too, was instructed to help, and eventually in October 1607 Antonio Manuele set out from Madrid, together with the nuncio, being joined en route by Tomás and Diego.

They reached Rome on 3 January 1608. As Adrian Hastings has said, there seemed at that moment 'a great and not entirely illusory hope for the conversion of Africa ... well, if ambiguously, symbolized' by the ambassador's arrival, 'that strangest of events in our history' (Hastings 1994, 126–7). Antonio Manuele was in a pitiable

---

[11] OCD archives in Rome 281e Cartapaccio f. 27–27v. See also Buri 237–253.
[12] Joseph de Santa Teresa, t.iv, libro xvii, cap. 39.

state. All but four of his attendants had died, among them at Livorno
a nephew to whom he was deeply attached. From Civitavecchia he
had been carried to Rome, where Fabio Biondi, now major-domo
to Paul V, had assigned to the ambassador the rooms in the Vatican
palace recently used by Cardinal Bellarmine. The pope visited him
on his death bed and administered the last sacraments. After his death
on the eve of the Feast of the Epiphany, Biondi personally arranged
and supervised a magnificent funeral in Santa Maria Maggiore
(Filesi, 1970).

Even before the ambassador had arrived in Rome, the papacy
was prepared for a public confrontation with Philip III over the
patronal powers of Spain and Portugal. Paul V had instructed the
secretariat of state to begin preparations for sending a Carmelite
mission to Kongo (Brásio V, 362–3), and had decided to receive the
ambassador in public consistory 'despite the opposition of the Spaniards
who maintain that this kingdom is tributary to them'.[13] Antonio
Manuele's death, followed by that of Pedro de la Madre de Dios in
August, delayed the preparations for the Carmelite mission, but eventually on 4 October 1610 Paul V informed Philip III that it was
setting out and asked for assistance for it (Brásio V, 617–9). A year
later Cardinal Borghese, the secretary of state, informed Diego de
la Encarnación that the news that he and the other Carmelite missionaries had been prevented from leaving Lisbon for Kongo had
caused the pope 'great displeasure'. (Brásio VI, 41). The papal collector at Lisbon was ordered to brush aside 'the pretext for this
impediment', and to emphasize to the authorities the damage that
this would cause to Christianity in Kongo and 'in preventing the
conversion of neighbouring kingdoms'.[14] The nuncio in Madrid was
reminded of 'the irreparable harm' that this obstruction would involve,
and he was told that 'since the affair is public knowledge, it would
damage the reputation of this Holy See' (Brásio VI, 42–3). Curial
concern over Ethiopia and Kongo, the two Christian kingdoms in
Africa, had thus become a matter of vital interest for the papacy.
Rome lacked the ships, finance and human resources immediately
to turn its missionary interest in Kongo into reality. The desire to
foster the development of Kongo Christianity had, however, become

[13] Vatican Library, Urb.Lat. 1076 Pt.1, f. 19, Avvisi di Roma, 9.I.1608. See also
Brásio V, 367 for report by the Portuguese agent.
[14] Vatican Archives, Confalonieri 43, f. 96v, Borghese to Collector, 12.X.1611.

an integral feature of the papal challenge to the Portuguese *Padroado*. A critical fracture had opened between Iberian colonial expansion and Catholic missionary enterprise.

When it became obvious that this papal missionary initiative was being effectively blocked by the patronal powers, Paul V began the search for financial resources. He summoned Jean de Brétigny to Rome. Jean had by no means forgotten the plea of the Kongo princess about which he had been told by María de San José in Lisbon over twenty years previously. In the meantime he had devoted much time, and a large measure of his considerable financial resources, in a patient, persistent effort to bring the Discalced Carmelite nuns across the Pyrenees to France and to Flanders. Several of the Spanish nuns who had been intimate assistants of St Teresa keenly supported his endeavours, but with the religious wars in France and the hostilities between the French and Spanish kingdoms it was no easy matter. In 1594 he had failed to obtain permission from Philip II and the authorities of the Discalced Order in Spain to allow the nuns to go to such hostile territory. In 1604, while Antonio Manuele was setting out on his mission to Lisbon, Madrid and Rome, Jean de Brétigny, ably guided by Pierre de Bérulle, finally obtained authority to bring four Spanish nuns to found the Carmel of Paris. Three days after the formal foundation of the Paris Carmel in October, Queen Marie de Médicis thanked him warmly for the present which he had brought to France (Sérouet, 107–198). By 1607 several other convents had been established in France with Jean's help, and in June, when he first heard of the presence in Spain of the embassy from Kongo, he was in Brussels as confessor to the first convent just being founded in Flanders.

Immediately, on 7 June 1607, Jean sat down to write to the ambassadors of the 'province of guinea' as he loosely described the area from which they came. He poured out his soul in the letter. He told them how he had held 'a special joy for a plan which for some years I have held for the salvation of souls in those areas of guinea'.[15] God had conserved within him 'for twenty two years' the idea of sending Discalced Carmelite nuns to those parts in order to instruct young girls (*las donzellas*), for he thought this was the best way to bring them to know and to love 'as their husband Jesus Christ and

---

[15] 'un particular gozo por un desseo que de algunos anos a tengo ala salud de las almas de aquellas partes de guinea'.

to offer him their virginity and service'.[16] He told the ambassadors that he was ready to do all that was necessary and to go to Africa himself. He asked them to let him know if they agreed, or at least to reply to him when they had returned, sending their letters care of the convents at Lisbon, Seville, Madrid or Salamanca. Antonio Manuele was never able to reply to this letter, but he took it with him to Rome along with many other treasured papers, which, on his death, were entrusted to Diego de la Encarnación, and are now in the Vatican archives.[17]

It was probably via this letter that Jean de Brétigny's interest in Kongo, inspired by the unknown princess, became known to the little group of missionary strategists gathered around Pedro de la Madre de Dios. The pope's summons to Jean was notified to him by a remarkable Spanish cleric, Juan Bautista Vivés, who had long been a friend of Gracián and had developed a keen interest in the work of overseas missions. Jean set out for Rome in March 1612 and lodged in Vivés's house during the months that he stayed there. In two audiences with the pope, he promised very considerable financial support for a mission to Kongo, and offered to go there himself to help, though he was then 56 years old (Sérouet, 286–8). His generous offers could not immediately be utilized, but his presence in Rome maintained and strengthened curial interest in Kongo. The following year in a letter to Paul V, dated 27 November 1613, Alvaro II formally appointed Vivés as his ambassador in order that he could render obedience to the Holy See 'with all the solemnity that is customary for royal ambassadors' (Brásio, VI, 128–130). The challenge to the *Padroado* involved in such a proclamation of Kongo's independence from Portugal would continue. Vivés was to make the initial approach to the Capuchins to send a mission to Kongo, and he was to play a notable part in the events leading to the foundation of Propaganda Fide.

Many factors and many people had combined together to produce in Kongo a firm commitment to the papacy as the institution which provided the focus and final legitimation of their identity as

---

[16] 'al esposo Jesu Christ y ofresçerles su Virginidad y servicio'.
[17] Vatican Archives Misc. Armadio I, 91, f. 222. Jhoan de quintana, uenas. The final five letters of his signature have been torn away, Brussels, 7.VI.1607. This letter provides further valuable proof of the sources quoted by Sérouet concerning the appeal of the Kongo princess.

African Christians. When eventually in 1645 Propaganda Fide managed to introduce its own emissaries into Kongo, they went not as evangelists to a non-Christian country, but as dedicated priestly reinforcements, bringing the sacraments of salvation and committed to strengthening the link with Rome. The Capuchins immediately recognized that Kongo, as represented by Garcia II and the male and female ruling elite, was a Catholic kingdom. These missionaries, like their confreres in many of those areas still ruled by Catholic monarchs in Europe, would find much to criticize and condemn in the faith and morals of the ruler and his subjects to whom they came as ministers. They rejoiced, however, to witness the strength of Kongo's loyalty to the pope. They even seem to have found it in no way remarkable that Garcia could believe that the papal monarch, so remote and difficult to contact, could be persuaded to alter radically, yet effectively, the established Kongo custom of electing and legitimating royal succession (Gray, 1997, 294–5).

The extraordinary hopes which the Kongo kings placed in the papacy were the result of much that had happened ever since Afonso Mvemba Nzinga had been baptized in 1491 by the Portuguese pioneers, who likewise accepted Rome as the final arbiter of their faith. The Catholic Church is nothing if not an institution, even if it may well be more than that. In that institution, the papacy has a position of undisputed primacy, however much its members may criticize and seek to manipulate or reform it. The ruling Kongo elite, like its Portuguese counterpart, did not dream of disputing the primacy of the pope. In cementing this linkage and the fundamental commitment to the papacy, the request of an otherwise unknown princess and the sacrificial death of an ambassador had played their part.

BIBLIOGRAPHY

Bal, Willy, tr. F. Pigafetta, *Description du Royaume de Congo et des contrées environnantes*, Louvain and Paris, Nauwelaerts, 1963.

Bontinck, F., 'Les Carmes Déchaux au royaume de Kongo (1584–1587)', *Zaïre-Afrique*, 262, 1992, pp. 113–123.

Brásio, A., *Monumenta Missionaria Africana. Africa Ocidental* (I serie). Vols. III–VI, Lisbon, Agência Geral do Ultramar, 1954–1955.

Buri, V., *L'unione della chiesa copta con Roma sotto Clemente VIII, Orientalia Christiana*, xxiii/2, no. 72, Rome, Pont. Institutum Orientalium Studiorum, 1931.

Cuvelier, J. and Jadin, L., *L'ancien Congo d'après les archives romaines (1518–1640)*, Brussels, Académie royale des sciences coloniales. Section des sciences morales et politiques. Mémoires, xxxvi, fasc. 2, 1954.

Filesi, T., *Le relazioni tra il regno del Congo e la Sede Apostolica nel XVI secolo*, Como, Cairoli, 1968.

————, *Roma e Congo all'inizio del 1600*, Como, Cairoli, 1970.

Florencio del Niño Jesús, *La Orden de Santa Teresa, la Fundación de la Propaganda Fide y las Misiones Carmelitanas*, Madrid, 1923.

Gray, R., *Black Christians and White Missionaries*, New Haven and London, Yale University Press, 1990.

————, 'The Papacy and Africa in the Seventeenth Century', *Il Cristianesimo nel mondo atlantico nel secolo XVII*, Pontificio Comitato di Scienze Storiche, Atti e Documenti, 6, Vatican City, Libreria Editrice Vaticana, 1997.

Hastings, A., *The Church in Africa 1450–1950*, Oxford, Clarendon Press, 1994.

————, 'The Christianity of Pedro IV of the Kongo, The Pacific (1695–1718)', *Journal of Religion in Africa*, XXVIII.2, 1998, pp. 145–159.

Joseph de Santa Teresa, *Reform de los Descalzos*, Madrid, 1684.

Mateo de Anguiano, *Misiones capuchinas en Africa*. I. *La mission del Congo*, with introduction and notes by Buenaventura de Carrocera, Madrid, Consejo Superior de Investigaciones Científicas, 1950.

Peers, E.A., *Mother of Carmel*, London, SCM Press, 1945.

Sérouet, P., *Jean de Brétigny (1556–1634). Aux origines du Carmel de France, de Belgique et du Congo*, Louvain, Bibliothèque de la Revue d'histoire ecclésiastique, 1974.

Suau, P., *Histoire de S. François de Borgia*, Paris, Beauchesne, 1910.

Thornton, John K., *The Kongolese Saint Anthony: Dona Beatriz Kimpa Vita and the Antonian Movement, 1684–1706*, Cambridge, Cambridge University Press, 1998.

Wing, J. van, *Études Bakongo*, 1, Brussels, 1921.

CHAPTER TWO

AFRICA AS THE THEATRE OF CHRISTIAN ENGAGEMENT WITH ISLAM IN THE NINETEENTH CENTURY

Andrew F. Walls

The nineteenth-century encounter between Europe and India was notable for the long and close engagement of Christianity in its western form with the traditional religious culture of India, with momentous consequences for both. The missionary impact, more than any other single factor, led the west into realms beyond all its previous experience. The nineteenth-century encounter with Islam, by contrast, was often shaped, not in the sphere of active engagement between Christian and Muslim, but by factors arising out of the long past histories of Europe and Asia, and in settings where genuine inter-religious exchange was well-nigh unthinkable. In the meeting with India, Europe was aware of its substantial ignorance, and the missionaries succeeded the early humanists of the East India Company as its sensors. In the meeting with the Islamic world, Europe, while sometimes changing its mind about Islam, believed it already knew all that was necessary, and the missionary was generally marginal in compiling that corpus of knowledge. It is the purpose of this paper to suggest that Africa was a partial exception, and to explore some of the ways in which West Africa, in particular, was a theatre of Christian-Muslim engagement and impinged on the changing debate in Europe.

'Some detest the Persians because they believe in Mohamed; and others despise their language because they do not understand it.'[1] Thus, Sir William Jones, the great impresario of Sanskrit studies, who handled the Hindu classics as his western contemporaries handled those of Greece and Rome, explained the neglect in his circles of Persian, the other great language of the Moghul Empire. The

---

[1] William Jones, *A Grammar of the Persian Language*, 2nd edn., London, J. Richardson, 1775, preface.

emotional charge in his words is evident: as Muslims the Persians 'believe in Mohamed', and to eighteenth-century Englishmen that is detestable. Behind that detestation lie centuries of hostility and terror. The contemporary folk image of Islam is evoked by Robert Burns, who describes the scene as the Devil comes into an Ayrshire town and marches off with the hated revenue officer. All the women of the town delight in the deliverance, crying 'Auld Mahoun', I wish ye luck o' the prize, man'.[2] In eighteenth-century Scotland, the Prophet's name was a demotic periphrasis for the Devil.

It was not only old ladies in Scotland who made the equation. The life of Muhammad best known to most educated people of the time was still probably that included in the work of Humphrey Prideaux, the title of which tells its own story: *The true nature of imposture fully displayed in life of Mahomet; with a discourse attached for the full vindication of Christianity from this charge.*[3] Prideaux's book, first published in 1697, was being reprinted as late as 1808, and someone thought it worthwhile to produce an American edition in 1798. Muhammad was above all the great impostor, or in Charles Wesley's phrase 'The Arab thief, as Satan bold', whose doctrine should be chased back to hell.[4]

There were not many reasons, even worldly ones, to take up the study of Arabic, the necessary prelude to any deeper engagement. Sir William Jones, enthusiast for languages as he is, urges Arabic only for those of his Company's staff who wish to become eminent translators. For all ordinary purposes, Persian would serve; and diligent use of his grammar for a year should enable the student to read and reply to any letter he might happen to receive in that language from an Indian prince.[5] It is noteworthy that when Dr Johnson and Boswell set up in imagination an ideal university, with chairs held by their learned friends, they thought of appointing a Professor of Sanskrit (Jones) but no Professor of Arabic.[6]

---

[2] Robert Burns, *The Deil's awa' wi' the Exciseman*.
[3] The real target of the work is not distant Islam but proximate English Deism; its popularity in this sphere of polemics made it one of the more accessible sources of information on Islam.
[4] Hymn 'For the Turks', first published in Bristol, 1758; *Poetical Works of John and Charles Wesley*, George Osborn (ed.), vol. 6, London, Wesleyan Methodist Conference Office, 1870, p. 137.
[5] Jones, ibid.
[6] 'Journal of a Tour to the Hebrides with Samuel Johnson', for 25 August 1773 in G. Birbeck Hill and L.F. Powell (eds.), *Boswell's Life of Johnson*, Vol. V, Oxford, Clarendon Press, 1964, p. 108.

Nevertheless, Arabic as a field for the learned never quite died out, just as the presence of the emotional charge which could produce detestation of Islam did not inhibit the activities of the Levant Company and other trading ventures in the Muslim East. An Arabic Psalter was produced in 1724 and a New Testament and a catechism thereafter by the Society for Promoting Christian Knowledge; but these were intended for use not among Muslims but by Eastern Christians, and the main burden of translation was borne by a Syrian Christian.[7] One of the correctors employed for the New Testament was the lawyer George Sale, who became the earliest major interpreter of Islam to the English-speaking world. Sale's *Koran*,[8] with its massive notes, was the standard English version for a century and a half. How unusual was such activity can be gauged from the fact that many people assumed, and Voltaire apparently actually said, that Sale had spent his life among the Arabs. In fact, he never left England.

By the early nineteenth century it was easier to identify some people who had genuinely lived among the Arabs, and not simply as travellers in the east, of whom there had always been some, but as interpreters of the life of Muslims. The most remarkable was probably E.W. Lane, who first went to Egypt for his health and to study the language and stayed on as Mansur Effendi to write *Manners and Customs of the Modern Egyptians*, published in 1836. Though Lane adopted a Muslim identity in Egypt, he never forsook the Christianity of his clerical background, but he was neither a missionary nor even an explorer of Islamic faith.[9]

By Lane's time, however, the new Protestant phase of the modern missionary movement was well under way. Not surprisingly, its American arm early directed itself to the area which had become prominent in American public consciousness as a result of American foreign policy, the Middle East.[10] This brought it to what the west

---

[7] The background is explored by Daniel L. Brunner, *Halle Pietism in England: Anthony William Boehm and The Society for Promoting Christian Knowledge*, Göttingen, Vandenhoeck und Ruprecht, 1993, especially pp. 154–165. English traders of the Levant Company resident in the East played a part in facilitating the project.

[8] *The Koran: commonly called the Alcoran of Mohammed, translated into English immediately from the original Arabic, with explanatory notes taken from the most approved commentary, to which is prefixed a preliminary discourse*, London, 1764.

[9] Lane's work is one of the key points of reference for Edward Said, *Orientalism*, London, Routledge and Kegan Paul, 1978. See especially chapter 2, section 5: 'Orientalism, structures and restructures: Oriental residence and scholarship. The requirements of lexicography and imagination.'

[10] See James A. Field, *America and the Mediterranean World 1770–1882*, Princeton,

generally saw as the heart of the Islamic world, where the Prophet's
deputy, the leader of the faithful, presided over the immense, if ram-
shackle, Ottoman Empire that extended over three continents. British
missionary interest in the area was much less sustained.[11] But, in any
case, the official position of the Turkish Empire was never to admit
missions to Muslims. Whatever the hopes for the future, missions
within the Turkish Empire owed their justification to the old Christian
minority communities of the Empire. For much of the nineteenth
century, writers on missions continued to lament the closed doors of
the world's greatest Muslim power. By the century's end only a frac-
tion of the world's Muslims were living within that empire, but old
habits die hard, and western perceptions of Islam continued to be
moulded by its association with the Ottoman Empire in decline, long
after the political reality had changed.

The exclusion of missions from what was seen as the heart of the
Islamic world, or their presence there on terms that made Christian
engagement with Islam at most indirect, meant that, though the
expanding missionary movement had by the 1830s reached many
parts of the globe, a very small number of its representatives were
closely involved with Muslims on any regular basis. First in point of
time were some in West Africa, where Sierra Leone, the first Christian
settlement, had Muslim neighbours and regular Muslim visitors.

From its inception, the 'Province of Freedom' in Freetown was
intended as a base for missionary operations, and through the 1790s
most of the new missionary societies sent representatives there, all
intended to reach beyond the colony. Most of the missions were dis-
astrous, but the most durable, first the Edinburgh Missionary Society,
and then from 1804 the Church Missionary Society, found a niche
among the Susu, who were in process of Islamization.[12] But as early
as 1794 representatives of the Sierra Leone Company, the colony's
evangelically minded sponsoring body, reached Futa Jallon. They

---

Princeton University Press, 1969; reprinted as *From Gibraltar to the Middle East*,
Chicago, Imprint Publications, 1991. Chapter 3 deals with the missionary impulse.

[11] The Church Missionary Society and the British and Foreign Bible Society were
early interested in developments which could bring renewal to the ancient Eastern
churches. William Jowett, later Clerical Secretary of the CMS, had been based for
15 years in Malta with this view; see, for example, his *Christian Researches in the
Mediterranean, Syria, or the Holy Lands . . .*, London, 2nd edn., 1826.

[12] Thomas Thompson, who visited the area in 1752, describes the Susu as 'a
mixt people of Pagans and Mundingos, which are a Sect of Mahometans'. *An Account
of the Society for the Propagation of the Gospel . . .*, London, 1758, p. 30.

were deeply impressed by the orderly Islamic state they found at Timbo. The king there professed himself interested in further contact with Europeans, while carefully establishing that he was not an independent agent; he was subject to a suzerain beyond. This simply increased the attractiveness of the idea of a mission. Let the gospel be preached in Timbo, and it might soon be preached in Timbuktu. No one supposed it would be easy; it would need to be a special mission, able to recommend itself by the productive methods of agriculture the company wished to see developed in Sierra Leone.[13] It was a task ready made for English Methodists, and Thomas Coke undertook to recruit an agricultural mission staffed by Methodists who could handle both the Bible and the plough.[14] The event had a comic opera outcome, for the party never got beyond Freetown. One of its members immediately created an incident by accosting a Muslim to denounce Muhammad as a false prophet and the rest were dismayed to realize the implications of the life to which they had committed themselves. The Governor of Sierra Leone, fearful for the colony's credit with its neighbours, easily persuaded them to go home. The first modern mission to a Muslim state collapsed before it began.

Despite the shame and embarrassment, the vision of the Muslim hinterland, the lure of Timbuktu, remained in missionary consciousness.[15] In the first two decades of modern West African missions there is little to suggest that either missionaries or their sponsoring societies thought of Muslims as being less likely to respond to the Christian gospel than others. The command was to preach the gospel to every creature, the promise was that Ethiopia would eventually stretch out its hands to God, and Timbo and Timbuktu belonged to Ethiopia as surely as Freetown. The facts of experience were that missions everywhere were difficult, slow and discouraging in their immediate results. Muslims at least acknowledged one God, so different

---

[13] *An account of the colony of Sierra Leone from its first establishment . . .*, London, 1795, contains a full report.

[14] See references in Christopher Fyfe, *A History of Sierra Leone*, London, Oxford University Press, 1962, and John Peterson, *Province of Freedom: A History of Sierra Leone 1787–1870*, London, Faber, 1969, and A.F. Walls, 'A Christian Experiment: The Early Sierra Leone Colony', in G.J. Cuming (ed.), *The Mission of the Church and the Propagation of the Faith*, Cambridge, Cambridge University Press, 1970, pp. 107–129.

[15] On the relation of Islamic movements in West Africa to Christian progress in this period see Adrian Hastings, *The Church in Africa 1450–1950*, Oxford, Clarendon Press, 1994, pp. 188–194.

from the dim mysteries of African traditional belief. And who could say that the Fulani of Futa Jallon (who had at least expressed interest in a mission from Freetown) would *not* be more responsive than the Susu or the Hindus? Experience elsewhere in the world counted for little, since the last significant Christian encounters with the Muslim world were long ago and under very different conditions.

The period of disengagement between Christianity and Islam which followed in West Africa thus arose, not from any avoidance of Muslims as unresponsive, but from the sudden burgeoning of new missionary tasks elsewhere. The most direct in its effect was the urgent need to respond to the crowds of recaptives being brought into the Sierra Leone peninsula from the slave-ships, which eventually caused the closure of the Susu mission and the transfer of its missionaries.[16] To this must be added the tantalizing prospects on the Gold Coast,[17] and later the link with the Yoruba states forged by Sierra Leonean recaptives making their way home.[18] These demands on a mission force which was never large, and which was subject in this period to particularly high mortality, broke the pattern of engagement with Muslim Africa that had earlier been envisaged. By the middle of the century Christians and Muslims were neither opponents nor competitors in Africa to any marked degree.

The second area of engagement, for a brief period, was the Russian Empire. The short-lived enthusiasm of Tsar Alexander I to involve Protestants in the conversion of the Tatars caused the Edinburgh Missionary Society, at least, to rate it a higher priority than West Africa. Its remaining missionary with the Susu, Henry Brunton, who had achieved the composition of the first grammar of a West African language, was transferred to the Russian Empire, taking his African assistant, Jellorum Harrison, with him. Harrison provides the spectacle of an African missionary to Russian Muslims in the early years of the nineteenth century.[19]

---

[16] On the shape of the Christian movement in West Africa at this time see Hastings, 1994, pp. 177–187; on Sierra Leone, A.F. Walls, 'A Christian Concordat: Two Views of Christianity and Civilisation', in Derek Baker (ed.), *Church, Society and Politics*, Oxford, Blackwell, 1975, pp. 293–302.

[17] See F.L. Bartels, *The Roots of Ghana Methodism*, Cambridge, Cambridge University Press, 1965.

[18] See Hastings, 1994, pp. 349–358, and J.F. Ade Ajayi, *Christian Missions in Nigeria 1841–1891: The Making of a New Elite*, London, Longmans, 1965.

[19] On Brunton and his work, see P.E.H. Hair, *The Early Study of Nigerian Languages*, Cambridge, Cambridge University Press, 1967, and William Brown, *History of Missions;*

More substantial was the encounter which took place in India, with the appointment to an East India Company chaplaincy of Henry Martyn, who brought a depth of scholarship previously unmatched in the Protestant missionary movement. With Martyn, and Samuel Lee, the Cambridge professor who presented his work to the world, comes the first literary response to arise out of direct encounter with Muslims since the Jesuit missionaries at Akbar's court in the early seventeenth century.[20] Martyn's early death, and the local and occasional nature of his controversy with Mirza Ibrahim, meant that it was not followed up. The nearest thing Martyn had to a successor was Karl Gottlieb Pfander,[21] whose own first encounter with Muslims had been in the Russian Empire. The first version of his best-known work, *Mizan-ul-Haqq* ('The Balance of Truth') was published in Persian in the Caucasus in 1835; five years later, Pfander joined the CMS in India. *Mizan-ul-Haqq*, a treatise in Arabic dialectic style, appeared in many editions and translations directed to every part of the Muslim world; the Religious Tract Society produced a revised English version in 1910 as a basis for further translations.[22] It provided, in fact, the standard Protestant missionary apologetic to Islam for almost a century. Arguing that of all world views only the Christian and Islamic *can* be true, since they alone recognize the one true God who is the source of knowledge, it pits Bible against Qur'an as the source of revelation. The argument is pursued in three stages: first that the Jewish Christian scriptures have not been corrupted nor abrogated; second that the teaching of these scriptures meets the criteria for true revelation, and third that the Qur'an is not miraculous, Muhammad not always estimable, the methods used in the spread of Islam questionable. The work moves on to establish the evangelical paradigm of sin-law-gospel-forgiveness.

Martyn, Pfander and their Muslim interlocutors were arguing about the truth of revelation, in works published in Asia and in Asian languages. In Europe, a Europe no longer menaced by Saracen or

---

or, of the propagation of the Gospel among the heathen, Edinburgh, 1816. Brown was Secretary of the Scottish, formerly Edinburgh, Missionary Society.

[20] Samuel Lee (ed.), *Controversial Tracts on Christianity and Mohammedanism . . . by the Rev. Henry Martyn*, Cambridge, 1824.

[21] Clinton Bennett, 'The Legacy of Karl Gottlieb Pfander', in *International Bulletin of Missionary Research* 20, April 1996, pp. 76–81.

[22] W. St Clair Tisdall, *Mizan-ul-Haqq, or Balance of Truth*, London, RTS, 1910. The argument is substantially that of Pfander's version.

Turkish bogeys, and disposed, indeed, to prop up the Ottoman
Empire as a check to Russian ambitions,[23] the depiction of Islam
was becoming more benign. A well-known literary landmark of the
change is Thomas Carlyle's *Heroes and Hero Worship*, published in
1840. Here Muhammad represents the Hero as Prophet: a true
prophet, a true man, no impostor, his utter sincerity declared by the
fact that more people now believe his word than believe any other
word. Islam, like Christianity, demands complete surrender to God;
indeed, it is definable as a confused form of Christianity, and a better one than that of the miserable Syrian sects squabbling about
christology. And if its morality is not always the highest, it is better
than that of penny-counting contemporary utilitarianism.

But the key assumption is revealed when Carlyle says, 'As there is
no danger of our becoming, any of us, Mahometans, I mean to say
all the good of him I justly can.'[24] That is, conversion to Islam is
culturally impossible for anyone partaking of western civilization. That
assumption was to shape a great deal of subsequent debate about
Islam. In the areas of engagement, the debate is about the truth of
revelation. By 1840, Europe was suspending that question, and turning
to the issue of whether Islam might have been good for *other people*.
That issue had more weight in determining attitudes than all the
Arabist historical-critical scholarship building up in Germany,[25] or
the incipient theology of religion being propounded by F.D. Maurice.[26]

The same middle years of the century which saw these developments in Europe saw the renewal of Christian-Muslim engagement
elsewhere. The Indian chapter of the story cannot detain us here;

---

[23] A writer in the *Edinburgh Review* in 1853 summed up contemporary attitudes
thus: 'Three centuries ago, the first vow of Christian statesmen was the expulsion
of the Turks from the city of Constantine and the deliverance of the Empire from
the scourge and terror of the infidel. In the present age, the absorbing desire of
the same cabinets is to maintain the unbelievers in their settlements; and to post-
pone the hour at which the Crescent must give way to the Cross.'

[24] All references are to the lecture 'The Hero as Prophet'.

[25] The effect of the new scholarship represented by Gustav Weil is reflected in
the popular *Life of Mahomet* by Washington Irving, a work which maintains the western reader's distance from the Prophet by treating him as the hero of an eastern
romance. It appeared more substantially in the new translation of the Qur'an by
a London clergyman, J.M. Rodwell, in 1861, and it made its fullest entry into the
English-speaking world in the large-scale works of the evangelical Indian civilian,
Sir William Muir.

[26] *The Religions of the World and their Relation to Christianity* appeared in 1847. See
A.F. Walls, 'Islam and the Sword: Some Western Perceptions, 1840–1918', *Scottish
Journal of Religious Studies* V, 2, Autumn 1984, pp. 88–105.

but there was also significant encounter in the Upper Niger area.
The central figure on the Christian side was the Yoruba clergyman
Samuel Adjai Crowther.[27] Already a veteran of the Niger Expeditions
of 1841 and 1854, and a seasoned pillar of the CMS Yoruba mission, he was in 1857 appointed to head the mission in the Niger
territories, becoming bishop there in 1864. His mission staff was
entirely African; most of them had, like Crowther himself, been born
in Sierra Leone or had been brought up there.

Sierra Leone, then the most sizeable Christian community in West
Africa to arise from the missionary movement, was also perhaps the
first to demonstrate how resistant to Christianity Muslim communities were; for in this Christian colony Muslim recaptives had maintained their separate identity. As a fervent young evangelist, keeping
school in a village where there were numbers of Muslim recaptives,
Crowther found a boy wearing a charm. Crowther cut it off, telling
the boy to take it home, as such superstitions were not permitted in
a Christian school. This brought the father with a wrathful com-
plaint. Crowther offered to answer him in front of the Muslim elders,
and duly appeared with his Bible and Sale's *Koran*. At the end of
his long life he could still recall the humiliation of that encounter.
All his well-marshalled arguments were useless. For Muslims, there
was only one argument: God did not have a son.[28]

The interesting feature of this story is the disjunction between
cause and outcome. The original point of conflict was not about
Islamic belief at all, but about the use of charms, an indigenous
African religious practice widely tolerated in Islam. In areas where
Muslim and non-Muslim peoples lived on close terms, Muslims often
had, paradoxically, a high reputation for the efficacy of their charms.
The origin of this reputation may well have lain in the Qur'an itself,
in the mystery of writing and its sacred character. Certainly scraps
of the Qur'an were often used as a prophylactic against disease or
misfortune, and it may thus have been a Qur'anic charm which
Crowther had cut from the boy's neck. Later, Christian missionaries came under similar pressures. Crowther himself as a missionary
on the Niger found a great demand from Muslim clerics and others

[27] Hastings, 1994, pp. 338–393, suggestively makes Crowther's life and significance
the frame for the mid-century chapter of African Christian history. On Crowther
see Ajayi, 1965. A major biographical study by Professor J.F.A. Ajayi is forthcoming.
[28] Samuel Crowther, *Experiences with Heathens and Mahomedans in West Africa*, London,
SPCK, 1892.

for Arabic Bibles. He was cautious about responding to expressions of interest in the Scriptures, fearing the use to which they might be put. He tells of an old cleric who had long begged for a Bible; Crowther declined, since he feared it would be cut up for charms. At last he gave in, but only after exacting a promise that the recipient would not use it 'for a bad purpose.'[29]

Crowther's early experience in Sierra Leone had taught him that confrontation, where one party cries 'Jesus is the Son of God' and the other 'No, he is not,' was useless. In his mature years on the Niger, he sought for common ground at the nexus of Qur'an and Bible: the themes of the status of Jesus as a great prophet, his miraculous birth, Gabriel as the messenger of God. Crowther seems to have had courteous and friendly relations with Muslim rulers, and to have nourished a hope of reaching beyond them, through the Christian community, to the as yet barely Islamized peasantry under their control.

He combines stories of his earlier and later attitudes at some length in a small posthumous work, *Experiences with Heathens and Mohammedans in West Africa*. The anecdotal approach adopted by the aged bishop is in fact very revealing; the stories also seem to accord reasonably well with accounts given at the time.[30] He describes, for instance, a meeting, which he dates as 1872, in the palace in Ilorin, which offers a striking contrast with his early encounters in Sierra Leone. Crowther

---

[29] A.F. Walls, 'Samuel Adjai Crowther' in G.H. Anderson et al. (eds.), *Mission Legacies*, Maryknoll, NY, Orbis, 1994, pp. 132–139.

[30] For instance, the account in the *Experiences* of the meeting at the court of the Emir in Ilorin is in line with its more contemporary report in CMS Archives CA3/04 A-B and the printed version, Bishop Crowther's report of the overland journey from Lokoja to Bida, CMS, 1872. See also P.R. McKenzie, *Inter-Religious Encounters in West Africa: Samuel Ajayi Crowther's Attitude to African Traditional Religion and Islam*, Leicester, University of Leicester, 1976, 57f. In a report made to the CMS Parent Committee in 1859 Crowther strongly urged that missionaries should refrain from any suspicion of attacks on Islam: '[Muslims] have great respect for the books of Moses, the Prophets, and the Psalms, and to some extent the Gospel of Christ also.... If they be quietly referred to these books ... in things concerning Christ Himself, we may have opportunity of bringing before their minds the wholesome substance of those blessed books. Our undue rashness in quarrelling with, and our untimely exposure of, Mohammedanism, can do no good; but may irritate, and prove most injurious to the heathen population ...' The CMS published this: Samuel Crowther and John Christopher Taylor, *The Gospel on the Banks of the Niger: Journals and Notices of the Native Missionaries Accompanying the Niger Expedition of 1857–1859*, London, CMS, 1859.

opened the debate[31] by asking the court if Jibrila (Gabriel) could
make a mistake; all agreed he could not. Crowther, showing the
Bible both in English and in Yoruba, then read from the first chapter of Luke the story of Gabriel's visit to Mary, the announcement
of the coming birth of Jesus Messiah. The court could assent to this;
the Qur'anic account has much in common with it.[32] Crowther passed
to the reading of two other New Testament passages, John 14 and
Matthew 28. The first was intended to indicate that the one whom
the court agreed had been pointed out by Jibrila had declared himself 'the Way, the Truth and the Life.' The second was to show that
he also commanded his followers to teach all nations about him,
and thus explain Crowther's own mission. The Emir now took a
hand, asking if Anabi (the Prophet Jesus) was not to be the judge
of the world? Crowther characteristically refused an answer in his
own words, but read Matthew 25, the parable of the sheep and the
goats, where 'all nations' are assembled before 'the Son of Man.'
The Emir asked when this will take place, and Crowther read three
passages in turn: Acts 1:7 ('it is not for you to know the times and
the seasons'), Luke 12:39 (the Son of Man comes as a thief in the
night), and Revelation 22:10 ('The time is at hand'). The succeeding silence was broken by a suspicious question from within the
court: 'What does your litafi say about Muhammad?' Crowther's
reply was that since the Prophet was born 622 years after Christ,
the New Testament is naturally silent on the matter. The next question suggests a Muslim rejoinder: 'Which is fuller, your litafi or the
Qur'an?': in other words, granted your book may be older, is there
a continuing need for it in the light of the Qur'an? What do you
have that we have not? Crowther again avoided pitting the Bible
directly against the Qur'an, saying that the Qur'an has selected certain topics from among the range treated in the Torah and the Injil.

The Muslims now asked Crowther for a prayer. The bishop's
choice is intriguing. He had his Church of England Book of Common
Prayer ready to hand, again in both English and Yoruba. From the
second he delivered the 'prayer for the Queen's Majesty' prescribed

---

[31] This was Sunday afternoon. Crowther had already read the morning service
of the Church of England in the compound where he was lodging, with a crowd
watching. McKenzie, 1976, p. 57.
[32] Sura 3:42–47; cf. Sura 19:16–21.

for every morning and evening service. It is worth setting out in full
the prayer in the English form which Crowther would have had:

> O Lord, our heavenly Father, high and mighty, King of kings, Lord
> of lords, the only ruler of princes, who dost from thy throne behold
> all the dwellers upon earth; most heartily we beseech thee with thy
> favour to behold our most gracious Sovereign Lady, Queen Victoria;
> and so replenish her with the grace of thy Holy Spirit, that she may
> always incline to thy will, and walk in thy way; endue her plenteously
> with heavenly gifts; grant her in health and wealth long to live; strengthen
> her that she may vanquish and overcome all her enemies; and finally,
> after this life, she may attain everlasting joy and felicity; through Jesus
> Christ our Lord.

Crowther explained that the Christian custom when outside the Queen's
dominions was to replace the name of Queen Victoria 'by the name
of the sovereign in whose dominions we are living'; that is, he lets
the Emir know, Christians in his dominions would pray for him in
these terms. The Court agreed that the prayer was very suitable.

'There was no argument,' says Crowther, 'no dispute, no objection made, but the questions were answered direct from the Word
of God.' This insistence on answering from Scripture, even when
another answer might be readily to hand, was essential to Crowther's
approach: 'After many years of experience, I have found that the
Bible, the sword of the Spirit, must fight its own battle, by the guidance of the Holy Spirit.'[33]

Taught by his early years in Sierra Leone, he recoiled from the
type of debate initiated by setting out the traditional formulations of
Christian doctrine which aroused hostility or suspicion. Not that he
departed from trinitarian doctrine, or thought it indefensible; but he
recognized the horror that Muslims felt at what they thought Christians
to be saying. Often, what Muslims shrank from as blasphemy was
not Christian doctrine at all. The way ahead lay in the words of
Scripture: establish the joint acknowledgement of the status of Gabriel
as messenger, and proceed to the prophecies of Jesus' messiahship,
Jesus' own words, and then the testimony of his disciples about him.
Crowther was an old and frail man when he wrote *Experiences with
Pagans and Mohammedans*, and the latter part of the book dissolves in
a shower of texts. But there is enough to show that Crowther, the
African leader of an African mission, had developed an African

---

[33] Crowther, *Experiences*, 28.

Christian approach to Islam in an African setting. It parted company from the assumptions about Islam that had been current in missionary circles in Crowther's formative years; there was no denunciation, no allegations of imposture or false prophecy. But his approach also differs markedly from the far more influential model being developed in another part of the Islamic world by Pfander, the leading missionary to Muslims in the ranks of Crowther's own mission. The dialectic of *Mizan-ul-Haqq* is meant to force a choice between Bible and Qur'an, to induce the conviction that the latter does not meet the criteria for a final revelation. Crowther steadfastly avoided posing that choice. He began with acceptance of what the Qur'an said of Jesus, and founded the body of debate on that premise. By using the actual words of Scripture he avoided many of the flashpoints that would immediately arise from the systematic exposition of Christian doctrine in the formulations of the day. His personal theology closely linked the activity of the Holy Spirit with the words of Scripture; and he correctly identified the emerging African Christianity as biblicist in character. For the future he looked to an African Christian community with an effective knowledge of the Bible; already the average African Christian knew the Bible better than the average African Muslim knew the Qur'an. His other ground of confidence lay in the vernacular principle in Christianity: the fact that the rule of faith was typically expressed in the vernacular, not enshrined in a special sacred language. (We have seen his careful recording of the fact that it was the Yoruba Bible, not the English one, which impressed the court of Ilorin). This difference reflected different understandings of the application of faith in life. It is a point which has become a focus of the modern debate about Christianity and Islam in Africa.[34]

The significance of the Upper Niger in the mid-nineteenth century as a meeting place of Christian and Islamic proclamation may deserve more attention than it has yet received. The contribution of Crowther, no Arabist and no formal scholar, and his group of African

---

[34] Far from being contemptuous of Crowther's not using an Arabic original, the Ilorin court were particularly impressed by the Yoruba Bible, and with how difficult it must be to read Roman script. The question of the different attitudes to the vernacular principle in Christianity and Islam is pursued by Lamin Sanneh, *Translating the Message: The Missionary Impact on Culture*, Maryknoll, NY, Orbis, 1989; *Piety and Power: Muslims and Christians in West Africa*, Maryknoll, Orbis, 1996; *The Crown and the Turban: Muslims and West African Pluralism*, Boulder, CO, Westview, 1997.

colleagues may deserve a place in the history of the debate alongside the more formally equipped Christian exponents such as Pfander
and Sir William Muir in India. In Persia, the *Mizan-ul-Haqq* could
be distributed only with discretion, and its arguments whispered. In
British India it could be scattered broadcast. Crowther and the black
missionaries of the Niger operated in an Islamic context quite different
from either, and, with little evident influence on, or indeed much
notice from, anyone outside, they developed a basis for continuing
operations in that context.

The opening they made was not followed up. The troubles that beset
the Niger Mission and clouded Crowther's last years are well recorded.[35]
The young Englishmen who succeeded the African missionaries, and
who sought to expand Christian missions into more Islamized territory than the Royal Niger Company was willing to allow, had a
different outlook and approach.[36] But the irony is that in this same
period West Africa for the first time became the theatre for a debate
about Islam, but once more the fruits of engagement on the field
were pre-empted by an academic debate in Europe that owed nothing to real conversations between Christians and Muslims.

One of the initiators of the debate was Reginald Bosworth Smith,
a Harrow schoolmaster who wrote for the newspapers. In view of
the reputation accorded to him at the time as some sort of special-
ist, it is worth noting that he was in fact one of nature's amateurs.
He knew no Arabic, had no cross-cultural experience, and was no
theologian. He wrote four books on entirely unrelated subjects.[37] If
we except a volume on ornithology, however, nearly all his writing
has a single theme: the responsibilities attaching to British imperial
and military power.[38] Patriotism allied to moral earnestness sounds
through his work. It is in this light that we must view his strangely
influential work, *Mohammed and Mohammedanism* (1874).

---

[35] See Ajayi, 1965; G.O.M. Tasie, *Christian Missionary Enterprise in the Niger Delta
1864–1918*, Leiden, Brill, 1978.
[36] Andrew Porter, 'Cambridge, Keswick and Late Nineteenth Century Attitudes
to Africa', *Journal of Imperial and Commonwealth History* 5, 1976, pp. 5–34; and 'Evangelical Enthusiasm, Missionary Motivation and West Africa in the Late Nineteenth
Century: The Career of G.W. Brooke,' *Journal of Imperial and Commonwealth History* 6,
1977, pp. 23–46.
[37] Apart from the work discussed here, they are: *Carthage and the Carthaginians*
(1878), *The Life of Lord Lawrence* (1883), and *Bird Life and Bird Lore* (1905).
[38] The theme of *Carthage and the Carthaginians* is the criminal folly of Rome in
destroying the province she had conquered; Lawrence is presented as the ideal representative of Empire.

His desire is that British power, beneficent in intent, shall be beneficent in reality. To act in the right way is to act in the Christian way, and Britain is a Christian country. Indeed, he declares that Christianity is the birthright of the Englishman. He has read F.D. Maurice and from him learned to affirm the positives of other faiths rather than to deny their negatives.[39] But to Maurician theology, Smith added two new elements. One was the new science of comparative religion. In default of the master, Smith himself undertakes to fit Islam into the systematic history of religion.[40] The other new element is a cheerful evolutionism. By adding Max Müller to Maurice within an evolutionary framework, Smith arrives at a formulation whereby all religions are moral, rather than theological, in origin. They have come into existence to meet social and national moral needs. They raise humanity gradually towards God.

Since religions arise from a particular need to establish the principle of righteousness at a particular period, one can readily acknowledge that Islam established righteousness at the time of its birth. For instance, while Christians commonly complain of the depressive effect of Islam on women, it can be shown that Muhammad significantly *raised* the status of women in early Arabia. But one can go further. Islam can still establish the principle of righteousness today, whenever it encounters a people at a lower stage of development than itself. Without, therefore, giving up the idea of the superiority of Christianity, and even leaving open the possibility that Muslims will eventually see the need for a higher ethical norm, Islam can be seen, not as the enemy of Christianity, but as its ally in the task of raising humanity.

This is not, of course, the vision of missionary Christianity; Smith's vision is that of birthright Christianity, the fortunate inheritance of Britain, which should be Britain's light in dealing with those who have not yet reached the same happy position. As Britain moved towards the high period of its imperial expansion, as that expansion brought British rule to more and more peoples where Islamic influence was already at work or at hand, Smith's book could be read as a tract for the times. The expansion of Islam might actually improve the lot of 'native peoples'. That was not to say that Islam was true,

---

[39] *Mohammed and Mohammedanism*, 45ff.

[40] The opening lecture of the series which formed *Mohammed and Mohammedanism* deals with 'the Science of Comparative Religion', acknowledging it is still in its infancy.

it was not to say that Islam was the highest religion, and it was certainly not to say that it had any relevance to western society. All questions of truth claims could be bypassed; the administrative convenience was that the general tendency of Islam was, or could be, socially elevating.

Once again western thought had become engaged, not in a debate *with* Islam, but in an internal one *about* Islam. Its new focus was less on comparative religion than on colonial policy. Smith's views were enthusiastically endorsed by the Afro-West-Indian man of letters, Edward Wilmot Blyden, who wrote with the authority of one who had himself been a Christian missionary.[41] He could give Bosworth Smith's argument a new dimension, detailing on the one hand the baleful effects in Africa of a Christianity heavily imbued with western values, and on the other the blessings already brought to Africa by Islam. Islam had brought unity instead of tribal division. It had kept foreign influence at bay; foreign nations had taken over every African state that had any foreign influence, Liberia alone excepted. Islam had provided a basis for economic and cultural progress. It had harmed the African psyche less than Christianity had, for western colour prejudice and the imposition of western cultural norms had confused African Christians and inhibited African artistic expression. Islam was less materialistic than Christianity, at least in its outworkings; in colonial society an African had little to gain by becoming a Muslim, everything to gain by connecting with the mission-dominated education system. Africans learned English to profit in this world, Arabic to enter the next:

> I believe that Islam has done for vast tribes of Africa what Christianity in the hands of Europeans has not yet done. It has cast out the demons of fetishism, general ignorance of God, drunkenness, and gambling, and has introduced customs which subserve the highest purposes of growth and preservation. I do not believe that a system which has done such things can be outside God's beneficent plans for the evolution of humanity.[42]

As a rhetorician, Blyden outpaces the gentle periods of Bosworth Smith, but it was Smith who haunted missionary writers and speakers

---

[41] See especially the collection of writings in *Christianity, Islam and the Negro Race*, London, 1887; 2nd edn., Edinburgh, Edinburgh University Press, 1967.

[42] J.G.G. Wilkinson, *The African and the True Christian Religion*, New York, 1892; the words are from a letter of Blyden to the author, printed as an appendix.

on Islam for a generation to come,[43] and their concern was not usually with his facile theology, but with his sociology. It is evident that
it was the sociology which was appealing to much of the educated
British public opinion which formed Smith's audience, opinion that
created the climate in which administrative decisions were made.

In West Africa, the growing empires of the western powers were
colliding with the great Islamic grassland empires, the fruit of a complex process of Islamic revival and expansion; in Egypt and the
Sudan, French and British interests were confronting each other; in
East Africa the western powers were absorbing the areas once claimed
by the Sultanate of Zanzibar.[44] Incremental changes in the rest of
the world now meant that the foremost ruler of the world's Muslims
was no longer the Sultan of Turkey but Queen Victoria. The Royal
Republic of the Netherlands also claimed vast numbers of Muslim
subjects; and the twentieth century was to bring a time, not far
ahead, when, with the Caliphate collapsed and Turkey secular, the
Emir of Afghanistan was almost the only genuinely independent
Muslim ruler in the world.

Thus in the age of imperialism which Smith heralded, most of
the Muslim world passed under the rule, or at least the dominance,
of powers that had always been thought of as Christian. But, despite
the optimism of some missionary commentators, such as Robert E.
Speer,[45] this did not usher in a great new era of accessibility, the
opening to missions of the doors the Caliphate kept shut; indeed,
the colonial powers were sometimes more efficient at gatekeeping
than the Sultan had been. Far more importantly, there seemed now
good reasons why public policy should control the access of missions, not only to areas that were Islamic, but to areas in which
Islamic influence was, or might soon be, at work.

---

[43] Blyden noted the progress of Bosworth Smith's views: *Christianity, Islam and the
Negro Race*, p. 189. The introductory paper of the Cairo Conference on missions
claims that 'many have been led to think of Islam as a mild oriental Unitarianism,
well enough adapted to Asiatics and Africans' largely through the 'misrepresentations of men like Bosworth Smith.' This was thirty years after Smith's book first
appeared. S.M. Zwemer, E.M. Wherry and J.B. Barton (eds.), *The Mohammedan World
of Today. Being Papers read at the First Missionary Conference on behalf of the Mohammedan
World . . .*, New York, Revell, 1904, p. 18.

[44] Hastings, 1994, pp. 397–492, under the title 'A Variety of Scrambles', relates
the political and religious aspects.

[45] E.g. *Students and the Missionary Problem. Addresses Delivered at the International Student
Missionary Conference, London, January 2–6, 1900*, London: Student Volunteer Missionary
Union, 1900, pp. 423–428. 'Dare we say that the Mohammedans are inaccessible

The era of imperial expansion is, of course, the era of missionary revival. Hundreds of new missionaries from the west pushed the frontiers of mission forward, seeking, in the eloquent title of a popular series of books at the time, the Conquests of the Cross.[46] As regards Africa, the idea developed of a race with Islam, a competition for the peoples of the continent. What appeared to the mission constituency to stand in the way was the colonial administration, so tender of Islamic susceptibilities, it seemed, and so misled by the spirit of Bosworth Smith about the social effects of Islam that it encouraged Muslim expansion and hindered Christian conversion. In the race for the soul of Africa, Christianity, it seemed, must contend with handicaps and heavy weights imposed by the administrative policies of Christian countries. The intellectual position of Christianity, the axiomatic character of its benefit to society, could no longer be taken for granted. It is in the heyday of imperialism that an unmistakable note of embattlement comes into missionary discourse.

That note of embattlement is very audible in the proceedings of the special missionary conferences, held in Cairo in 1906 and in Lucknow in 1911, called to consider missions in Muslim lands. Fifty years earlier the mission constituency had complained that British administration in India was trying to maintain neutrality in India when it should be declaring support for Christianity. At the Cairo conference W.R.S. Miller, one of the most eloquent missionary figures associated with Northern Nigeria, complained not that the British government practised neutrality in religion, but that it did not. Were the government truly neutral, Islam would not be making the progress it was in Nigeria, where the Plateau people had long experience of harsh treatment from Muslims. But, while Muslim missionaries were allowed to go anywhere under British administration, Christian missionaries were restricted. 'The inevitable results of a slave-ridden land, laziness, oppression and dirt have fallen upon West Africa.'[47] An American, C.R. Watson, made a general observation about colonialism and missions:

---

until we have tried?. . . . When Islam has been won to Christianity we shall be able to give the world missionaries. Who dare say that they will not be even better than the Jews?'

[46] *Conquests of the Cross: A Record of Missionary Work throughout the World*, London and New York, Cassell, 1890. The series of three volumes was compiled by Edwin Hodder.

[47] 'Islam in West Africa,' in Zwemer, Wherry and Barton, 1904, pp. 43–50.

> The displacement of pagan governments by western governments has
> generally been to the advantage of the missionary enterprise as a whole.
> Yet, when we consider only the way in which that change affects the
> status of Islam . . . the change from a pagan to a western government
> has generally been to the advantage of Islam.[48]

The distinguished CMS missionary in Egypt, Temple Gairdner was
more direct. Contemporary British colonial policy was 'cowardly and
unchristian . . . The British official may one day see that all this sub-
servience to the Muslim and neglect of his own faith gains him neither the respect, gratitude nor affection of the people, but the very
reverse.'[49]

The World Missionary Conference in Edinburgh in 1910 produced
a documentation of the discrimination practised by western governments
against Christian missions in Islamic contexts, and made an official
protest to what was seen as the chief culprit, the British government.[50]

In a period when the idea was developing of competition with
Islam for the soul of Africa, the conclusion was that competition was
unfairly skewed towards Islam by colonial policy. The missionary
constituency itself became involved in the debate about the social
effects of Islam, a theme which is very apparent in discussions in
the mission conferences of the last decade of the nineteenth century.
The enemy were those like Bosworth Smith (frequently mentioned
by name long after the appearance of his sole book on the subject)
who claimed a Christian standpoint yet urged that the effects of
Islam on 'primitive' peoples were beneficial. What made this so dis-
tressing was the opinion now widely canvassed by European observers,
and loudly proclaimed by Blyden, that the social effects of Christian
missions were, to say the least, ambiguous. It had once been a key-
stone of Christian thinking about Africa that Christianity and legitimate commerce would spread together, commerce choking that
slave trade which itself was one of the impediments to missions. But
at the end of the century, with the Atlantic slave trade ended, commercial relations with Europe well established, and Christian missions

---

[48] 'Statistical and Comparative Survey of Islam in Africa', ibid., pp. 281–285.
[49] 'Islam under Christian Rule' in E.M. Merry, S.M. Zwemer and C.G. Mylrea
(eds.), *Islam and Missions: Being Papers read at the Second Missionary Conference on behalf
of the Mohammedan World at Lucknow*, New York, Revell, 1911, pp. 195–205. The
quotation is from p. 205.
[50] World Missionary Conference 1910 Vol. VII: *Missions and Governments*, Edinburgh
and New York, 1910, p. 113.

in most of the trading centres, the most notable article of trade was
ardent spirits. As the pyramids of gin bottles mounted in African villages, the word began to be heard that alcohol was a new slave
trade even more devastating than the old one. And the areas in
which this was most evident were the coastal territories, the most
missionized. What if the gin traders were Christians, whether from
Christian Europe or Sierra Leone? (In the latter case they might
well be teaching the people to sing hymns on Sunday.) If an alco-
holic haze was truly hanging over West Africa as a result of the
confluence of Commerce, Christianity and Civilization, was it really
to be assumed that the social effects of Christianity were better than
those where alcohol was renounced? Might not the spread of Islam
be to the moral and temporal benefit of Africa?

A little book by C.H. Robinson[51] excellently represents a good
deal of missionary writing. Robinson had been a member of the
'Soudan Party', an early mission to Northern Nigeria; he became
Lecturer in Hausa at Cambridge; and as Editorial Secretary for the
Society for the Propagation of the Gospel he was a prolific writer
on missionary topics. His specific target in this work is 'Christian
apologists for Islam', and his purpose is to show that the reality of
Islamic lands is not what ought to follow from Bosworth Smith's
premises. Interestingly he does not take the traditional line of denounc-
ing Ottoman corruption: the Mediterranean lands were formerly Christian, and no index to the social effects of Islamic civilization. The
theatre for judging that is Hausaland.

Hausaland proves that Islam does not halt the new slavery of
drunkenness: Muslims get as drunk as anyone. Certainly, the further
north one goes, the less the incidence of drunkenness; but this simply represents distance from the source of pollution, western trade,
a trade due, not to Christianity but to the highly secular Royal Niger
Company. Nor does the experience of Hausaland suggest that Islam

---

[51] *Mohammedanism, Has it any Future?*, London, Gardner Darton, 1897. Many of
the same themes are addressed in Robinson's larger book, *Hausaland or Fifteen Hundred
Miles through the Central Soudan*, London, Sampson Low, 1896. Chapter XII, or
'Mohammedanism in the Central Soudan', sets out to counter 'a considerable number of apologists in England, who, whilst professing Christianity themselves, have
maintained that for a large portion of the human race, Mohammedanism is not
only as good, but a distinctly better form of religion than that which they themselves profess.' He quotes a letter to *The Times* by Sir William Carter, Governor of
Lagos, arguing for the spread of Islam as an answer to the alcohol problem.

creates an advanced civilization: the celebrated Hausa cloth is pre-Islamic. What Islam has brought to Hausaland is slavery. A third of the Hausa are slaves, one in 300 of the world's population is a Hausa-speaking slave. To the argument that Christians were for centuries responsible for the slavery of Africans, Robinson replies that slavery is integral to Islam, fundamentally antipathetic to Christianity.

This raises the link between theory and practice, by which the 'Christian apologists for Islam' must be tested. Islam, Robinson concludes, may indeed raise 'degraded savages' through the idea of the transcendent God and the practice of Arabic literacy. But it has little to offer 'civilized heathenism', a category which seems to comprehend the Hausa. The reason is that Islam has a built-in block to cultural progress *beyond a certain point*.

> Unless we are prepared to contemplate the African civilization ... of a thousand years hence being on a level with that of the Arab even of today, we cannot look with other than grave mistrust and apprehension at the progress, be it great or small, which Islam is now making in Africa.[52]

In this way a significant element of mission thinking became drawn into the western debate about the social effects of Islam in a period in which mission strategy became concerned with the idea of competition with Islam. In evangelical circles the German traveller Karl Kümm popularized the idea of competition in the whole 'Sudan' (i.e. *Bilad es-Sudan*) region. The object was not to lock horns with Muslims, but to concentrate on non-Muslim peoples before they came under Islamic influence. The Sudan United Mission was one outcome of such thinking.[53] Other missions begged for missionary reinforcements to stem an expected tide of Islamic advance (an expectation not always justified by the event).[54] In these new crusading days, the immediate challenge was to 'occupy', meaning to get there first.

All this activity and controversy about Islam did little to advance direct Christian engagement, encounter and conversation with Muslims. True, there were new developments in germ. The year 1911 saw

---

[52] Robinson, *Mohammedanism*, p. 27.
[53] See Hermann Karl Wilhelm Kümm, *The Sudan: A Short Compendium of Facts and Figures about the Lord of Darkness*, London, Marshall, 1906; *Khont-hon-nofer: The Lands of Ethiopia*, London, Marshall, 1910; *From Hausaland to Egypt*, London, Constable, 1910.
[54] J.D. Holway, 'CMS Contact with Islam in East Africa before 1914,' *Journal of Religion in Africa* IV.3, 1972, pp. 200–212.

the birth of both the journal *The Moslem World*[55] and the Kennedy
School of Missions, which together (the latter through its Muslim
Lands Department under Duncan Black Macdonald) were to have
a deep influence on Protestant missionary thinking about Islam. But
to a remarkable extent, and for a variety of reasons, the nineteenth
century is a time of disengagement between Christians and Muslims.
Every exception is significant, and one of them is Samuel Adjai
Crowther and the African missionaries of the Niger.

Adrian Hastings, in the course of a characteristically discerning
portrait of Crowther, says:

> It might well be claimed that for all-round pastoral maturity he has
> no peer among nineteenth-century Anglican bishops in Africa.... A
> combination of learning, zeal, sound judgement, regular visits to Britain,
> and the towering status provided by his bishopric set Crowther in a
> place apart until the end of his life. For his contemporaries, both black
> and white, he appeared to represent all that they could hope for.[56]

And with all the rest that he represented, he was also one of the
nineteenth century's most significant Christian conversationalists with
Muslims.

---

[55] This journal, the work of Samuel Marinus Zwemer, was designed to be 'a
quarterly review of current events, literature and thought among Mohammedans,
and the progress of Christian missions in Moslem lands.'

[56] Hastings, 1994, p. 340.

CHAPTER THREE

THE BUGANDAN CHRISTIAN REVOLUTION: THE CATHOLIC CHURCH IN BUDDU, 1879–1896[1]

John Mary Waliggo

On ne connait pas assez en Europe la Mission de
l'Ouganda: elle est unique au monde.
(Fr Auguste Achte, White Fathers missionary in Buganda)[2]

The Background

The 'Christian Revolution'[3] that took place in late nineteenth-century Buganda is one of the best known episodes of African history, but has often been viewed from only one perspective: that of the capital, the Protestant party, the European missionaries, the written sources, the period preceding the war of 1892 which gave the Protestants power in Buganda. This chapter aims to correct the balance by focusing on Buganda's most south-westerly province, Buddu, which in the 1890s became the centre of the Catholic Church in Uganda, and by using the full range of Catholic sources for the period. While many of these were written by missionaries, this is not a mission history. I have taken the term 'church' to mean not so much the organized institution with set rules and regulations, but rather a community of Catholics, baptized, catechumens and postulants, dedicated and wavering members, saints and sinners, clergy

---

[1] This essay is based on parts of chapters two and three of the author's unpublished Ph.D. thesis, 'The Catholic Church in the Buddu Province of Buganda, 1879–1925' (Cambridge, 1976). Kevin Ward's help in editing it is gratefully acknowledged. For the purposes of this volume, the author's very detailed references to archival material and interviews have been reduced, and some recent references have been added.

[2] G. Leblond, *Le Père Auguste Achte des Missionnaires d'Afrique (Pères Blancs)*, Algiers, Maison-Carrée, 1912.

[3] D.A. Low, *Religion and Society in Buganda, 1875–1900*, Kampala, East African Institute of Social Research, 1957; C.C. Wrigley, 'The Christian Revolution in Buganda', *Comparative Studies in Society and History*, II, 1959, pp. 33–48.

and laity, young and old, elite and non-elite. The concentration is
on the period after 1892 when the Catholics, defeated in the struggle
for political power, turned to create a Christian province instead of
the Christian kingdom which they had been denied. From 1892 to
1925, the provincial chief (*Pokino*) of Buddu was Alikisi Ssebowa, one
of the Catholic leaders in the earlier civil war. This period is known
in Buddu as 'the times of Ssebowa', the heroic age of the Catholic
Church.

The White Fathers, founded by Charles Lavigerie (then Archbishop
of Algiers) in 1867,[4] and recruited chiefly from rural France, had
reached Buganda in 1879. They were the Catholic Church's missionaries in Buddu, which was their 'darling mission',[5] the pioneer
of African advancement within the universal church. Within a single generation Christianity became the province's predominant religion. When Buddu's first African priests were ordained in 1913 they
were the vanguard of the Catholic Church's first successful attempt
to create an indigenous African priesthood. Eight years later the first
African superiors took charge of former mission stations. In 1934 all
European missionaries withdrew from Buddu, and in 1939 Joseph
Kiwanuka became the first African bishop of the Catholic Church
in modern times.

The Aftermath of War

Between 1888 and 1892, Buganda was convulsed by a series of violent
changes in its traditional and constitutional situation. This 'Christian
revolution' began as a bid for power by leaders of all three of the
new religions, Muslim, Protestant and Catholic. The Muslims were
militarily and numerically strongest in 1888 and they soon engi-
neered a coup that forced the Christians into exile in Kabula, on
the western border of Buganda with Ankole. From there a Christian
coalition of Catholics and Protestants staged a counter-revolution,
which in turn ousted the Muslims. Very quickly Catholics and
Protestants quarrelled over the division of the political spoils, until

---

[4] See Adrian Hastings, *The Church in Africa 1450–1950*, Clarendon Press, Oxford,
1994, pp. 254–255.
[5] Livinhac to missionaries, 1 January 1895, in *Lettres de Monseigneur Livinhac*, Algiers
1912, White Fathers' Archives (henceforth WFA); Livinhac to missionaries, 14
September 1909, WFA.

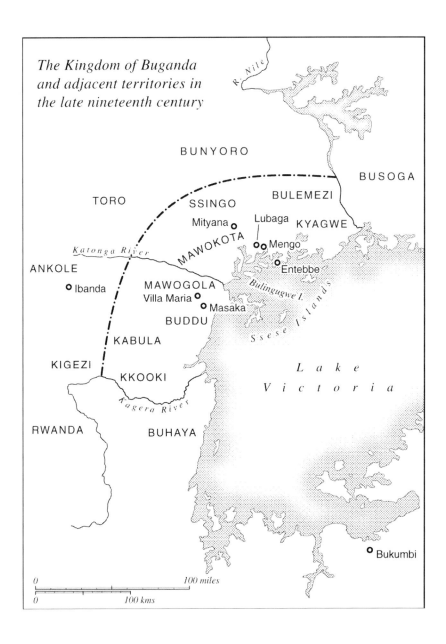

The Kingdom of Buganda and adjacent territories in the late nineteenth century

in 1892 the Protestants settled the matter by invoking the military aid of the British, in the person of Captain Frederick Lugard of the Imperial British East India Company. Defeat in the war of 1892 began a new era for Catholics. Lugard offered them the county (*ssaza*) of Buddu as compensation for their defeat. Buddu, on the southern fringes of Buganda, was rich and strategically important, but far from the centre of political power. The opportunity to rebuild their fortunes, spiritually rather than politically, was to redirect and renew Catholic energies over the next decade and beyond. From all sides, Catholics migrated towards Buddu in a 'trek' and there emerged an exile mentality, which became a distinguishing feature of the Buddu church.

From the beginning of 1891, Buddu had seemed to both Catholics and Protestants the most promising province for further evangelization. Mgr Joseph Hirth, recently appointed Vicar Apostolic of Nyanza and head of the White Fathers mission in the Great Lakes area, selected the trusted Fr Henri Streicher to start a Buddu mission in March, and a month later the Protestants also set up a mission there. When Hirth visited Buddu in August 1891, he was so impressed by the work that he hoped the province would be predominantly Catholic by the end of 1892.

During their negotiations with Captain Lugard in the period just before and immediately after their military defeat, the Catholics insisted that Buddu had already become theirs *de facto* and could not be taken away. They wanted the neighbouring provinces only in order to form a natural unity. Nikodemo Ssebwato, the *Pokino* at the time, supported by his Protestant chiefs and missionaries, declared that to give Buddu to the Catholics was to invite them to continue the revolt, to receive arms from the Germans, to plot against the king and to extend their control to the west and south. Lugard was for a time inclined to agree, but, seeing that the Protestants did not act fairly in awarding the Catholics enough provinces, he decided to use the Catholics' insistence on Buddu as his bargaining position: they must accept either two other provinces or Buddu alone. They chose the latter, and, though they felt cheated, they were relieved that no further migration need take place. Lugard now realized that Buddu would be a test of Catholic loyalty. If Catholics received guns or ammunition from the Germans, if they attacked the neighbouring small kingdoms, or if they refused to come and work for the king at the capital, he would have strong grounds for using all other parties to crush them.

In the exodus of Catholics to Buddu, relatives and families usually went together, tenants followed their landlords and the baptized, catechumens and postulants their religious teachers. The migration continued for over nine months, the worst period being from January to April 1892 when there was no official protection along the route. As to the number of exiles, sources differ substantially, but from interviews, missionary documents and, especially, a survey of the hundreds of villages in which exiles lived, it is clear that no fewer than 15,000 Catholics and their adherents left other parts of Buganda for Buddu in the course of 1892.

Kabaka (King) Mwanga's own group was the first to leave the capital, followed by others under the leadership of Victoro Kiddukanya, Zoeli Mutibwe and Isodoro Mbugeramula. Travelling was mainly by night and in silence, except when the rosary and prayers were recited. Food, the main problem, was obtained wherever possible through pleas to relatives, friends, blood brothers and sympathizers along the route. Sometimes threats were needed. Most traditionalists were sympathetic to the migrants, although they were equally afraid of the consequences of helping them.

The group of the Catholic *Pokino*, Alikisi Ssebowa, consisted of over 4,000 people. He was at the extreme northern end of Kyaggwe fighting the traditionalists when he heard of the Catholic defeat. He separated peacefully from his Protestant warriors and marched westwards through Singo, Bulemezi and Butambala to cross the Katonga to Buddu. As he marched, others joined him, including several Catholics. On 31 January news reached Kampala that he was on his way with a large group to join the rebels in Buddu. The Protestant leaders asked Lugard to help them attack him, and Kakungulu was chosen to lead the forces. They were much outnumbered by Ssebowa's, and about thirty Protestants were wounded before Kakungulu retreated, leaving Ssebowa to march unchallenged to Buddu. On the following day the two opposed groups of exiles approached each other around dusk. The Buddu Protestants, travelling northwards, were in a valley, and at the sight of Ssebowa's group they kept silent. Ssebowa passed about a quarter of a mile from them, and continued his march towards Buddu.

During the following months the migration continued. The wife of Stanislas Mugwanya, another of the Catholic leaders, represents many women who took a lonely route but arrived safely in Buddu. Auguste Achte, one of the White Fathers, wrote of her arrival:

Towards evening I was sitting in the doorway of my hut meditating on the sad state of our mission efforts. Suddenly a child appeared on the road with a woman following it. But what a lamentable condition she was in! She walked but leaning on a stick, her garments were dirty and all in rags, her face bruised and covered in blood. Approaching me she fell on her knees weeping 'Father, God has saved me! The Blessed Virgin has helped me! I have run a long distance and have escaped the Protestants who were chasing me but Donatilla and Josephine my poor daughters have been captured by them.'[6]

Only then did Achte recognize who she was. A few weeks later her daughters joined her, but many were less fortunate. As 1892 came to a close the hope of finding missing people waned. Bishop Hirth received permission from Rome to remarry people wherever it was most probable that a partner had died. Several widows, however, refused to remarry and offered to work for the church at the mission stations or within the chiefs' enclosure.

Three important conclusions can be drawn from the exodus of Catholics to Buddu. First Lugard, unlike most Protestants and their missionaries, showed great generosity to the defeated Catholics and facilitated their withdrawal into Buddu. Second, all those who participated in the exodus, whether for religious or other motives, adopted a similar attitude to the Protestants and the Company's rule, which was used by the Fathers and the Catholic chiefs in creating a Catholic province in Buddu. Lastly, if the number of exiles was between 15,000 and 20,000, about a third of Catholic adherents must have stayed behind, for by mid-1891 the total Catholic population was claimed to be 30,000. The Catholic missionaries and chiefs were greatly worried about these since they were in situations easily capable of leading to 'heresy'. The fact which seemed forgotten was that the treaty had assured freedom of religion to those Catholics who chose to remain in Protestant provinces. Several took this option, so that by mid-1892 there were local Catholic communities running smoothly under their catechists in Kyaddondo and Busiro, while by September Lubaga, near the capital, had no fewer than 150 catechumens. Yet these were Catholics in diaspora, for Buddu had become at least for a time the natural home of Catholicism.

Once the Katonga River became the political as well as the religious frontier separating the communities, taunting began again. Protestants sang:

[6] Leblond 1912, p. 186.

I don't want to sit where a papist sits
I don't want to eat where a papist eats
I don't want to dip my fingers in the same plate with a papist
For we the English defeated the papists.

Catholics responded

The man who will ever cross Lweera
Will open the mouth of our guns.

Even the drums summoning Catholics and Protestants to church were made to spell out their attitudes. The Protestants boasted:

We ate Buganda, we ate it, we ate it,
We ate it secretly, but we ate it.

The Catholic drum looked to the future:

Leave them alone, we shall share later, we shall share later.

Buddu Society and Christianity, 1879–91

'The more a nation is fatigued, oppressed and unhappy, the better it is disposed to embrace our holy religion and aspire to the goodness it promises to its children.'[7] Buddu fitted that description when the Catholic exiles arrived to settle in 1892. Yet they found a basis already laid for the extension of the church.

By the time Europeans reached Buganda, Buddu, although in many ways a typical Ganda province, still preserved its own distinctiveness. In order to reach 'Uganda proper', wrote the explorer James Grant, one had first to cross the Katonga river.[8] Buddu's language differed both in accent and in several words and expressions from the standard Luganda. Many of its social customs, deities and clans were exclusively Kinnabuddu. Some of its Bataka chiefs were of Bunyoro origin and preserved certain privileges after Buddu's incorporation into Buganda by king Jjunju in the eighteenth century. Some areas were inhabited by the Bahima from Ankole who herded their own cattle and that of the kings of Buganda. They remained a group apart from the Bannabuddu. From the 1860s several Baziba princes and their people settled in southern Buddu. By

---

[7] Brard to Lavigerie, 19 July 1891, in *Chronique Trimestrielle* (White Fathers review), 1892, pp. 110–111.
[8] J.A. Grant, *A Walk Across Africa*, W. Blackwood and Sons, Edinburgh, 1864.

1880 they were ruled by five influential princes, and dealt directly
with the king, remaining distinct from the local people. There were
other border areas many of whose citizens lived within Buddu, notably
the kingdoms of Kooki and Bweera, Ssese Islands and Mawogola.
Since Buddu's incorporation into Buganda, many Baganda had settled in Buddu. They were distinct from the Bannabuddu 'Saafi',
occupying the central and coastal areas of Buddu, who were essentially agriculturalists, though fishing, hunting and bark-cloth-making
were popular professions among men. Buddu's heterogeneity had
one great advantage to any central power. Since no one group was
strong enough to rebel, all groups cultivated good relationships with
representatives of central authority. Unlike Kyaggwe, Buddu gave
little opposition to the establishment of Christian rule in 1889. Likewise
in 1892 it did not oppose the Catholic takeover.

By the reign of Muteesa,[9] Buddu's political administration had
long followed the pattern of other Ganda counties. In it, the king
(*Kabaka*), queen mother and queen sister each had a complete hierarchy of chiefs from the provincial chief (*Pokino*) downwards, each
ruling independently of the others. The head of each hierarchy had
his provincial execution site and power to judge cases in the name
of the royal person he represented. Because of these parallel hierarchies and the numerous sub-divisions of chieftaincies, Buddu had
several hundred chiefs of varying influence. This system had three
consequences for Christianity. First, because each chief and clan-
head sent pages and gifts to the king, went to do homage accompanied by many of his tenants, and supplied warriors and food for
military expeditions, Buddu was never isolated from the capital. This
mobility helped Bannabuddu to know each other and to come into
contact with the European missionaries at the capital. While the
interaction between Christianity and the Baganda was taking place
at the capital in the presence of missionaries, it was also happening
in Buddu through converts or those who had only heard of the presence of European religions. Second, when the Christians shared all
chieftaincies among themselves in 1889 they replaced the three hierarchies of power in Buddu with their own men, making it easy for
Christianity to expand quickly. The expectation of Mgr Leon Livinhac,
until 1890 superior of the Uganda mission and later first Superior-

---

[9] The father of Mwanga, died 1884.

General of the White Fathers, became true: 'L'organisation politique de L'Ouganda peut être d'un grand secours pour l'évangélisation du pays.'[10] Lastly, Buddu, a land of plenty, dense population and skilled specialists, manifested characteristics of generosity, pride and wealth that marked out its inhabitants from the rest of the Baganda. These qualities were to be used by Christianity in setting up more elaborate mission-buildings and a self-sufficient church in the early years. Buddu was greatly coveted by all chiefs. To be appointed *Pokino* was regarded as a very high royal favour. Katikiro Mukasa for several years had combined being premier and *Pokino*. All this helped in giving Buddu a strong leadership after the Christian victory of 1890. Each Christian party appointed to Buddu many of its best men, and the missionaries became very anxious to establish centres there.

In outlining the impact of Christianity on Buddu between 1879 and 1891, it is important to bear in mind that Buganda's population was very mobile, because of frequent expeditions, revolutions and migrations. The first Buddu aspirants to Catholicism lived at Kyaato in Chief Mawulugungu's enclosure. The chief was an excellent warrior and collected around him a number of youths from all parts of Buddu. Five of the boys he trained became very prominent in the Catholic Church: Mutagwanya, Ssemugooma, Lwanga, Sserunkuuma and Buuza. On one of their frequent errands to carry royal gifts to Mengo, they visited the CMS missionary, Alexander Mackay, soon after his arrival in 1878. In December of the same year, Mutagwanya was promoted and became a royal page. He continued to visit Mackay's mission and visited the White Fathers too, when they arrived in 1879, soon becoming the Fathers' pupil exclusively. Whenever his Buddu friends came to the capital, they stayed with him and together they went to the Fathers. At Kyaato, those who had begun to pray kept their activities secret and never admitted anyone into their small group until they were sure of his determination and discretion. The 'readers' usually had a member in each delegation to Mengo and it was his duty to pass on what he learned from the Fathers there. Because of the many gifts to the king and successes in battle, Muteesa promoted Mawulugungu to Ssingo county in December 1879. He went with all his young warriors. From there they continued to pray at the capital. When their master died in battle in 1882 the

---

[10] Livinhac to Lavigerie, 24 September 1879, WFA.

group was scattered, only to be reunited in the royal palace as pages. Lwanga and Sserunkuuma were executed in Mwanga's purge of Christians in 1886, while their remaining three companions survived to become leaders during and after the Christian victory.

The second group of Catholics in Buddu were members of Matia Mulumba's household, but their stay was short and their impact difficult to assess. Mulumba was the leader of the Mityana church during the Fathers' absence from Buganda. A few months before his death, Muteesa transferred the county chief of Ssingo to Buddu. Mulumba, the deputy county chief, went with his overlord and lived at Bulawula, two miles from Kyaato, where the first group of Catholic converts had lived. Here Mulumba continued to be the Catholic leader of those around him. Towards the end of 1885 his overlord was restored to his former post of Mukwenda (county chief of Ssingo), and Mulumba and his family returned to Mityana, leaving very little tangible Catholic impact in Buddu. But the Christian martyrdom created sympathy for Christianity in Buddu. Of the twenty-two Catholic martyrs, three were from Buddu and their families were extensive.

Before the Christians' exile to Kabula in 1888, there were two outspoken Catholic chiefs in Buddu: Petro Kyononeka and the young successor to the post of Mukudde, Inyasi Lule. It is likely that some Christians, especially women and children, remained in Buddu, hidden among friends and relatives, while the men were in exile at Kabula. Throughout their period of exile the Christians did not consider Buddu as hostile, though the *Pokino*, Muguluma, a Muslim, was their arch-enemy. When Mwanga landed in Buddu and was enthusiastically joined by Bannabuddu traditionalists, feelings of loyalty and resentment of Muslim control were united in the Christians' favour. At the Battle of Bbajja several traditionalist chiefs and Kamuswaga, the ruler of Kooki, fought on the side of the Christian army and many died. When Mwanga fled to Bulingugwe, Ssebowa and many other Christians remained in Buddu, where they were again joined by Bannabuddu and inflicted a major defeat on the Muslims.

The Christians' chief priority after their victory over the Muslims was to extend their religion throughout the provinces. There was demand for missionaries from all counties but the missionary personnel was very limited. The work of conversion therefore fell on the Christian chiefs. Among the Catholic chiefs appointed to Buddu fourteen were outstanding within the Catholic party. It was they who carried out the evangelization of Buddu before the missionaries' arrival. They were geographically evenly distributed to cover the main and densely populated centres of Buddu. Eleven of them erected village chapels within their enclosures for prayer and teaching the catechism. Although there were only thirty-eight baptized men in Buddu in 1890, all were men of influence, with numerous tenants and servants, and were imbued with zeal for converting Buddu.

In January 1891 new Catholic missionaries reached Buganda. It was thus time to start a mission in Buddu. Thanks to the Luganda grammar and dictionary of Leon Livinhac and Simeon Lourdel, the new men arrived already knowing enough of the language to begin active work. On 10 March Fr Streicher and Fr Gacon left Lubaga for Buddu. On 19 March they reached Mukudde's headquarters in Nnyendo. The Catholics had started constructing mission buildings on Kiwaala Hill, four miles from Masaka and two from Mukudde's headquarters. The fact that the Fathers' house was not yet completed and there was no chapel or catechumenate classroom greatly annoyed Streicher, who blamed it on African laziness and threatened to leave unless the work was finished soon. The chiefs, however, had several good reasons for the delay. They were not sure the missionaries would come; their men were all trying to settle down after years of war and famine; most of their young men were guarding Buddu frontiers against Muslim attacks.

Streicher's initial disappointment did not prevent him from immediately admiring the people's extraordinary generosity, politeness and ardent desire for baptism, and the missionary zeal of the already baptized or instructed. Here in Buddu, he wrote, a missionary found all that his ambition desired. Here he was dealing with rural people, simple and sincere, who brought goats, sheep, bunches of bananas and potatoes. One man presented Streicher with a parcel of white ants: 'I am a poor *mukopi* [peasant]. I have no goats, not enough bananas, but for a present at your welcome arrival, I offer you this.'[11] Delegations of chiefs from all parts of Buddu began to arrive to welcome the newcomers. Open-air catechism classes started immediately, attended by about a hundred people, who returned every morning to learn, despite the heavy rains of March. Special afternoon sessions were held daily for those living at a distance. On Sundays people began to arrive at the mission from 4 a.m., and by

---

[11] Villa Maria diary, April 1891.

8.30 a.m. several hundreds were there. The attraction of a white
missionary was great. Whenever a catechism class or Sunday service
was over, there was great disorder as everyone tried to get hold of
the missionary. Some wanted just to look at him close to, some
avowed they had a secret to tell him in private or advice to seek,
and all without exception wanted a favour, chiefly a medal or a
rosary. Streicher had brought a thousand medals and, despite his
policy of giving them only to those who had mastered the prayers,
within a month all were taken. When the chapel was completed in
April, the Fathers, fearing fever, moved the catechism classes inside.
Of the 300 catechumens, they could select only about thirty-five.
Streicher was determined to use this to achieve a quicker completion of the large church. One influential chief brought up several
candidates he had instructed: 'For a long time we have awaited your
coming. I have brought these men. They have been praying for two,
three or four years. They know the catechism well and I entreat
you to select them.' To these pleas, which were numerous, Streicher
always had the same reply: 'You have brought me ten or fifteen
candidates today. I shall choose not more than one or two. I shall
choose the rest when the church is completed.' Those selected would
prostrate themselves in the traditional way and thank the missionary, the unfortunate would await another occasion.[12]

On one occasion, all thirty-five catechumens entered Streicher's
room and pleaded: 'Father, we beg you to give us baptism ... We
desire it fervently: we don't want to remain any longer slaves of
Satan.' Although Streicher admired their sincerity, he was not prepared to break the rule of four years' instruction before baptism.[13]
The eagerness for baptism in Buddu was experienced at both missions, on the initiative of the people, not the missionaries. Several
instances of successful missionary work by the ordinary converts
taught Streicher a lesson that was to determine all future development of the Buddu church. In May 1891 a young catechumen,
Galiira, introduced himself to Streicher as a cook of the Protestant
chief of Kayanja. 'You are in a dangerous position', Streicher told
the boy. 'Ah, no', he replied, 'I accepted the post in order to be
able to instruct the Protestants.' 'And have you succeeded?', asked
Streicher. Full of joy, Galiira introduced his 'troop' of forty men

---

[12] Ibid.
[13] Ibid.

whom he had instructed in the Protestant chief's enclosure. Every evening they would meet secretly for prayer and instruction, and to 'adore the God of the Catholics'.[14] A few days later, an old blind man who had once been a flute player at the royal palace came to see Streicher. Having heard how he came to lose his sight, Streicher comforted him: 'You can no longer see the light of the sun, but in heaven there is a sun much more beautiful, and that you will see.' 'But in order to see that beautiful sun', responded the blind man, 'one must receive baptism'. Then, putting his hands together and kneeling down, he explained the reason for his visit: 'I have come here that you may select me for baptism. I have prayed for five years. It is a long time since I mastered the catechism, and if you leave me out I will go the whole way to the capital, blind as I am.' He then beckoned 'his troop of blacks', thirty-two in number, whom he had instructed. 'They told me', he said to Streicher, 'that you love those who teach others to pray; on coming I have brought these whom I taught prayers that you may see them.'[15] These experiences taught Streicher to use full-time catechists in Buddu. 'The first efficient plan of evangelization of Africans by fellow Africans', he wrote later, 'came to us from the Africans themselves.'[16]

Streicher now made the existing method of conversion in Buddu into official policy. When Bishop Hirth's letter came, stressing the urgency of converting the whole of Buddu before the end of 1892, Streicher was even more encouraged to use this policy. Having received the statistics of the religious affiliation of Buddu chiefs from his Catholic chiefs, Streicher decided to send his own catechist-messengers first to traditionalist chiefs in Buddu and the neighbouring areas. The Catholic chiefs supplied him with trusted men for the mission, and to these he added young men from Lubaga whom he had been training since his arrival in Buddu. In all 107 catechists were sent out with gifts to the traditionalist chiefs and with instructions to establish friendly relations with them on behalf of the 'European of Masaka'. They were to bring back sons or trusted men of the chiefs to be instructed and sent back as catechists to their own people. Catechists went to the Baziba princes, to Kooki, Bweera, Ssese, Ankole and several other areas. Except in Kooki, they received a

---

[14] Ibid., May 1891.
[15] Ibid.
[16] Ibid.

warm welcome and Streicher's offer of friendship was accepted. Several chiefs sent their sons or representatives to Streicher for instruction. Many sent gifts in return for his. A few pleaded that they were too old to learn the new religion, but nonetheless sent their younger men to be instructed and to report back to them Streicher's teaching.[17]

By June 1891 Streicher's travelling catechists had converted 1,365 people from traditionalism or Protestantism.[18] They were all expected to arrive at the mission soon, but the impending war between Catholics and Protestants throughout July prevented them. When Hirth visited Buddu in August he admired the work of God accomplished in the province. He returned to the capital and recalled his missionaries from Kyaggwe and Busoga in order to concentrate on Buddu, Ssese, Kooki and Kiziba. By the end of 1891 Streicher had extended Buddu mission using the foundation which had been provided by the Catholic chiefs from 1890. The Catholic chiefs had agreed to act as catechists in their own areas. A group of full-time catechists dependent on Streicher had been formed and the preparation of future expansion to neighbouring districts already started. Over 150 candidates had been baptized and thirteen couples married,[19] while between two and three thousand catechumens were under instruction in the chiefs' enclosures and at the mission. Motives for conversion had been various. A few had come to the mission merely out of curiosity. Many came with sincerity desiring to identify themselves with the new religion which also meant identification with the new political order. Several were attracted by Streicher's personality, his free medicine, especially for eye disease, and his free distribution of religious objects. The fear of hell dominated those who insisted on quick baptism. But the majority of Buddu people had simply followed their immediate overlords in choosing their new religion. The young were ready to follow whatever was fashionable. The traditionalist chiefs realized they would have more to gain from accepting a European's initiative for friendship than by rejecting it. Time was running out for non-Christians. The future in all aspects was in favour of the new European religions.

In November 1891 Streicher left Buddu for Kooki, where Kamuswaga rejected his proposals for a mission. On 8 December Streicher

---

[17] Ibid.
[18] Ibid., June 1891.
[19] Villa Maria baptismal and marriage registers for 1891.

moved on to the extreme south of Buddu. As he was about to set out to found a mission in Kiziba, news reached him of the Catholics' defeat at the capital. The work he had accomplished in Buddu provided the necessary basis on which the Catholic exiles were to erect a church that proved to be unique.

The Consolidation of Buddu Catholicism, 1892–6

When the Catholic missionaries returned from their exile in Kiziba in March 1892, they found Buddu ready to cooperate actively with them in setting up a new pattern for the Catholic Church. All Protestants had evacuated the province.[20] Having lost the original ideal of a Catholic kingdom, both the Fathers and Catholic exiles were determined to create a Catholic province based on zealous Catholic chiefs. This was made easier by the treaty of 5 April 1892 which gave them Buddu as their exclusive religious and political centre.

In the distribution of Buddu chieftaincies and villages, certain principles were fostered. First, the former Buddu Catholic chiefs remained in their posts. They knew their people better. They had done so much for the propagation of Catholicism. To remove them in favour of the exiles could lead, it was feared, to resentment and disunity among the Catholic chiefs. Second, the Buddu traditionalist chiefs who were or could be well disposed towards Catholicism were left undisturbed. The Buddu clan-heads also continued to rule their lands along the lake. To interfere with these traditionalists was considered undiplomatic and an obstacle to the quick spread of Catholicism. Together with the indigenous people of Buddu as yet untouched by Catholicism, they were to be won over to the church through friendship and missionary zeal. The exile leaders took the chieftaincies evacuated by the Protestants or vacant through death. These posts, however, were not given to the top men in the Catholic party but rather to lesser chiefs to prevent the temptation of apostasy for political reasons. Alikisi Ssebowa became *Pokino* by order of Lugard and recommendation of Protestant chiefs. Gabrieli Kintu became *Mujaasi* of Buddu. The top Catholic leaders then began to choose villages which appealed to them for settlement with all their men. Since

---

[20] Streicher to Livinhac, 24 March 1892, *Chronique Trimestrielle*, 1892; Walker to his family, 20 February 1892, CMS Archives.

chiefs were now also catechists, they spread themselves rather evenly through Buddu's main corridor. In all, about 950 villages were divided among the exiles. No-one who had played an important role in the past events was left without some sort of chieftainship in these villages or within the chiefs' enclosures.

The next step was to spread the mission stations equally to serve the whole province. By July 1892 three stations had been set up, their location dictated principally by the concentration of the exile population and the size of land available for large expansion. Streicher found his original mission at Kiwaala Hill in complete ruin. Kiwaala had originally been chosen because it was on the main route through Buddu to the capital, near the ports most used when travelling by the lake route, and above all it was beside the powerful Catholic chief, Inyasi Mukudde. But from the beginning Streicher had found it too removed from the centre of Buddu's dense population and too narrow for further extension.[21] With the chiefs' help, Streicher now removed the mission to Villa Maria, ten miles north of Masaka, and Ssebowa's exiles settled around it. Thus Villa Maria was to serve the central and northern parts of Buddu. Several exiles had settled in the southern region and from March Fr Auguste Achte was working there at Chief Nsingisira's enclosure. A mission was built first at Kampungu and later at Bikira, thirty miles from Masaka. In addition to exiles, it served the Baziba princes and hundreds of Buddu catechumens who had started instruction before the war. Bujaju opposite Ssese Islands had settled the entire population from Ssese with their chiefs. They were over a thousand and all embraced Catholicism. Here a third mission was erected to serve them and receive the incoming exiles from across the Katonga.

The three stations were headed by men who were highly regarded by the Catholic chiefs and their fellow missionaries. Streicher we have already seen. Achte, the superior of Bikira, was no less outstanding. From the beginning of his work in Buganda in February 1891, he had shown a singular personality that attracted the Baganda and made him confront difficulties with great confidence. Hardly two months after his arrival in Buganda he had volunteered to lead the 'travelling mission' to Ssebowa's county of Kyaggwe. While there, on Sundays he used to teach no fewer than 4,000 catechumens. On

---

[21] Villa Maria diary, April 1891, WFA.

other days he instructed between 400 and 500. Every month he baptized an average of forty-five candidates chosen from a group of 200.
He was soon surrounded by eager young men, most of whom
remained with him, moving wherever he went until his death. Like
Streicher he immediately realized the missionary nature of the Baganda
and utilized it. 'Here', he wrote home, 'a missionary does not teach
the letter of the catechism, the postulants teach each other. We do
nothing except examining the religious knowledge [of the catechu-
mens] and giving them more adequate explanations.'[22] Because of
the division of Ssese Islands, Achte had been recalled from Kyaggwe
in July 1891 and sent to Ssese, which now had a higher priority.
By the time of the war of January 1892 he had 3,000 to 4,000
Basese catechumens. Such was the man who was to dominate the
southern half of Buddu during this period. Fr. Brard who headed
the mission of Bujaju had also arrived in Buganda in February 1891.
A month later he had gone to open a mission in Busoga, where he
had less success than his colleagues in Buddu and Kyaggwe. The
Basoga disliked the Baganda catechists he brought. But by the time
he was recalled to Buganda and sent to replace Streicher in Buddu
in November 1891, he had won the friendship of several Basoga
chiefs and was planning to erect a mission in chief Mutabingwa's
headquarters. During the civil war, he was in Buddu continuing
Streicher's work.

The type of Catholicism that emerged in these years was based on
four main elements: the religious instruction received and the special
characteristics developed before the wars; the intensification of both
aspects after the defeat; the type of Catholicism the White Fathers intended to set up, given an ideal situation of a rural Catholic province;
and finally the adaptation of aspects of Kiganda religious and social
sentiment and symbolism into the Catholic faith and practice.

Having lost the political kingdom, the Catholics were exhorted to
seek the heavenly one. They began to accept all the sufferings of
Buddu—plague, famine, jiggers, influenza—for the sake of their religion. Writing to Livinhac, the chiefs stated their determination. 'We
are not going to say that God abandoned us therefore let us also
abandon Him. We shall never do that. We know that God tempts
us in that way, so that He may see those who love Him. We therefore

---

[22] Leblond 1912, p. 139.

have accepted all. . . . Let them kill us because of our religion of
Jesus Christ who died for us.' Their subsequent letters affirmed the
same determination to face death rather than see their religion dis-
appear.[23] Having explained how numerous people were dying in
Buddu of the plague, Mugwanya assured Livinhac that suffering had
produced a great sense of unity and love among all Buddu Catholics
which was envied by Protestants. He concluded: 'So pray for us very
much to our Mother the Virgin Mary that we may get still more
love in our party and also we may love those who don't love us.'[24]

The Catholics and their missionaries had interpreted the treaty of
April 1892 as an intended death-blow to Catholicism. Protestantism,
they believed, was going to spread in all the other nine provinces
of Buganda, and this strengthened their determination to make the
total conversion of Buddu their first priority. Chiefs were already
missionaries to their people, and they now began to compete with
their colleagues in the numbers of candidates they presented every
month for baptism at the mission station. Nsingisira proudly informed
Livinhac that he had presented eighty-three men and eighteen women
for baptism at Pentecost.[25] He had instructed them all himself. At
first all chiefs sent their advanced catechumens to the missions to
be prepared for baptism. Villa Maria had over 1,500, Bikira over
2,000, Bujaju over 1,000.[26]

The work of building the mission stations was taken up fully by
the Catholic chiefs. Since most had been royal pages, they copied
the royal departments to facilitate the work. Thus in July 1892 Alikisi
Ssebowa set up four departments around Villa Maria for the work
at the mission: a department for planning, dividing the work among
the chiefs according to the number of their subjects; a warriors'
department, to encourage all Catholics to be courageous and hardworking; a construction department, including the supervision of
brick-building and carrying (after mass on Sundays every able-bodied
Catholic was supposed to carry at least ten bricks to the construction
site); and the fining department, led by Ssebowa himself, which fined
all who were lazy or disobedient, and tried to explain to all Catholics
and traditionalists that it was not by force that they should work,

---

[23] WFA.
[24] Ibid.
[25] Letter, Nsingisira to Livinhac, 3 November 1892, WFA.
[26] Leblond 1912, pp. 188–189, 196; baptismal registers, Villa Maria and Bikira.

but for the love of God. These departments fulfilled a real need in the mission, enabling the Fathers to concentrate on spiritual welfare, and continued to function until 1909 when the permanent church was completed. At Bikira and Bujaju mission stations the same work with the same means was being undertaken by the chiefs.

The structure of the missions that emerged showed that the Catholic chiefs had constructed nothing less than an imitation of the royal palace, except that the mission buildings were stronger and more elaborate, owing to the new devices of the White Fathers who insisted on using sunburnt bricks and very thick walls. Villa Maria set the pattern for all other White Fathers' missions in Uganda. The church, which dominated the large compound, was the new *Twekobe*, the house for the King of Kings, and also the royal assembly hall. To work on it was considered a high privilege. The pride the Catholics had had in Lubaga Cathedral, burnt down on 24 January 1892, was now transferred to Villa Maria church. Next to the church was the Fathers' residence. It was built with the same attitude: the priests were the representatives of God, their house had to be decorated and surrounded with beautiful fences. In front of it, but outside the fence, a special open house was constructed for each priest. Here he would meet people, settle disputes, examine catechumens and receive important guests. The houses for mission catechists followed. Streicher had by now about fifty young men he had trained as missionary catechists. These were placed at a distance behind the Fathers' residence. There were four large living quarters, two for women catechumens and neophytes and two for men. The catechumens were under instruction while the baptized served the material needs of the mission. The largest buildings, apart from the church, were the audience halls for the morning and afternoon instructions, in front of the church. A school for baptized children was placed in front of the Fathers' house. Finally, about a quarter of a mile from the church stood the house for the sick and aged. A wall was constructed in 1894 to enclose all these mission buildings and by 1898 it had been completed. Following their vision of the mission station as a royal palace, each Catholic chief of influence constructed a house near the mission. The chiefs' houses were to serve neophytes who came for sacraments or for settling disputes at the mission, those who came for refresher courses or feast days, and above all the chiefs' catechumens attending instruction. Each chief found women ready to volunteer to look after his mission property and feed his subjects.

During Easter retreats chiefs resided in their mission houses. By 1896 Villa Maria had about 300 chiefs' houses and Bikira 200, while Kooki had only 50. The hut tax proposed by Sir Harry Johnston, the British Commissioner, in 1899 was vigorously opposed by the Fathers as a threat to this structure.

The missionary's timetable left him little time for rest: masses, catechism classes with hundreds of candidates, distribution of both medicine and of advice on civil and religious matters, regular visits to outstations and influential chiefs. As Fr Achte wrote to his parents, 'Sometimes we cannot say our breviary until 9 p.m. because all other business takes so long . . . You see, my dear parents, we have no leisure to be ill.'[27]

A change of policy by Bishop Hirth early in 1893 increased the missionary involvement of the chiefs. In order to save the missionaries from exhaustion, he ruled that each mission should not accept more than 300 candidates for the morning catechism or more than 100 for the afternoon session. This was a sad decision for the hundreds of catechumens at the stations. Their desire for baptism was great. They had waited for a long time and baptism had become the passport for social acceptance and promotion in Buddu. Fear of hell and living under 'Satan's control' brought strong pleading for baptism by the candidates themselves and their chiefs. An old woman who had taken a lonely route of exile to Buddu came to Fr Achte and begged: 'My father, I am an old woman. I am about to die, but I still have the demon in my heart. Make me a child of God.' 'Good mother', replied Achte, 'it is very true that you are very old but to ask for baptism do you know the essential prayers?' 'I know the Our Father, Hail Mary, the Creed and the three fundamental words: Only One God; three Persons in one God; the Word was made flesh and died to save us.' Achte promised her baptism within a month of instruction. 'My father, my young friend', replied the woman, 'I am about to die; I am almost as dead already. Have pity on me and give me baptism. I am too feeble to wait that long.'[28] Achte broke Lavigerie's rule and baptized her the following day. Within fifteen days she was dead and Achte was happy to have gone against instructions in this case. At Villa Maria the same desire for baptism dominated. Before examination of candidates for baptism,

---

[27] Leblond 1912, p. 196.
[28] Ibid., pp. 187–188.

some promised eight days fasting to thank the Virgin Mary if they passed. What was happening in Buddu at this time was best summed up by Achte: 'On ne connait pas assez en Europe la Mission de l'Ouganda: elle est unique au monde.'[29]

Hirth's decision to reduce the number of mission catechumens led to the increase in the numbers instructed in the chiefs' enclosures. From an intensive study of religious practice and instruction in the enclosures of five prominent chiefs, the picture which emerged was almost identical. Alikisi Ssebowa's enclosure consisted of a big house in the middle of the compound for himself, his wife Birabwa and his important guests, including the visiting priests. On its right were the quarters of the boys sent to him as pages. By 1893 they were about 80. Behind the house stood the quarters of the girls being trained in Birabwa's service. They were about 60 in 1893. Farther south were several small houses for the respectable old women who had been left to Ssebowa by his dead friends and relatives, or who had chosen to offer him their free services. Directly in front of the chief's house was the chapel/catechumenate. Beside it stood the audience hall where cases were heard, visitors received and chiefs' meetings held. At the entrance to the enclosure was the Ssabakaki's house. His duty was to keep out undesirable people and to introduce visitors to the chief. Surrounding the chiefs' buildings was a fence which left out only the banana groves and food plantations.

It was to such enclosures that the surplus catechumens were now sent. Those who lived within the enclosure had to follow Ssebowa's timetable to the last detail, from five in the morning to six in the evening. What made his enclosure feared and respected most was his moral code. Fighting and quarrelling were heavily punished. Ssebowa's famous stick, *kazigo*, was always ready to chastise transgressors. Strict obedience was demanded. No unnecessary mixing of boys and girls was tolerated. The moral code also applied to the traditionalists, who had to respect Sunday observance. No practice of witchcraft or what Christians regarded as public superstitions was tolerated. The old traditionalists were not forced to embrace Catholicism, but their children were regarded as *de facto* Christians and had to be instructed. For a traditionalist parent to object was to oppose religious freedom. Unmarried men were not allowed to build their

---

[29] Ibid., p. 198.

own houses, but had to stay with their parents. A man using inde-
cent language was heavily fined.

Catholicism dominated ordinary family life. Every Catholic was to
say prayers on waking, after greeting the members of the family, at
midday, in the evening and before going to bed. A family rosary
became a daily practice. The more devoted Catholics went to confession every Saturday. Feasts of popular devotion were numerous
and had special attractions: the Saturday masses in Our Lady's
chapels; the feast of Purification when Christians carrying burning
reeds climbed the hill to Mary's chapel; Ash Wednesday, attended
by as large a crowd as Easter and called by the Fathers the 'eighth
sacrament',[30] since all baptized and catechumens received the ashes
on the forehead and preserved them throughout the day; Rogation
Days, when processions were made and Christians brought goats,
cows, sheep, hens, bananas and crops of every kind to be blessed
by the priests; Holy Thursday, when male Christians spent the entire
night in the church to 'guard' their master Christ (women were
excluded). The Feast of God (*Corpus Christi*) was by far the most
traditionally celebrated. The drums used only for the king were
employed and the men who had played in the royal palace were the
only ones who drummed on this occasion. Christ the King was carried through the villages near the mission and all people were expected
to show reverence. Several traditionalists were converted on these
occasions as they joined in the celebrations. The feast of All Saints
and of All Souls appealed to everyone. People travelled from afar
to pray to their patron saints and for all their dead relatives. The feasts
of Easter, Ascension, Pentecost, the Immaculate Conception of Mary,
and Christmas were most solemn and adapted to the traditional pattern of the people. Thus from January to December the White
Fathers set up an intensive Christian programme to which people
responded eagerly. In view of the great stress on uniformity in the
universal Catholic Church of the time, one must conclude that the
Buddu Catholics took the initiative to make Catholicism their own,
and the Fathers, with Lavigerie's instructions to support them, were
not always unwilling to cooperate in the work of adaptation.

From mid-1893 the church of Buddu began an active evangelization of other areas. The first move came as a result of Sir Gerald
Portal's treaty of April 1893 (rectifying the religious division of the

---

[30] Kannabulemu Mission diary, Palm Sunday, April 1906, WFA.

country), which gave Ssese Islands, Mawokota County and Buwekula to the Catholics. Danieli Ssematimba left Buddu to become the county chief of Mawokota in August 1893. He went with over 800 Catholics[31] and several followed later. When he occupied the county without resistance from Protestants, the Catholics thought the impossible had happened. They wrote to Livinhac: 'Our Father we tell you the extraordinary event has happened in our country—the Protestants to leave their villages and the Catholics to come in without fighting ... the Lord has rectified our situation.'[32] By the end of the year there were 400 baptized Catholics and the Fathers were planning a mission station in Mawokota, which was opened in 1899. Ssese Islands were given to Nova Jjumba Naluswa. Most of the Basese, over 2,000 in number, migrated from Buddu back to their original land. The original aim of Bujaju mission no longer existed, so the Fathers went with their Christians to the Islands to reopen the mission that had been destroyed in 1892. The new county chief of Buwekula was Cypriano Mutagwanya, who took 200 baptized Catholics and several hundred catechumens. Streicher had already made friends with the chief of Kitagwenda and was at the moment of sending missionaries there. Now Fr Achte left Bikira for Buwekula to found the mission of Bukuumi in 1894. In addition to these counties, Portal's treaty had given several villages on the route to Mengo to the Catholics and a few plots in the capital itself. Their holders were expected to look after Catholics who went to work at Mengo. This assured a Catholic presence in the Protestant counties of Busiro and Kyaddondo.

From January 1894 Buddu church began to look beyond Buganda. Catechists were sent from Villa Maria to Busoga, Ankole, Toro, Bunyoro, Kooki, Bweera and Mawogola. They took gifts to the chiefs, requesting them to accept Streicher's offer of friendship and to send their own men to be instructed in Buddu as catechists. The results were satisfactory.[33] From Busoga several chiefs sent candidates to Streicher to be educated and most of them returned to evangelize Busoga. Kitagwenda, the quasi-independent chief of Bunyoro, enthusiastically accepted Streicher's offer and requested a mission: 'Tell the European of Buddu ... all my subjects who want to pray will

---

[31] See Lubaga Mission diary, September and October 1894, WFA.
[32] Letter of Catholic chiefs to Livinhac, 1893 (no specific date), WFA.
[33] Villa Maria diary, 1 January to 29 May 1894, WFA.

do so freely and I will also pray.'[34] Following this good news more
catechists were sent and Bishop Hirth decided to found a mission
there. From Ankole the king, while detesting the foreseen arrival of
colonial representatives, was anxious to make blood brotherhood with
Streicher. This was sealed in December 1894 between the Mugabe's
son and Fr Guillermain. Kooki still presented great obstacles to the
Fathers but pressure began to build on Kamuswaga from Villa Maria,
Bikira and Kiziba missions as well as from the Buddu chiefs. By
mid-1894 Kamuswaga had accepted Achte's building of a mission
in his kingdom and in January 1895 it was opened. With the acquisition of this mission, Buddu's three main centres had been covered.
What now remained was for each mission station to have other
daughter missions to share the heavy work. In Bweera the traditionalist chiefs accepted catechists and women were sent to open a
catechumenate there. In Mawogola male catechists set up catechu-
menates and the Fathers of Villa Maria started to visit these distant
centres regularly.

Seeing the great success of Buddu missionary efforts, Bishop Hirth
wrote his important circular[35] addressed to all the missionaries on
the training of the home and missionary catechists and on the education of baptized children and young men in every mission station.
Henceforth church and school were to go together in all Buddu missions and in the village chapels.

In addition to being sacramental and missionary, Buddu Catholicism
of this period was devotional and disciplinary. Devotional life had
been one of the basic characteristics of the Catholics from the beginning. Since they had no scripture books to read, and since Lourdel's
catechism was to be memorized, right from the time of the Fathers'
self-exile in 1882[36] the self-reliant Catholic community that had remained behind became attracted to the devotion of Our Lady. This
was intensified during the wars of religion and after their defeat.
Many who escaped to Buddu attributed their safety to Mary. Medals
and rosaries were widely possessed. Thus the most elaborate devotion
in Buddu became Marian. People wanted to thank Mary for favours
obtained and to ask her for more. The White Fathers were willing

---

[34] Ibid., 20 February 1894.
[35] Hirth to missionaries, 10 April 1894, WFA.
[36] From November 1882 to July 1885, the White Fathers left Buganda, withdrawing to a station south of the lake. The reason is not clear, but it appears that
they had become discouraged and frightened. Hastings 1994, p. 376.

co-operators. Lavigerie, their founder, had built shrines to Mary and St Anne in Algiers and Jerusalem, and had often visited the Marian shrines at Nancy, Lyon and Lourdes. In his letters and instructions to his missionaries he insisted on this devotion. The White Fathers dedicated the whole Uganda mission to the Immaculate Virgin Mary on 21 November 1879, the feast of the Presentation of Mary.[37]

In his second *Instructions*, Lavigerie had left the veneration of saints and religious images, as well as the distribution of medals, to the discretion of the superior. He had been quick to realize that Africans, being so 'superstitious' as the first reports presented them, could abuse such aspects of Catholic devotion. But the competitive principle between Catholics and Protestants, which directed each to stress what distinguished it from the other, made Marian devotion only more predominant. The medal became the symbol of anyone willing to become a Catholic. After baptism, it remained a symbol of being a child of Mary. The Fathers believed without hesitation in miracles performed by Mary, especially in times of peril. This was quickly accepted and adopted by the Baganda Catholics. When the fathers returned from exile to find their mission more flourishing, it was seen as a miracle of Mary. When their young readers showed the courage of martyrdom, it was regarded as another miracle by Mary, as was the victory of the Christian army against the Muslims. Finally, when the Protestants failed to eliminate the Catholics, it also appeared to be because of Mary's protection. Now in Buddu in 1892 both the Catholics and missionaries felt it was time to thank Mary for all the favours obtained and to rely on her for protection from plagues and for successes in the future. What emerged was a Marian devotion that had its origin in the White Fathers, but fully adapted to Ganda culture and mentality, to an extent that Lavigerie's fear of superstition was in some ways proved right.

The Baganda's devotion, respect and love for the queen mother were the tools used to explain the Marian devotion. The queen mother (*Namasole*) was 'king' in her own right, ruling a kingdom within a kingdom. She was the most effective door for those seeking special royal favours, and the ardent upholder of the purity of the nation's traditions. All these qualities were attributed to Mary with very little theological consideration. The queen mother's titles were used for Mary: *Namasole, Naluggi* (head-door), *Nnabijjano* (full of

---

[37] Lubaga Mission diary, 21 November 1879, WFA.

surprise). Each title explained a reality to the Baganda better than any Marian book could have done.

Catholics therefore set up a geographical and ceremonial counterpart of the queen mother at the capital. No sooner did Streicher arrive at Villa Maria than the chiefs, led by Lui Kibanyi, suggested a chapel for the Virgin Mary on the top of the neighbouring hill, Kyawangabi. It was a little over a mile from the mission. The chiefs co-operated in building the chapel, which was finished in July 1892. Here the neophytes went to thank Mary for the gift of baptism, wives begged for children, catechumens asked for the 'miracle' to pass the baptism examination. Every Saturday from July 1892, mass was said at this chapel. The congregation was larger than on ordinary days. Every Sunday after mass, groups of Christians with their chiefs climbed the hill to pay homage (*kukiika*) to Namasole. Before and after examination for baptism, it had become a practice to go up the hill running to ask or to thank Mary. Those who had passed would run up shouting, singing and at full speed, while those who had failed walked slowly, often weeping but at the same time not completely discouraged.

On all Marian feasts of solemnity, after mass at the mission processions climbed the hill to Kyawangabi, singing hymns or reciting the rosary. At the top, Benediction was celebrated, a homily given and guns fired. All other Buddu missions followed the same practice. At Bikira the chapel was completed at the end of 1893, that of Kooki in May 1896. Henceforth all the White Fathers' missions in Uganda were named after Mary despite Livinhac's original wish in 1879 to put the second mission under the protection of the Sacred Heart and another under the patronage of St. Joseph.

The Marian devotion became so important and popular because it was accessible to all categories of Catholics—postulants, catechumens and neophytes—and was similar to the practice of mediation in traditional religion. The medal with the red thread appealed greatly to women. It was both 'a shield against the devil' and a decoration for beauty. Boys began to sing 'The girl without a medal, whom will she marry?' As soon as one could recite the basic three prayers of the rosary plus the mysteries one was given a rosary. After 1892 this was usually not a free gift. Many secured it by bringing fifty or a hundred bricks from a distance of one mile to the mission compound, in the case of Villa Maria up a steep hill (named *Sikamidaali*, 'I won't die for medals', after those who gave up the struggle). The rosary became a daily prayer, but rosaries and medals also became protective religious articles, in a way Lavigerie would not have approved, a borrowing from Kiganda traditional religion. They became medicine for headaches and fevers: people would dip them in water and drink it. They became weapons to terrify lions and leopards on the way to church in the early morning. They became articles to ward off evil charms. In the morning a man would open the door, swing the rosary or medal in all directions and ask the Virgin to keep out evil spirits and spells. Medals and rosaries, as well as blessed palms, were thrown into the courtyard or placed on the threshold to stop thunderstorms, tempests and hailstones. They were also used to secure good harvest, for good luck in general, and to help barren women conceive.

The second devotion which became important was the adoration of the Blessed Sacrament, less popular than that of Mary because catechumens and postulants were largely excluded, but like Marian devotion a synthesis of the White Fathers' spirituality with the Baganda's love of and respect for the king. Catholics applied the titles of the king to God. He was *Kabaka, Ssalongo, Mukama, Ssebintu, Ssemanda, Kamalabyonna*. They were to treat him as they would their king, with the one difference that he was King of Kings and anyone baptized could visit him without having to be admitted by royal pages. The term for paying homage to the king, *kukiika*, was employed. Benediction was called *lukiiko*. The same reverence was enforced in church as in the *Twekobe* of the king. The compound of the church was seen as a royal palace: only good behaviour was tolerated, the church had its own royal pages to look after it and the chiefs exercised discipline.

Many Catholic chiefs behaved exactly as they would be expected to do at Mengo, at the king's court. They came to do homage as often as possible, to secure special favours. On such visits they would go to the church first, then greet the priests and, if time allowed, visit the Queen Mother's chapel. Important chiefs spent Holy Week in retreat at the mission. The title 'Christian' was higher than that of *Kabaka*.

Above all the traditional concept of kingship resulted in great reverence for the Fathers, the visible representatives of the king, and for anyone who had religious duties: catechists, sisters, sacristans, seminarians. This was one of the chief factors in encouraging vocations: to have a son or daughter in the church's service became an honour and symbol of social status. From this period chiefs, even Ssebowa, began to kneel in greeting the Fathers. The era of equality in which they addressed priests as *wattu*, my friend, was over.

Four other minor devotions developed as the number of the baptized increased. The crucifix was the symbol that distinguished the baptized. It became even more elitist after 1892 when influential chiefs and catechists, the Christians who had professed their faith in the religious wars, were given bigger crucifixes than the rest, worn on the same string as their medals. Chiefs and catechists wore them over their tunics for all to see. In many cases, crucifixes were used in the same way as medals in times of danger or need.

Holy water had traditional significance. In pre-Christian days the master of the house sprinkled water early in the morning in all four directions to keep away evil spirits. The head-wife did the same when the husband was away. Holy water now began to be drunk to cure disease, or to be sprinkled on children to bless and protect them. It was used at the time of planting to ensure a rich harvest and protect the crops from evil charms. Those travelling used it for a safe journey.

The guardian angel also found a counterpart in Kiganda tradition. He was called the blood brother (*ow'omukago*), and accompanied one wherever one went. He was presented in catechisms as a Christian's intercessor and accuser. Many Christians during this period were determined to befriend him. This devotion was especially instilled among children below the age of thirteen. Their religious sodality was known as that of Angels, and in their monthly instruction the theme of guardian angel appeared frequently. The patron saint was another figure whom Christians took seriously. By receiving a new name in baptism, converts became members of the new religion and those without a 'European name' were despised. Many converts prayed to their patron saints and tried to learn their life-histories.

The spiritual fervour that manifested itself in such devotions was not universal, however, and some of the less devout Catholic chiefs found it difficult to tolerate their exile in Buddu. There was a group, led by Gabrieli Kintu, Yoanna Mubinge, Leo Bisogolo, Felix Kitatta and Alipo Mutenda, which tried to console its men, most of whom had come to Buddu because of their political and military connections with their chiefs, by providing feasts of banana beer (*mwenge*), continuing through the night. They were soon known as '*Mwenge* drinkers' and a rival '*Mubisi*'[38] group, led by Alikisi Ssebowa, was

---

[38] Banana juice (i.e. non-alcoholic).

formed to oppose the scandal of drunkenness. Gabrieli argued that his men were soldiers and he had a right to entertain them. Moreover, drinking was not a sin nor was it condemned by the Fathers. His men went to church regularly, received sacraments, said their prayers. But Hirth and Streicher disciplined Gabrieli and by the end of 1892 the *Mwenge* group seemed to have disappeared.

It reappeared, however, during the Lent retreat of 1894, when all Catholic chiefs and their men were at the mission for instruction. Silence had been imposed throughout the retreat, but during the night of 19 March shouts were heard from Gabrieli's house, where his men were drunk and firing guns into the air. Chief Mubinge's men were also drinking. Streicher's catechist, who had gone to investigate the disturbance, was beaten and wounded by Chief Mutenda's men. Next morning Streicher read out in church the names of the chiefs involved, informing them they were not to receive Easter communion and that they must await the bishop's decision on their misconduct. Mutenda was forbidden to set foot in church until he received a written pardon from the bishop, and was fined 10,000 cowries for the attack on the catechist. Streicher ordered Gabrieli and his 'whole scandalous group of rebels' to return to their villages so that 'our Christians may prepare themselves better for Easter'.[39] The chiefs left, but next day Gabrieli and his men returned to the mission to ask for pardon. Streicher showed great displeasure at what they had done, but pardoned them, though adding that they would have to go to confession, abstain from Easter communion and await the bishop's decision. Other rebel chiefs wrote letters, asking for forgiveness.[40] The punishment the bishop gave was for them and their men to construct the mission fence.

This incident highlights not only the disciplinary power of the missionaries, and the importance of their sanction of withholding sacraments, but also the strength and character of the Buddu church, from which separation was impossible, because it would mean the loss of a sense of belonging to Buddu. The harmonious cooperation between church and state strengthened the missionaries' authority and the exile mentality united chiefs and commoners in the daily struggle to become heroic Christians.

The results of the five years of intensive Catholic evangelization in Buddu appear clearly in the figures for baptism at Villa Maria

---

[39] Villa Maria diary, 20 March 1894, WFA.
[40] Ibid., 21 March 1894.

and Bikira. At the former, the numbers of adult baptisms rose from 147 in 1891 to 2,729 in 1896. At Bikira, there were no adult baptisms in 1891, but numbers reached 1,553 in 1894, dropping to 1,089 in 1896.[41]

In his annual report for 1895, Bishop Guillermain, who had succeeded Hirth, outlined the position of the Catholic Church in Buddu and Buganda. The favourable terms imposed by Portal and the defeat of the Muslims had offered the church in Buddu a wonderful opportunity to expand outside and develop its missionary character. Wherever Buddu chiefs and catechists went, they erected the same kind of Catholicism.

In Mawokota county there were 1,500 baptized, all from Buddu, and 420 catechumens under instruction at Lubaga mission. There was a school for reading and writing at the county chief's headquarters which catered for 110 pupils. In Buwekula county, under Cypriano Mutagwanya, there were about 500 neophytes and 2,000 catechumens and a school of boys at the Bukuumi mission. Ssese Islands were even more flourishing under the Bumangi mission and the leadership of Nova Naluswa, Ssemuggala and Ssewalala. The baptized were 750, the catechumens 1,500. A hospital and school had been erected at the mission. In Bulemezi county, the Catholic Church had made an important conversion of Princess Elizabeth and her people. Around the capital there were only 42 baptized and 750 catechumens at Lubaga mission. The seminary with its seventy pupils was the main preoccupation of Lubaga Fathers. Kyaggwe county was given to the Mill Hill Fathers and disappeared from the Fathers' reports.

The years of exile in Buddu had done great good: the Catholics had grown strong in unity before dispersing elsewhere.

---

[41] Baptismal registers at Villa Maria and Bikira.

CHAPTER FOUR

'TAKING ON THE MISSIONARY'S TASK': AFRICAN SPIRITUALITY AND THE MISSION CHURCHES OF MANICALAND IN THE 1930s

Terence Ranger

Introduction

During one phase of his extraordinarily varied career Adrian Hastings was Professor of Religious Studies at the University of Zimbabwe. This did not, alas, result in a book on local religious history. But it did familiarize him with the literature about it and, as a result, his magisterial history, *The Church in Africa 1450–1950*, contains a number of references to Zimbabwe that another author would not have made. Those of us who have worked on Zimbabwe's religious history were surprised but delighted that, after describing the mass conversions of the Igbo and in the Lower Congo, as well as the similar movements in Ijebu and in and around Buganda, Hastings added:

> What happened in those years . . . was happening, if just a little less dramatically, . . . in Manicaland, the eastern part of Rhodesia where Anglicans, Methodists, and Catholics were all multiplying fast by 1910 and where the pace was very clearly being set by African demand rather than by missionary hard work . . . What was happening in place after place was a spiritual revolution sparked off by native evangelists in conditions created by the unsettlement of early colonial rule.[1]

Hastings turns to Manicaland again when he comes to discuss apostolic 'independency' in the 1930s, and sees it as a repetition of the early colonial mass movements that led to the establishment of the mission churches. Where so much of the literature has emphasized a schismatic breach with tradition, Hastings stresses 'continuity in experience', and illustrates this with the Manicaland case of the Anglican baptism of Shoniwa in July 1896, followed thirty-six years

---

[1] Adrian Hastings, *The Church in Africa 1450–1950*, Oxford, Clarendon Press, 1994, pp. 452–453.

later by the emergence in the same area of the prophetic baptizer, John Shoniwa, founder of the Masowe Apostolic Church. In the inter-war period, when financial stringency was compelling the abandonment of many missionary activities, 'the prophet was essentially taking on the missionary's task because it seemed so important'. The new visionaries employed the old missionary methods: baptism in local Jordan rivers and focus on the Bible. The 1930s, as unsettled as the time of the early colonial conquest, required a second spiritual revolution, and the prophets provided it.[2]

This paper is designed not as a refutation of Hastings's argument, with which I profoundly agree, but as a development and illustration of it, using a series of Manicaland case studies, drawn particularly from Makoni district. I have already published a great deal on the development of popular Christianity in Manicaland in the early twentieth century, but not, hitherto, on Manyika 'independency'; in doing so now I focus on the way African visionaries sought to 'take on the missionary's task' in the 1930s.[3]

---

[2] Ibid., p. 530. For Masowe see p. 521; for other Manicaland 'prophets' see pp. 522 and 533.

[3] I have dealt with all three of the major Manicaland missions in 'Medical Science and Pentecost: The Dilemma of Anglicanism in Africa' in W.J. Shiels (ed.), *The Church and Healing*, Oxford, Blackwell, 1982, and in 'Religion, Development and Christian Identity', *Neue Zeitschrift für Missionswissenschaft*, 42/1, 1986. I have dealt particularly with the Anglican 'conversion' of the Manica landscape in 'Taking Hold of the Land: Pilgrimages and Holy Places in Twentieth Century Zimbabwe', *Past and Present*, 117, 1987. I have discussed the significance of the missionary creation of the Manyika dialect in 'Missionaries, Migrants and Manyika: The Invention of Ethnicity in Zimbabwe', in Leroy Vail (ed.), *The Creation of Tribalism in Southern Africa*, London, James Currey, 1987. For a study of the American Methodist Church in Manicaland, see 'The Dialectic of Conversion: Protestant Missions in Africa' in T. Blakeley, Walter van Beek and Dennis Thomson (eds.), *Religion in Africa*, London, James Currey, 1994. A general account of my current interpretative conclusions, supported by a prophetic Manicaland example, may be found in the Appendix of Terence Ranger, 'Religious Movements and Politics in Sub-Saharan Africa', *African Studies Review*, 29,2, June 1986. Taken together, these and other articles and chapters amount to a study of the emergence of a popular Anglicanism, a popular Catholicism and a popular Methodism in eastern Zimbabwe. I draw on all this material for the section that follows on popular missionary Christianity in Manicaland. I have not published, however, on the prophetic challenge in the 1930s except in the general account of that decade presented in Terence Ranger, *Peasant Consciousness and Guerrilla War*, London, James Currey, 1985. This article draws upon an unpublished seminar paper, 'Poverty and Prophetism: Religious Movements in Makoni District, 1929–1940', SOAS, 1981, and on subsequent research.

The Mission Churches of Manicaland

The early mission history of Manicaland was, perhaps, a little less dramatic than that of Uganda. Much of its drama was implicit rather than realized. Certainly the rival mission churches disliked and denounced each other as much as those of Buganda. The sermons of the contesting Anglican and Methodist missionaries at Chief Mtasa's capital were reminiscent of the debates at the court of Kabaka Mutesa. But in eastern Rhodesia the colonial regime was established before rival Christian armies could emerge. There was yet greater tension between Anglicans and Catholics. Relations between the Trappist mission of Triashill in Nyanga and the Anglican mission of St Faith's in Makoni were, said one Catholic priest, like those of Rome and Carthage. When the first world war broke out in 1914, local Africans were reported to believe that the 'English' Christians of St Faith's would march to destroy the 'German' Christians of Triashill. Once again, the British South Africa Company regime stepped in to intern the German missionaries and interpret the war in secular rather than religious terms. To complete the cycle of rivalry and mutual hatred, the American Methodist Episcopal Church (AMEC) missionaries believed that they had a divine mission to save Africans in Rhodesia and Mozambique not only from slavery and paganism but also from Catholic superstition.

But despite all this antipathy, and despite the self-consciously different theologies and missiologies of the three churches, they had many things in common during the Manicaland Christian revolution. First, the success that all three enjoyed was due to African evangelists and teachers, who partly responded to and partly stimulated mass demand for spiritual change. All three missions came across congregations gathered around schools and churches that had been founded by returning labour migrants and were only later brought formally into the fold of one or other mission church. All encountered Africans who wanted to surrender witchcraft medicines to them or who demanded to be touched for healing. Despite the focus on white priests and ministers in church publications and histories, the missionaries themselves were partly aware that the rapid spread of Christianity in Manicaland was due relatively little to them and much more to African initiative and the mysterious providence of God. Many missionaries believed that it would take a number of

generations for a Manyika Church to emerge. God and the African
Christians achieved it in one.

The second common factor was that within each church there co-
existed an 'official' and a 'popular' Christianity. Anglican missionaries tried hard to repress African desires for spiritual healing, but
it developed within popular Anglicanism anyway. American Methodist
missionaries strongly disapproved of holy places and pilgrimages,
which they associated with Catholic superstition, but AMEC converts turned the Revival Campgrounds into Pentecostal holy places.
Catholic priests presented Mary as the patroness of virgin African
girls who pledged themselves to the church as nuns; African patrons
crept into the church at Triashill to beg Mary, as a mother, to give
them their children back.

The third common factor was that the missionaries made use of
missiological techniques which either drew upon the popular religion
of nineteenth-century Europe or went consciously back to the Pauline
(or Augustinian) church. The Trappists erected Lourdes Grottoes;
the American Methodists organized Revivals and Camp Meetings
and thus triggered off the descent of the Holy Spirit on their African
agents at the great Pentecost of 1918; the Anglicans baptized by
immersion in Jordan rivers and 'took hold of the land' by turning
Christian cemeteries into places of power and pilgrimage. None of
this looked proper to later theorists of inculturation, and indeed much
of it was undertaken either in ignorance of or hostility to African
religion. Yet this missionary populism interacted in complicated ways
with African demands for spiritual change to produce a popular
Catholicism, a popular Methodism and a popular Anglicanism in
Manicaland. As I have summarized it elsewhere, 'this popular Christianity was imaginatively founded by symbolically sensitive missionaries . . . and also by their first teacher/evangelists who set up villages
of their own, made rain and adopted the plough.'[4]

---

[4] Ranger, 'Religious Movements and Politics in Sub-Saharan Africa', p. 57. I
have argued also that 'one can make some sort of equation between types of popular religion and socio-economic groupings in the eastern Zimbabwean countryside.
Three main mission movements spread and contested with each other for influence.
They obtained foot holds all over the place and won converts of many different
sorts, but the areas in which they established their core followings were those in
which the teaching and liturgy of a particular mission resonated especially with the
aspirations and economic opportunities of the people. Thus, folk American Methodism
grew up around [centres like] Gandanzara in eastern Makoni, where a group of
entrepreneurial Methodist elders had ready access to urban markets, adopted the
plow and thrived on American Methodism's mixture of intense religious emotion

The fourth common feature was that the initiatives of all three mission churches, in conjunction with the creativity of African Christians, had profound social and ideological effects. All three churches worked on producing a written vernacular, for example, with the American Methodists in particular laying emphasis on literacy and literature as a key dimension of the 'richness' that Christianity would bring to an impoverished people. The American Methodist station at Old Umtali, the Anglican College of St Augustine and the Trappist mission at Triashill were the three powerhouses of *chimanyika*, the dialect of the literate progressives of eastern Zimbabwe. Their shared investment in this Christian 'language' did in the end do something to modify their early rivalries. The investment in the new language by African teachers and catechists did more than anything else to produce a sense of distinct Manyika identity.

If the mission churches thus helped to 'make' ethnicity, so too they contributed to the emergence of the Manyika peasantry. The American Methodists, trading Bibles and tracts for grain at their rural stations, did most to propagate the Gospel of the Plough, but all three churches were committed to developing a network of peasant villages, each around its school and church. Thus they helped to make not only a new socio-economic class but also a new landscape.

Finally, all three churches began as communities of young men and ended as congregations of girls and women controlled by a few resident elders. The impact of mission Christianity on gender relations in Zimbabwe is a complex and much debated subject. My own view has been that the emergence of uniformed Christian women's organizations—the Anglican Mother's Union, the Methodist *Rukwadzano*, the Catholic sororities devoted to the Virgin Mary—were only partly a means of instilling restrictive and inappropriate doctrines of sexual constraint and female subordination. They were also about women's power. *Rukwadzano* women had their own Pentecost and their own prophetic foundress rising from the dead; they took an aggressive line in challenging male domination of the church. Catholic women were the guardians of the shrines of rural folk Christianity, Anglican women were credited with saving their church between the wars when it

---

under strict discipline. Folk Anglicanism grew up in areas of middling peasant production, spread out across a wide area of out-schools, each under its own trusted teacher-evangelist; folk Catholicism grew up in areas of subsistence production and labor migration, where Catholic pilgrimage to the local holy places brought men back from the towns and where a largely feminine popular religion of Marian devotion developed.' Ibid.

was suffering from fiscal crisis and the challenge of the prophets.

Thus Africans became deeply and enthusiastically involved in a number of 'new' identities: the ethnic identity of being Manyika; the social identity of being a peasant; the gendered identity of being a monogamous Christian wife. They also became involved in theological and biblical debate. It was African teachers and evangelists, after all, who played the crucial role in translations of the Bible into *chimanyika*, and who pondered the key questions of what vernacular terms to use for fundamental Christian concepts.

The Decline of the First Christian Movement in Manicaland

Yet this first Christian Movement, with all its vitality, innovation and debate, was running out of steam in the 1920s and early 1930s. Those who believed that missionaries themselves had been crucially important to the emergence of Manyika Christianity thought that the fiscal crisis, which in the late 1920s and early 1930s afflicted all the churches alike, leading to reduced numbers of missionaries, schools and stations, had weakened mission Christianity and left the people open to new preachers. Certainly this was an element in the prophet's taking up of the abandoned missionary task because it was so important. But the crisis was much more complicated: it was also a generational crisis within the African churches. By 1930 the bright young men and women who had been the makers of the first Christian Movement had become elders and were seen as repressive of their juniors. A new Revival was needed, no longer to legitimate and empower the first evangelists but to allow a second generation to speak and to work its own miracles. Canon Edgar Lloyd, for thirty years the dominant Anglican figure at St Faith's, summed up this change:

> The Mission Church has come to the second generation of Christians and begins to manifest many of the weaknesses and inconsistencies of all Mass Movements . . . Something of the ardour, undisciplined though it may have been, of the earlier converts has been lost. The very emphasis on education, primary and secondary, . . . and a simple native disposition to take all European ways and manners as necessarily the higher way, have dulled the African spirit . . . Obedience to social convention is a deeply inherited characteristic not to be questioned by the pagan African. He has carried it so far into his idea of Churchmanship.[5]

---

[5] Edgar Lloyd, Report for May to October 1936, USPG Archives, Series E, Rhodes House, Oxford (henceforth RHO).

Missionaries themselves seemed to have lost what enthusiasm they had had for energetic manifestations of popular religion. By 1930 they had come to concentrate on improving the educational qualifications of their teachers, a challenge both to the founder generation of evangelists and to less well qualified youth. An Apostolic convert, looking back on this period, says that within the mission churches they

> used to read about the works of Jesus Christ, how he had sent out his disciples who visited all lands spreading the gospel and also placing hands on those who were sick ... Those with evil spirits were prayed for and the evil spirits driven out. People received the Holy Spirit ... We Africans, however, who were being instructed by white people, never did anything like that. We just worshipped an idol. We were taught to read the Bible, but we ourselves never did what the people in the Bible used to do.[6]

Moreover, the socio-economic achievements that had sprung from the first Christian revolution now all seemed to be endangered and discredited. Prosperous peasants had few markets for their surplus, and settler legislation imposed constraints on their sale of maize and cattle. An American Methodist hero and role model, Abraham Kawadza, who had bought a white farm, had to give it up under the Land Apportionment Act. On the other hand, if men travelled to South Africa for work they usually came back empty-handed. There was need for a new, religiously sanctioned, economic model.

Finally, many of the ideological achievements of the first Christian movement seemed under threat. African agency itself seemed to be increasingly repressed as a new generation of missionaries appeared to go back on the promises of 'Christian Civilization' offered by their predecessors.[7] Manyika Catholics found themselves taken over by *zezuru*-speaking Jesuits, who had traded their stations in Matabeleland for the Trappist/Mariannhill eastern missions. Even the newly imagined

---

[6] I cite Clive Dillon-Malone's summary of a sermon given in St Mary's township in 1974 in Dillon-Malone, *The Korsten Basketmakers: A Study of the Masowe Apostles, An Indigenous Religious Movement*, Manchester, Manchester University Press, 1978, p. 26.

[7] I have dealt with the profound sense of betrayal during the 1920s and 1930s among the pioneer African leaders of a mission church in *Are We Not Also Men?*, London, James Currey, 1995. In this case it was the Wesleyan Methodist Church that frustrated the aspirations of men like Thompson Samkange and Esau Nemapare. In their letters they reminded each other what the radical pioneer missionary, John White, had taught them in their theology courses at Waddilove. There were no more missionary prophets left, he told them. African Christians would have to produce prophets for themselves.

ethnic identity seemed under threat. The apparent collapse of expectations of growth and progress led missionaries, as well as administrators, to develop a new conservatism, supporting elders against youth,
men against women.

All this disillusionment, immiseration and ideological turmoil meant
the revival of fears of witchcraft, which the first Christian movement
had set out to suppress. A key claim of the early missionaries had
been that conversion freed Africans from fear—fear of their ancestors,
fear of evil spirits, fear of witches. If these fears had indeed been
subdued at key moments of Christian triumph in Manicaland, they
were all back again by 1930. Indeed, it seemed to African Apostolic
visionaries that the missionaries and their evangelists, despite their
rhetoric, had never got to the bottom of witchcraft belief and practice; had never rooted out ancestral veneration; had lived with the
patriarchal system of in-marriage and *lobola* (bride-price) which under-
wrote both witchcraft belief and offerings to the ancestors.[8] It needed
African prophets to carry Christianity deeper into African society.

Thus it seemed clear to many thoughtful African Christians that
a new movement of mass transformation was needed. It might happen within the mission churches, but if necessary it would happen
outside them. African visionaries arose to articulate what was needed.
The three examples that follow come from the Reserves of Makoni
and Manyika, and thus leave out the religious history of eastern
Manicaland and in particular the remarkable Johana Maranke, founder
of a great international Apostolic church. They are the Catholic,
Patrick Kwesha; the Anglican, Francis Nyabadza; and the Gandanzara-
born Shoniwa, John of the Wilderness (Johana Masowe), and between
them they run the whole gamut. Kwesha stayed within the Catholic
Church to the end; Nyabadza tried as hard as he could to remain
an Anglican but was forced out of the church; even Johana Masowe
told police that he had hoped the Catholics might licence his African
movement before he broke off on his own to found his huge Apostolic
movement. But all three men believed the work of missionaries was
too important to leave solely to them.

---

[8] Pieter Nielsen, Native Commissioner for Melsetter, found that at mission stations in Melsetter in 1932 a widespread belief in *mademoni* was 'supported by many
passages in the book which they are taught to accept as the final word of God to
man.' Annual Report, Melsetter, 1932, S 235/510, National Archives of Zimbabwe
(henceforth NAZ).

The Challenge of African Visionaries within the Mission Churches
of Manicaland: Catholicism

The depression of the late 1920s and early 1930s hit Catholicism
particularly hard, because so many young men from Triashill and
other Catholic stations had gone to South Africa in the hope of mar-
keting their literacy in English.[9] As the South African economy went
into crisis these young men were forced to return to Manicaland.
They were resentful and many of them were politicized. Thus in
1930 one Tobias Mandichomira returned to Nyanga after six years
away in South Africa where he had joined the South African National
Congress. The Native Department suspected that he was 'probably
an emissary of the Industrial and Commercial Workers' Union'.[10]
Mandichomira was friendly with teachers at Triashill. Two years
later, three residents of Triashill farm returned from South Africa.
The Provincial Secretary of the Western Province committee of
Congress wrote on their behalf from Cape Town to complain that:
'We have it by atmospherical rumours that three of our men, namely
Messrs Makana, Tobias; Chikomba, Bonifas; Makoni, Windring, have
been arrested on their arrival home.'[11] In fact the three were not
arrested, but they were evicted from Triashill, 'owing to the fact that
they are members of the African National Congress, which is not
approved of by the Mission people'.[12]

Father Jerome O'Hea, one of the Jesuits newly in charge of Triashill, wrote with alarm about the political atmosphere around the
mission:

> There is a certain amount of trouble of a Bolshi sort, brewing and
> coming to the surface among the Manyika ... The Young Ethiopians, the
> ICU and a few local societies are talking a great deal of hot air in
> the Reserves ... Boys back from Capetown and Johannesburg are par-
> ticularly active and it is really astonishing to hear the clear echoes of
> Moscow out here in the wilds. The missionaries, of course, are merely
> for the sake of drugging the blacks to make them the slaves of the
> whites ... A fairly good grasp of the theory and practice of the 'class

---

[9] See footnote 4.

[10] Superintendent of Natives, Bulawayo to Chief Native Commissioner, 5 June 1930;
Native Commissioner, Inyanga to CNC, 23 June 1930, S 138.22.1930–32, NAZ.

[11] Secretary, ANC, Cape Town to Resident Magistrate, Nyanga, 25 May 1932,
S 138.22.1930–31, NAZ.

[12] Native Commissioner, Inyanga, to Chief Native Commissioner, 6 June 1932, ibid.

war' being in the hands of the black . . . it is easily to be understood
how the slightest grievance is seized upon and ventilated to the full.[13]

One of these grievances was the arrival of the Jesuits themselves.
Throughout the 1920s the Jesuits had consistently criticized the language, education and missiological policies of the Mariannhill fathers
of Triashill. They disliked the Mariannhill emphasis upon *chimanyika*,
which they regarded as the result of a perverse desire to be as
different as possible from the *chizezuru* language of the Jesuit station
at Chishawasha. They disliked the emergence of a mission-fostered
Manyika ethnic identity, which they believed gave the Africans of
eastern Zimbabwe altogether too high an opinion of themselves.
Monsignor Robert Brown, the Jesuit Prefect Apostolic, who had
authority over the Manicaland Province, demanded in the mid-1920s
that the Triashill missionaries should abandon their *manyika* prayer
books and adopt 'the Chishawasha language'. He particularly disliked the Mariannhill use of the traditional name, *Mwari*, to stand
for God in the Triashill liturgy. This gave too much encouragement
to local culture. Brown insisted that *Jahve* be used instead. The
Triashill missionaries objected that 'no-one here knows the word
Jahve—except as a cry of pain'.[14] Brown was not amused. 'I have
written to Bishop Fleischer and Fr Arnoz today', he told a Jesuit
correspondent on 23 September 1924, 'telling them that unless Mwari
is eliminated and Jahve substituted I will suspend the priest-in-charge
and if necessary close the mission of Triashill.'[15]

The Jesuits also disliked what they believed was a mistaken
Mariannhill emphasis on higher education. They refused to allow
Latin lessons at Triashill to boys who might 'later on become Priests.'
The Jesuit father in charge of Chishawasha scoffed that it was absurd
to think of teaching 'even a few of them Latin . . . They are steeped
in superstition . . . Human respect makes cowards of them . . . Perhaps
their children will be fit for something higher.'[16]

The Mariannhill fathers felt blocked at every turn. They first
approached Rome to have Manicaland declared an autonomous

[13] O'Hea to Mgr Brown, 20 March 1930, Box 195, Jesuit Archives, Harare
(henceforth JAH).
[14] Interview with Fr Conrad Atzwanger, Macheke, 17 March 1981.
[15] Mgr R. Brown to Fr Johanny, 23 September 1924, Box 195. Entry for 4
October 1924, 'Chronicle of Triashill', Triashill, JAH.
[16] Fr A. Reinhard to Mgr E. Parry, 12 November 1920; Fr J. Apel, memo, 18
November 1920, Box 125, JAH.

Mariannhill Province. When this failed they began negotiations for an exchange of territory. Reluctantly, they were prepared to hand Manicaland over to the Jesuits in return for independence in Matabeleland. But the Triashill Christians were not prepared to accept new missionaries who would undercut *chimanyika*, frustrate aspirations for higher education, and seek to humble the proud Manyika. Triashill men working in Johannesburg sent a deputation to the Apostolic Delegate asking that the transfer not be made. They were ignored. On 30 August 1929 two Jesuit Fathers arrived to take over Triashill; the last Mariannhill priest preached a sermon telling the people that the decision had been taken by the church in its wisdom and that they must obey the new missionaries. Then he left.[17]

The Jesuits arrived in no conciliatory mood. 'These Manyikas want and seem to expect incessant propulsion *a tergo*', wrote O'Hea a few months after their arrival. 'They are an awfully slack crowd and they find good medicine in Fr Schmitz who won't stand any nonsense and tells them often and clearly what he thinks.'[18] Partly because of the depression and partly because they had so low an opinion of the local teachers, the Jesuits closed down a number of the outschools. They made it clear that the African seminarians and the girls who had been sent to Natal for training as priests and for a projected Sisterhood of St Francis would not be received back at Triashill. Some of them spent their whole lives as priests and nuns in Natal rather than Manicaland. This was not merely a loss of missionary impetus. It seemed a wanton destruction of what had already been achieved.

At any rate it was too much for the young Catholics of Triashill to endure. Affronted in their new ethnic patriotism, and in their aspirations for advancement in school and church, they began to rebel. Combining with the insecurity caused by the depression and the political influence of returning labour migrants, their protests took some interesting forms.

In October 1929 Triashill men in Johannesburg wrote to the teachers of the mission calling upon them to organize resistance to the Jesuits. Triashill, they wrote, 'belonged to us black people, not to the whites.' The Jesuits had come:

[17] Entry for 30 August 1929, 'Chronicle of Triashill', JAH.
[18] O'Hea to Brown, 20 March 1930, Box 195, JAH.

> to spread divisions, because they have come like intruders to despise
> us, as we have no agreement with them ... See how these Jesuits are
> stepping into our possessions and snatching them from us! We, the
> owners of these things, how are we being treated by them? We are
> being looked upon as nobodies ... Teachers, let it be known that the
> blacks can reason frightfully; therefore strengthen yourselves in being
> of one mind with your children.

The teachers were to write 'many and countless letters' to the Mariannhill Bishop Fleischer in Natal 'for he knows Chimanyika' and would
take their case to the Pope.[19]

The Jesuits intercepted and suppressed this letter. The young men
tried again. The Jesuits 'came to despise us'; 'this stranger walks about
our home [but] we do not know where has he come from'; 'the
Jesuits have not even informed us nor asked us whether we consent.
Is a beast asked?' These protests, clearly, were not against Catholicism
but against the abandonment of the old missionary programme:

> We are treated as nothing. Now, what do they want nothing for? ...
> We say that the SJ came to teach us, let them go for we have been
> taught long ago ... Let them tell us how they wish to make us bet-
> ter than we are being made.[20]

This letter was also suppressed.

But by now articulate dissent had returned home from Cape Town
and Johannesburg with the return of the labour migrants. O'Hea
reported that he heard everywhere in the Reserves the cry 'You are
taking away our language ... our King Mtasa ... the religion of our
fathers' (which meant popular Catholicism rather than traditional
religion). Some teachers had 'openly declared that they will never
teach children from a Chizezuru book'. O'Hea's indignation exploded:

> Nothing but a rod of iron is any use for these people ... They are
> utterly blinded by the most foolish vanity. It is a poison that has its
> roots in history—they, the most despicable of the despised Mashona,
> are given a chance at last, owing to the coming of the white man;
> and they now openly declare that they are the cream of the black
> race!!! Trouble that has its roots deep down in history is big trouble.
> As far as I can gather Brother Aegidius [the legendary Mariannhill
> itinerant evangelist] fostered this idea, if he did not hold it himself.[21]

---

[19] Admin. Apostolic to Deleg. Apostolic, 18 March 1931, Box 195, JAH.
[20] Translation of a letter written by Triashill Christians on the Rand, Box 195, JAH.
[21] O'Hea to Brown, 11 September 1930, Box 195, JAH.

At this point Patrick Kwesha entered the controversy. The Jesuits treated his letters as merely more political agitation. And indeed he took up many of the same points raised by previous labour migrant protesters. He complained that people at Triashill were 'forbidden their own tongue and forced to use a tongue which we never knew nor our fathers'; the Jesuits were closing schools and 'are not the means of teaching us or serving us or raising us, but the means of destroying us and killing us'; they 'mean to deny to the members of our race access to the higher life, of the church.'[22]

In fact Patrick Kwesha was a very unusual man, a mystic and visionary rather than an urban agitator. What he aspired to above all was 'access to the higher [Catholic] life'. He saw himself as an instrument of God and of folk Manyika Catholicism. The Mariannhill missionaries had been forced to abandon their work. Kwesha, as Catholic prophet, thought that this work had been so important that it had to be taken up and extended.

Kwesha was born around 1900. He fell victim to the influenza epidemic of 1918, that seedbed of so many African visions and prophecies. 'From that time onwards', he wrote later in his book of spiritual meditations, 'I never really got well. The disease grew and grew until it has almost taken me ... But I am glad to say Praised Be God because after I got this disease I got many blessings, great blessings that if I had not been humbled by this illness I might not have been given.'[23] After his recovery, Patrick became a fervent Catholic, absorbing the devout Marianism and radical Franciscanism which were the staples of popular religion under the Mariannhill fathers.

In 1922 he went to Johannesburg to work. But he was a very unusual labour migrant: for the next twenty-eight years he worked as gardener to the Irish nuns at Parktown, and dedicated himself to a state of celibacy. 'In Manyikaland there is great wonder with people talking about me wondering why I did not marry', he wrote later. 'I have given them the reply that the Catholic Church is my wife. I ask them, why are you surprised? *I* am really surprised by the way you people are devoted to your wives. I have lived all my

---

[22] Admin. Apostolic, to Deleg. Apostolic, 18 March 1931, Box 195, JAH.
[23] Notebook of Patrick Kwesha containing spiritual reflections and dedication to an imitation of the life of Christ, in the possession of Augustine Kwesha, St Xavier's, Manyika, translated by Sister Emilia Chiteka.

life not for the natural family you think of but for the family of the
whole church.'[24]

In Johannesburg Patrick became himself a missionary to the
Manyika:

> He used to convert people in Johannesburg [says his brother Augustine].
> He used to teach people the catechism. Many, many were baptised.
> These people were nearly all labour migrants from Manyikaland. There
> may have been some South Africans too but what he was really inter-
> ested in was the Manyika. Patrick never married himself but what was
> really important was that all those instructed by him married in church.

The Mariannhill missionaries had planned an African Sisterhood of
St Francis. Kwesha also felt that the example of Francis was needed
as a response to poverty in Manicaland. 'While he was in Johannesburg', says Augustine, 'he joined the Third Order of St Francis and
so did some of his converts.'[25]

In a real sense Kwesha had been extending the work of the
Mariannhill missionaries in Johannesburg. The articulate young Manyika Catholics who wrote to protest against the Jesuits—'the boys
of Johannesburg (probably all rotten Christians)', scoffed O'Hea[26]—
had been shaped as much by Patrick Kwesha as by Mariannhill.
But what he really wanted was to expand the work of the missionaries into the border areas of Manicaland, and particularly into
the Samanga valley.[27] He set out his aspirations while he was in
Johannesburg:

> My only wish which led my whole life is this of going back to Rhodesia
> and start[ing] an out-school of Our Lady of Lourdes in the valley of

---

[24] 'To Renew the Face of the World', black memo book in possession of Augustine
Kwesha, translated by Emilia Chiteka.

[25] Interview with Augustine Kwesha, St Xavier's, Manyika, 28 February 1981.

[26] O'Hea to Brown, 11 September 1930, Box 195, JAH.

[27] Although the plateau areas of Manicaland had experienced a great movement
of mass Christianity in the early twentieth century this had not spread to the remoter
border areas. Thus David Maxwell has shown that although Brother Aegidius had
itinerated the area it was not until the 1950s that Catholic missions were set up in
Katerere in north-eastern Nyanga (*Christians and Chiefs in Zimbabwe. A Social History
of the Hwesa People c. 1870s–1990s*, Edinburgh, Edinburgh University Press, 1999,
chapters 2 and 3). Heike Schmidt has shown that there was little missionary penetration of the Honde Valley until the 1950s. Just as Kwesha chose Samanga Valley
for the work of African missionaries, so African members of the American Methodist
Episcopal Church chose the Honde Valley as the site of an African-controlled mission and school ('The Social and Economic Impact of Political Violence in Zimbabwe,
1890–1990', D.Phil. thesis, University of Oxford, 1996).

Samanga, which also would mean the opening of the world's second Lourdes, or Lourdes of Africa. I wanted that school to be a mission and a training centre for boys and girls and a centre of religious civil-isation, but all to be conducted by African priests, brothers and sis-ters, as the valley is very hot for Europeans. And the order of the religious group was to be the Franciscans of the family of St Joseph. I wanted Our Lady to be served fully in this valley like she is served at Lourdes of France, or more than that. I wanted God to be fulfilled with His covenant by these children of Mary of this her valley, and His great servants to rise up among them, and that some of them, as apostles, may swarm over the whole of Manyikaland, as the bees, and banish all heathenism, protestantism and superstition, and establish a pure and holy Kingdom of God and glory of Mary, so that from that our God may be called God of Manyikaland as He was called God of Israel, and Our Lady to be called Queen of Manyikaland as she is called Queen of angels and saints.'[28]

Until his death in 1963 Kwesha never ceased to elaborate upon the rules of conduct, the habit, and the foundations of the spirituality of his longed-for African missionary order of St Francis. It was to lay hold of Samanga valley as the Trappist/Mariannhill missionar-ies had taken spiritual and symbolic command of the landscape around Triashill. There were to be 'convents, monasteries, missions and hospitals.' 'We also want a grotto or a huge crucifix some-where . . . because, my dear brethren, our places must be very reli-gious to attract our brethren, just as the angels in heaven are attracted by the sight of God.' The members of the order were to conduct themselves as though Mary was

> . . . their own mother like to her being the mother of Jesus . . . They are to be children of her immaculate conception and of her whole life, of her passion, death and her assumption . . . So their missionary work shall be identical or more than that of the apostles who preached the gospel of our Lord with her in their midst.

This Apostolic Marianism would bring 'joy, gaiety, mirth and won-derful richness and pleasure.'[29]

This was a temperament that could never be at home outside the Catholic Church nor fully at home inside the Southern Rhodesian missionary Catholicism of the 1930s. The Jesuits scorned Kwesha's

---

[28] Red notebook 'Written by Patrick Kwesha. 1943 Johannesburg', in possession of Augustine Kwesha.
[29] Ibid.

'rambling misrepresentations . . . so characteristic of his race at this early stage of its development.' He raised questions 'of religious policy upon which he is quite incompetent to express an opinion'.[30] Kwesha's spiritual reflections and his Marian ambitions, however impossible of achievement in colonial Rhodesia, suggest that the Jesuits were misrepresenting him. Kwesha was a living proof that the Manyika were readier for 'the higher life' of the church than the Jesuits were prepared to allow.

It is interesting to speculate on what might have happened if Kwesha had returned in 1931 to give leadership to the Manyika opposition. In fact, he waited out the whole Jesuit period at Triashill and returned to Manicaland only after the Irish Carmelite fathers had taken over the mission field there. He opposed this take-over also on the same grounds that African Christians had not been consulted.[31] But he found it possible to work with the intensely Marian Carmelites:

> When we took over [says the Carmelite Father Peter Turner] we were accepted with great reserve at [Triashill, St Barbara's and St Killian's] because of Patrick Kwesha's influence. But Father Jacky Roche came to strike up a close alliance with Patrick and would do nothing without consulting him. In fact they were astonishingly alike in temperament and aspirations and they both had a deep Marian devotion. They battled against Anglicans and Methodists in the Honde Valley and in Samanga. They found a particular rock in Samanga, Masamiki rock, where they thought they saw Mary in profile, which they called Madonna Rock. Roche would cry and laugh with the people and he would travel for miles with men like Patrick Kwesha, men of little education but very shrewd and devout.[32]

Kwesha did not achieve his African missionary order but he did set up his own *Chita* of St Francis, a Manicaland guild of the Franciscan third order which was very much his own creation and under his own command. In its modest way the *Chita* extended the work of the missionaries and deepened the life of the Manyika church.[33] Samanga was won for Catholicism, after all.

[30] Admin. Apostolic to Deleg. Apostolic, 18 March 1931, Box 195, JAH.
[31] Interview with Fr Peter Turner, Umtali, 14 March 1981.
[32] Ibid.
[33] Interviews with Erika Karimupfumbi and Rafael Makutangwi, members of the *Chita* of St Francis, St Xavier's, Manyia, 28 February 1981. Bereft of Kwesha's leadership some of the returned Triashill migrants turned to Watch Tower and preached its doctrines on Triashill and St Barbara farms.

Deepening Anglicanism: Francis Nyabadza

There is no doubt, then, that Patrick Kwesha was profoundly Catholic. Equally Francis Nyabadza's African Church of St Francis was deeply rooted in Anglicanism. Indeed, the difficulties that in the end drove Francis out of the Anglican Church arose because he was an old-style Anglican finding it hard to accommodate to the new atmosphere of the 1930s.

There was no direct equivalent in the Anglican Church to the Jesuit take-over of the Mariannhill missions. Nevertheless, Anglicanism in Manicaland experienced a thorough shake up in the 1930s. Many of the issues were the same in the Anglican as in the Catholic case. Just as the Jesuits believed that Manyika Catholics had been given too much freedom and encouraged to have too high an opinion of themselves, and that too many compromises with traditional religion and culture had been made, so Edward Paget, who became Bishop of Mashonaland in 1925, was determined to break the power of the leaders of 'folk Anglicanism' in Manicaland. This meant dispensing with old-style teacher-evangelists and replacing them with young Government-approved teachers, just as the Jesuits were doing at Triashill. It also meant bringing to heel the old white clergy who had presided over popular religion for so long. Modernization, rationalization and centralization were Paget's watchwords, just as they were the watchwords of the Jesuits.

The Anglican Mission of St Faith's had been under the guidance of Edgar Lloyd since 1905. He had played the leading role in imagining a Christian landscape; instituting Jordan baptisms, turning mission graveyards into places of spiritual power, itinerating the Makoni countryside on donkey-back, his stalwart old evangelists at his side, making St Faith's a great centre of pilgrimage from its surrounding outstations.[34] Lloyd was a great friend and admirer of the radical missionary, Arthur Shearly Cripps, with his dedication to Franciscan poverty. Like the Mariannhill missionaries, and like Patrick Kwesha, Lloyd aspired to create an African order of Franciscans in Manicaland.

Paget would have none of this. He thought St Francis an entirely inappropriate model for African Christians. When he visited St Faith's

[34] For Lloyd's part in the construction of popular Anglicanism and for his differences with Paget see Terence Ranger, 'Taking Hold of the Land: Holy Places and Pilgrimages in Twentieth Century Zimbabwe', *Past and Present*, 1987, p. 117.

in June 1933 to take part in one of Lloyd's invented rituals based
on traditional religious custom, Paget was highly critical. While Lloyd
might recall how 'In the old days the wisdom and humanity of the
Church made pagan observation and rite subserve Christian practices',[35] like a Jesuit sniffing out heresy in the use of *Mwari*, Paget
was more aware of 'pagan observation' than of 'Christian practices':

> The atmosphere at St Faith's is none too good [he wrote in September
> 1933]. A Sister, who does not work at St Faith's but paid a visit there,
> said to me the other day apropos of the Devil's hold in this country,
> 'I've never felt the Devil so much as at St Faith's'.[36]

In the same month, Lloyd's wife, Olive, noted in her journal that Paget

> had no sympathy for the older generation of missionaries [or evange-
> lists]. Give youthful, inexperienced men the responsible jobs seems to
> be the craze, promote them over men (of black or white skins) whether
> they know anything about the language or history or the racial intri-
> cacies of the natives here or not.[37]

By 1933, three hundred small village schools had been closed, partly
for economy and partly because their standard was thought too low.
Lloyd was fighting to keep the rest open. He lamented the down-
grading of the old teacher-evangelists, men of little learning but much
zeal, and leaders of their villages. Lloyd hated the trained young
teachers, rootless and urbanized. 'Dear Sir', wrote one of them in
November 1934, 'having stayed in a bit far-sighted places I dare to
confess that this country is too far behind . . . and I should like to
be in a place where there is life and where things are progress.'
Lloyd drew the young man's attention to the St Faith's Pastor-
Teacher's Handbook, item 5: 'Our Blessed Lord lived for nearly the
whole of His life . . . in the little village of Nazareth. Let us then
think it is a great honour to work for Christ in a little village and
to work for our own people and to lead the life of our own people'.[38]

Francis Nyabadza was a man after Lloyd's own heart. He was
very much one of the old-style, unlearned but charismatic teachers.

---

[35] Edgar Lloyd, 'St Faith's Rusape: the Archbishop's Visit', June 1933, USPG
Missionary Correspondence, RHO.
[36] Edward Paget to A.C. Knights, 13 September 1933, Paget Out-Letter Book,
ANG 1/1/5, NAZ.
[37] Olive Lloyd, circular letter, 23 September 1933, ANG 16/11/1, NAZ.
[38] Olive Lloyd, circular letter, 17 November 1934, ANG 16/11/1; St Faith's
Teacher's Handbook, 1935, ANG 16/1/10, NAZ.

When Lloyd had gone on his great donkey safaris around the St Faith's out-schools in the 1920s, Francis Nyabadza's school at Tswatswa in north-west Chiduku Reserve had been one of his first and favourite stops.[39] In the early 1930s Francis was at St Faith's itself and still an ally of Lloyd's; he was not going to make the fuss the other teachers were making over the salary cuts necessitated by the depression, and it is clear that what distressed him in the early 1930s was not anything that Lloyd was forced or chose to do. It was his own relationship with the African teachers and clergy, who represented partly African tradition and partly the new-style Anglicanism.

Francis was a man of real spiritual power, who, in his own world of the villages, drew rapt hearers. But among the other teachers, especially the young men with formal qualifications, he was treated as an inferior. The chronicler of the church that Francis founded, Sekuru Nyamapfene, tells us that:

> From the time Baba Nyabadza became a true Evangelist whenever they go on trek with Canon Lloyd, all the people were told to listen to his valuable teaching . . . Baba Nyabadza could now read the Bible and sing church songs with all his family but he did not understand or speak English. When the churches came together at St Faith's for special services that occurred during Christmas, Easter and Harvest, a number of teachers would come for such attendance but when the church bells rang in the morning prayers these teachers commanded Baba Nyabadza to fold and pack their sleeping bags and blankets . . . because these teachers were anxious to go in the service in time and Nyabadza would come late because his degree was very low among them all.[40]

The African clergy at St Faith's felt it inappropriate that this unlettered catechist should command a large personal following. Moreover, they disliked what they regarded as the crudity of his old-style message. They were very much men of the new compromise, while Francis was a man of the old certainties of popular Anglicanism. Here again he was following Canon Lloyd.

Lloyd had always campaigned against drunkenness and rewarded those who became abstainers. Nyamapfene tells us that at Tswatswa, under the combined exhortations of Lloyd and Francis, 'people began to make vows for refusing beer. They took red crosses on their

---

[39] Interview with Fr Isaiah Gosho, 5 February 1981.
[40] B. Nyampfene, 'Baba Tafatsiru Nyabadza', ms., February 1981.

garments and Canon Lloyd blessed them'. Francis continued his uncompromising condemnation of beer at St Faith's itself, where some of the clergy and teachers took a very different view:

> Drunkenness is just as much a national vice among our African natives [wrote Lloyd in 1936] as in the England of our youth. An old lay Christian teacher, Francis Nyabadza, acquired and indeed exercised a very remarkable influence among certain men and many women and girls. It could be said perhaps that it was exercised in a puritanic direction and expressed with a good deal of unconventionality of lay religious services, and with a ritual and pageantry not dissimilar to that of some guilds etc. in the Church of England. Indeed this in itself became a matter of real concern to some of our African Christians, priests and lay pastors. They were scandalised much as the 18th century pastors and Churchmen were by the manner and speech of the early Wesleyan preachers . . . and later of the Salvation Army and Church Army . . . The really serious matter of offence . . . concerned more the reactions on 'social life' and ways alike of African priests and teachers. The candidates for Francis's 'Chita' (lay guild) were required to abstain from all beer, and not only were they not to drink but not to touch . . . which in practice meant that their wives and daughters were not to brew beer or give any help whatsoever in the preparation of beer . . . Very determined efforts were made by African priests, teachers and the majority of Christian natives to make this impossible.[41]

What was at stake here was not only sociability, but the removal of women from participation in the ancestral cult and its offerings of beer.

Finally, Francis took up and developed Lloyd's own devotion to Franciscanism. His lay guild was called the *Chita* of St Francis. He reacted to the elitist ambitions of the bright young teachers and to the compelled poverty of the great majority in the 1930s by adumbrating a doctrine of voluntary and shared communal poverty and 'littleness'. In this, too, he infuriated the African clergy. In July 1937 Father Elfric Matimba set down his condemnation of the insistence on community in Francis's *Chita*:

> I think it is wrong for any Chita to receive the Holy Communion for salvation of [the] Chita and not for the salvation of each individual person with his or her true contrition of sins. If Francis's people come to receive because he told them to do so it will be what I say, salvation of [the] Chita . . . I am sure Francis's is not work of the Church, but his own glory.[42]

---

[41] Edgar Lloyd, Report for May to October 1936, USPG, Series E, RHO.
[42] Elfric Matimba to A.C. Knights and C. Tambo, 27 July 1937, ANG 16/1/1/1, NAZ.

As he developed his position, which he took to be the position of the Anglican African church, it proved to be the case that the old lay Christian teacher was speaking to the needs of many young people, especially young women. They responded to his opposition to middle-aged compromise with beer drinking as a customary social institution; his repudiation of progressive individualism and elitism; to his recreation of community; and to his intensely personal religion of wonder and miracle.

Philida Madani, now Sister Clara, was a teenager in the 1930s. Her family lived on European farm land near Rusape and she went as a pupil to Francis Nyabadza's school at St Matthews, Rusape. She recalls the power of his preaching and became one of the young people who clustered around him. They joined the *Chita* and came to church three times a week. When Francis left St Matthews, in disgust at the continuing jealousy of the priests and teachers, he went to live on ten acres of land at Makoni Farm, given to him by Chief Makoni, whose village was nearby. Philida and the others from Rusape used to walk all the way to Makoni Farm and back three times a week. 'The men got tired', she says, 'only the girls kept on.' Their parents objected and refused them food; boys mocked them and threw stones. But 'we wanted to live there all the time and pray.'[43]

Then came the moment when they could not go home any more. Nyamapfene describes it:

> In the year 1939 Baba Lloyd retired from his ministry... He soon obtained a plot which he called *Zuwa radoka* (the sun is now set). One day the Guild found it necessary to visit him and be preached to and receive Holy Communion served by their favourite priest... The whole Guild left *Zuwa radoka* for their homes. When the people had come to the junction for each group to lead home, the power of God came down to capture some of the girls to be Sisters of his will. Philida and Grace fell on the ground... Emma of Nyagumbo kraal became the same. Unless she faced St Francis things would not be well with her... We had 6 [Sisters] to start with at the African mission. Their relatives tried to bring them home but once they came at the gate of the church they fell down and became very ill.[44]

With Lloyd's retirement, the sun of the old folk Anglicanism had set. Francis Nyabadza sought to make it rise again. He built his church, founded his Sisterhood and in fear and trembling took the

[43] Interview with Sister Clara, 6 March 1981.
[44] 'Baba Tafatsiru Nyabadza'.

sacramental role of priest upon himself. These acts were held to be schism from Anglicanism, but in a very real sense his new church was a continuation and extension of Lloyd's work.

There are obvious parallels between Francis Nyabadza and Patrick Kwesha. Both wanted their own Franciscan order of nuns. But while Patrick dreamed of it, Francis instituted it. Perhaps it was because the sacramental power of the Catholic priest was too awe-inspiring for anyone to assume for himself: Francis went through agonies before he decided to act as a priest and to give communion to his people. Perhaps it was because in the end Catholicism proved more flexible than Anglicanism. At any rate, Kwesha stayed in the Catholic Church, while on 19 May 1942 formal notice of the excommunication of Francis was posted at the gates of his church.

St Francis African Church has always remained small, but it was founded in an atmosphere of miracle and prophecy which echoes that of the larger prophetic movements. As Nyamapfene writes:

> During this time of the prophets the Guild expected to hear warnings and teachings from God . . . Rodah Chimhowa was a prophetess from 1933 until her death [in] 1980. She lived in St Faith's with her husband, Joseph . . . They were expelled by the priests . . . Chamasimba means powerful. Francis obtained that name from devotional prayers, judgement times. Poverty and kindness. Francis was very humble. He did not want to live with the rich and the great. The man was inspired. This is a place of power, a holy place. It was difficult for anyone to walk outside at night. There was a heaviness, a presence.[45]

Adrian Hastings counts Nyabadza's movement as 'Ethiopian'. And it is true that it issued an early manifesto claiming to be 'the church of all black people born in this country . . . an Harbour for Africans. For example, the Church of England—means was started by a man of England . . . Therefore let us turn back to our starting point'. But it was an odd kind of Ethiopianism: spirit-filled, loyal to Canon Lloyd to the last. To this day the services and life at St Francis summon up the atmosphere of 1930s folk Anglicanism much more powerfully than any present-day Anglican station.

---

[45] Ibid.

A Prophet for the Sons of Ham: Johana Masowe

Patrick Kwesha and Francis Nyabadza were visionaries from within the mission churches of Manicaland. Through all his years in Johannesburg Kwesha lived among Manyika and dreamt incessantly of returning to evangelize. Francis Nyabadza lived and died in Manicaland. Kwesha was a quintessential Catholic. Nyabadza was forced out of a rationalizing Anglican Church to whose earlier forms he remained devoted. Shoniwa Masedza Tandi Moyo, founder of the Masowe Apostolic Church, seems the odd man out in their company.

Although he was born in Manicaland, in Makoni, Shoniwa's epiphany in 1932 took place on Mount Marimba near Norton, not far from Salisbury. Thereafter he evangelized in Mashonaland before being compelled to return to his home in Makoni by the Chief Native Commissioner. He did not remain there for long. By the early 1940s Shoniwa, now known as Johana Masowe, had taken many of his followers first to Bulawayo, then into Botswana, the Transvaal and finally to Port Elizabeth, where they remained for many years. The evangelical aspirations of the church ranged more widely still. 'We are the Church who rose at Marimba', wrote Evangelist Jack Sitole in September 1959, 'and it was said that we must go all over Africa at first and then overseas. *Izwi Ndizwo zwakata wurwa ne izwi kwetiri. The word said this to us, that we should preach to all nations.*' The Deacons of the Church were commissioned to 'Go all over north, south, east and west of Africa and Overseas, Day and Night'.[46] Nor was this mere rhetoric. While they were in Port Elizabeth the Masowe Apostles asked Israel for asylum; when forced to leave the city Johana Masowe went to Lusaka, to Dar es Salaam and to Nairobi.[47] By this time, the movement which had begun with Johana Masowe's forty days and nights in the wilderness, which had drawn members from rural Mashonaland and Manicaland, had 'become urbanized as an urban people'.[48]

---

[46] Jack Sitole to Chief Native Commissioner, 2 September 1959; Deacon Certificate; S 2824/3, NAZ.

[47] The best account of the history of the Masowe Apostles is Dillon-Malone's *The Korsten Basketmakers*.

[48] Enock Dube, Ephreim Moyo, Josam Sibanda to Minister of Native Affairs, 24 July 1962. 'We must be located near a city' wrote the three Masowe spokesmen, S 2842/3, NAZ.

Nor was Masowe reared in a single folk mission tradition. He was born to Anglican parents, was nurtured by a Wesleyan Methodist uncle, admired the Catholic Church, was greatly influenced by the Apostolic Faith Mission, and drew deeply on the ideas of traditional Shona religion.[49] In the cities of their exile the Masowe Apostles read widely in both Old Testament and New Testament apocryphal books. When they applied for asylum in Israel they declared that 'they consider themselves true Jews . . . because their religious beliefs and strict code of living are based on the Jewish faith.'[50]

Patrick Kwesha and Francis Nyabadza were fated to remain confined within Manyika Catholicism and Manyika Anglicanism. Out of his religious syncretism and his wanderings about Africa Johana Masowe created a great international church, now several million strong. Nevertheless, Johana Masowe *did* emerge from Manicaland, at much the same time as that other Manyika John the Baptist, Johana Maranke. Native Commissioners in Manicaland had anticipated the emergence of wandering prophets from folk mission Christianity; missionaries in Manicaland had longed for a great African prophet to arise there.

Pieter Nielsen, Native Commissioner for Melsetter in eastern Manicaland, described in his annual report for 1932, the year of the emergence of both John the Baptists, how prophetism sprang out of the mission churches. Indeed, the eschatological biblicism and the belief in witches and evil spirits that characterized the Apostolic movements had clear folk mission precedents.[51] Nielsen held that the focus on the Bible in mission schools led to 'endless and barren debate about points of doctrine.' At Chikore Mission, for instance,

---

[49] When questioned by the Chief Native Commissioner in 1932 Masowe declared: 'I associate myself with the Roman Catholic Church . . . It was my intention to gather natives around me and then obtain the necessary authority of the Roman Catholic Church to have a separate native Church'. Dillon-Malone, *Korsten*, p. 14. David Maxwell has recently explored Masowe's connections with the Apostolic Faith in 'Historicizing Christian Independency: The Southern African Pentecostal Movement 1908–1950', *Journal of African History*, 40, 1999. Bella Mukonyora has argued cogently for Masowe's use of Shona religious concepts in 'The Complementarity of Male and Female Imaginary in Theological Language: A Study of the Masowe and Valentinian Systems', D.Phil. thesis, University of Oxford, 1998.

[50] *Sunday Mail*, 2 December 1956.

[51] Dillon-Malone comments on the close study not only of the Bible but also of the Old and New Testament apocryphal books within the Masowe Church. The Masowe Apostles drew on the Bible to authenticate belief in both witches and evil spirits. Dillon-Malone, *Korsten*, p. 62.

two 'parties of Native schoolmen' debated whether African girls 'should obey the injunctions of the lady missionaries to keep the hair of their heads short'. It was objected that 'if the women will not let their hair grow' they could not 'wipe the feet of the Saviour' at his Second Coming. Moreover, thought Nielsen, belief among mission Christians in *mademoni* (demons) was 'supported by many passages in the book which they are taught to accept as the final word of God.'

In this context were felt the 'frustrations resulting from the present economic dislocation.' 'There has been of late', wrote Nielsen, 'a feeling in the air':

> It is a feeling never openly expressed but often obliquely voiced in the course of prayers and local preachings by way of metaphor and parable . . . The discontented natives tend to look heavenwards for the change they desire from their earthly conditions.

Out of all this there emerged in Melsetter in 1932 yet a third Manyika Apostolic prophet: Jeremiah, with his Zion Apostolic City. Jeremiah made 'a ready display of the gift of speaking in tongues', citing St Paul as an authority. He presented the image of the 'Saint, with its implication of oppression suffered from the powers that be.' 'Tall and gaunt', in a long robe, with 'eyes unnaturally large and bright' and 'a small beard like those in Sunday-school pictures of the Saviour', Jeremiah made an imposing prophetic figure.[52] But unlike Johana Masowe, Jeremiah's influence remained localized.[53] Masowe was a far more convincing candidate to fulfil, however ironically, missionary longings:

> Someday, I dream [wrote Father O'Hea in 1932 at the end of his tirade against the Manyika], a great Apostle of God will rise up from among them; a man whom God will fill with great things and who will be able to change them, knowing them, one of them, and yet all God's.[54]

Despite unreliable oral testimony that Masowe preached an atavistic revolutionary gospel against white rule, his main objective was precisely this divine transformation of the African people.[55]

---

[52] Annual Report, Melsetter, 1932, S 235/510, NAZ.
[53] Adrian Hastings contrasts in *The Church in Africa* the purely local influence of prophets based on Zion Cities with the international influence of the Apostolic movements.
[54] Fr Jerome O'Hea to Mgr Brown, 20 March 1930, Box 185, JAH.
[55] Dillon-Malone quotes one Andrea of Nyamweda both to the effect that Masowe told his followers to return to traditional religion, to drink beer, and 'eat the meat

Masowe's founding vision was of his death; his journey to heaven; his witness of dead African twins, 'suffocated by their ancestors', and other children killed by witches; the clamour of these slain innocents that 'the world would come to an end so that they could bring their case against their fathers'; and Christ instead commissioning him to return and purge the African people of witchcraft and evil spirits in preparation for the Second Coming.[56] This was an African prophet, sent to the African people, the people of Ham. 'We never had a prophet of our own', says Cyprian Nedewedzo, Masowe's right-hand man. 'The light has never shone on Africa right from the time of Adam onwards [but] in 1932 the word of God came and made it clear that it had come to the race of Ham. We received this word with great joy, because we knew that God had begun to visit the people of Africa.'[57]

Masowe's work, seen in this light, was not so much a continuation of the missionary's work, the taking up of a task in which the missionaries were faltering. It was rather that the missionaries had been incapable of redeeming the African people. Only an African prophet could do that and thus achieve what the missions had proclaimed but could not do.

The early days of Masowe's movement in Mashonaland and Manicaland are reminiscent of those first mass movements of Christian expectation which Hastings describes for Igboland, Buganda and Manicaland itself. There were great gatherings at which the Holy Spirit descended and Africans flocked to surrender their witchcraft charms and to see them consumed by holy fire.[58] So far from returning to traditional religion, many Africans were giving it up for Christianity for the first time. 'One enthusiastic native adherent', it was reported in 1936, 'said [the Mazowe Church] had helped him

---

blessed by our forefathers', and also that he told them that Moses and Elijah would drive the whites from the country. In fact, the brewing and drinking of beer was strictly prohibited within the Masowe movement and Masowe sought to ignore whites rather than to confront them. Dillon-Malone himself finally concludes that 'the central emphasis was placed on destroying the evils of the traditional Shona religious system rather than on attacking the white world.' *Korsten*, p. 133.

[56] Johana's vision, as narrated by Onias Bvuma, can be found in Dillon-Malone, *Korsten*, p. 147.

[57] Dillon-Malone, *Korsten*, p. 60.

[58] Assistant Native Commissioner, Wedza, to Native Commissioner, Marendellas, 27 June 1933, S 1542/M8, NAZ.

to give up heathen practices and that he was afraid he would return to them if encouraged to forsake the movement'.[59]

In this sense, Masowe's movement was a fulfilment of both white and black expectations and dreams in Manicaland. Dillon-Malone tells us that once his movement had become firmly established, Johana Masowe 'began to praise the white mission churches for preparing those who were to become his followers . . . [and familiarising] his followers with his word before he had come in person to lead them'.[60] But I want to argue for more than these general connections to folk mission Christianity in Manicaland. I want to argue that for many of his followers the Masowe Church was particularly a critique and continuation of Manyika folk American Methodism.

Johana Masowe and the American Methodist Pentecost

Masowe was, after all, born in Gandanzara, that key American Methodist station. Despite all his wanderings and concealments under other names and identities, his converts consistently claimed 'John Masowe of Gandanzara's kraal, Makoni' as the founder of their Apostolic Faith.[61] His own extended kin-group always remained at the centre of the church. His close friend, Sailos Kutsanzira, became head-preacher for the Apostles in Gandanzara and thus enjoyed seniority in the movement. Most of his followers in Makoni district lived in Dewedzo in the Chiduku Reserve, another zone of American Methodist activity. Onias Bvuma, whose account of Johana Masowe's vision I have quoted above, 'was the first head-preacher to be appointed in Dewedzo and was, hence, regarded, as the head-preacher of all the Apostles.'[62] Although many Apostles remained in Gandanzara and Dewedzo after Masowe began his great migration to South Africa and beyond, sons and daughters of the first Dewedzo converts constituted a significant proportion of those who followed Masowe out of Rhodesia.[63] After Masowe's death in 1967 the man who emerged as leader of the 'loyalist' faction of Apostles was Cyprian

---

[59] Annual Report, Hartley, 1936, S 235514, NAZ.
[60] Dillon-Malone, *Korsten*, p. 60.
[61] Monthly Report, Urungwe, August 1946, S 1619, NAZ.
[62] Dillon-Malone, *Korsten*, p. 51.
[63] Statement of Nyamayaro, Mawodza kraal, April 1958, S 2824/3, NAZ.

Nedewedzo, who conducted a burial ceremony at Gandanzara attended by 16,500 people. Cyprian also presided at the Gandanzara Synod which laid the foundations of the post-Masowe church. Gandanzara thus became, even if it had not been before, the focal point of pilgrimage for Masowe Apostles. So it is worth looking at Gandanzara in the 1920s in order to understand the religious and socio-economic situation within and against which Masowe developed his ideas.

The American Methodist Church differed from the other missions in one very important respect. While they looked back to the movement of mass enthusiasm at the beginning of the twentieth century, American Methodism also had a second mass movement in the great Revival of March 1918. It then seemed to the African evangelists that 'the Holy Spirit had come down upon them as it did to the Apostles': this was an exclusively African Pentecost which left the white missionaries untouched. The spirit-filled evangelists fanned out across Manicaland, preaching and healing. Inevitably one of the places they came to was Gandanzara, a cherished stronghold of American Methodism.

The Pentecostal news was carried there in July 1918 by one Johanne Mafuta, a converted diviner, now an American Methodist evangelist.[64] When Johanne visited Gandanzara,

> they had prayers from Sunday to Monday ... A kopje in the vicinity was called 'Sinai' and [it was said] that the ten commandments came from this kopje. [This was] the kopje known by the natives as 'Gwidza'. The natives were told that the Holy Spirit descended from it and that therefore they should confess their sins. Dougwa Pass was called 'Galilee Pass' and [it was said] that the Lord Jesus came through that Pass to bring the Holy Ghost to the Hill Gwidza. They fasted for three days and made confessions of Adultery, Theft, Bewitching.' [65]

One might easily mistake this description for an account of the arrival of Masowe in 1932, and Johanne Mafuta was treated by the Native administration much as Johana Masowe was treated in the 1930s. He was arrested for being without a pass, and the Native Commissioner sent his Messengers to Gandanzara, fearing that 'open confession ... may result in murders, arsons and assaults.'[66]

---

[64] Mafuta's career is described in 'Here are Spirits that Will Set this Land on Fire', *African Advance*, 2, 1, April/June 1918.

[65] Native Commissioner, Rusape, to Superintendent of Natives, Umtali, 6 August 1918, N 3/1/3, NAZ.

[66] Ibid.

Thereafter the Pentecostal idiom regularly recurred at Gandanzara. It was adopted both by the sub-chief, Philip Gandanzara, who refused to pray to ancestral spirits for rain and invoked the Holy Spirit instead, and by the prosperous agrarian entrepreneurs who dominated Gandanzara society. In the early 1920s 'many wagon-loads of maize' left for the Umtali market and there were more than a hundred plough-owners there. 'God's blessing truly rests upon the people of the Gandanzara circuit', wrote the missionaries. It was a centre of Christian literacy, with pupils exchanging grain for books.[67]

But the 1930s were a very different matter in Gandanzara, as everywhere else in Manicaland. In 1931 the price of grain fell to record lows and 'at most of the trading stores it is impossible to sell for cash, but only in exchange for goods.'[68] The world of the Gandanzara *kulaks* suddenly came to an end, and the connection between Pentecost and prosperity was broken. Within the church itself there was a cutting back and clamping down. There had been a good deal of missionary suspicion of the 'excesses' of the 1918 Pentecost. Now the slogan was to be 'slow but sure'.[69] The situation came to a crisis point in 1934. By the end of that year, Gandanzara was 'so far behind in its 1934 collections that even the people themselves did not wish to have schools until the debts were paid.' Morale was at its lowest ebb. The African ministers, meeting in the Native Christian Conference of the AMEC in July 1935, stressed 'the hard task of the people in our out-stations'; asked that central mission funds be used to support either the pastor or the evangelists so that villages had only one man to carry; 'asked for advice from the missionaries since there are so many stations being closed. This was not answered.' And they debated the proposition that 'it is apparent that our Christian people are gradually withdrawing themselves from the Church and they regard it as an instrument of oppression.'[70]

The second mass expansion of the folk Methodist Church had come to a sudden end. Even its essential idiom, the Revival Camp

---

[67] The annual proceedings of the Church, including detailed reports from its various circuits, were printed and published. A full set is located at Old Umtali Mission. *Rhodesian Annual Conference*, American Methodist Episcopal Church, Old Umtali, 1923, pp. 33, 67, 68; 1924, pp. 36, 37; 1925, pp. 54, 55 (henceforth *Conference*).

[68] *Conference*, 1931, pp. 36, 37.

[69] W. Bourgaize to Chief Native Commissioner, 23 March 1942, S 2810/4233, NAZ.

[70] 'Christian Conference, Agenda and Minutes, July 3 1935', Green file, Old Mutare Archives; *Conference*, 1935, pp. 248, 253, 255.

Meeting, was losing its vigour. Pentecost, once a habitual experience, was now manifested annually at the special campsite of Nyatende,
near Gandanzara. At Nyatende there was an attempt to draw upon
the Holy Spirit to repulse the power of witchcraft. In September
1930, for instance:

> the Holy Spirit was present in great blessing and power. Many peo-
> ple, some of them church members, confessed that they had been
> under the power of witchcraft. Under the power of the Spirit they
> began to surrender their charms . . . An open fire was burning outside
> the tabernacle. At the conclusion of each testimony, the charm was
> placed on the fire.[71]

In the old days of widespread agrarian prosperity the Methodist
Camp Meeting would have been enough to check fears of witchcraft. But in the early 1930s, as the depression immiserated the
smaller peasants in Gandanzara and elsewhere and accentuated the
difference between them and the *kulak* Methodist elders, it seemed
less plausible that the sin of witchcraft could be dealt with within
the American Methodist Church.

Masowe's movement cannot be reduced to a response to the crisis within one mission church in a single village or province.
Nevertheless, it can be seen both that Masowe took up many of the
idioms of Manyika folk Methodism and that he sought to continue
and deepen its work by offering his own resolution of its problems.
His movement addressed both the economic and spiritual crisis of
Manyika Methodism.

The depression had shown up the danger of depending either
upon colonial food markets or on colonial labour demand. Kwesha
and Nyabadza responded by glorifying Franciscan poverty. Masowe
took a different path. He proposed to his followers a new style of
economic existence that demanded of them a great deal of dedicated labour. They must become independent of the colonial economy by means of shared agrarian and craft labour.

At the two centres of his influence in Makoni, Gandanzara and
Dewedzo, Masowe set up church fields. In Gandanzara he also set
up a carpentry and wood-working shop. The proceeds of both were
common.[72] A Makoni Apostle, Amon Nengomasha, says:

---

[71] *Conference*, 1933, pp. 36, 37.
[72] Later, in Port Elizabeth, the Masowe Apostles practised a 'religious distribution of labour'. Children were instructed in the Bible by unwaged teachers, who
were sustained from the proceeds of 'basket-making, blacksmith, gardening, poul-

> Baba Johan had the conviction that one could not lead a proper and holy life unless he could fend for himself. That is the most important belief expressed by Baba Johan. If he satisfied his material needs, he would be able to satisfy his spiritual ... The first message to these people was, 'First of all, all you people must learn to work together. Have a common field ... designed for the church.'[73]

In fact, Manicaland in the 1930s was little more propitious to Apostolic self-help than to peasant agriculture and labour migration. Official policies of land centralization and allocation broke up the church fields: 'the church failed to receive land', says Nengomasha, 'because it was neither a family nor was it one individual. So everywhere the church lost land.' Moreover, there was little market for craft production. These two factors in combination with administrative repression of the church led to the extraordinary exodus of the Masowe Apostles from their rural homes and their urbanization. But the wandering craftsmen were still linked to the original base of the church. Thus in 1975 Headman Nedwedzo wrote to the District Commissioner, Makoni, about the far-flung Apostolic movement. 'They work their own jobs; handwork, carpentry, builders. Some are painters, contractors and blacksmiths ... They are not allowed to work for somebody, they work their own jobs.' They worked all over Rhodesia and southern and eastern Africa. But 'all this congregation I am their Mambo, because of my father who welcomed John the Baptist, the Messenger of God.'[74]

As for spiritual deepening, Masowe offered continual rather than occasional rituals of repentance, exorcism and protection. By the time he was ordered back to his home district by the Chief Native Commissioner, everyone knew the story of how he had died, gone to heaven, asked God for time to save the African people from the sin of witchcraft, and how he had returned with redemptive power. Healing of individuals and of societies riven by witchcraft fear was at the very centre of his work. Amon Nengomasha, born in Chiduku and General Secretary of the Apostles after Masowe's death, describes the prophet's return home:

---

try, furniture.' 'Inside information on the Rhodesian Basket Makers', Edward Nheta, 9 November 1959, S 2824/3, NAZ. A Rhodesian memorandum of 1962 found that 'property is in the main communal, and their money earning efforts are all communal, with income going to the group'.
[73] Interview with Amon Nengomasha, 17 February and 2 March 1977, National Archives Oral History Project, AOH/4, NAZ.
[74] Headman Nedewedzo to Provincial Commissioner, Umtali, 30 April and 2 May 1975, file 'Headman Nedewedzo'. District Administrator's office, Rusape.

Now instead of going to Gandanzara he went westwards to a certain hill ... When he sang 'Hosanna' from this hill people started converging on him and he started preaching ... 'Get rid of all evil concoctions and magic, repent from your evil deeds because the day of judgement is nigh'. Many people were converted. From here he went to Nyamatanga near Devedzo ... When they were knelt down and praying, they were all possessed by the Holy Spirit ... All those with medicinal beads, charms and other concoctions threw them away ... heaps and heaps of evil concoctions ... were thrown away. From the very beginning he condemned such things as mashavi [animal spirits]. Worship of tribal spirits was forbidden ... Some of those people possessed by the Holy Spirit were also given the powers to prophesy and started identifying the evil people ... Witches and wizards ... when picked out by these prophets did not deny their evil.[75]

Masowe's 'Camp Meetings' were thus not only much more frequent but also much less inhibited than those in the American Methodist Church. Witches were identified, and then healed by exorcism and prayer. Women flocked to the Masowe church, enduring the shame of being identified as witches because of the release of being exorcized. They were also liberated from having to brew beer for patriarchal ancestor ceremonies.[76] Young men flocked to the church partly because it ordered the abandonment of brideprice, which had become in the 1930s an increasingly burdensome instrument of control by the elders. In Dewedzo 'it had been ruled that the believers or followers were not to receive anything on the marriage of their daughters ... The congregation was told to return any of the bridewealth they had received.'[77] Masowe's teachings struck deeper into Manyika society than American Methodism had ever done.[78]

---

[75] Interview with Amon Alwen Nengomasha.
[76] Interviews between P.M. Chakanyuka and Mai Mapani Mupfururi, Nedewedzo, 9 January 1981; and Mibidzeni Luciah Chakanyuka, 18 January 1981.
[77] Interview with Mibidzeni Luciah Chakanyuka.
[78] Edward Nheta's 'Inside information on the Rhodesian Basket Makers' of 9 September 1959 stressed that 'if I have a grown up daughter in my house a member of the church however old he may be and no matter how many other wives he may already possess can come to ME THE FATHER and TELL me that he would like to add his dependents this daughter as his wife. This request is immediately presented to the church which almost in all cases approves the request and in the same evening one has the daughter brought to him to be wife.' Nheta was a clerical assistant to the official Rhodesian delegation sent to Port Elizabeth to inquire into the Masowe Apostles. His use of capital letters reveals how scandalized he was by their marriage practices. On his return to Rhodesia he recommended to the Chief Native Commissioner that the church should only be admitted back into the country provided they gave an undertaking to accept brideprice. S 2824/3, NAZ. Meanwhile members of the church still in Rhodesia sent their

Most of this was seen as heretical by the mission churches, and their clergy certainly saw the situation as one of confrontation. In 1934 Father Yakobo Mwela of the Anglican mission at St Faith's embarked upon a Mission of Revival in the rural areas of Makoni:

> Our trek came to a station where there were some people, men and women who called themselves 'Apostolics', followers of Peter who calls himself 'Johanne the Baptist'. These are a mixed lot of lapsed Christians from the American Methodists, the Roman Catholic and our church. 'We came out here', I said, 'to bring back to Church these Christians who left their Church.' Before finishing to speak these words there came howls and shoutings to find chapters and verses from the three first Gospels and 1 Corinthians. They claimed themselves to be the true followers of the Apostles, and the other Christians of other churches are false, their priests are not true ministers of Christ. 'You are not true ministers of the word because you sell it for money. Our Lord did not do that nor His Apostles. But you do. Our Lord cast out devils and evil spirits, you cannot.'[79]

To others it looked a little different: more like continuation and intensification of folk Christian idioms than confrontation. 'In this district', wrote the Native Commissioner, Wedza, in 1939, 'one recognized church [the American Methodists] holds annually on the summit of Mount Wedza a meeting at which boys and girls attend, spending at least one night at this sport away from parental control. The so-called Apostolics do the same, only more frequently.'[80]

Conclusion

In the end the mission churches of Manicaland survived the 1930s. Continually harassed by the administration, Johana Masowe left the country, taking many of his followers with him. Patrick Kwesha was contained by the Catholics, Francis Nyabadza was marginalized by the Anglicans. Movements, especially of women, arose within mission folk Christianity. Within the American Methodist Church in Makoni, the women's movement in many ways paralleled Masowe's. Mrs Kanyangarara of Muziti in Chiduku Reserve 'had died for 12 hours and during her trance . . . she was told to come back to earth

daughters down to Port Elizabeth to be disposed of without brideprice. Statements of Naume Marufu and Nauma Kanyoka, 19 July 1962, ibid.

[79] Yakobo Mwela, 'The Mission of Renewal', 1934, USPG Archives, Series E, RHO.
[80] Annual Report, Wedza, 1939, S 235/517, NAZ.

and carry on God's work. She visited almost every church giving her testimony of what she had been shown in heaven by God.' Gandanzara Methodist women who 'used to go in the forest to pray' made contact with her, and in this way the *Rukwadzano* began in Makoni. These militant Methodist women defended Christian mono-gamy against Masowe's subversive ideas on marriage and re-con-verted sub-chief Gandanzara away from ancestor veneration back to Methodism.[81] A rain-making and healing minister completed the return of Gandanzara to fervent Methodist loyalty. The Anglican Church in the 1930s developed the pilgrimage cult of the 1896 mar-tyr, Bernard Mizeki, with all its opportunities for miracles and heal-ing, and in 1942 it at last succeeded, where it and all the other churches had previously failed, in baptizing a Chief Makoni. In the 1940s the recovery of cereal prices and labour employment reduced some of the fears and tensions of Manicaland.

But the emergence of these three African visionaries emphasized that the mission churches needed to return to the well-springs of folk Christianity and African agency. The spiritual geography of the Makoni Reserve is deeply marked by the visions of Kwesha, Nyabadza and Masowe. In this relatively small part of the larger Makoni dis-trict lie the burial hill of the Makoni chiefs and the burial ground of the Makoni princesses, both revived in importance with the cul-tural nationalism of recent years. There stand the key mission sta-tions, the Anglican St Luke's, the Catholic St Killian's, the Methodist Gandanzara. But there also lie the graves of the visionaries. Patrick Kwesha is buried in St Killian's cemetery, his prominent tomb a place of pilgrimage for the members of his Franciscan third order. Francis Nyabadza is buried in the family mausoleum at St Francis Church, where his *bira* is joyously celebrated every year. Johana Masowe is buried near Gandanzara on Mazowe hill, and every September thousands of Apostles flock to his grave. The Makoni Reserve is marked, too, and very obviously and physically marked, by the effects of rural poverty. It seems fitting that it should be in this eroded and scarred landscape, rather than in the fat commer-cial farmlands, where the prophets now lie.

[81] Shepherd Machuma, 'Women', Oral History collection, Old Mutare Archives. 'Chief Gandanzara', *On Trek with Christ in Southern Rhodesia*, Rhodesia Mission Press, 1936, pp. 31–33.

CHAPTER FIVE

CHRISTIANITY AND THE LOGIC OF NATIONALIST ASSERTION IN WOLE SOYINKA'S ÌSARÀ

J.D.Y. Peel

Two things might well strike an Africanist, particularly one interested in religion, in regard to the vigorous debates about the character of nations and nationalism that have blossomed in the last ten
or fifteen years. The first is that they largely ignore the literature on
African nationalism of the 1950s and 1960s. One cogent reason
might be that, since their main historical stimulus has been the re-
emergence of old ethno-linguistic nations from the wreckage of the
Soviet bloc, the emergence of a 'nationalism' whose potential nations
had no existence prior to the colonial states which they challenged
seemed a phenomenon of a wholly different character. The second
is that their handling of religion as a factor of national identity is
so uncertain and skimped. On both counts Adrian Hastings's book,
The Construction of Nationhood: Ethnicity, Religion and Nationalism (1997),
does much to re-connect things. To an extent equalled only by
Terence Ranger, he has eloquently insisted both on the relevance
of the African experience to the humanities at large, and on the
centrality of religious concerns in the definition of nationhood. On
the latter point, basic to his argument has been his attack on the
'modernism' of such influential theorists of nationalism as Gellner,
Anderson and Hobsbawm: the view that nations are more the product than the source of nationalism, and that neither essentially pre-
dates the last three centuries. Their neglect of religion as a factor
of nationhood seems connected with this, since modernity is seen to
entail a more secular form of society. Because he is prepared to
place the emergence of national identity much earlier, Hastings
emphasizes the religious shaping of culture, in the national histories
of peoples who are Christian. His argument moves forward from the
case of England and other European nations to some African cases,
such the Baganda and the Yoruba, where the cultural intervention
of missionaries was crucial for the shaping of ethnic identities.

Yet African divergences from the European model are still great. What matters here is not so much that the ethno-linguistic quasi-nations which Hastings discusses seldom coincided with the ex-colonial states which became Africa's 'new nations', but that African nationalism had to place itself in relation to two, largely opposed, religions: Christianity and 'paganism' (otherwise 'African traditional religion'). Christianity sowed the seeds of nationalism in two contrasting ways. Positively, it promoted the idea that ethno-linguistic units were natural or God-given, polities *in posse*; through Bible translation it standardized the languages that gave them voice; and through education it produced the nationalists. Yet by its disparagement of the 'pagan' roots of indigenous cultures and its complicity, willy-nilly, in colonial domination, Christianity also provoked in nationalism something of a negative reaction against itself. Conversely, the values, symbols and idioms of traditional religion tended to be revived in nationalist discourse as the highest expression of the 'soul of the people'. Here, the place of traditional religion in African nationalism rather recalled the significance of long-held forms of Christianity in some European nationalisms (Polish, Irish, Greek for example). But the attachment of African nationalism to 'paganism' could not but be highly selective, often indeed not much more than rhetorical, since it was also crucially a modernizing project; and in most local African contexts, modernity means Christianity.

This essay presents a case-study of how this general logic of African nationalism worked itself out concretely in a particular Yoruba and Nigerian setting, through an analysis of Wole Soyinka's quasi-fictional account of the early-1940s milieu of his father, in *Ìsarà: A Voyage round 'Essay'*. Soyinka, now in his mid-60s, is undoubtedly Nigeria's best-known intellectual, not merely on account of the writings—poems, plays, novels, critical essays and several volumes of autobiography—which won him the Nobel Prize for Literature in 1986, but also because of his high public profile over the years as a critic of the corrupt, incompetent and (latterly) brutal military regimes which Nigeria has had to endure.[1] His courage has brought him periods of imprisonment and exile. Though on his mother's side he comes from an old Christian family replete with clergymen, and

---

[1] The literature of Soyinka is vast, but see Wright, 1993; Ogunba, 1994; Maja-Pearce, 1994; Quayson, 1997. *Ìsarà* does not seems to me to have yet received the close and informed critical attention that it deserves.

grew up in an intensely evangelical-Anglican environment, he grad-
uated easily to a post-Christian cultural nationalism that was much
in the *zeitgeist* of the Nigerian universities in the late 1950s where
he began his career. On his mature religious convictions I cannot
go into much detail,[2] though his regard for Ogun (the Yoruba god
of iron) seems to be for an icon of cultural value and the artist's
creative struggle rather than for an object of 'religious' devotion. But
if Soyinka has personally left Christianity behind, it still remains central to the two volumes (*Aké: The Years of Childhood* and *Ìsarà*) in which
he recalls and reconstructs the milieu in which he grew up. The
implication of this nationalist intellectual's reflection on the origins
of nationalism is that its thematic was no less religious than it was
political or economic: perhaps even more so, since a nation is always
at its core a religious project.

Fact and Fiction

Ìsarà is a complex book, on account of the narrative strategies used
by Soyinka and of its large and elusive cast of characters. (For ease
of reference, the story and its 'cast' are summarized in two Appendices.)
As a sociologist-cum-historian of the Yoruba, I found it enormously
informative and 'true' (for all that in the literal sense it is fictional).
It gives a wonderfully vivid and detailed evocation of the ethos and
lifeworld of a key sector of Yoruba society at a major turning-point
in Nigeria's history: the youthful educated elite in the years around
1940, when they took over leadership of their local communities
from the chiefs who had held sway under Indirect Rule, and went
on to fashion the nationalist movement. The title, *Ìsarà*, refers to the
small town in Ijebu Remo, population in the 1940s probably around
5–6,000, whence Soyinka's father hailed.[3] It thus complements *Aké*,
which is set in the much larger Abeokuta, the town of Soyinka's
mother and the site of his father's work as a teacher.

   Ìsarà's subtitle, *A Voyage round 'Essay'*, incorporates a punning reference to the initials and nickname of his schoolmaster father S.A.

---

[2] But see Soyinka, 1991, the text of the first of the Olufosoye Lectures on religion at the University of Ibadan.

[3] Little has been published on the history and ethnography of Ijebu Remo, with
the exception of an excellent thesis by Insa Nolte (1999). Though it mainly deals
with Ode Remo, a town of similar size, in general terms much of its analysis is
applicable to Isara. She briefly reviews the Isara Ọḍẹmọship dispute on pp. 240–243.

Soyinka's maternal relatives at Abeokuta

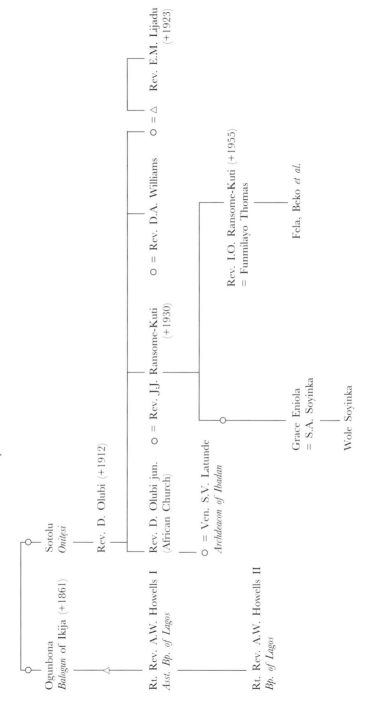

Soyinka, memorably depicted from another angle in *Aké*. In fact it was based on the contents of a metal box left by his father, opened by Soyinka only in 1986, which contained 'a handful of letters, old journals with marked pages and annotations, notebook jottings, tax and other levy receipts, minutes of meetings and school reports, programme notes of special events, and so on.'[4] A full appreciation of Soyinka's creative alchemy is clearly not possible without access to these documentary materials. But what were probably two of them have been independently preserved in the papers of the late Bishop A.B. Akinyele,[5] both being the programmes of plays staged in connection with the centenary of the CMS Yoruba Mission in 1942–43. One of these is the programme for a dramatic pageant presented at Abeokuta in which Mr and Mrs Soyinka took minor parts, which must surely be the source of the fictionalized version that occurs in *Ìsarà*, pp. 179–192.[6]

Reading such documents as these was, he goes on, 'a tantalising experience, eavesdropping on this very special class of teachers of our colonial period', and he was drawn 'to flesh out these glimpses

---

[4] *Ìsarà*, p. v. This source intrigued me, since I was once given access to a similar cache of personal documents, in fact one left by a somewhat older acquaintance of S.A. Soyinka's: W.F. Sosan (died 1957), then Clerk of the Egba Council. This was a big breakthrough in the research which led to my book on the Aladura (Peel, 1968).

[5] Held in the Kenneth Dike Library, University of Ibadan.

[6] The front page reads:

YORUBA CHURCH CENTENARY
CELEBRATIONS
IN
ABEOKUTA
(ANGLICAN)
1843–1943.

===============================

S K E T C H of P A G E A N T

Representing the First arrival of the

Rev. Henry Townsend

and the Reception by

Chief SODEKE

===============================

Held on Tuesday, January 5th 1943
at Ake Mission Yard, at 3.30 p.m.

on a very different level of awareness and empathy from that of *Aké*. The most immediate difference from *Aké* is that in *Ìsarà* Soyinka does not use real names for the central characters, since he wants to 'eliminate any pretence to factual accuracy in [the] attempted reconstruction of their times, thoughts and feelings'. So Soyinka's father becomes Akinyode Soditan, or Yode for short. In fact much of *Aké* too might—actually must—be fiction, since Soyinka cannot have remembered all those childhood conversations verbatim; but it is still written as a recollection of the real, and has a style to go with this, a naturalistic forward-moving narrative, whose scope broadens as the world of the growing child expands. The inventions and fictions of *Ìsarà* come with a much more complex emplotment, intended to convey a reality more multiple, layered and segmented than the child's world of *Aké*.

Soyinka suggests two reasons for his decision to fictionalize *Ìsarà*. One is methodological scruple: to make the story, he had to add to the information contained in that metal box (supplemented, no doubt, by personal knowledge and family traditions about the people and places involved). The other is to permit an account of more general truth to be written: '"Ilesa" [the fictional location of Soditan's teacher-training college, the original of which was St Andrew's College, Oyo] is . . . not simply one such institution nor Isara one such community' (p. vi). His message here is a nationalist one addressed across the nation: he hopes that 'surviving "ex-Ilés" [the members of Soditan's circle] all over the nation will understand this compulsion to acknowledge . . . their seminal role in the development of present-day Nigerian minds . . .'[7] Soyinka's 'fiction' (*poiesis*) thus hints at Aristotle's claim for poetry as conveying a higher truth than history, precisely because it rises beyond the particular, and at the same time it echoes the social scientist's construction of typical cases or ideal types to convey general phenomena.

In fact the boundary between real and fictional names used in *Ìsarà* is complicated, and sheds some light on the author's use of his raw materials. The landscape of most of the action, the Lagos/Abeokuta/Ijebu triangle, is real and specific. Virtually the only fictional

---

[7] 'Ex-Ilé' is an Anglo-Yoruba pun. The word *ilé* means 'house' or 'home' in Yoruba, so 'ex-*ilé*' means 'those away from home', as most of the youthful educated elite of an Ijebu town would be for most of their active adult lives. But unlike 'exiles' they would regularly come back and involve themselves in their town's affairs.

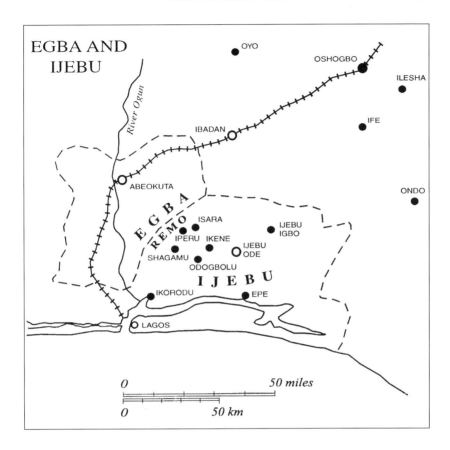

place-name is the site of St Simeon's Seminary at Ilesa, which is somewhere to the north (for the journey there starts by the train) but it is neither the well-known Ilesa to the east of Ibadan nor the less known one on the far northern border of Yoruba country.

When we come to the people, those at the centre of the narrative, Soditan's family and friends, are nearly all given fictional names. Soditan's wife, the splendid 'Wild Christian' of *Aké*, appears (somewhat reduced, I feel) as Morola. It is those in the background, those who place the story in a real historical context, who have real names: international figures of the day (Mussolini, Haile Selassie), nationalist notables (Anthony Enahoro, Dr C.C. Adeniyi-Jones, Ladipo Solanke, Eyo Ita) and some prominent churchmen (Bishop Vining of Lagos, Archdeacons Phillips and Howells). Two key figures in their own names bridge foreground and background: the Revd I.O. Ransome-Kuti, the formidable 'Daodu' of *Aké*, the uncle of Soyinka's mother, and S.A. Akinsanya or 'Saaki', the nationalist trade-union leader, who is the candidate of Soditan and his friends to become Ọdẹmọ or king of Isara. Three other local names are real: Erinle, the rival candidate for the Ọdẹmọ-ship; Rokodo, his compound in the town; and Chief Olisa, leader of the faction opposing Akinsanya's candidature.[8]

The most intriguing cases are those names that have migrated from fact to fiction. So an English Director of Education is called Melville-Jones, which was the name of the Principal of St Andrew's, Oyo, while S.A. Soyinka was a student there; he later became Bishop of Lagos (1920–41). Onayemi, the name of the trader who has access to the Spirit of Layeni, which the ex-Ilés wish to consult, was the real-life name of the Clerk of Isara Council, a zealous partisan of Akinsanya in his bid to become Ọdẹmọ. The name of one of the ex-Ilés, Osibo, is the same as that of the stage manager of a play whose programme seems very likely to have been among the contents of S.A. Soyinka's tin box.[9] Then there is the early European missionary recalled as 'Goloba', which Soyinka re-anglicizes as 'Gollmer' (p. 179). But this is a case of mistaken identity, since 'Goloba' was the Yoruba rendering of Glover, the British Governor of Lagos, whose policies the Egba detested, while Gollmer was always known

---

[8] The Ọdẹmọship contest can be minutely reconstructed from the files of the colonial administration: IJEPROF I/2428, vols. ii–iii ('Ọdẹmọ of Isara') and 2742 ('Isara Affairs'), Nigerian National Archives, Ibadan.

[9] The programme title reads in full:

Centenary of the Yoruba
Mission
1842–1942.
—o—
Programme
OF
A SHORT PLAY
depicting the arrival and early work of
C.M.S. Missionaries in Nigeria,
staged at the
GLOVER MEMORIAL HALL
on FRIDAY the 15th of January, 1943,
at 8.30 p.m.,

UNDER THE DISTINGUISHED CHAIRMANSHIP OF
HIS LORDSHIP
THE BISHOP OF LAGOS
(Rt Rev. L.G. Vining, M.A.).

to Yoruba as 'Alapako'.[10] What these cases suggest is that Soyinka, whether or not he was aware of their original reference, drew freely on names that circulated orally or that he had at some time encountered in print, in his father's talk or in documents, and that many of these names came from church or local political contexts.

These documents might suggest incidents as well as names, as in the following little detail. The play programme places 'An Apology' after its cast list, stating:

> The original characters in this human drama of early Missionary life in Nigeria comprised both Africans and Europeans. This sketch was rehearsed at short notice, and the difficulty of arranging for Europeans to take the part of white Missionaries could not be surmounted. The audience are therefore requested kindly to excuse the substitution of Africans for Europeans in the play.

There seems to be a distinct echo of this in *Ìsarà*, where Soyinka describes the preparations for the fictional play:

> Various individuals had been marked down for various roles—Osibo, the dispenser, was, for instance, a natural one for one of the white visitors; his long face and hooked nose eliminated most of the competition. So did the light-skin complexion of the shy, normally retiring court registrar from Igbore, Bandele Dosumu . . . (p. 179).

Finally, chronology. Soyinka himself tells us that he has taken liberties here, taking events from a fifteen-year period. Still, the bulk of the action, or at least the public events that can be historically dated, belong clearly to 1941–43. That was the period of the interregnum in the Isara *Odemo*-ship, though Soyinka has greatly simplified and contracted the contest to fill the vacancy, and it coincides with the centenary celebrations of the CMS mission in 1942–43, which is given a hilarious treatment (pp. 178–181). References to the second world war occur often. So I infer that it is in relation to the events of private life that most of the chronological liberties have been

---

[10] Captain Glover enraged the Egba by using rockets to break up their forces besieging the Lagoon port of Ikorodu in 1865, an action which led to the expulsion of European missionaries from Abeokuta in 1867. Glover's action might have been taken more kindly at Isara, since it was then an ally of Abeokuta's enemy Ibadan. C.A. Gollmer served as a CMS missionary between 1845 and 1859. His sobriquet *Alapako* means 'Owner of the plank house' and came from the prefabricated mission-house at Badagry which he had re-erected at Lagos in 1852.

taken. The fictional Soditan family seems to be younger than the real-life Soyinka family would have been in 1942–43; for example the Deinde of the book (p. 126), who may be intended to portray Wole Soyinka himself, seems younger than Wole (born in 1934). Whatever chronological liberties Soyinka took, their main point was surely to enable him to align significant events in the characters' private lives with the public events to which, as we shall see, they stand in telling counterpoint.

Stories and Structures

Ìsarà is much more complexly organized than Aké. It is written in four distinct narrative registers:

1. The master narrative, which provides the framework to the whole, deals with the public sphere, with the struggle of Soditan and his ex-Ilé friends or 'the Circle' to get their man Akinsanya selected as the Odemo of Isara.

2. Then there is a sequence of minor narratives, episodes or incidents in the private lives of Soditan, his family and friends, which are interleaved with phases of the master narrative. A good part of their function is to thicken the cultural description, and make the politics of the master narrative more fully intelligible by grounding them in what is, in effect, a depiction of civil society.

The minor narratives are not so firmly rooted in 'progressive time' as is the master narrative: appropriately so, since they convey 'a way of life', not unchanging but much less proactive in relation to change than the ex-Ilés' project to get Akinsanya chosen as Odemo and drive Isara forward to nationalist modernity. But still, these first two narrative registers, skilfully interwoven, together carry the reader forward. There are, however, two other registers, which seem to pull against them, checking the forward pace of the story by taking the reader back in time:

3. There are flashbacks, where the *narrator* turns back to present past experiences in the lives of the main characters. This device works to deepen the historical intelligibility of the story by extending its time-span beyond the year or so that it evidently covers.

4. Finally there are sections where the *characters* dream, reminisce or fall into reveries. While the content of these various inward states of consciousness does mostly refer to the past, this pastness is less

significant than their role in the present, which is to constitute the subjectivities that underlie the characters' actions.

While the use of these four registers adds greatly to the textured richness of *Ìsarà*, it also makes great demands on the reader's attention, and seems to explain why many people, to judge from my casual impressions from conversations about it, both inside and outside Nigeria, find *Ìsarà* a difficult book to 'get into' or 'get through', particularly after the seductive charm of *Aké*. For the flashbacks and reveries/dreams/memories both make the action slow to get under way (Parts I and II, roughly the first third of the book, consist almost entirely of them) and seem to slow it further by their later interpolation.

So while one is easily led to compare *Ìsarà* with *Aké* because of their overlapping themes and characters, *Ìsarà* is so different that it seems to belong to an altogether different genre. It recalls two others in Soyinka's body of writing. In both form and theme it echoes his first novel, *The Interpreters* (1964), which circles round the interlocking lives of a group of friends, young intellectuals on and around the campus of the University of Ibadan. Since that is also pretty much a *roman à clef*, it anticipates the merging of fact and fiction that we have in *Ìsarà*, though in a less challenging way. The other generic affinity of *Ìsarà*, much more than any other of Soyinka's autobiographical writings, is with his plays. Soyinka is a highly versatile writer, but is he not a dramatist above all? Certainly it was through thinking of *Ìsarà* as a kind of play that I found it came alive for me. The reader is perhaps encouraged to think of *Ìsarà* like this by the fact that it is not divided into chapters in the conventional way, but into six long, titled Parts, which are further divided into substantial sections, not titled but clearly indicated by a break in the text. These we may consider as operating like the Acts and Scenes of a Shakespeare play. The story gets under way slowly, as the first few sections or Scenes lay out the setting and introduce the main characters; the markers are laid down for the future development of the main line of the plot; the pace of the middle of the book, Parts (or, pursuing the dramatic analogy, Acts) III and IV, quickens, with a focus on the minor, personal narratives gradually building up to the master, public narrative; this takes over in Acts V and VI, now with little deflection, and one dramatic tableau succeeds another, up to the triumphant entry of Akinsanya into Isara as *Odemo*-elect and Soditan's climactic meeting with his alter ego from overseas. This way of reading *Ìsarà* is perhaps further validated by the fact that it contains that familiar Shakespearean device, the 'play within a play' (like those in *Hamlet* and *A Midsummer Night's Dream*), at Act V, Scene 3.[11] That this scene is also played for laughs should not lead the reader to ignore the serious point of its subject. Staged by Soditan and his friends as part of the centenary celebrations of the Church Missionary Society, the play touches on a core theme of the entire book, the assessment of the cultural impact of Christian missions in Yoruba history.

Coordinate to the issues of memory and the temporality of action are the spatial structures through which they move. The action of *Ìsarà* turns on a number of key spatial oppositions. These include: (i) the public sphere of the master narrative vs. the domestic or personal spheres of the minor narratives; (ii) local events in Isara vs. the distant, global events of the second world war; (iii) chieftaincy politics vs. nationalist politics; (iv) Isara the backwater vs. Abeokuta the local fount of education and enlightenment, which correlates with (v) the contrast of home and work for Soditan, and (vi) the paternal and maternal sides of Soyinka's own family; and (vii) the orderly bureaucratic world of clerks and teachers vs. the enticing but uncertain world of the independent entrepreneur. Several of the leading characters, for all their personal individuality, also serve to typify these oppositions. Akinsanya straddles local and nationalist politics, Pa Josiah (Soditan's father) the claims of Christianity and local knowledge, Sipe Efuape the reality of his work as a tax inspector and his hopes to make money as a trader.

Through their actions, various kinds of interchange, transition or encompassment are worked out between the local and the global. A unique role here is played by one of the most remarkable characters in the book, Soditan's American pen-friend, Wade Cudeback, from Ashtabula, Ohio. (Whether he is based on a real person, or is a pure invention of Soyinka's, I cannot guess.) Ashtabula is the Alpha and the Omega of *Ìsarà*. The book opens with Soditan reading a letter from Cudeback and musing on his and the town's past, and it concludes with their meeting: macrocosm united with microcosm, imagination with reality.

---

[11] On which see further Hubert, 1991, a reference for which I am indebted to Karin Barber.

Religion in Cultural Politics

Ìsarà is a study in cultural politics. As a cultural product itself, it is a contribution by Soyinka to the project of making the Nigerian nation. That it is so largely about religion at once indicates the centrality of that particular sphere of cultural endeavour to the politics of Yoruba communities, the struggles of individuals, groups and communities to gain and to wield power. While we may distinguish between the exercise of power over the environment or external circumstances and over other people (a distinction which underlies the contrast in Western political thought between power as a quantum which can be increased absolutely, and power as a zero-sum property of the relations between social actors), the contrast is misleading in relation to how the Yoruba think about power. For external circumstances, like sickness and a good trading or farming year, are themselves regarded as being strongly influenced by the activity of hidden 'spiritual' powers, or by the different degrees of 'spiritual' power inherent in other individuals. Because 'power' and 'spirit' are largely interchangeable terms, religion as the drawing down of the power of Spirit is deemed crucial to the framing of political choices, of policies and identities in the public sphere.

So it is not surprising that *Ìsarà* is saturated with references to religion. The formative experiences of Soditan and the ex-Ilés, what gave them their distinctive identity as 'enlightened' elements (*ọlaju*) in the town, derived from their engagement with mission Christianity and its agencies. They remember the time they were together at St Simeon's, training to be teachers. They dream of its absurd or formidable figures like the Revd Mr Beeston. They continue their lives much involved in church institutions: Opeilu as the Bishop's trouble-shooter, Mariam's circle of church women, the diocesan Synod as an important arena of public debate, the centennial pageant of the CMS. They draw on the Bible for symbols—Pharoah, Job, Anathema and Maranatha as a curse, the Ijebu as Jebusites—and they get all sorts of ideas from *In Leisure Hours*.[12] They speculate about the magical Sixth and Seventh Books of Moses.

---

[12] A monthly magazine published by the CMS Bookshop in Lagos between 1910 and around the late 1950s. It contained Bible study notes, articles on current affairs or of Christian interest, church news, crosswords and puzzles, cultural items etc. Articles were in English or Yoruba, its Yoruba title being *Nigbati Ọwọ Ba Dilẹ* ('When Hands Are Idle').

Local Christianity at this period drew much of its social distinction, as the religion of progress and modernity, from its opposition
to traditional religion. The latter figures as a diffuse presence in *Ìsarà*,
in the background rather than the foreground of the characters' lives,
though one likely to break with fresh insistency at moments of personal or social crisis. Yet it is striking that, except for one brief reference to Ogun, there is hardly any mention in *Ìsarà* of the *orìṣa*, or
deities, who usually figure prominently in accounts of Yoruba religion. Much more salient are the ancestral cults, Oro and Egungun,
which played a large role as sanctions of public order; the mystical
powers wielded by the societies of elders, Osugbo or Ogboni; and
those elements of traditional religion which gave people a sense of
practical power and control in their lives: techniques to divine (*awo*)
and then to ward off or assuage evil forces (*ẹbọ* and *etutu*). Of the
presence of Islam the indications are only brief.

I want to take two episodes in the book where the processes of
confrontation and substitution in the field of religion are shown to
be central to the definition of the nationalist agenda. One episode
comes from the major narrative, Act VI, Scene 3 (pp. 228–237),
close to the climax of the whole book. In fact, it is really the turning point of the narrative, since it is here, in a confrontation between
the spokesman of the ex-Ilés and the ancient chief who speaks for
the values of the pre-colonial past, that the plot as a whole becomes
fully intelligible, as the meaning of recent and immediate events are
placed in the longer historical span of Yoruba history.

The other episode, part of Act IV, Scene 2 (pp. 124–129), comes
from the minor narratives of family life, and does not at first seem
to be of strategic significance to the plot, but just part of the general cultural scene-setting. It is a conversational joust between Soditan
and his wife Morola about what form of treatment might be best
for her medical problem. At the same time, it presents, in an apparently non-political context, the same cultural choices that were
addressed at the public level in the ex-Ilés' arguments for the candidature of Akinsanya for the *Ọdẹmọ*ship. Its effect is to remind us
that colonialism was a total phenomenon for those who experienced
it, realized as much in the mundane dilemmas of private life as in
issues of politics or macro-economics, and that nationalism was necessarily more than merely a movement for political independence.
Underlying the outcomes of both episodes is a common, distinctively
nationalist, logic of resolution.

Morola's Dilemma: Etutu, Sàráà *or Surgery?*

The Yoruba concepts that occur most frequently in *Ìsarà* are *etutu* and *sàráà*.[13] *Etutu* may be defined as sacrificial offerings made to assuage or placate the anger of a deity or other spirit agency that has manifested itself in some kind of sickness or misfortune. As such they are a sub-category of *ẹbọ*, which are sacrifices in general. Sacrifice was perhaps the cardinal mode of interaction between the Yoruba and their gods: to 'worship' (*bọ*) a deity was essentially to sacrifice to it. *Sàráà* is a term of Islamic provenance, whose original meaning was 'alms' (which it still carries, especially in Muslim circles) but which in the Yoruba context has developed other meanings, particularly as a virtual synonym of the indigenous words for 'sacrifice'. Perhaps the most common reference of *sàráà* in modern Yoruba, among Christians as well as Muslims, is to a thank-offering feast made for mercies received, to be shared by one's family, friends and co-religionists. It may be suggested that, while the indigenous terms *etutu* and *ẹbọ* (as well as still referring to 'pagan' rituals) have tended to take on additional, more secular meanings, under the influence of the growing numbers of Muslims and Christians *sàráà* has expanded in the opposite direction, as Islamic practices have been widely understood in the prior terms of Yoruba religious culture.[14]

This semantic lability is doubly evident in the text of *Ìsarà*, both in Soyinka's own glosses of the words and in what he puts into the mouths of his characters. So when he defines them in a footnote on p. 127, he brings the meanings of *ẹbọ* and *sàráà* very close to one another: *ẹbọ* is 'ritual offering' (which somewhat downplays its religious character, as 'sacrifice'), and *sàráà* is 'ritual feast' (which is one common form which 'alms' have taken in Yoruba society). In fact both of these definitions are contained within the character of Yoruba sacrifice, since the sacrificial offering to the deity is typically followed by a meal shared by the participating worshippers. *Etutu* is not given

---

[13] A note on Yoruba orthography, since in one respect I have departed from Soyinka's usage. In the printed text of *Ìsarà* Soyinka puts in very few tone accents, and omits to use any of the subscript dots or strokes which distinguish the two phonetic values of *ẹ, ọ* and *ṣ*. Fully rendered, *Ìsarà* would be *Ìṣarà*. The word which Soyinka writes as *saara* is rendered in its more conventionally phonetic form as *sàráà*, to convey the drawn-out pronunciation of the second syllable—really two syllables, one on a high, the other on a low tone.

[14] For a fuller historical account of the relations between *sàráà* and *ẹbọ/etutu*, see Peel, 1990.

such a footnote gloss, but emerges only in contextualized use. So when Node's new lorry is dedicated (p. 5), a triple offering is made: '*etutu* rituals' are performed by Chief Jagun, while Pa Josiah says a Christian blessing and the town's imam reads from the Koran. The pagan character of *etutu* is reiterated when Pa Josiah later objects to his wife's request for money towards her kinsman Tenten's funeral expenses on the grounds that it will go 'to make all the *etutu* and other things which you know are forbidden to me' (p. 100). He would rather just dig the grave himself and say a prayer over it. But whereas *etutu* is here contrasted with the religious practices of Christians and Muslims, elsewhere a completely *ẹbọ*- or *etutu*-style ritual is performed, but called *sàráà*. Sipe, anxious to make money, is intrigued by the 'mystic services' that his friend Onayemi has been hoping to enlist from the medium of the Spirit of Layeni. But he still remains sceptical of 'poor Onayemi expending his commission [as a salesman for the John Holt company] on goat, yams, palm oil or whatever, dutifully carrying them to the medium as *saara* every full moon' (p. 73).

These semantic ambiguities are exploited to the full in Morola and Soditan's discussion of whether to use *etutu* to deal with her abdominal pains and failure to conceive another child. It is Pa Josiah, Soditan's father, who has hitherto figured as a Christian strongly opposed to having any dealings with such pagan things, who has been pressing it on them. They do not want to use it, but they have already been to several clinics and doctors to try European remedies, without success. The argument develops through a number of stages:

1. Soditan says, in a wholly pragmatic spirit, that if European remedies don't work one last time, and the pain starts again, then 'Father will be set to place his *ẹbọ* right against the church gates if that is what his *oniṣẹgun* [traditional healer] recommends'.

2. Morola expresses her worry at getting involved in 'this pagan business'. Like the staunch fourth-generation Christian that Soyinka's mother was in real life, she is anxious to separate sharply pagan and Christian practices.

3. Soditan starts to get argumentative: 'Pagan? Why pagan? All right, what if it is pagan? Tell me don't Christians make *saara* on occasion?' He counters Morola by exploiting the fact that *sàráà* was often conceptually assimilated to *ẹbọ* and *etutu*.

4. Morola fights back: 'The way I see it, *saara* is a kind of thanksgiving. A child has been ill, recovers, so we make *saara* ... People

have a good harvest or they arrive safely after a long journey . . . all that is different. What Father is saying in this letter is something else; *etutu* is like a secret ritual.' Here she both reasserts the distinctively Muslim or Christian meaning of *sàráà*, and adds a further point to strengthen the difference: the secrecy of *etutu* is morally dubious, unlike the openness of Christianity.

5. Yet again Soditan bounces back to rebut this claim to difference between *etutu* and Christian practice: 'there is nothing secret about *etutu*'. This is at best a half-truth, since though the use of an *etutu* was not necessarily secret, its ingredients did typically depend upon esoteric knowledge.[15] But he then goes further, and tries to outflank Morola's position altogether by likening *etutu* to the white man's surgical operations, which he says are even more secret. 'Those doctors, do they allow anyone in the theatre when they start cutting up people and sewing them up and removing their insides?'

6. Seized by a spirit of jocular mischief, Soditan speculates on what the surgeons do with the organs they remove: 'How do you know they don't use them to make some white man's *etutu*?' Morola tries to head him off by going along with the joke, but Soditan is now unstoppable. He turns the tables on European disparagement of African medicine by likening the parts removed by the surgeon to the dried snakes and monkey skulls sold as ingredients in the juju market; 'and why do these Europeans look down on them as instruments of devilish rites?'

7. As the exchange winds down, Soditan scores a last rhetorical point against European medicine. When his wife expresses a concern about the cost of hospital treatment, he expostulates: 'I know why you are so dead against Father's kind of cure [*ẹbọ/etutu*]. With European treatment, you eat all the medicine by yourself. In our own, we all get to share it [alluding to the sharing of the sacrificed animal by the family group]. That's it! Selfish woman. And me fooling myself that your appetite has not yet returned!' Thus the moral superiority of African culture is asserted by means of a criterion that Christianity could not but endorse.

Though this vividly realized exchange between husband and wife is apparently inconsequential and purely concerned with domestic issues, it is organized by the same dialectical logic of argument that

---

[15] On secrecy in Yoruba medical practices, see Buckley, 1985.

we find in the master narrative. This logic has a tripartite structure: (i) something traditional is posited (here, *etutu*); (ii) this is then opposed by something from the world religions, the external harbingers of cultural modernity (here, *sàráà*); (iii) this religious antithesis is then negated by something that arises from the external source of modernity (here, surgery) but also 'loops back' to valorize the traditional. While in this episode the point is disguised by its jokey, seemingly unserious character, its structure points the same nationalist argument that is made at the narrative climax of the book.

The Pain of the Past: The Agunrin Meditates on Ijebu History

The final Act of *Ìsarà*, entitled 'Ashtabula!', brings the personal and the public narratives together, as the contest for the *Odẹmọ*-ship culminates in the success of the progressives' candidate, S.A. Akinsanya, and at the same time Soditan's pen-friend Wade Cudeback unexpectedly arrives in the town. Thus at one stroke Isara moves decisively into the nationalist future, and its microcosmic reality becomes one with the macrocosmic and the imagined (as symbolized in the exotic stranger from Ohio). It was in fact rather exceptional in the early 1940s for someone as much in the vanguard of Lagos politics as Akinsanya, Vice-President of the Nigerian Youth Movement and Secretary of the Nigerian Motor Transport Union, to contest for the *ọba*-ship of a small Yoruba town.

The contest in real life was protracted and, at its outset, complicated by half-a-dozen candidates claiming affiliation to the royal lineage. Soyinka's fictional account simplifies it to a struggle between two factions, led respectively by Chiefs *Jagun* for Akinsanya and *Olisa* for his rival Erinle, of Rokodo 'ruling house'. There is an implicit significant contrast between these two titles. *Jagun* is a warrior title, and is presumably the head of the line of military chiefs, like the *Balogun* of an Egba or Oyo town, while *Olisa* is one of the senior Osugbo or Ogboni titles, which relate to judicial or other 'civil' functions. In many Yoruba towns, such as Abeokuta in the 1850s, it was the military chiefs who sponsored missionaries and 'progress', because they were concerned with the external relations of the community, with its viability in the context of the wider world; while the Ogboni chiefs, concerned with its internal relations and so with its normative traditions, were generally much more opposed to cultural innovation.

How to reconcile the commitment to progress of the *Jagun* faction and the conservatism of the *Olisa* faction is the agenda of the nationalist argument which is presented in the climactic confrontation between the two sides. Fighting has broken out in Isara, and after an innocent sanitary inspector has been beaten up on suspicion of being a spy by the members of Rokodo's compound, the ex-Ilés of *Jagun*'s party decide they must send a delegation to face their opponents at their headquarters, Chief *Olisa*'s house. A key resource of Chief *Olisa* is that he holds, as a virtual prisoner, the aged and speechless *Agunrin* Odubona. The *Agunrin* (the title is unique to Ijebu towns) were palace officials and emissaries, and the main repositories of tradition.

> Old and gnarled as the bunched open roots of the *odan* tree, he was the last surviving tome of Isara, and indeed of Ijebu, history from before the settled phase of missionary incursion. He lived with his memories, a still-active but closed circuit within the tight-skinned independency of his head. The Olisa was his sole link with the present ... (p. 229).

Odubona is 'the collective will of all of Isara', but his authority has been appropriated by his masterful keeper, the *Olisa*.

The ex-Ilés have chosen as their spokesman the emollient church politician, Opeilu. Soyinka portrays the clash of views by the brilliant device of intersplicing fragments of Opeilu's speech with longer passages that convey the unspoken thoughts of the listening elders, and particularly of *Agunrin* Odubona. As Opeilu urges on the chiefs the advantages of choosing as *Odẹmọ* a man like Akinsanya, who 'knows the white man but ... belongs to Isara' (p. 233), so will serve as an effective champion of Isara's communal interests, Odubona is reflecting on the course of Ijebu history. He sees it as a tale of spiritual catastrophe. He remembers how he supported the resolve of Ijebu in the last century to reject missionaries and the corrupt and polluting manners of their converts, unlike the Egba who 'had ruined everything' by encouraging the importation of the white man's ways. Opeilu's mention of Governor Carter triggers more intense reflection on the effects of 'Kata-kata's' invasion of 1892, which finally broke through Ijebu's cultural defences. The ideological difficulty the ex-Ilés had to surmount was that in the *Agunrin*'s eyes a man with the attributes of Akinsanya was the logical outcome of what Carter had started:

> And was this *Odẹmọ* they wanted to inflict on Isara not their way of finishing off what they began forty years ago? Was it not enough that

the missionaries now strutted through the proud land, their churches
and schools everywhere, their products mincing on feet suffocating in
thick socks and leather through their council halls? Was it not enough
that they had to obey laws imposed on them by Kata-kata and his
black servants? Must they now permit one of these godless ones to
come and sit on the throne of Isara? (p. 232).

As if he hears his unspoken thoughts, Opeilu seeks to reassure *Agunrin*
Odubona and the other chiefs:

> Akinsanya will abide by your wishes, the wishes of the people of
> Isara . . . he has sworn to preserve the ways of Isara while carrying
> our voice to the highest councils of the land, and beyond the seas . . .
> The Ibadan, Egba, the Ekiti, the Ijaiye or Oyo never defeated us in
> war. They will not now mock our defeat at our own hands.

Opeilu's artful attempt to appropriate the traditional rhetoric of Ijebu
pride, as undefeated in war and able to control its own frontiers,
triggers in Odubona another round of painful recollection of the
debacle of 1892. He recalls that, as one of the *Agunrin* at the time,
he had reluctantly taken the message of the Ijebu paramount king,
the *Awujale*, to Governor Carter; and that Carter's treaty, which the
four *Agunrin* had refused to put their marks to, had been signed by
Ijebu Christian residents in Lagos. And would not Akinsanya be 'a
"Lagosian" king sitting on Isara's throne', the true successor of those
traitorous Ijebu with their preposterous names—Christians like Otumba
Payne and Jacob Williams—'the mincing spawn of tainted Ijebu
blood' who had signed the treaty in Ijebu's name?

When Opeilu goes on to recommend 'a peaceful way' to the chiefs,
Odubona reflects that this was how the missionaries always talked
when they wanted to push their way into Ijebu. He recalls the
provocative behaviour of Bishop Tugwell—'Togiwe' as the Ijebu
called him—and his associate Tom Harding, the CMS superintendent at Ibadan, whose heads the Ijebu had demanded of the Ibadan
chiefs as a price of their friendship. Odubona's imagination now
drifts wider afield, to other Yoruba groups and beyond, to their rep-
utations in war and to their several responses to the white man's
pressure. When finally Opeilu gets to his peroration, he insists that
not only does the colonial administration oppose the *Olisa*'s bid to
install Erinle as *Odemo* of Isara, but so does the *Awujale*. At the mention of the Ijebu paramount, Odubona suddenly jerks into a spasm
of movement and brief speech, the first for ten years. 'Aaa-wujale

Tunwase!', he cries out, naming the king of 1892. As *Olisa* gently reminds him that was long ago, he slumps back and dies with the words '*O ti fọ n'ojú!* [It is smashed beyond redeeming]'.

As the tension of this sustained encounter drains away, and the reader is finally apprised of the historical antecedents of the nationalist project in Ijebu, *Ìsarà's* narrative picks up speed and moves to its climax. And again there is a crucial parallel between events in the major and the minor narratives: *Agunrin* Odubona's death soon has its counterpart in the death of another representative of the ancient order of things, Soditan's 'Old Granny', Iya Agba. Simultaneously Wade Cudeback, the symbol of global modernity, arrives in town, and we learn that, whether thanks to *etutu* or the white man's medicine, Morola is expecting a baby.

There is more to these coincidences than some general notion that without death there can be no life, or that by dying the dead make space for new lives. There is the specific Yoruba idea of *atunbi*, the idea that the dead are reborn in their descendants, and particularly a grandparent in a grandchild born shortly after its death. Such a boy child will be called *Babatunde* ('Father returned') while a girl will be *Yetunde* ('Mother returned'). And here the coincidence of Iya Agba's death and Morola's pregnancy works to remind us that, though they seem so opposed, Akinsanya is a kind of grandson to Odubona. Odubona represents the old, autonomous Ijebu: he resisted the imposition of colonialism, and was never reconciled to its values. Though Odubona can see in Akinsanya only a product of the colonial order (as indeed he was), Akinsanya is a nationalist, who aspires to restore independence to Ijebu, but as part of a new, higher-order entity, Nigeria. Odubona's backward-looking vision must die before it can be reincarnated in the forward-looking one that Akinsanya will promote as the first educated *Ọdẹmọ* of Isara. Soyinka has earlier trailed this interpretation in front of the reader when, at the first news of Morola's pregnancy, he has her friend Mrs Esan predict that it will be a boy, 'and you can only name him Obatunde' (p. 152). *Ọbatunde* means 'the king has returned'; and *ọba* ('king') stands metonymically for sovereignty, which nationalism would recover for the colonized people of Nigeria.

Yet with the essential paradox of dialectical processes, the passage from the old vision to the new one was critically dependent on the cultural role of the middle, intervening generation, which had had to come to terms with colonialism. That meant actions in the cultural sphere, notably conversion to Christianity and learning the white man's ways, which were felt as betrayal by an Odubona, but were essential to the formation of an Akinsanya. It is the same dialectical triad that came up in the argument between Soditan and his wife about *etutu*, *sàráà* and modern medicine, but here it is projected more surely onto the three-generation span of the colonial period.

Postscript: A Dog that Didn't Bark?

The embarrassment of African nationalism at its Christian roots may perhaps explain, if it needs explanation, one curious detail absent from Soyinka's representation of the exchange between Opeilu and Odubona. This absent detail would have provided a further, and absolutely clinching, link between the public and the domestic narratives of *Ìsarà*, highlighted the contrast between the Egba and the Ijebu sides of Soyinka's family and perfectly encapsulated the irony of Christianity's links with nationalism. As Odubona reflected, the responses of Abeokuta and Ijebu towards Christian missions had been very different. Abeokuta had welcomed them in the late 1840s with the Christian Egba returnees from Sierra Leone and, despite temporarily expelling them in 1867, had been greatly influenced by them, acquiring a sizeable Western-educated elite long before any other Yoruba town. The missions were kept out of Ijebu until after 1892, but a few years later reported a mass movement to Christianity, as young Ijebu rushed to make up what they now saw as a serious cultural deficit. Soyinka's father, entering St Andrew's College in 1910, was part of this Ijebu flood.[16] His mother, by contrast, was a fourth generation Christian: her great-grandfather Daniel Olubi had been 'given' by his uncle Ogunbona, the chief patron of the missionaries, to the Revd David Hinderer in 1849 to be his houseboy. Olubi went with Hinderer to Ibadan, was later ordained—the first home-grown Yoruba Anglican priest—and eventually succeeded him as the pastor of the Ibadan church. So the contrast between the historical experiences of Abeokuta and Isara has its direct counterpart in the Egba and Ijebu sides of Soyinka's ancestry.

The intriguing absence is this. When the Ijebu authorities took offence at the doings of Christian clergymen in the run-up to the

---

[16] For a fuller account, see Peel, 1977.

invasion of 1892, the figure they most objected to was neither of the two Europeans who figure in Odubona's reflections, Bishop Tugwell in Lagos and the Revd Tom Harding at Ibadan, but none other than Soyinka's own Egba great-great-grandfather, the Revd Daniel Olubi. The Yoruba wars were then in their end-game, and the Ibadan army was still in its war-camp at Kiriji, desperately short of ammunition because the Ijebu had closed the trade route from Lagos. Urgently needing to reach an accommodation with Ijebu, in April 1892 the Ibadan chiefs received envoys from the *Awujalẹ* demanding the expulsion of Olubi and Harding. Olubi, wrote Harding, was held 'in great respect' at Ibadan, and the chiefs resisted the demand. The Ijebu then sent a man to pronounce a solemn curse on Olubi. When a third delegation came, the Ibadan chiefs reluctantly told Olubi and Harding to go; but gave them a stay when they protested their innocence of the Ijebu charges. These negotiations were only cut off by the British invasion of Ijebu in mid-May. When the news of that reached Ibadan, there was no end of visitors to the mission compounds at Ibadan to offer congratulations on the Ijebu defeat.[17]

It is not surprising that Olubi, as the leading Yoruba Christian pastor in Ibadan, was identified with the colonial presence, even that he was called *oyinbo* ('white man') by ordinary non-Christian Yoruba.[18] But this still does not explain why the Ijebu chiefs had such a peculiar antipathy to him. The reason appears to be that in 1881–82, when Ijebu had been torn by a civil war between an anti-Ibadan party led by the then *Awujalẹ* and a pro-Ibadan party led by the senior war-chief, *Balogun* Onafowokan, Olubi had built up friendly relations with some of the Ijebu exiles in Ibadan, and succeeded in converting the war-chief's son.[19] Ten years later, Ijebu could neither forget nor forgive Olubi an act that it saw as tantamount to fomenting treason. As I have said, *Ìsarà* makes no mention of these circumstances of Olubi's life, which have such an ironic potential. Was it

---

[17] Journal Extracts of W.S. Allen, African catechist at Ibadan, for 2–4 April, 26 May 1892, and of T. Harding for 11 April 1892, in G3A2/1892: CMS Yoruba Mission Papers, Birmingham University Library.

[18] African CMS agents often noted in their Journals that they were called *oyinbo*, the term's cultural connotations taking precedence over its racial ones. Olubi was even seen (wrote his friend Samuel Johnson) as 'the white man's representative' in parts of eastern Yorubaland, where he had played a role in several British diplomatic missions: S. Johnson to Governor, 6 January 1882, in G3A2/1882/7.

[19] Journal Extracts of D. Olubi, for 10 September 1880, in G3A2/1881/99, and for 18 September 1882 and 17 June 1883, in G3A2/1884/100.

a deliberate decision of Soyinka not to make use of them, or was he just unaware of them? If the latter, was it that in the traditions of Olubi's descendants, Soyinka's mother's side, the memory of his conspicuous alignment with the forces that imposed the colonial order was erased? Was it felt to be incompatible with the self-image of a family that made so notable a contribution to the nationalism which destroyed that colonial order?[20]

Author's Note

An earlier version of this essay was intended for a volume in honour of Terence Ranger, which in the event was not published. Since the subject of the relations between Christianity and politics has equally been an interest of Adrian Hastings, I was happy to accept David Maxwell's invitation to place the paper in the present volume. I regard it as paying homage to the achievements of both men.

---

[20] See the account of Soyinka's radical political aunt, Mrs Ransome-Kuti, by Johnson-Odim and Mba (1997), which frequently ignores or underplays the Christian sources and idiom of her campaign. For example, they do not comment on (or even translate) the slogan on the banner on the front of the building of the Egba Women's Union, of which they show a photograph: *Ojo Irapada Egba de: obinrin Egba, e fi ope f'Oluwa* ('The day of Egba redemption is come. Egba women, praise ye the Lord').

APPENDIX I: *Dramatis personae*

Akinyode Soditan, 'Yode', headmaster at Abeokuta

Ex-Ilés, or The Circle

Sipe Efuape, a tax clerk, college friend of Soditan
Osibo, 'Genie of the Bottle', a pharmacist
Ogunba, a schoolteacher
S.A. Akinsanya, 'Saaki', a trade unionist in Lagos, the ex-Ilés' candidate to be *Ọdẹmọ*
Opeilu, a produce inspector and church politician
Sotikare, a court clerk

Family (Ile Lígùn)

Morola, Mrs Soditan
Pa Josiah, Soditan's father, a farmer and church elder
Mariam, Soditan's mother
Iya Agba, Soditan's grandmother
Pa Node, family friend, a wealthy but paralysed timber dealer
Tenten, Morola's late brother, who worked for Node
Carpenter, head of Mariam's family at Sagamu
Damian or Wemuja, driver of Node's lorry
Rev. I.O. Ransome-Kuti, 'Daodu', Morola's uncle at Abeokuta

Others

Chief *Jagun*, Josiah's friend and Saaki's main backer for the *Ọdẹmọ*ship
Chief *Olisa*, main backer of Erinle, the rival candidate
Agunrin Odubona, the oldest chief in Isara
Goriola, a sanitary inspector
Fatuka, a public letter writer
Onayemi, a literate trader with access to the Spirit of Layeni
Akanbi Backley, a truculent pupil, and his angry father
Mrs Esan, Morola's friend, a teacher and cloth trader
Jose Santero, the wastrel scion of an old 'Brazilian' family in Lagos
Madame Santero, Jose's mother and head of the family
Ray Gunnar, a Trinidadian confidence trickster in London
Bishop Vining of Lagos
Revd Beeston and Dr Mackintosh, teachers of Soditan's at St Simeon's
Wade Cudeback, Soditan's American pen-friend

APPENDIX II: *The plot*

I: EX-ILÉ

1. Soditan visits Isara off-season, and reads a letter from his pen-friend Wade Cudeback in Ashtabula, Ohio. He reflects on travel and history.
2. Soditan recalls his youthful journey by train to St Simeon's seminary at Ilesa, accompanied by Damian.
3. How Damian came to Isara and became Wemuja, Node's driver. *Jagun* and Pa Josiah talk to Soditan about the impending death of the *Ọdẹmọ*.
4. Soditan reflects on his life. His grandmother anticipates her funeral.
5. Soditan muses on his life as a teacher, and the issues of the day debated by teachers and his friends of the Circle.
6. Soditan recalls his days at St Simeon's.

II: EFUAPE

1. Sipe Efuape, ex-Simeonite and tax-clerk, dreams of a great money-making project.
2. Sipe's attempt to get to a friend's wedding ends disastrously. On the way back, he reflects on his expulsion from St Simeon's, and on his schemes to get rich. His trader friend Onayemi's use of magic, through the Spirit of Layeni.
3. Sipe falls asleep and dreams of the Cherubim and Seraphim, Mammy Wata and the Revd Beeston at St Simeon's.

III: LÍGÙN

1. Mariam and Josiah squabble over her missing money box. She worries about her brother Tenten's funeral, and gets a letter-writer to write to Soditan at Abeokuta about her troubles.
2. Further dealings of Mariam with her family, Node's household, her companions and the Osugbo society over Tenten's funeral.
3. How Node's paralysis was caused by his wife's infidelity. Tenten's loyalty to him. Mariam seeks Josiah's help in approaching Osugbo, who say they can't bury him because he was an albino.
4. The Osugbo elders return the missing box.

IV: TISA

1. Soditan's ways as a teacher at Abeokuta. He talks politics with Osibo the pharmacist.
2. Morola's gynaecological problems, and family pressure to use *etutu*. Soditan deals with Beckley, a delinquent pupil. He prepares to give a speech to the Owu National Society.
3. Pa Josiah comes to Abeokuta to get the things to make *etutu*. He and Soditan talk about Isara affairs.

V: HOMECOMING

1. Mrs Esan calls to congratulate Soditan on the expected baby. They talk politics. Message comes from Saaki.
2. Isara fills up with people returning for the New Year festivities. Soditan and Sipe talk about their fortunes and the War. The war's local impact: shortages, fund-raising, nationalist hopes. Pa Josiah breaks in to announce that the *Olisa* faction has illicitly installed their man as Ọdẹmọ.
3. Ray Gunnar's career and contacts with West Africans in London. His correspondence courses in drama attract Nigerian subscriptions. Soditan and colleagues at Abeokuta prepare to stage a musical drama as part of the CMS centenary celebrations. Sipe puts on a successful pantomime in Lagos, assisted by Jose Santero.
4. Soditan and Sipe go to Lagos to see Saaki. They talk about their hopes for the development of Isara. Sipe asks Soditan for his views on the Spirit of Layeni. They talk about Opeilu.
5. Opeilu talks church affairs with Bishop Vining at Abeokuta. With the help of Psalm 21 he narrowly escapes from drunken soldiers at Ibadan.
6. Soditan and Sipe tell Saaki to go easy on his nationalist politics till the Ọdẹmọship is his.
7. They go on to the Santero house in Lagos, and agree with old Madame Santero that they will take a white horse, a prized family possession, to repay the money which Jose took from Sipe's theatre funds to send to Ray Gunnar. On this Saaki will ride into Isara as Ọdẹmọ.

VI: ASHTABULA!

1. Sipe and Soditan return to Isara with news of Saaki's commitment. Fighting breaks out between the two factions, and a man is killed. Wemuja dresses for action.
2. Goriola goes to inspect Rokodo compound, a stronghold of the *Olisa* faction, and is beaten up on suspicion of being a spy. The ex-Ilés decide to confront the *Olisa*.
3. *Olisa* has the ancient and speechless *Agunrin* Odubona in his house. As Opeilu puts the case for Saaki, Odubona meditates on Ijebu history and the coming of the white man. At the name of the Ijebu paramount king, the *Awujale*, Odubona bursts into brief speech and then collapses dead.
4. *Jagun*, coming from divination in the Osugbo house, receives news of Odubona's death.
5. Wemuja prepares his lorry to go and get Saaki from Lagos, while Sipe sets off to consult the Spirit of Layeni. The night before, the ex-Ilés had talked things over, and Soditan revealed he had attended a consultation a few years back: the message was 'Find Asabula', and the same day the first letter arrived from Ashtabula.
6. Isara prepares to receive the District Officer to confirm Saaki's selection as *Odemo*. While Soditan is with the dying Iya Agba, Wade Cudeback arrives unexpectedly in town.
7. The processions of the rival factions enter town. Saaki, on the white horse, is triumphant. Soditan greets Cudeback with the words: 'Welcome to Ashtabula'.

BIBLIOGRAPHY

Ajayi, J.F. Ade, 'Nineteenth Century Origins of Nigerian Nationalism', *Journal of the Historical Society of Nigeria*, II, 1961, pp. 196–211.
Anderson, Benedict, *Imagined Communities: Reflections on the Origin and Spread of Nationalism*, London, Verso, 1983.
Buckley, Anthony D., *Yoruba Medicine*, Oxford, Clarendon Press, 1985.
Gellner, Ernest, *Nations and Nationalism*, Oxford, Blackwell, 1983.
Hastings, Adrian, *The Construction of Nationhood: Ethnicity, Religion and Nationalism*, Cambridge, Cambridge University Press, 1997.
Hobsbawm, E.J., *Nations and Nationalism since 1780: Programme, Myth, Reality*, Cambridge, Cambridge University Press, 1990.
Hubert, Judd D., *Metatheater: The Example of Shakespeare*, Lincoln, University of Nebraska Press, 1991.
Johnson-Odim, Cheryl, and Mba, Nina Emma, *For Women and the Nation: Funmilayo Ransome-Kuti of Nigeria*, Urbana, University of Illinois Press, 1997.
Maja-Pearce, Adewale, *Wole Soyinka: An Appraisal*, Oxford, Heinemann, 1994.
Nolte, Margrit Insa, 'Ritualised Interaction and Civic Spirituality: Kingship and Politics in Ijebu-Remo', Ph.D. thesis, University of Birmingham, 1999.
Ogunba, Oyin, *Soyinka: A Collection of Critical Essays*, Ibadan, Syndicated Communications, 1994.
Peel, J.D.Y., *Aladura: A Religious Movement among the Yoruba*, London, Oxford University Press, 1968.
———, 'Conversion and Tradition in Two African Societies: Ijebu and Buganda', *Past and Present*, LXXVII, 1977, pp. 108–141.
———, 'Poverty and Sacrifice in Nineteenth-Century Yorubaland', *Journal of African History*, XXXII, 1990, pp. 465–484.
Quayson, Ato, *Strategic Transformations in Nigerian Writing*, London, James Currey, 1997.
Soyinka, Wole, *Aké: The Years of Childhood*, London, Rex Collings, 1981.
———, *Ìsarà: A Voyage round 'Essay'*, London, Methuen, 1990.
———, *The Credo of Being and Nothingness*, Ibadan, Spectrum Books, 1991.
Wright, Derek, *Wole Soyinka Revisited*, New York, Twayne, 1993.

CHAPTER SIX

KIKUYU CHRISTIANITIES:
A HISTORY OF INTIMATE DIVERSITY

John Lonsdale

Argument[1]

Christianity in Kikuyuland, of central Kenya, is a century old. From
the outset there have been many Kikuyu Christianities.[2] They have
differed over theology; over spiritual, mental, marital, dietary and
bodily disciplines; forms of worship and formulae of self-government;
and how far personal salvation needs social justice. Religious plurality is in part due to an imported motley of Christian missions:
Italian, French and Irish Catholics, English Anglicans, Scottish
Presbyterians, American Baptists. It also reflects Christianity's basic
mystery, its many 'contestable possibilities' open to individual readings of the Bible.[3] Deeper still, Christian diversity has tapped an
already disputatious local culture, with a history of moral and, probably, theological, enquiry. In all, the Kikuyu case confirms Adrian
Hastings's general thesis, that Africans have had a large, indeed

---

[1] Many have helped me by discussion over the years and in criticism of earlier
drafts of this essay. I am grateful to Revd Paddy Benson, Professor Bruce Berman,
the late Revd Canon Peter Bostock, John Casson, Dr Yvan Droz, Revd Griphus
Gakuru, Right Revd Dr Gideon Githiga, Dr François Grignon, Dr Amrik Heyer,
Professor John Iliffe, Bildad Kaggia, Revd Dr Grace Karamura, Revd Dr John K.
Karanja, Professor Greet Kershaw, Revd Canon Graham Kings, Revd Dr Ben
Knighton, Professor Paul Landau, Mungai Mbayah, Professor Godfrey Muriuki, Dr
Jocelyn Murray, Right Revd Stephen Mwangi, Right Revd Daniel Munene Ng'oru,
Professor John Peel, the Revd Dr Carrie Pemberton and Revd Jeremy Pemberton,
Dr Derek Peterson, Dr Malcolm Ruel, Dr Galia Sabar, Professor Richard Waller
and George K. Waruhiu. I have taken advantage of David Maxwell's invitation to
amend the original article (in *Journal of Religion in Africa* XXIX-2, 1999, pp. 206–229)
to ask how far Kikuyu held a pre-Christian 'theology', and to discuss more fully
popular and establishment Christianities in the present day.
[2] A more correct orthography would spell Kikuyu (a Swahili and British colonial corruption) as Gikuyu. I use the familiar Kikuyu for the people, Gikuyu for
the language.
[3] Stephen Sykes, *The Identity of Christianity* (London, 1984), pp. 254–7, quoted in
Gray (1990), p. 77.

decisive, say in making their Christianities—even in an era when they look to have lost all narrative power over their lives, under the seeming hegemony of white missionary and colonial control.[4] More recently Kikuyu have found that lack of land, work and political power has sapped the bases of self-realization and growth in personal responsibility. To achieve full manhood has become even harder than winning a proper womanhood. But this moral impasse has made their Christianities all the more urgent in their variety.[5] Meanwhile, in an exercise that Hastings puts at the heart of nationhood, Kikuyu have read the Bible as an allegory of their own history—a story of servitude and salvation, exile and return.[6] This primer in communal responsibility has helped them face up to the socially, even theologically, divisive test of finding themselves, more consciously than ever before, to be a nationality, a people.

Kikuyu Christianity's historical variety is easily sketched out, in its origins and institutional growth, its theologies and nationalisms, its contemporary relations with the Kenyan state. First, the early sociology of Kikuyu adherence to Christianity (of which the historian can write with more certainty than of conversion) defies any attempt at pattern-making. The pioneers came from a stateless society, one with no concerted power to decide who could, or could not, aspire to a new therapeutic community or knowledgeable authority.[7] Many sorts of young men, kinless and well-connected alike, and, initially, many fewer women, first tested the new faith, or at least its ritual practices, and its learning. They then led different lives, some remaining close to their mission, others careless of or opposed to it. Many black Christians scarcely met a white missionary, and were decreasingly likely to do so over time. Missionaries remained few while Christians multiplied in number and matured in age. From the 1920s, Africans themselves began to enter ordained, denominationally divided, ministries; and Kikuyu penalized those missions slow to start such church building.[8] In the realm of culture, Christian elders then divided on

---

[4] Hastings (1994) pp. 437–92.

[5] For important studies on the gender crisis and religion: Droz (1999), Heyer (1998). For its Kikuyu agrarian history: Mackenzie (1998); and its sociology: Thomas-Slayter and Rocheleau (1995), Weisner et al. (1997).

[6] Hastings (1997).

[7] Motivations for adhesion or conversion suggested by Neckebrouck (1978), pp. 316–18 (a sadly neglected work) and Droz (1999), pp. 293–6.

[8] By contrast with the Presbyterians and Anglicans, with traditions of autonomy and few missionaries, who led the way in African church-building, the growth of a Catholic community was slow to match its large missionary numbers, thanks to

how far faith should reform custom. Whether Christ condemned clitoridectomy, a surgery hitherto essential to female initiation, was the
question of 1929. In the 1930s some left the missions to lead independent churches with a Christian-national project. Others had already
founded 'praying' churches for whom any politics was an offence to
the Spirit. Others still were later swept into the mission churches'
Revival, which fostered love for those white brethren who were similarly 'broken', born again, converted. The nationalism of Christians,
churchgoers and non-Christians alike was still more contested after
1945. Some Christians fell martyr to the seemingly pagan insurgency
called 'Mau Mau'; others, with Bible in pocket and gun in hand,
took to the forest as guerrillas, there to deplore the tactical influence
of traditional diviners. Finally, today, the theology of power could
not be more divided. Some Kikuyu churchmen pray for Kenya's
President as God's agent on earth and allow a legitimate sphere for
Caesar's reasoned rule; others fear that the state is in league with
the Devil and rest their Pentecostal hopes on a Second Coming.

But to what purpose is this parade of local Christian sectarianism? Hastings's own work suggests three questions to which it may
be relevant. The first is the nature of 'the long conversation' between
Christian and African cosmologies;[9] the second is how far one can
identify a church history, a developmental narrative which influenced
actors in their time; and, finally, whether doctrinal variety was inter-
related, debated and perhaps mutually modulated, rather than a
cacophony of different voices forever out of tune. All three issues
are fraught with controversy.

First, the discursive relationship between Christian and African
cosmologies has attracted a spirited historiography. The question is,
how far Christianity's message and domestic practices were hegemonic, that is, persuasive enough to transmute colonialism's racial
inequality from an injustice demanding its subjects' resistance into a
ladder of cultural ambition. Any answer must respect the contingency
of history. Cases differ. There are many variables: such as the social
vigour of indigenous 'moral knowledge',[10] a term perhaps preferable

the high, universal, qualifications required of African Catholic priests (Njoroge, 1999).
Conversely, adherents of the (mostly) Baptist and American Africa Inland Mission
(AIM) were always few. The AIM lagged in indigenous church building; its Kijabe
mission has long been the largest mission station in Africa (Sandgren, 1989).
  [9] For my terms (but not my argument) see Comaroffs (1991, 1997).
  [10] A term I owe to James (1988), especially pp. 143–56. I discuss below how far
Kikuyu moral knowledge was also 'religion' or 'theology'.

to 'traditional religion'; or the readiness of a colonial regime to respect or exploit African authorities; or the nationality and doctrines of the local mission societies; and so on. The Kikuyu case is one among many. Its internal diversity nonetheless suggests three general points.[11] The first is that the terms of the religious conversation were argued out among Africans as well as with whites. In debating their own changing moral economy, Kikuyu generated between themselves the discursive energy which fired their dialogue with colonial Christianity. Some converts were as 'enthusiastically confrontational' toward indigenous inequities as in other parts of Africa.[12] But, secondly, there was compromise as well as confrontation in the cross-cultural encounter. Each protagonist, white missionary or black enquirer, found uncertainties in the other's position, perhaps particularly on the question how far God, whoever he might be, poured his blessings only on the deserving: people of self-disciplined social virtue.[13] Finally, not least in Kenya with a settler minority bent on building a 'white man's country', colonial projects were rarely agreed between colonizers. Missionaries shuddered at the proletarian future offered by settlers to Africans, and tried to foster the local peasant farm economies that would nourish a living church.[14] A would-be colonial hegemony thus foundered on competing white ideologies which, in turn, overlapped with African debate. The mutual conflicts in the conversation between white and black could not long support, let alone disguise, their unequal power relations.

But, to take the second broad issue, may diversity animate a church history or did it reflect only a multivocal clamour? Kikuyu Christianities do indeed seem to have shared a gathered history of difference, a mutual sense of polemical periods, even stages of growth,[15] in which the terms of debate changed, if never silencing the old. Some historians renounce the use of narrative, seeing it as a distorting mirror to past actors who in their own day had little idea whence they came or whither they went. This very proper reservation is in the present case outweighed by the vocational pull of personal, institu-

---

[11] I discuss the first two points at greater length in Lonsdale (2001).

[12] Hastings (1994), p. 448.

[13] The best known African doubt was sown in an Anglican mind when William Ngidi questioned Bishop Colenso of Zululand on the truth of the Pentateuch: Guy (1983).

[14] As new research has emphasized: Peterson (1996); Casson (1998).

[15] For which Taylor (1958) provides a model. Karanja (1999), pp. 263–9, contrasts Ganda and Kikuyu experience, in a work without which this essay would scarcely have been possible; Hastings (1994), pp. 371–85, 464–8, 472–5, 571–6, 596–9, augments Taylor's model for Buganda.

tional and political contexts. Individuals who at great social cost
change their explanations of the world, and their place in it, may
develop a strong narrative sensibility. The accidents of life may seem
in retrospect to be providential steps. Young churches which invoke
a newly incarnate, historically active God will also possess the fervour of their 'calling'.[16] The conviction of living within a purposive
story can be the more powerful when, to recall the third issue suggested by the Kikuyu case, a new political community is in the making. Christian diversity seems to have expressed conflicting interests
and subjectivities, to which an emergent ethnic nationalism made
Kikuyu sensitive as never before. A prophetically charged arena lent
to the base metal of human self-interest a hallowed narrative of duty
to the dead and the unborn.

It is however difficult, perhaps indeed wrong, to give social shape
to the first decade of the twentieth century, when Kikuyu made their
earliest enquiries into and creative appropriations of Christianity.
They 'came forward'—to adopt a Kikuyu view which rejects all
thought of being 'colonized in mind'—often in *Rebellion* against differing
kin pressures or political bullying, out of personal crisis or social cal-
culation. Nonetheless, the second decade of Christian life, the 1920s,
may, without constricting its variety, be seen as an energetically discursive project of *Reconciliation*. Many of the first generation of *athomi*
or Christian 'readers' translated the pre-colonial moral discourse of
social obligation into the cradle of a new people whose redemptive
colonial narrative of endurance, improvement and salvation was
prefigured in the Bible. It was to them axiomatic that to save true
Kikuyuness from extinction (two notions novel in their cultural clarity)
one had to be what their parents disprized: a Christian. To be both
Christian and Kikuyu was to control an otherwise destructive modernity. Ethnic nationalism was a moral project, a reworking of the
internal terms of social belonging and personal maturity, before it was
a political one. After this 'stage of growth' in consciousness there could
be no looking back. The demanding discourse of 'moral ethnicity',
this collective debate on how to uphold the hegemonic tenets of local
moral economy in new times, could never be ignored in the future,
however private one's hope of salvation.[17] The oral fragmentation of

---

[16] Peel (1995).
[17] Lonsdale (1996 b). For elaborations of the concept: Tamarkin (1996); Berman
(1998); Hastings (1997), ch. 7; Peterson (2000). For critiques: Campbell (1997);
Mamdani (1996) p. 188.

pre-colonial times had allowed much variation in Kikuyu ritual practice; now, with growing literacy, one could the more easily appraise
differences in religious observance and social achievement.

This adoption of Christianity into the customary context of moral
knowledge provoked the next, costly, phase of growth, from the
1930s. This was *Revival*, a refining fire which infused several different
movements as Christianity deepened its hold on Kikuyu imaginations. I do not by that ethnic adjective impute a primordial 'essen-
tialism' to Kikuyu; on the contrary, they renegotiated social duty as
changing times required; their aspirations were formed by history.
They had previously been driven to tame the wilderness, their forested
hills, and dig the fields of fertile civilization. Their new moral compulsion was to prove themselves as civilized as their self-proclaimed
white civilizers. Social labour still pleased ancestors; engendered a
wealth which, as before, was justified by repaying its social debts;
and, if it is the case that past moral knowledge speculated on divinity,
made the old God's gifts bear fruit in new times. Like other Africans,
frontiersmen in a harsh, capricious continent, Kikuyu upheld a theology, or at least a morality, of abundance.[18] In the 1920s the readers'
project of Reconciliation began to Christianize its hegemonic terms
and images. Soaped skin, squared stone houses, frocks and trousers, tea-
drinking, defecation in pit latrines, all competed with the old wealth's
symbols: goat's fat and ochre cosmetics, oiled cloaks of animal skins,
the thatched and smoky huddle of a beery polygynous hospitality.[19]
But from the 1930s Kikuyu had to argue out their morality of abundance afresh, for its context began to change more radically and,
with that, its own capacity to inspire or console. Divisions of wealth
were arising, more cumulative than before. Rural capitalisms emerged,
black as well as white. Private property, which often repudiated its
social debts, evoked a rising fear of envious witchcraft between Africans
no less than a growing resentment of white settlerdom.

Christians faced new social division in a variety of ways. To missionary dismay, their leading Protestant adherents, members of what
was now a prosperous Christian establishment, continued to expound
the old moral equation between openly laborious household wealth

---

[18] Iliffe (1995) rests on this view. African moralities, or theologies, of abundance
demanded more laborious obedience from their adherents than does the modern,
Pentecostal, gospel of prosperity: Gifford (1990).
[19] Lonsdale (1992), pp. 380–88.

and civic virtue; they had nothing with which to reproach themselves. The new 'praying' churches, the *akurinu*, rejected even this
well-earned mammon. Their puritanism owed nothing to missionary
or even Kikuyu thought, and all to unaided scriptural study. Theirs
was a truly subversive, counter-hegemonic, Christianity. By contrast,
the 'independent' churches, which feature so largely in histories of
'the growth of nationalism', were deeply conservative. Founded by
people who had left the missions, they valued wealth conventionally,
and cleansed it by investing in public improvement, principally in a
network of fee-paying schools. Revivalists proper, 'born again' within
the mission churches in a movement coming from Anglican Uganda,
also warded off the contamination of jealousy but by very different
means, by confessing their rebirth in the Blood of Jesus. Later, in
the effort to cement a militant new political loyalty, Mau Mau initiation fended off the same fear of jealous sorcery, this time with the
old cleansing medium of the blood of goats. All these approaches to
contagion tackled the same problem of growing social inequality at
a time when a single moral community, with a coherent political
voice, was increasingly in demand. Discordant these beliefs and practices may well have been, but they were intimately related, often
critical of each other.

With Kikuyu prominent in their Catholic, Presbyterian and Anglican
leaderships, Kenya's churches have fully faced the issue of the state
only since independence. While leaders in colonial times might compare their struggles with the test of freedom God had set in Exodus,[20]
it was not until sovereignty passed to Africans that hard questions
were asked about its earthly purpose. Imaginations of exodus did
not fade but were joined by evocations both of exile, under Darius
or Nebuchadrezzar, and of the Devil. In the late 1980s the churches
were the state's only open critics, an established yet popular voice
of *Reproof*. Involvement in their congregations' daily lives gave them
authority to test the increasingly strident claims of secular power
against the freedoms rightly due to the people of God. As was
inevitable in Kenya's competitive ethnic arena, these latter were only
too easily construed as the Luo children of Ramogi (as it might be)
or the children of Gikuyu and Muumbi, not as the citizens of Kenya,
a plural whole. It had been within Kenya's rural vernaculars, not

---

[20] Walzer (1984).

in its urban, Swahili, lingua franca, that Christianity's possibilities were first tested in all their moral seriousness.[21]

Rebellion

The earliest surviving Kenyan African painting in western style portrays the parable of the prodigal son.[22] Its artist, in 1929, was a Kamba college student, member of an ethnic group closely related to the Kikuyu. It represents the desire of many pioneer Christian men, on entering into marriage and elderhood, to recover the reciprocal ties with non-Christian kin and neighbours which they felt they had broken by previous moral rebellion. The rupture was only partly due to the stringency of missionary demands; it also reflected a militant Kikuyu response to a new faith. Christianity would not have so divided African peoples against each other had not many found its message to be personally compelling.[23]

In explaining how missionary faith became indigenous belief, one can do no better than follow Taylor for the Baganda, or Karanja for the Kikuyu, through a fourfold process of congruence, detachment, demand and crisis.[24] Missionaries thought Kikuyu cosmology had points of *congruence* with their own; conversely, their many denominations matched the competitive patronage networks of Kikuyu 'big man' culture. Equally, native Kikuyu conflicts—generational and gendered friction, the moral failings of the recent great famine—*detached* young people from their kin and allowed them to associate with other moral dissidents, or 'enquirers'; colonial dislocations also occurred, but were slower to take effect. The urgency of the *demand* which 'readers', *athomi*, 'felt the Gospel laid upon them' to disown normal family ritual often startled their white pastors. Nonetheless, *athomi* never quite faced the *crisis* or test of faith in which Ganda converts had to choose between imported saviour and native king in 'a fiery moment of martyrdom'. In its decentralized social context, with

---

[21] Hastings (1997), p. 165, contrasts Tanzania's experience here.

[22] In the Margaret Trowell archive, School of Oriental and African Studies, London, an observation I owe to Dr Elizabeth Dunstan.

[23] The crux of Murray (1974).

[24] Taylor, (1958), pp. 43–9. What follows holds more true for Anglicans and Presbyterians than for Catholics and Baptists.

households less greedy for victims than a royal court, the Kikuyu church nonetheless 'wrestled with its conscience for years.'[25]

Many missionaries saw hopes of *congruence* in what they thought was Kikuyu 'belief'; Catholics and liberal Protestants saw in its supposed monotheism a basis for dialogue. While Kikuyu recognized lesser powers, they seemed to believe in a bountiful creator, to whom effective sacrifice could be made by upright elders. Missionaries also admired Kikuyu ethics: generosity, sense of duty, hatred of anti-social forces. While their ideas of an afterlife seemed vague, Kikuyu had already considered the notion of resurrection. To liberal missionaries it seemed there was much for the gospel message to build on. But they also felt much had to be rebuilt, in both social practice and religious belief. Whites thought Kikuyu were too narrow in their affections, abused sex and alcohol, ridiculed the afflicted, were terrified of death. As to initiation rites, circumcision was tolerable to Britons who were even then adopting it for their sons, but clitoridectomy seemed a cruel, dangerous mutilation. In the sacred realm the Kikuyu God, *Ngai*, 'divider of good things', was deplorably aloof; his prophets had dubious claims to revelation; prayer, sadly, was a communal cry of despair, not a routine of private devotion. Kikuyu seemed to trust God less than they feared sorcery; external contagion substituted for a sense of sin, of personal accountability to God. They knew nothing of God's loving accessibility. Their failings were summed up in their ritual of atonement: animal sacrifice performed by close kin was the antithesis to the one true sacrifice, made for all, on the Cross.[26]

Liberal missionaries presupposed a discursive equivalence between Christianity and Kikuyu 'religion'. They assumed that by the term 'God' (for example) Kikuyu also imagined a transcendent being, if unrevealed and unincarnate. But such equivalence is by no means certain. There are three areas of doubt. Our evidence for the inter-cultural conversation is tainted; other cases suggest that missionaries may have brought not so much a new religion as the very concept of theological 'belief'; finally, like all forms of human experience,

---

[25] Karanja (1999), p. 269.
[26] This paragraph summarizes A.R. Barlow, 'Notes on Points of Comparison and Contrast between Kikuyu Religious Beliefs and Customs, and Christianity' (n.d., but c. 1908): Edinburgh University Library, Barlow papers, Gen 1786/1/52. Barlow's assumption of continuity between Old and New Kikuyu Testaments has coloured modern Kikuyu scholarship: see Kibicho (1978) and Wanjohi (1978).

pre-colonial Kikuyu moral (or religious) thought must have had a history, rather than an immanent essence. With our present data, however, we can do no more than speculate about the arguments or crises on which that history may have turned.[27]

As to our evidence, the liberal missionaries who are our chief witnesses admittedly paid tribute to the fellow humanity of Africans by assuming that they too believed in a creator God with a transcendent power that required some human response. African religion, however blind, was a seedbed providentially prepared for planting biblical truth. On this assumption, missionary accounts imposed what may (or may not) have been misleading Judaeo-Christian categories. If Africans 'sacrificed' to make 'prayer' effective before 'God' it was the easier to 'baptize' African ideas and practices into Christianity. African Christians, politicians and theologians, not to mention western anthropologists and historians, have since become accomplices in this self-deception, if that is what it is, by treating missionary evidence as sober proof, not optimistic thinking.

In truth, it is cognitively not possible to grasp any cultural practice, even one's own, without private preconceptions. Misperception shapes all perception. Missionaries were naturally prone to see other cultures in a theistic light. Yet all knowledge is also a dialogic process of negotiation; and the missionaries' construction of Christian-Kikuyu congruence shows caution, as well as an evidentially suspect generosity of spirit.[28] We cannot assume they were entirely wrong in the lessons they drew from their Kikuyu dialogue, just as we cannot know how far, or how soon, Kikuyu learned to become misleadingly intelligible by adopting what they thought were Christian analogies. We can be certain of one thing only. No religion is so divisively demanding as Christianity over what its adherents ought to believe on the nature of God. Kikuyu cosmology rested on implicit understandings rather than the reasoned beliefs which missionaries thought they found—and found wanting. Missionaries were better attuned to hear symbolic meanings than Kikuyu were practised in

---

[27] For the dubious knowability of African 'religion' see Landau (1999); for observation of African 'moral knowledges', independent of a divinity, James (1988), Beidelman (1986), Ruel (1996); for African religious change, Shaw (1990) and, specifically, Peterson (1999); also Leakey (1977), pp. 1074–1119. Kenyatta (1938), pp. 231–68, could not conceive of past religious change but saw Kikuyu 'belief' as equivalent to the Judaeo-Christian Old Testament. For a partial discussion of Kenyatta: Bernardi (1993).

[28] Fulford (2000) has clarified my ideas here.

their exegesis. Since our first evidence is from missionary pens and from Africans who had absorbed most from mission teaching, their Christian conviction is bound to influence our perceptions of the encounter more than any Kikuyu hesitation.[29]

Did missionaries then bring the very idea of religious belief to Kikuyuland? There is certainly reason to suggest that Kikuyu life was premised not so much on a transcendent religion as on moral knowledge of how bodily power and vital will, the matter and mind of existence, were best generated, protected, and passed on to successor generations.[30] Moral knowledge was materially based, not divinely derived. Kikuyu labour theory, a hegemonic morality of abundance, placed a twofold value on the fruits of farming. They were the material means of ordered life but also its moral product, proof of the discipline, sweat and skills to which juniors were apprenticed in their elders' rationally managed households. Domestic order rested on a binary distinction between material powers, bodily and vegetable. Some were clean, cool and fertile, if consumed or used in their proper social place; others hotly malevolent and death-dealing, in themselves or when used by sorcerers, people of ill-will. Substance and society made each other. Kikuyu were ever wary of incurring *thahu*, the pollution caused by handling hostile matter, or even clean substances out of their proper place.[31] Risk of *thahu* represented the tricksy battle, moral and material, between culture and the wild, health and decay. What missionaries called sacrifice can often (not always) be read as an attempt, by expending society's currency, the blood or stomach-contents of goats, to cleanse the impurities one inevitably stirred up in daily life. The rules of purity were no doubt subject to debate and change. Certainly, the diviners who uncovered the nature of any offence were said to be subject to public scrutiny and liable to challenge from clients.[32]

Kikuyu material disciplines underpinned a moral knowledge that was arguable precisely because of the ordered behaviour it prescribed.[33]

---

[29] Ruel (1996), pp. 36–59, for Christian belief; James (1988), p. 7, for lack of dialogue between 'older wisdom' and 'newer religious systems'.

[30] For earlier thoughts here Lonsdale (1992), pp. 332–46. I have since learned from Kershaw (1997), Peterson (2000); and, comparatively, from Beidelman (1986), James (1988), and Ruel (1996).

[31] Generally, Douglas (1966).

[32] Leakey (1977), pp. 1146–50.

[33] Kenyatta (1938) is a compendium of social rules.

Men were enjoined to master their passions in order to rule their households, the sole means of production. Successful men, *hommes accomplis*, as the French well put it, should foster in others a similar will to straightness.[34] This required an honourable obedience. Enjoined on children by parents, its terms had to be negotiated between men and wives,[35] patrons and clients. Life was a struggle, from childhood's irresponsibility to persevering adult courage, and on to the calming wisdom of elderhood. Material wealth must remember its moral debts, if, in an uncertain world, it was also prudent to do so. Ambition ought not to forget kin, age-mates or clients. It is difficult to imagine a social ideal more productive of dissent about the scales of duties and claims, but it did not in logic demand the presence of a God of distributive justice, let alone amazing grace. Moral knowledge had its own reciprocating checks against anti-social behaviour, both in this life and in a shadowy afterlife, from which one's ancestors kept jealous watch.

But what is redundant in moral logic is not debarred in living practice, especially in a tolerant world of oral thought. There is some evidence, if not much, that Kikuyu used to argue about a being it seems appropriate to call God. He had four names, each bearing a different human character. Possibly his oldest name, *Murungu*, may mean 'divider' (of gifts).[36] Other named qualities, like *Mwenehinya*, 'holder of power', or *Mwenenyaga*, 'possessor of brightness'—an apt term for one whose favourite earthly seat was the snows of Mount Kenya—are hard to explain in the absence of religious speculation. And its theology may have changed. The most common name, the one which missionaries adopted for God, was *Ngai*, again meaning the divider of gifts among peoples. But *Ngai* is a Maasai term; its linguistic ascendancy attests to the long history of exchange between Bantu-speaking Kikuyu farmers and the Nilotic and Cushitic pastoral peoples of the Kenya highlands, trading wives, goods and ideas.[37] *Ngai* is in a neuter class of nouns, neither male nor female, as is right for a being so hard to imagine.[38] It is difficult to say more,

---

[34] Droz (1999). The Gikuyu terms *muramati, muthamaki, muigwithania, mutongoria* catch aspects of 'the self-mastered, self-made man'.

[35] On which see Brinkman (1996).

[36] Inference from the verb *rung'a* in Benson (1964), p. 411; thanks to Derek Peterson for evidence of association with a hornless cow.

[37] For Kikuyu names of God, Leakey (1977), pp. 1075–6; and Peterson (2000). For possible highland religious history, Iliffe (1995), p. 121.

[38] Gathigira ([1934] 1959), p. 29: thanks to John Karanja for translation.

but it does seem that the theological encounter to which missionaries invited them a century ago was not the first in which Kikuyu had engaged. Nor do 'sacrifice' and 'prayer' seem misleading terms for some at least of the repertoire of religious acts they performed from time to time, as distinct from the ritual routines that underpinned their moral knowledge.

While only a few American Baptists demonized Kikuyu religion, while Catholics and liberal Protestants saw in it an unconscious African yearning for truth, most whites recoiled from the social and ritual practices of moral knowledge, especially those to do with sexuality and gender.[39] A measure of household rebellion thus seemed necessary to Christian observance. Missionaries in central Kenya would have agreed with John Willis to the west of them, when he called for a boarding school: 'God himself does not attempt the practically impossible. He did not attempt to give Israel the law in Egypt: He first brought them out, then He taught them . . . ordinary village life is dead against Christianity.'[40] But some young Kikuyu also welcomed such *detachment*, this probably new opposition between the demands of God and the rules of men. One 'reader' was attracted to Christianity because elders excluded the young from religious practice, believing them incapable of grasping 'the personality of God'. Another thought parents sent their most disobedient children to school, so that they could be 'let loose like the English'.[41] Christianity thus 'harnessed the energy [of] generational conflict' that was always latent even in the most ordered of households.[42] Many readers in any case had detachment forced on them, orphaned by famine, with no parents to stop them taking the path to school, or with wicked uncles whose hostility drove them to it for protection. The first Anglican marriage joined two such waifs.[43] There could be no greater detachment: a new family formed without benefit of kin, cut off from common ritual practice, dependent on outside patronage. It was clearly no foundation for a local church.

---

[39] Ward (1976), p. 99. For missionary cultural distaste see Murray (1974), Neckebrouck (1978), ch. 8.

[40] J.J. Willis to F. Baylis, 24 Nov 1910: CMS Archives (University of Birmingham), A.7/08. For similar missionary sentiments in Kikuyuland, see Harry Leakey, 1908, quoted by Karanja (1999), p. 57; Hulda Stumpf, 1914, quoted by Sandgren (1982), p. 197.

[41] Mockerie (1934), p. 27, Wanyoike (1974), pp. 25, 57.

[42] Iliffe (1979), p. 228.

[43] Murray-Brown (1972), pp. 37–9; Kariuki (1985), p. 17; McIntosh (1969), p. 151; Ward (1976), p. 111; Feldman (1978), p. 76; Karanja (1999), pp. 19–21.

Yet many *athomi*, not themselves orphans, opposed household
authority, the pillar of Kikuyu civilization, with what they believed
were the gospel's *demands*. Missionaries marvelled at their courage
and feared for them. Several embarked on their own evangelistic
journeys, without missionary sanction or to areas from which missionaries had withdrawn, armed only with a vernacular gospel.[44] A
few burned down prayer-trees, destroyed diviners' equipment, buried
the corpses from which Kikuyu recoiled, even dug up ancestral skulls,
daring contagion. One gang of readers beat up people they found
cultivating on Sundays. The most common Christian insult was refusal
to share in household sacrifice, an abstention which ruptured its ritual wholeness, making it invalid.[45] Conversely, *athomi* could use mission patronage to steal a march on age-mates by getting circumcised
early, a crucial step in personal growth.[46]

This last example raises the question what purpose these delinquent
actions served. Why did elders curse readers?[47] Missionaries saw in
these rebellions the proofs of grace, responses to gospel demands for
a redeemed way of life. That one cannot know; but one can say
that they were offensively *indigenous* assertions of dissent, or upstart
claims to self-mastery, *wiathi*, which in the past had been more hardly
won. For their forms were not far removed from ordinary Kikuyu
practice: indigenous prophets had attracted followings, diviners had
had to watch their words, clan prayer trees were destroyed on the
death of the senior responsible elder, proverbs attested to the right
of a younger generation to change custom, the adoption of alternative
patrons was nothing new. There was little as yet to suggest that
Christianity was more than an addition to an existing range of cosmic
enquiry or moral assurance, adopted for Kikuyu ends. Orphan marriages were few; more generally missionaries sought connections. With
African interpreters, they preached to large audiences long before the
first baptisms, and tested public reactions to Bible translation. There
were no early Kikuyu martyrs. The absence of divine jealousy, amid

---

[44] For example, Archbishop Gitari's memory of how his father responded to
God's summons in 1919, in Smoker (1994), pp. 200–02; and a (fruitless) teenage
missionary journey, in Fadiman (1993), pp. 231–36.
[45] Strayer (1978), p. 82; Sandgren (1989), pp. 42–3; Karanja (1999), pp. 22–8;
McIntosh (1969), p. 408; Ward (1976), pp. 129, 113.
[46] Thuku (1970), p. 8.
[47] Wanyoike (1974), p. 85.

much moral disapproval, makes the Kikuyu experience akin to most others in Africa. In the diffuse flux of household fortune, opportunities for reconciliation between kin were always available.

Reconciliation

There was, then, a mutual field of enquiry between old and new moral knowledges, or theologies, in which missionaries encouraged *athomi* to take the lead by public preaching. Dialogue spared Kikuyu churches from *crisis* in their early years.[48] But if the word was crucial, so too was bread. Some of the most dynamic readers came to mission schools because a prior experience of wage labour made them hungry for the communicative knowledge of the 'red strangers'.[49] Literacy added value to external wage labour. It also conferred power in internal Kikuyu politics. A new vital force, material and mental as before, literacy was the core of Christian reconciliation with everyday life.

The higher pay of literates contributed to their own and household stores of bridewealth, the lubricant of social influence; fluency in colonial courts won the day in property disputes with neighbours; readers evaded colonial conscription of labour for local roads. Christian literacy was a ritually encoded skill with which to pursue status and power by other means. As much anti-colonial as colonial, one could even call it neotraditional in its parochial, clannish, resistance to state demands. Elders reciprocated by coming to terms with *athomi* over property and marriage; parents welcomed back truant sons when circumcised, even if at the mission; subclans dedicated land and labour, the means of Kikuyu civilization, to build the mission outschools that opened gates to the new epistemology of power. Within a decade of the first baptism, unlettered populations were content to be ruled by young Christian chiefs.[50]

Christianity soon became a mass movement such as Hastings has seen elsewhere in Africa at this time. Its origin can be dated precisely, to 1915–16, when the annual sale of scripture portions leapt

---

[48] The best account of the Christian-Kikuyu dialogue is in Wanyoike (1974), ch. 4.
[49] Lonsdale (1995).
[50] Clough (1990), Feldman (1978), Karanja (1999).

from 755 to over 10,000, at 30 cents each, a day's pay.[51] In 1916, too, 1,600 readers went off to war in German East Africa (now mainland Tanzania) under missionary officers, as military carriers. Almost all returned, proof of the beneficially material substance of the word. Tens of thousands of unlettered porters died, having no prophylactic protection of scripture in their kit.[52] But 'Kikuyu time' was in ritual motion, too. During the war years a new candidate generation, one of the ritual moieties into which Kikuyu were divided, began to pay goat fees to the outgoing elders, as had been done every thirty years or so, since time began. The incoming elders were restarting the ritual transition of generational power, *ituika*. In this they cleansed household wealth, commuting it into public responsibility. Readers joined in with their generation mates, once they had ensured that their goats were eaten rather than 'sacrificed', as they now understood it. Hundreds of subclans, *mbari*, unbidden by missionaries, started to invest in schooling. Cyclical Kikuyu generational time and new Christian linear time were locked together in the search for ordered social growth.[53]

The first world war was of high significance, then, for old ritual time as for new, church-building, time. Kikuyu seized on Christianity while Christianity took hold of the land. After the war, in a ferment of anti-colonial politics, even non-Christian chiefs took offence when called Judas. Some imagined the political leader, Harry Thuku, to be Messiah, others saw him as Moses; still others linked him with the rainbow-dragon which used to hallow *ituika*.[54] This was not a manichaean but a theologically plural world. Some missionaries called revival meetings, to stiffen Christian faith against its dangerous social popularity. They wanted their readers to face a crisis which most readers seemed just as keen to avoid.[55]

One can now see why the boldest politicians in the 1920s, the 'young Christians' of the Kikuyu Central Association (KCA), whom some Scots dismissed as Anglican dupes, adopted reconciliation as their internally hegemonic project. The KCA's general secretary, Johnstone Kenyatta, was one of many orphan *athomi*. Its first

---

[51] Karanja (1999), p. 157, table 4; p. 165, fn. 69. For comparison, Hastings (1994), pp. 443–78.
[52] Hodges (1986), pp. 176–83.
[53] Discussed more fully in Lonsdale (1995).
[54] Lonsdale (1992), pp. 369–74.
[55] Ward (1976), pp. 312–5.

Presbyterian office-holder, in 1928 he started the vernacular party paper. He called it *Muigwithania*—one who makes people listen and agree together, a reconciler and, implicitly, a respected elder.[56] Kenyatta thus asserted the KCA's seniority, its right to be heard as internal conciliator: religious and ritual peace had to come before there could be any effective anti-colonial representation.

The Gikuyu New Testament's publication in 1926 is said to have given the KCA their newspaper's title. The term *muigwithania* appears six times in its pages, and carries an authority lacking in the mere *mjumbe* or 'messenger' of the Swahili Bible, available since 1909, and read by many Kikuyu. The references are to Christ the mediator, either between God and man (I Tim. 2: 5),[57] or between new and old cosmic covenants (Gal. 3: 19–20; Heb. 8: 6; 9:15). At a time when intergenerational negotiation was in everybody's thoughts, *athomi* clearly asked why new faith should not mediate God's promises to the ancestors in a new age. In such proposals of equivalence to white colleagues one can glimpse the intellectual delight with which Kikuyu scholars explored ways to squeeze the most intimate old meanings (as they saw them) into newly standardized, sacralized, words.[58] The excitement of translation stemmed from a cultural encounter filled with as much surprised self-recognition as mutual misunderstanding. Among world religions it appears to be Christianity's peculiarity thus to sacralize the local while introducing the global.[59]

The passage remembered as the KCA's authority for adopting the title *muigwithania* comes from Hebrews (12: 24),[60] where Jesus the mediator is said to have been in himself a more eloquent sacrifice than that of Abel who, like Kikuyu, had offered only livestock. This was a useful text, fusing ideas of old cleansing and new sacrifice, for *athomi* who wished to identify the old Kikuyu *Ngai* with the new missionary God, also *Ngai*.[61] Kenyatta himself stressed the continuity.

---

[56] Benson (1964), p. 183; and instruction from Godfrey Muriuki. This section summarizes Lonsdale (1996a).

[57] This is the only place where the Swahili Bible translates Christ the mediator as *mpatanishi* or peacemaker, equivalent to *muigwithania*.

[58] Karanja (1999), ch. 5. For another view, Peterson (1997).

[59] Sanneh (1990), Hastings (1997).

[60] Murray (1974a), p. 100; Gideon Mugo in *Muigwithania* i-3 (July 1928), p. 10. *Muigwithania* is in Kenya National Archives (KNA) file DC/MKS. 10B/13/1. Translations from the Gikuyu by A.R. Barlow (for information of the police).

[61] Karanja (1999), pp. 131–2. Fadiman (1993), p. 233, for an early Kikuyu sermon distinguishing the blood of a ram from the blood of Christ.

On it rested the two-stage argument with which he and his friends urged reconciliation. Their premise was that urban wage labour, that is, disorderly behaviour (not Christianity, a rebellious belief) presented modernity's main threat to Kikuyu. Their thesis called on *athomi* to return to filial obedience; but turned the tables on elders by claiming that repentant readers were the better able to safeguard true Kikuyu civilization.

Athomi found no difficulty in making terms with the unlettered in the pages of *Muigwithania*. Many had already repaired relations with their kin. Their favourite simile compared pen and spear, weapons new and old for defence of property. But legal utility was not social hegemony. George Ndegwa, a later KCA secretary, put the problem. He was proud to be one of the new ritual generation, expected to 'straighten' Kikuyu from the moral disorder associated with the waning of an incumbent moiety's power. But how could he, a 'prostitute', without kin, thanks to his 'mission clothes', presume to straighten society? His answer was that this was a false antithesis, based on appearances only. Supported by his editor, Kenyatta, he was prepared to separate faith from matter. Since *Ngai* was the God of other races, one could be Christian or Muslim while remaining 'Original Kikuyu'.[62] Christian practice did not have to mean corruption; and ethnic virtue, moral knowledge, had self-evidently to come to terms with the modern world.

Muigwithania's readers found a marvellously apt biblical allegory for discussing how to harmonize the prostitution of foreign ways with true Kikuyuness in the parable of the prodigal son (Luke 15: 11–17). It was the most commonly cited folktale, old or new.[63] It taught the virtues of obedience to a tolerant tradition, but only as a preparatory step towards asserting *athomi* superiority over the elders whom the Bible enjoined them to obey. For readers soon concluded that social harmony must be a modern rather than traditional project. As modern men themselves, *athomi* were the best representatives of their people's cause.

Muigwithania argued this with the logic of all conservative reform: Kikuyu faced new dangers; they needed new defences. Readers com-

---

[62] George Ndegwa to *Muigwithania* i–4 (Aug 1928), p. 10. Kenyatta gave editorial assurance that sartorial difference was immaterial: ibid., p. 5.

[63] Karanja (1928) p. 11; Kiongo wa Kahiti in *Muigwithania*, i–10 (Feb-Mar 1929), p. 15; M.J. Muchikari in ibid., i–11 (April 1929), pp. 9–10

pared the prodigal's private dissipation with the public fecklessness of age-mates who followed 'the road of wilful ways' to Nairobi. Men were absconding from home; women who did so would neither hon-our fathers nor fear husbands. Town reached into the core of Kikuyudom, destroying kin and property by debauching gender; the moral cords of social order were being unloosed. Yet townspeople should not be deceived: they might take new names but could never remove their black skin nor cease to be Kikuyu.[64] Male migrants could overcome their rulers' racial contempt only by strengthening the moral fibre of filial duty. Female constructions of self-mastery in town and trade, as opposed to household farm production, made women only more reprehensible in men's eyes.[65]

Athomi admitted that they had led the way to urban corruption; but only they could avert its fate, which was to 'peter out among the *chomba*' or strangers—the Muslim Swahili, Kenya's first towns-folk. Migrant labour, a new seduction from the economy of obliga-tion, needed a new antidote, a debate on ethnic virtue that literacy alone made possible. Kenyatta's generation believed that any claim for equality in a racially ordered colony must rest on a patriotic modern ethnicity; and only readers could awaken it. A self-interested thesis, it turned repentant Christianity into leadership of the Kikuyu common weal. *Athomi* asked how one could reproduce moral self-mastery when the absence of migrant workers frustrated the oral transmission of social norms. Literacy, however, widened sociability in step with mobility; literacy made strangers friends.[66] Charles Ng'undo best put the *athomi* case to be better guardians of society than the elders. As elegantly as any anthropologist he linked mate-rial practice and moral knowledge. Social order, he wrote, had once been inscribed on consciousness by rituals now falling into decay. 'A man will not speak to his child or a child address his father for want of a sign.' Christians must renew the rituals of instruction, and with a subversive new substance, tea. Many readers had forsworn beer, the liquid of gerontocratic authority. Tea-parties, Ng'undo proposed, could unite parents and children at circumcision; they would 'rec-ognize' each other and thank God. He called on all to 'wake up

---

[64] These sentiments, expressed by wa Kahiti and Muchikari, were similar to those of 'Red' Xhosa in South Africa, classically in Mayer (1961).

[65] White (1990), Robertson (1997).

[66] Cf. Ong (1982), p. 74.

and turn over the fallow-land of your brains'—a wonderful mix of matter and mind—to invent new ways of conveying social memory.[67] And he had good cause to think that print-religion could do so: Kikuyu proverbs, most of them gems of improvement, were first collected by student competition in mission schools.[68]

Kenyatta agreed on the conservatively patriotic role of mission education. From London, where he went in 1929 to represent his people, he reminded them of their prodigal's duty to the Almighty, in whom he combined Gikuyu and Christian names of God.[69] Townsmen must not think their ethnic identity irrelevant; to despise one's history invited stagnation. They must unite and thatch, with new grass, the leaking roof of the house of custom. *Muigwithania* was full of calls to record custom, to avert the ignorance of posterity.[70] Kikuyu were already talking Swahili, a 'foreign jargon' once seen as gibberish; only print could save the Gikuyu tongue from extinction.[71] And Christianity was better than Islam as a buttress of identity. To take a Muslim name only made one a Swahili, a double disgrace: a 'stranger' and yet still a subject people. Christian names made Kikuyu 'of the one clan of Christianity', equal to all.[72]

But Christianity also divided. One can sense Kenyatta's anger when he described the KCA struggle for 'all Kikuyu to attain unity, educated and uneducated, ceasing to ask each other, what Mission do *you* belong to? or, you are not a reader. For if there could be an end of things like these the country of Kikuyu could go ahead in peace.' But why did he anchor this plea to the text Galatians 6: 2?[73] No Kikuyu could have objected to the first clause of this Pauline injunction: 'Bear one another's burdens'; it epitomized the best of their inheritance. But what about the rider, 'and so fulfil the law of Christ'? Kenyatta could have chosen from many biblical texts, or proverbs, that called for cooperation but did not invoke Christ. He appears to have seen religious division as a reflection of other Kikuyu quarrels rather than inherent in Christianity. He could apparently evoke no more unifying sanction for a patriotic project than the son

---

[67] Ng'undo (1929), p. 5. Thanks to Derek Peterson for alerting me to the distinctions between beer and tea.

[68] Barra (1939).

[69] Kenyatta to *Muigwithania*, i–11 (April 1929), p. 5; ibid., i–12 (May 1929), pp. 8–10.

[70] Karimu (1928).

[71] Njuguna wa Karucha (1928).

[72] Kagika (1928), prefiguring Sanneh (1990) and Hastings (1997).

[73] Kenyatta (1928).

of the newly trinitarian *Ngai*. Gideon Mugo, a leading Anglican, backed Kenyatta up. He agreed that churches were cattle-kraals, protecting Kikuyu values from the hyena of colonialism—the old duality of civilization and the wild. Indeed, Kikuyuland was itself a church, part of a world-wide communion. *Athomi* were not a separate clan, merely those who had heard the gospel first. Mugo pleaded for ethnic unity in Christian, incarnational, terms. Missionaries were wrong to condemn politics as worldly, for 'we are all of us of the world.' Christ's parting words to his disciples had been 'that the church was to be built here on earth until he should take us to his home above.' In a delightful change of image, showing how the terms of moral knowledge could permeate 'the long conversation' between missionary and African cultures, Mugo concluded that 'the people of the little digging stick', a moral-material nickname for Kikuyu, should agree together like the smoke that mingled over their huts at the time of cooking the evening meal.[74] *Athomi* could not imagine 'the country of Kikuyu' without either its moral economy of survival and sociability or its (fractured) framework of church organization and Christian hope.

The best evidence that such reconciliation was now a hegemonic project lies in the outcome of the 'female circumcision crisis' of 1929. Some Protestant missions lost ninety per cent of their members when they demanded that Christians forswear clitoridectomy for their daughters.[75] The Baptist African Inland Mission (AIM) never recovered; their schools were poor and white authority unyielding. Other mission church and school rolls more than revived within five years. Even dissent was Christian. The defenders of clitoridectomy invested not only in independent schools but also in churches without which they could not imagine education. They kept up the cross-cultural 'conversation' too, and asked the Anglican bishop to confer the apostolic succession on their ordinands. Only when he refused did they turn elsewhere for legitimacy, and to a still older church, the African Greek Orthodox.[76] This they did, not in deference to a supposed colonial Christian hegemony but, rather, as a local claim to global equality in a world thronged with competing ethnicities, only one of which, the British, had thus far had the audacity to proclaim itself universal.

---

[74] Kagika (1929).
[75] From a large literature see, especially, Murray (1974); Ward (1976), chs. 5 & 6; for my own approach, Lonsdale (1992), pp. 385–97.
[76] Welbourn (1961), ch. 8.

Revival

Much has been written on the East African Revival of the 1930s, by Hastings among others.[77] Two reminders are in order: that Revival was but one, perhaps minor, strand in the thread of Kikuyu Christian revival; and that this period of church-building seems best grasped as an era of moral conflict between new biblical readings and rural capitalism's violations of the hegemony of obligation between wealth and poverty. The publication of the Gikuyu New Testament in 1926 was the originating date of revival, not the coming of saved Ugandan evangelists a decade later, as is conventionally thought. The independence of the Bible-reading mind, and the contestability of Christian possibilities in a self-consciously divided society, could not be more vividly displayed. On one hand the Gikuyu scriptures spurred the reconciliation attempted by *Muigwithania*. On the other, two years of devoted study in caves gave birth to a totally different Christianity, embodied in the earliest 'praying' or *akurinu* church. This was the first Kikuyu body to realize that the Holy Spirit was the most demanding person of the Trinity; he condemned both political activity and material wealth, and left clitoridectomy to the private conscience.[78] In all respects this teaching ran counter to the KCA project of *muigwithania*. KCA were reconcilers; *akurinu* were revolutionaries, dissident Kikuyu in every sense other than an insistence on ritual purity; even here they were more Levitical than Kikuyu. Kenyatta (by now Jomo) voiced a common, internally critical opinion in calling them 'a bunch of lunatics'.[79] It was also early in the 1930s that perhaps the most remarkable among several Kikuyu itinerant preachers, Mwangi wa Nyarere, first proclaimed the culturally subversive demands of Christ. He deliberately distanced Christ from the old Kikuyu cosmology, and was thus utterly opposed to the KCA—and missionary—vision of theological continuity.[80]

Ironically, it was the 'independent' churches, their numbers swelled by the 1929 crisis, who most closely followed the liturgy of the missions from which they had parted. But then, alone among the several revivals, they deepened their fidelity not to Christ but to a

---

[77] Hastings (1994), pp. 596–600.
[78] Murray (1973); Njiri (1984).
[79] Kenyatta (1938), p. 277. Berman and Lonsdale (1998) survey his oeuvre.
[80] Ward (1976), pp. 323–34.

pre-Christian prophecy that stressed the importance of acquiring the wisdom of the Europeans rather than their faith;[81] indeed they expelled *akurinu* prophets and refused a hearing to Mwangi, Kikuyu who could be said to possess more faith than the missionaries. Christian rebirth *within* the missions could nonetheless revalidate African practice and belief; the energetic differences in the African side of the 'long conversation' are endless. When Revival 'proper' came to the mission churches, its brethren not only attested to the cleansing power of the Blood of the Lamb, they confessed sin publicly in what looks like a locally African defence against suspicions of witchcraft.[82] A leading revivalist, later Bishop, Obadiah Kariuki was also morally-materially 'Kikuyu' in committing himself to God in gratitude that he and his age-mates had been spared in the Spanish influenza pandemic of 1919.[83] These were all marks of considered Christian division in face of the most contentious issue of Kikuyu moral ethnicity, the mutual obligations of wealth and poverty. Missionary teaching had little to do with it. Rather, the gospel's contestable demands had revived Christian faith in some, African ritual practice in others, public service in yet more. Social inequality was even more contentious by 1950.

By 1950 all Kikuyu leaders were familiar with Christian images, not least the militant leaders of Mau Mau. Whites charged Mau Mau with militant paganism. I have argued elsewhere that this charge was unfounded.[84] The best proof is found in the movement's teachings with respect to moral ethnicity, in comparison with the teaching of the several Kikuyu Christianities. Of these there were by now three distinct Protestant strands. Mau Mau's relations with them were governed by the churches' views on moral ethnicity's implicit contract between rich and poor.

The first Christianity was the establishment's. Missionary in origin, it was practised in parishes now almost wholly African in leadership. Worldly in belief and practice, it was conventionally Kikuyu (if also bourgeois) in seeing wealth as a reward for using God's talents, just as poverty was the price of neglecting them. Its sensibilities were closer to the Old Testament than the New. Missionaries

---

[81] Lonsdale (1995).
[82] A view I owe to the Revd Grace Karamura.
[83] Kariuki (1985), p. 22.
[84] Lonsdale (1992), pp. 441–5.

denied it but Mau Mau owed much to this first Christianity. The
Christianity of reconciliation was under threat not so much from
Mau Mau as from its own rural capitalist, even sorcerous, subver-
sions of the old reciprocities between wealth and poverty. The movement's militants grappled with the establishment religion's failures
and widened its popular appeal.

The chief missionary failure was an inability to share the peasant's
moral knowledge of personal evil. With their belief in original sin
and a scientific attitude to disease or the caprice of nature, Europeans
could not grasp the full horror of the occult power that Kikuyu knew
to be available to their enemies. Prayer to God was no answer to
the evil willed by men on earth, and the latter was growing in parallel with a social inequality that neglected duty. Furthermore, missionaries were disgusted by the material of Mau Mau oaths: merely,
and conventionally, the meat, blood, and vegetables of personal reputation and household sustenance. Mau Mau oaths did not so much
oppose Christianity as supplement it in a magical field that missionaries could not enter. A major element in Mau Mau ideology
was therefore non-Christian rather than anti-Christian.

On the other hand, Mau Mau gave Christian ideas a wider currency. Its politics was voiced in hymns, called *nyimbo*. Their theology seems to have come from the independent churches. These
believed, with the missions and the old moral knowledge, in justification
by works. In all other respects the *nyimbo* were eclectic. As in the
days of Harry Thuku thirty years earlier, it was a theologically plural
world. Belief in the old God, *Ngai*, in Jehovah, in a political Christ,
anger against sorcery, all played a part, coloured by a civic religion
of ethnic nationalism. The *nyimbo* were no more anti-Christian than
the prayers that conscript God to a national cause at time of war.
They compared Kikuyu to the children of Israel and the British to
Pharaoh's Egyptians. Echoes of an Exodus undertaken by a people
already knowing God were made the more resonant with the publication of the Gikuyu Old Testament in 1951; missionary and black
Christian linguistic effort thus fed political dissent, an unwitting exercise in translation.[85] *Nyimbo* compared Kenyatta to a Moses who led
to freedom and wealth, the materiality of personal growth, not to
salvation. Yet in one song he was also, implicitly, Messiah: 'he gave

---

[85] Leakey (1954), pp. 57, 63, 71; Wa Kinyatti (1980), pp. 18, 39, 40; cf. Sanneh
(1990).

his life to save us'.[86] Mau Mau hopes thus rested in a purposive tradition that owed much to the Christianity of reconciliation. As expressions of political faith, *nyimbo* were full of witheringly Kikuyu, but
also biblical, calls to good behaviour: men were known by their fruits,
the prodigal must return to his people, the lazy could expect no
freedom, nor wastrels 'free things'. Only toil gave a right to land
which the British must return.[87] This-worldly religion, whether of the
Christian establishment or of remembered moral knowledge, was
pressed into political service. But the effort was scarcely more hegemonic than the missionary project before it.

For there was also dissident belief, as there had been since at least
the 1920s. The praying churches, emerging from the caves of 1926,
had by now split into two traditions. One, the *dini ya Jesu Kristo*,
came to notice in 1947. Its members cut up a Kikuyu tailor who
refused to make them a flag free of charge; then killed three policemen. The *dini* (sect) said that government had fallen; the police were
Satan's soldiers. Respectable Kikuyu, Kenyatta included, thought the
sect worse than mere lunatics by now: they were animals.[88] There
was no evidence, other than in inflamed British imaginations, that
the *dini* had anything to do with Mau Mau; and it was quite unlike
the other praying churches. These continued to separate themselves
from normal life. Unlike the missions, they actively opposed sorcery
and were obsessed with ritual cleanliness. They refused to drink blood
or to mix 'godliness with politics'. One of their prophets advised his
followers to turn to Kenyatta only if they found it too hard to obey
God.[89] The praying churches, *akurinu*, were alone in bringing consolation to the poor; but they did not preach action on their behalf.

Some missionaries explained Mau Mau as a political response to
Christian Revival. That is not proven; I have argued that both sprang
from similar roots of social anxiety. Revival attracted some of the
few Kikuyu who enjoyed material success. They listed their deadly
sins as worldliness, anger and envy, to be cleansed in the blood of

---

[86] Leakey (1954), p. 69; also pp. 57, 59, 66–8, 70–3; wa Kinyatti (1980), pp. 47,
56–7; Githige (1978), p. 284; Wanyoike (1974), pp. 180–5.
[87] Leakey (1954), pp. 60, 68–7; wa Kinyatti (1980), pp. 18, 19, 26, 31, 38, 45,
90; Ogot (1977).
[88] Henry Muoria's reports in *Mumenyereri*, 29 Dec 1947, 5 & 12 Jan and 9 Feb
1948: KNA, MAA. 8/106; Wamagatta (1988), pp. 265–7.
[89] Joseph Ng'ang'a Kimani, 'Rules written on 3 March 1950' and 'Things to be
observed by all Godly people', in Sandgren (1989), pp. 161–74.

Christ. Mau Mau members were similarly freed from imputations of
witchcraft, if by the blood of a ram, as in the moral-material practices of former days.[90] The *akurinu*, Revival and Mau Mau look to
have had different answers to sorcery in the new money economy.
This does not mean the missions were right to see Mau Mau and
its Kikuyu resistance as locked in religious conflict. Just as Kikuyu
knew many Christianities, so too a decentralized society harboured
different Mau Maus. Some gangs did fight Christianity; a dead goat
desecrated at least one church altar.[91] Many church-school teachers
died, and one or two pastors. In 1953, the first year of the Mau
Mau 'Emergency', over sixty teachers were attacked; nearly half of
them were killed.[92] This was a small minority of the hundreds of
teachers employed but revivalists felt especially threatened. Some
were martyred for refusing to drink goats' blood. Two Anglican
revivalists were killed for giving tea to thirsty policemen; others were
spared because they could be trusted not to help the police.[93] Catholics
felt that Mau Mau fears of the confessional put them especially at
risk; yet their church was the asylum of first resort for the independent churches, proscribed for their allegedly seditious teaching;
and the senior insurgent commander, Dedan Kimathi, went as a
Catholic convert to the gallows, his last words being as much Kikuyu
as Christian: 'Farewell to the World and all its belongings.'[94]

Had Mau Mau leaders ordered a general attack on the churches,
there would have been many more martyrs. Without wire, guns or
searchlights they had no defence. Almost all African clergy survived,
perhaps because most of them refused to bear arms. Those who died
were probably killed not on account of their faith but because refusal
to take the oath breached insurgent security; disputes over church
property also took their toll. White missionary school-supervisors,
who motored hundreds of miles a month with their teachers' pay-
packets during the Emergency war, were never ambushed; an Anglican,
Cyril Hooper, whose missionary father's typewriter had produced
the first KCA petition a generation earlier, left his car's broken

[90] Wanyoike (1974), pp. 165, 167.
[91] *East African Standard* (Nairobi) 8 Aug 1952.
[92] Fazan (1960), pp. 9, 80.
[93] Wiseman (1958), Smoker (1994). Hastings (1994), pp. 599–600, is right to call
Revival and Mau Mau 'symbolically incompatible', but too narrow.
[94] Githige (1978), pp. 52, 182–3; Wanyoike (1974), pp. 193–6; Wiseman (1958),
pp. 15–17; Bottignole (1984), p. 232; Njoroge (1999), pp. 163 80.

exhaust-pipe unrepaired so that Mau Mau, on hearing him coming, would let him pass unharmed.[95] Mau Mau forest fighters complained that some of their generals were too Christian; some generals complained that their guerrillas paid too much heed to witchdoctors.[96] Religious belief, it appears from this summary of its complexities at the time of Mau Mau, was both transcendent, beyond politics and yet, at the same time, a concentrate of political thought, deeply contested, appealed to by all, and the hegemonic property of none.

Reproof

> All scripture is inspired by God and profitable for teaching, for reproof, for correction and for training in righteousness.

David Gitari, then one of the Kikuyu Anglican bishops, quoted this Pauline dictum against those who condemned his political use of scripture in 1987. Some churches, not least his own, were becoming increasingly critical of Kenya's state, reproving its corruptions and training its subjects in citizenship.[97] This new trend has caused further splits in Christian thought and action, as churchmen have faced the issue of how secular and sacred power should co-exist. Africans wield much more of both than when under British rule. That ended in 1963; as, soon after, did white ecclesiastical control. Kenyatta then ruled until his death in 1978, trying to re-enact his youthful role of *muigwithania*, conciliator of intra-Kikuyu and inter-ethnic divisions. Both had deepened in the era of Mau Mau and decolonization. His presidential method, the patronage of other men's energies, followed that of the Kikuyu big men who had once competed in managing the settlement of their forest frontier, and the outcome was a similar inequality. His own people, centrally located as they were, blessed with fertile coffee land, with educated elites well connected in trade and politics, gained disproportionately from Africa's now fading boom-time. The envy of other peoples and unrest

---

[95] Oral information from the late Cyril Hooper and from John K. Karanja.

[96] Lonsdale (1994), pp. 142–50: 'a forest debate'.

[97] 2 Tim. 3: 16, in Gitari (1988), pp. 47–54. Here follows a mere sketch of post-colonial church-and-state relations. A more complete history can be patched together from Benson (1995), Bottignole (1984), Chepkwony (1987), Githiga (1997), Hearn (1997), Kariuki (1985), Lonsdale et al. (1978), Ngunyi (1995), Njoroge (1999), Sabar (2000), Sabar-Friedman (1997), Throup (1995).

among the Kikuyu poor made Kenyatta's lieutenants nervous. Their
anxiety caused the first clash of church and state. In 1969 they tried
to bind their ethnic voters with an oath campaign that recalled Mau
Mau. The churches, led by conservative-evangelical Baptists who
were less inhibited than others by any links with power, condemned
an earthly totalitarianism that no Christian conscience could accept.
But clerical voices were silent when Kenyatta banned the parliamen-
tary opposition party soon after. The churches were closely engaged
with government in running works of improvement, schools, farm
institutes and so on, and voiced few criticisms of a regime that had
brought freedom and, now, a quite widely shared 'development'.[98]

The churches had at first welcomed Kenyatta's successor, Daniel
arap Moi. He was a professed Christian, and promised to curb the
public and private inequities of Kenyatta's later years. But relations
between church and state soon cooled. The terms of trade turned
against agrarian Africa; economic decline envenomed a political piracy
that favoured ethnic groups who had lost out in the Kenyatta boom;
increased coercion contained the anger of those excluded from state
bounty. Foremost among these, Kikuyu were vulnerable to being
divided by the power they had formerly enjoyed, now lacked, and
coveted again.

Such is the political background to the new sectarianism. But to
politics must be added a new phase of church growth, and a new,
more devastating, moral fracture than the growth of rural capitalism. Church growth is twofold and contradictory. In general Christianity
has expanded greatly, until in the 1990s Kenya was over 70 per cent
Christian. This was largely due to increases in educational spending,
and the state's desire for Christian discipline in school. The main
beneficiaries are the Catholics and the two Protestant churches once
part of the colonial establishment and now with the most confident
African leaderships, the Anglicans and Presbyterians. But a very
different growth has also occurred. This is the huge increase in
American Pentecostal and other evangelical missionaries. In the 1990s
Kenya had 1,300 of them, an astounding figure, twice as many as
any other African country, and a second missionization none would
have foretold in 1963. The charismatic liturgy and gospel of prosperity of the new Pentecostal churches—'sheep stealers' as they are

---

[98] Lonsdale et al. (1978), Chepkwony (1987), Githiga (1997), Njoroge (1999),
p. 257, Sabar (2000), chs. 3 to 9.

called—have won them many members from the 'mainstream' churches, Catholic, Anglican and Presbyterian.[99] The third change is ominous, a rising poverty and population which have finally cut off many Kenyans from a landed base. Property used to link the moral economy of self-realization within a continuity of kin, between the dead and the unborn, and Christian hopes of individual salvation. Landlessness, a moral as much as a material closure, has ushered the Devil on to the stage of popular religion. Church-formation offers one of the few openings for community leadership; and the Second Coming the only hope.[100]

Kenya's Christianities, then, have never been more different than they are today. Political antagonism, church growth, private despair, all play their part in a threefold segmentation. The people of God are divided by ethnic political competition; by theological strife; and by traditions of moral ethnicity which, although confined within discrete vernacular arenas of debate, do in reality (and not so paradoxically) unite all Kenyans in their efforts to recreate a persuasively hegemonic moral knowledge. This chapter concludes by examining these divisions in unity.

Christianity is divided, first, by political ethnicity. Ethnic conflict helps to make the long-established conservative evangelical churches, mission-derived and 'independent' alike, into loyal supporters of the state. To them it is a divinely sanctioned authority, as Paul reminded the Romans. Conversely, the more liberal churches (a relative term) preach against what they see as the state's abuses of power, its breaches of God's mandate. Political and ecclesiastical history have together produced this denominational contrast in secular affairs. The formerly pastoral peoples who flank the northern Rift Valley provide the core support for the Moi regime. It is here that the AIM and other evangelical American missions had most success. Their African churches, both successor and secessionist, have come together in the Evangelical Fellowship of Kenya (EFK), on which the government has relied for clerical support. The EFK separated from the National Christian Council of Kenya (NCCK) as long ago as 1976. The grounds were theological, replicating the disputes that prevented evangelical and liberal white pastors from forging a full mission alliance in colonial times. The evangelicals believed that the

[99] Hearn (1997), Njoroge (1999), pp. 251–4.
[100] Heyer (1998), Droz (1999).

time was too short before Christ's return to deflect energies from
saving souls; liberals, with an indefinite timespan, argued for the
needs of 'the whole man' on earth. Today the separation is also
political. The NCCK is dominated by the Presbyterian Church of
East Africa (PCEA), almost entirely Kikuyu, and the Anglican Church
of Kenya (ACK), in which the Kikuyu and Luo peoples jointly pre-
dominate. Recent political history has cast Kikuyu and Luo into the
opposition camp. The NCCK churches' call for an earthly citizenship at present denied to God's people is inspired as much by political ethnicity as by their theology.[101]

Political ethnicity is not the whole story. Theology matters too. It
is not that Kenyan churchmen are skilled theologians; no more than
are most Christians in other countries. It is still a world of implicit
understandings; but it contains new moral images and narratives,
biblical ones. The Bible is the only universal literature Kenyans possess, more often heard than read. It tells the same stories, with their
various teleological possibilities, in all the main vernaculars. It shapes
both popular and educated minds. A veteran missionary, revisiting
his embattled flock during Mau Mau, exclaimed of Kikuyuland, 'This
is Gospel country!' and listed the parables he could see daily enacted
there.[102] Africans had made that journey of the spirit long before. It
is impossible to understand Kenya's political culture otherwise. Bishop
Gitari had no need to explain who St Paul was. No more can Ngugi
wa Thiong'o, Kikuyu novelist and avowed atheist, escape biblical
imagery, as he has himself complained.[103] Still less can Kenya's politicians. Kenyans live in a world where the Bible is familiar allegory,
whether in the age of Old Testament prophecy, or of Christ's moral
teaching, or the terminal tumult of Revelation.

Biblical imagery informs two opposed Christian traditions, a liberal trinitarian theology on the one hand and an evangelical dualism on the other. In the first, it is believed that an incarnate God
suffers with the world he has created, allowing freedom to human
responsibility while remaining ultimately in charge. Man cannot know
the day of Christ's Second Coming; and meanwhile justice must be
pursued on earth. For dualists the struggle between good and evil

---

[101] Ngunyi (1995). Until 1998 the ACK was the CPK (Church of the Province
of Kenya).
[102] Bewes (1953), pp. 18–19.
[103] Wa Thiong'o (1972), p. 3.

is more anxiously balanced, as Christ foretold of the Last Days before his return. The contemporary power of evil confirms the imminence of that Second Coming. Justice can await Christ; personal faith alone will secure his mercy.[104] Kenya's history has shaped these theologies more than scriptural scholarship. Trinitarian thought is 'liberal' in its situation of salvation in a secular environment of justice, not in any sceptically 'modernist' understanding of the human provenance of God's word. Dualist theology has only to draw its lessons from the increasing despair with which good people struggle to survive with dignity and hope in the Kenyan world of the every day.

To take the liberal tradition first, educated Kikuyu (and those of other Kenyan nationalities) have long quarried the Bible for contemporary comment on justice and peace, but it is important to remember that in the creative task of Bible translation they first put their own images *into* its word. Kikuyu *athomi* imagined Boer farmers as Pharaoh's taskmasters and both as *kaburu*, a corruption of the 'corporals' of police who collected tax or conscripted labour. Gideon Mugo had said of Thuku's arrest in 1922 that Goliath had come against him; a generation later Mau Mau saw the Philistine giant as a British general.[105] Since independence, hymns of Exodus have persisted: like 'Water is bitter', *mai ni maruru* which contrasts the politicians' failure to refresh people with the life that Moses released from the rock.[106] These images were all expectant of a moral relationship between leader and led, subject and ruler, and thus critical where it was lacking. They illustrate the tradition on which 'mainstream' church leaders, Catholic and Protestant, draw to authorize their critique of state power.

But there is a very different tradition at work, more visibly than in colonial days. Most Kikuyu Christians are probably now not only conservative evangelicals but more immediately believing Pentecostals, gathered mostly in tiny churches that satisfy ambition by secession. They are sustained by a most striking change in intimations of evil. Despair at the prospect of any sort of moral economy between power and poverty, patron and client, state and citizen, even laborious virtue and its just reward, leaves people staring evil in the face.

---

[104] I am grateful to Graham Kings, Ben Knighton and Jeremy Pemberton (all with African pastoral experience) for theological instruction at this point but hold myself responsible for any error.

[105] Lonsdale (1992), pp. 383–4, 458.

[106] Chepkwony (1987), p. 156.

Nairobi Pentecostalists metaphorically cast Jesus as David's stone against a Goliath of the generalized evil manipulated by their enemies.[107] Dread of the Devil has been added to fears of witchcraft, to organize the world of the occult into a new hierarchy of the Pentecostal imagination.[108] In most of the older evangelical and newer Pentecostal churches, the conflict of good and evil is seen to be within and between persons rather than structured in society; and, since governments can therefore do little, they must be allowed the authority that scripture (if one takes certain texts) commends. But in some parts of the country, popular Christianity has no difficulty in identifying the state itself with evil. Political ethnicity is as important as theology. Among Kikuyu, the economic decline of recent years is all too plausibly associated with the wasting powers of sorcery, the life-draining will of the Devil.

In Kikuyuland people resent having to bend before politicians who have made an idol of money.[109] Money now destroys relationships; it is seen as a new substance for sorcery. The tea, *chai*, of Christian sociability and ethnic memory in the 1920s, euphemism for Mau Mau oaths in the 1950s, as for the Kikuyu oath of 1969, has become slang for the bribes one must pay state officials in order to satisfy one's daily needs. It is thus a poison rather than a sustenance to one's posterity.[110] Only the Devil could have told the regime to destroy slum settlements or kill its citizens in the recent campaigns of 'ethnic cleansing', in both cases to make land available for its chief supporters, and in both mainly at the expense of the Kikuyu poor. Resentment of oppression has brought a new readiness to take the part of the poor, whom the gospel of prosperity can accommodate as people undergoing a time of moral trial. Taped songs, sung in Gikuyu and relayed in mini-bus *matatus*, have asserted that, 'God, a person who hates the needy hates you, because you are the one who created the needy.' And hatred has increased because 'money has driven this country mad . . . you have assumed that money is your God.' 'We feel very bad when people are praying to the power of the Devil here in Kenya. Banish the Devil to go away from us.'[111]

---

[107] Droz (2000).

[108] Gray (1990), p. 105; Ciekawy (1998); generally, Ciekawy and Geschiere (1998); for Ghana, Gifford (1998), ch. 3, and Meyer (1998).

[109] Oral information from the Right Revd Dr Gideon Gichuhi Githiga.

[110] Droz (1999), pp. 364–73.

[111] Thanks to François Grignon for providing me with translated transcripts of these songs.

As elsewhere in Africa, Pentecostalism is spreading like a fire among the apprehensive poor of Kenya. The centralization of the source of evil, with sorcerers as satanic hellhounds, has quite undermined the hegemonic morality of abundance which inspired the Christian project of reconciliation. Then, between the wars, Christian and Kikuyu moral responsibility were joined. Now, for many of the poor, any hope of personal responsibility, of self-realization, is illusory. Believers trust that faith will bring wealth or, if disappointed, trust in a Second Coming, not in reward for toil. While popular memory of *thahu* has disappeared,[112] Pentecostal Christianity has made over into a terrifyingly transcendental form the material manichaeism of African moral knowledge. In this it is utterly foreign to the practical, worldly hermeneutics with which Kikuyu earlier reconciled revealed belief and moral economy. Pentecostalism indeed echoes the state's own destruction of moral knowledge, its separation of merit from reward.

This popular biblical imagination, which cuts churchgoing politicians to the quick, gives resonating power to the very differently reasoned, trinitarian, critique of the state taught by David Gitari, now Archbishop, and other leaders of the mainstream churches. Conversely, in a continuing echo of indigenous moral economy, the churches would have little authority without their constant help given to parishioners in daily struggles with poverty and powerlessness.[113] But Gitari and other establishment leaders have no dealings with Pentecostal dualism. They render to Caesar his proper due, and ascribe no satanic power to the state. Their critique contains Old Testament prophetic fire, not the torments of Revelation. King Rehoboam, who threatened Israel with whips and scorpions, or the emperor Darius who enacted a decree of which he soon repented but could not amend, have both been taken to typify the ruler of a one-party state who consults no one. There is a conscious dissent from President Moi's own vision of a consensual state leadership that nurtures the energies of its clients.[114] Moral knowledge thus remains contested. In 1987 both press and parliament debated the hermeneutics of Darius's tyranny, following one of Gitari's sermons. His life was threatened, apparently by ruling party thugs; but he persevered in his critique of power and asked, amongst other awkward questions, why there

---

[112] Droz (1999), pp. 211–19.
[113] Sabar (2000).
[114] Benson (1995).

was 'No Naboth to say No' to corrupt land seizures. The arguments
over rural capitalism in the 1930s have taken on fresh urgency in
an era of state kleptocracy.[115]

Despite the differences between Christianities which declare, with
the EFK, that salvation has nothing to do with social justice; which
wait for the Second Coming to rid the world of evil; or which, with
the NCCK, plead with the state for justice within a shared mandate from God, there is, to conclude, much implicit understanding
that is common to all Kenyans. It does not look as if it is held in
common, for it is articulated in different vernaculars, in ethnically
separate moral arenas. To give an example, Gitari's love of Old
Testament prophecy makes him a child not only of Christian training, fruit of a long international conversation, but also of Kikuyu
cultural history. His God is driven to anger against injustice by love
of his material creation; catastrophe awaits the unjust state, as in
pre-Christian times human hatreds were known to bring drought.
Establishment Christianity's concern for justice has ecological, material roots in the old moral knowledge.

Those roots are common to all East Africans. To that truth the
new, 1989, Anglican service of Holy Communion bears witness in
one of the official national languages, English. Its prayers make more
mention of manna, bread and grain than does metropolitan usage.
Prayers for the ancestors, those who drank from the Rock of Exodus—
'and the Rock was Christ'—build a bridge between pre-Christian,
Old Testament, Africa and Christian, New Testament, Africa.[116]
Muigwithania's reconciling work continues, and not in the Gikuyu
tongue alone. At a more vulgar level, and in Gikuyu this time, one
can now sing, and reverently, of a God who 'gave his only son to
be sacrificed *like a goat* so as to bring understanding to his people':
a simile which I am sure could not be found in the previous eighty
years of recorded Gikuyu literature, unless in derision. It is the ultimate reconciliation between Christian theology and Kikuyu moral
knowledge, but not Kikuyu alone; the goat is everywhere in East

---

[115] For Rehoboam, I Kings 12. Canon Kings, to whom I owe much eyewitness
insight and documentary ephemera from recent years, tells me that theology students drew their own analogy between Rehoboam's and single party rule; see also
Kings (1996). For Darius and the subsequent public debate, Gitari (1988), pp. 35–46;
for Naboth, Gitari (1996), pp. 102–10. For context: Benson (1995), Throup (1995),
Githiga (1997), Sabar (2000).
[116] Church of the Province of Kenya (1989).

Africa a medium of social intercourse and its cleansing. The same
unifying point is made in the NCCK's voter-education pamphlet of
1992. Its opening text was from Exodus 18: 'choose able men from
all the people, such as fear God, men who are trustworthy and who
hate a bribe.' Nobody could in that injunction see ethnic bias. But
one of the leaflet's cartoons showed the state as an ogre. With a
mouth at the back of its neck with which to eat the unwary, this
was a common figure of Gikuyu folktales, to deter any idle wandering into the wild, especially on the part of young girls.[117] But,
again, it is a widespread image. Kenya has a new Christian political imagination. Its continuities remain divisively, that is to say, ethnically, Kenyan; but the images are shared, all the same.

The regime complains, not without reason, that Kikuyu and other
leaders confuse ethnic self-interest with the cause of the Kingdom
of God, and use universal biblical reproof for particularistic ends.[118]
Kenya's political calculations do become increasingly ethnic.[119] But
one may end with two suggestions that its Christian discourse may
be evolving in more expansive, if still seemingly ethnic, ways. At a
memorial service held in March 1995, in London, on the twentieth
anniversary of the radical Kikuyu politician J.M. Kariuki's unsolved
murder, the lesson was from Amos 5:4–15. The prophet's condemnation of those who afflict the just, take bribes and oppress the
poor had a general resonance; a prayer applied this text to the 'ruthless leadership by the late dictator Kenyatta', as well as the then
almost entirely non-Kikuyu government.[120] For Kikuyu overseas exiles
to condemn, on biblical authority, the Kikuyu father of the Kenyan
nation suggests that Christian universalism is still as appealing as in
the days of Gideon Mugo, and can be used by Kikuyu to criticize
one whom non-Kikuyu would call a Kikuyu tribal hero.

Criticism of Kenyatta's dictatorship represents a universal concern,
however local the Kikuyu moral economy may be in its own formation. Universality and ethnic particularity can pull in opposite
directions. It seems, for instance, that many Kikuyu Christians today
do more than compare themselves with the Jews, as in the ordeal
of Exodus; many see themselves as, literally, one of Israel's 'lost

---

[117] National Christian Council of Kenya (1992); Brinkman (1996).
[118] Ngunyi (1995).
[119] Throup and Hornsby (1998).
[120] Order of service seen by courtesy of Wanyiri Kihoro, MP for Nyeri.

tribes'; seventy years ago that belief was confined to the puritan
akurinu, the praying 'lunatics' as most Kikuyu saw them.[121] Yet even
a lost tribe has men and women. Of all common concerns none is
deeper than gender. In Kikuyu country a new value is being accorded
to formerly 'loose' women, unmarried mothers, urban houseowners.
Muigwithania saw them as wasters of male substance, Kikuyu seed,
in their liaisons with non-Kikuyu men. It is different now. Prominent
in local churches, townswomen are in some areas being welcomed
back as a source of commercial credit for their rural clans, formerly
the domain of patriarchy. 'Nowadays', one woman has explained,
'the church is your clan.' On the eve of a new millennium, another,
Wairimu, a seller of maize and beans, observed, 'We are a nation
of single mothers. It all started with the [Mau Mau] Emergency and
it will only end with the Second Coming!'[122] Perhaps here, in the
reluctantly realistic reconciliation of men towards independent women
as a source of social order, some might see the beginning of a new
stage of growth. The self-realization of both genders, stunted by
poverty and oppression, is forcing each to recognize their need for
the other. Some elderly Kikuyu might say the churches were merely
sponsoring a return to the household gender equality which once
upheld pre-colonial moral economy.[123] Others will say that equality
only makes the war between the sexes more open.[124] The long conversation continues, often angrily—and most eloquently, as always,
in the vernacular—between a changing indigenous moral order of
the every day and the transcendence of the denominationally divided
word. To present the separate anxieties of moral ethnicity as a matter of universal concern is an aspiration in which Kenya's churches
still have much to achieve.

BIBLIOGRAPHY

Barra, G., *1000 Kikuyu Proverbs*, Nyeri, Consolata Mission, 1939.
Beidelman, T.O., *Moral Imagination in Kaguru Modes of Thought*, Bloomington, Indiana
    University Press, 1986.
Benson, G.P., 'Ideological Politics versus Biblical Hermeneutics: Kenya's Protestant
    Churches and the Nyayo State', in Holger B. Hansen and Michael Twaddle
    (eds.), *Religion and Politics in East Africa*, London, James Currey/Nairobi, EAEP/

---

[121] Kenyatta (1938), p. 275; Heyer (1998), p. 291; Droz (1999), p. 343.
[122] Heyer (1998), chs. 11 and 12; quotes from pp. 238, 264.
[123] Shaw (1995), ch. 2.
[124] As observed in Kikuyuland by Ben Knighton.

Kampala, Fountain/Athens OH, Ohio University Press, 1995, pp. 177–99.

Benson, T.G. (ed.), *Kikuyu-English Dictionary*, Oxford, Clarendon Press, 1964.

Berman, Bruce J., 'Ethnicity, Patronage and the African State: The Politics of Uncivil Nationalism', *African Affairs*, 97, 1998, pp. 305–41.

———, and Lonsdale, John M., 'The Labors of *Muigwithania*: Jomo Kenyatta as Author, 1928–45', *Research in African Literatures*, 29–1, 1998, pp. 16–42.

Bernardi, Bernardo, 'Old Kikuyu Religion, Igongona and Mambura: Sacrifice and Sex. Re-reading Kenyatta's Ethnography', *Africa*, XLVIII-2, Rome, 1993, pp. 167–83.

Bewes, T.F.C., *Kikuyu Conflict: Mau Mau and the Christian Witness*, London, Highway, 1953.

Bottignole, Sylvana, *Kikuyu Traditional Culture and Christianity: Self-examination of an African Church*, Nairobi, Heinemann, 1984.

Brinkman, Inge, *Kikuyu Gender Norms and Narratives*, Leiden, Research School CNWS, 1996.

Campbell, Aidan, *Western Primitivism, African Ethnicity: A Study in Cultural Relations*, London, Cassell, 1997.

Casson, John, '"To Plant a Garden City in the Slums of Paganism": Handley Hooper and the Future of Africa', *Journal of Religion in Africa*, XXVIII-3, 1998, pp. 387–410.

Chepkwony, Agnes, *The Role of Non-Governmental Organizations in Development: A Study of the National Christian Council of Kenya 1963–1978*, Uppsala, Studia Missionalia Upsaliensia, XLVIII, 1987.

Ciekawy, Diane, 'Witchcraft in Statecraft: Five Technologies of Power in Colonial and Postcolonial Coastal Kenya', *African Studies Review*, 41–3, 1998, pp. 119–41.

———, and Geschiere, Peter, 'Containing Witchcraft: Conflicting Scenarios in Postcolonial Africa', *African Studies Review*, 41–3, 1998, pp. 1–14.

Clough, Marshall S., *Fighting Two Sides: Kenyan Chiefs and Politicians 1918–1940*, Niwot CO, University Press of Colorado, 1990.

Comaroff, Jean and John, *Of Revelation and Revolution*, I: *Christianity, Colonialism and Consciousness in South Africa* and II: *The Dialectics of Modernity on a South African Frontier*, Chicago and London, Chicago University Press, 1991, 1997.

Douglas, Mary, *Purity and Danger: An Analysis of Pollution and Taboo*, London, Routledge, 1966.

Droz, Yvan, *Migrations Kikuyu: des pratiques sociales à l'imaginaire*, Neuchâtel, Editions de l'Institut d'ethnologie/Paris, Editions de la Maison des sciences de l'homme, 1999.

———, 'Des Origines vernaculaires de réveil pentecôtiste Kenyan: Conversion, guérison, mobilité sociale et politique', in André Corten (ed.), *Imaginaires politiques et Pentecôtisme: Afrique et Amérique Latine*, Paris, Karthala, 2000.

Fadiman, Jeffrey A. *When We Began, There Were Witchmen: An Oral History from Mount Kenya*, Berkeley, Los Angeles and London, University of California Press, 1993.

Fazan, S.H., *History of the Loyalists*, Nairobi, Government Printer, 1960.

Feldman, David, 'Christians & Politics: Origins of the Kikuyu Central Association in Northern Murang'a 1890–1930', Ph.D. thesis, University of Cambridge, 1978.

Fulford, Ben, 'An Igbo Esperanto: The Making of the Union Igbo Bible', BA (History) Dissertation, University of Cambridge, 2000.

Gathigira, Stanley K., *Miikarire ya Agikuyu* (Nairobi, 1934), London, Sheldon, 1959.

Gifford, Paul, 'Prosperity: A New and Foreign Element in African Christianity', *Religion*, 20, 1990, pp. 373–88.

———, *African Christianity: Its Public Role*, London, Hurst, 1998.

Gitari, David M., *Let the Bishop Speak*, Nairobi, Uzima, 1988.

———, *In Season and out of Season: Sermons to a Nation*, Carlisle, Regnum, 1996.

Githiga, Gideon, 'The Church as the Bulwark against Extremism: Development of Church-State Relations in Kenya 1963–92', Ph.D. thesis, Open University, 1997.

Githige, Renison Muchiri, 'The Religious Factor in Mau Mau', MA thesis, Nairobi University, 1978.
Gray, Richard, *Black Christians and White Missionaries*, New Haven and London, Yale University Press, 1990.
Guy, Jeff, *The Heretic: A Study of the Life of John William Colenso 1814–1883*, Pietermaritzburg, University of Natal Press/Johannesburg, Ravan, 1983.
Hastings, Adrian, *The Church in Africa 1450–1950*, Oxford, Clarendon Press, 1994.
———, *The Construction of Nationhood: Ethnicity, Religion and Nationalism*, Cambridge, Cambridge University Press, 1997.
Hearn, Julie, 'The Development Implications of American Evangelism in Kenya', Ph.D. thesis, University of Leeds, 1997.
Heyer, Amrik, 'The Mandala of a Market: A Study of Capitalism and the State in Murang'a District, Kenya', Ph.D. thesis, School of Oriental and African Studies, University of London, 1998.
Hodges, Geoffrey, *The Carrier Corps: Military Labor in the East African Campaign, 1914–1918*, Westport CT, Greenwood, 1986.
Iliffe, John, *A Modern History of Tanganyika*, Cambridge, Cambridge University Press, 1979.
———, *Africans: The History of a Continent*, Cambridge, Cambridge University Press, 1995.
James, Wendy, *The Listening Ebony: Moral Knowledge, Religion, and Power among the Uduk of Sudan*, Oxford, Clarendon Press, 1988.
Kagika, Gideon Mugo, 'Hold Fast to Tribal Names', *Muigwithania*, i–7, Nov 1928, p. 1.
———, 'Setting Forth What is Right', *Muigwithania*, ii–1, June 1929, pp. 7–8.
Karanja, John K., *Founding an African Faith: Kikuyu Anglican Christianity, 1900–1945*, Nairobi, Uzima, 1999.
Karanja, P.K., 'Those who Take Counsel Together Do not Come to Destruction', *Muigwithania*, i–4, Aug 1928, p. 11.
Karimu, S., 'The Blessing of the Ancestor', *Muigwithania*, i–4, Aug 1928, p. 12.
Kariuki, Obadiah, *A Bishop Facing Mount Kenya*, Nairobi, Uzima, 1985.
Kenya, Church of the Province of, *A Kenyan Service of Holy Communion*, Nairobi, Uzima, 1989.
Kenya, National Christian Council of, *Why You Should Vote*, Nairobi, Uzima, 1992.
Kenyatta, Johnstone, 'A Message from *Muigwithania* to the Leaders and Workers of all the Missions which are in Kikuyu Country', *Muigwithania*, i–4, Aug 1928, p. 3.
Kenyatta, Jomo, *Facing Mount Kenya*, London, Warburg, 1938.
Kershaw, Greet, *Mau Mau from Below*, Oxford, James Currey/Nairobi, EAEP/Athens OH, Ohio University Press, 1997.
Kibicho, Samuel G., 'The Continuity of the African Conception of God into and through Christianity: A Kikuyu Case Study', in Edward Fasholé-Luke, Richard Gray, Adrian Hastings and Godwin Tasie (eds.), *Christianity in Independent Africa*, London, Rex Collings, 1978, pp. 370–88.
Kings, Graham, 'Proverbial, Intrinsic, and Dynamic Authorities: A Case Study on Scripture and Mission in the Dioceses of Mount Kenya East and Kirinyaga', *Missiology: An International Review*, XXIV-4, 1996, pp. 493–501.
Landau, Paul, '"Religion" and Christian Conversion in African History: A New Model', *Journal of Religious History*, 23–1, 1999, pp. 8–30.
Leakey, L.S.B., *Defeating Mau Mau*, London, Methuen, 1954.
———, *The Southern Kikuyu before 1903*, 3 volumes, London and New York, Academic Press, 1977.
Lonsdale, John, 'The Moral Economy of Mau Mau', pp. 265–504 in Bruce Berman and John Lonsdale, *Unhappy Valley: Conflict in Kenya and Africa*, London, James Currey/Athens OH, Ohio University Press, 1992.

————, 'Moral Ethnicity and Political Tribalism' in Preben Kaarsholm and Jan
    Hultin (eds.), *Inventions and Boundaries: Historical and Anthropological Approaches to the
    Study of Ethnicity and Nationalism*, University of Roskilde, Institute of Development
    Studies, 1994, pp. 131–59.
————, 'The Prayers of Waiyaki: Political Uses of the Kikuyu Past', in David
    Anderson and Douglas Johnson (eds.), *Revealing Prophets: Prophecy in Eastern African
    History*, London, James Currey/Nairobi, EAEP/Kampala, Fountain/Athens OH,
    Ohio University Press, 1995, pp. 240–91.
————, '"Listen while I Read": The Orality of Christian Literacy in the Young
    Kenyatta's Making of the Kikuyu', in Louise de la Gorgendière and Kenneth
    King (eds.), *Ethnicity in Africa*, Edinburgh University, Centre of African Studies,
    1996a, pp. 17–33.
————, 'Moral Ethnicity, Ethnic Nationalism and Political Tribalism: The Case of
    the Kikuyu', in Peter Meyns (ed.), *Staat und Gesellschaft in Afrika*, Hamburg, LIT,
    1996b, pp. 93–106.
————, 'Kenyatta, God, and the Modern World', in Jan-Georg Deutsch, Peter
    Probst & Heike Schmidt (eds.), *African Modernities*, Oxford, James Currey and
    Portsmouth, NH, Heinemann, 2001.
————, with Booth-Clibborn, Stanley and Hake, Andrew, 'The Emerging Pattern
    of Church and State Cooperation in Kenya', in Edward Fasholé-Luke, Richard
    Gray, Adrian Hastings and Godwin Tasie (eds.), *Christianity in Independent Africa*,
    London, Rex Collings, 1978, pp. 267–84.
Mackenzie, Fiona, *Land, Ecology and Resistance in Kenya, 1880–1952*, Edinburgh,
    Edinburgh University Press, 1998.
Mamdani, Mahmood, *Citizen and Subject: Contemporary Africa and the Legacy of Late
    Colonialism*, Kampala, Fountain/Cape Town, David Philip/London, James
    Currey, 1996.
Mayer, Philip, *Townsmen or Tribesmen*, Cape Town, Oxford University Press, 1961.
McIntosh, Brian G., 'The Scottish Mission in Kenya, 1891–1923', Ph.D. thesis,
    University of Edinburgh, 1969.
Meyer, Birgit, 'Modernity and Enchantment: The Image of the Devil in Popular
    African Christianity', in Peter van der Veer (ed.), *Conversion to Modernities: The
    Globalization of Christianity*, New York & London, Routledge, 1996, pp. 199–229.
————, 'The Power of Money: Politics, Occult Forces, and Pentecostalism in Ghana',
    African Studies Review, 41–3, 1998, pp. 15–37.
Mockerie, Parmenas Githendu, *An African Speaks for his People*, London, Hogarth, 1934.
Murray, Jocelyn, 'The Kikuyu Spirit Churches', *Journal of Religion in Africa* V.3, 1973,
    pp. 198–234.
————, 'The Kikuyu Female Circumcision Controversy, with Special Reference to
    the Church Missionary Society's "Sphere of Influence"', Ph.D. thesis, University
    of California at Los Angeles, 1974.
Murray-Brown, Jeremy, *Kenyatta*, London, Allen and Unwin, 1972.
Neckebrouck, Valeer, *Le onzième commandement: Etiologie d'une église indépendante au pied
    du Mont Kenya*, Immensee, Nouvelle revue de science missionnaire, 1978.
Ng'undo, C., 'One Does not Part from One's Clan or Circumcision Guild',
    Muigwithania, i–12, May 1929, p. 5.
Ngunyi, Mutahi G., 'Religious Institutions and Political Liberalisation in Kenya', in
    Peter Gibbon (ed.), *Markets, Civil Society and Democracy in Kenya*, Uppsala, Nordiska
    Afrikainstitutet, 1995, pp. 121–77.
Njiri, Philomena, 'The Akurinu Churches: The History and Basic Beliefs of the
    Holy Ghost Churches of East Africa 1926–1980', MA thesis, Nairobi University,
    1984.
Njoroge, Lawrence M., *A Century of Catholic Endeavour: Holy Ghost and Consolata Missions
    in Kenya*, Nairobi, Paulines, 1999.

Njuguna wa Karucha, S., 'Kikuyu Time', *Muigwithania*, i–6, Oct 1928, p. 10.

Ogot, B.A., 'Politics, Culture and Music in Central Kenya: A Study of Mau Mau Hymns 1951–1956', *Kenya Historical Review*, 5–2, 1977, pp. 275–86.

Ong, Walter J., *Orality and Literacy: The Technologizing of the Word*, London and New York, Routledge, 1982.

Peel, J.D.Y., 'For Who Hath Despised the Day of Small Things? Missionary Narratives and Historical Anthropology', *Comparative Studies in Society and History*, 37–3, 1995, pp. 581–607.

Peterson, Derek, 'Dancing and Schooling: Missionaries, Athomi and the Outschool in Late Colonial Kenya', MA thesis, University of Minnesota, 1996.

———, 'Colonizing Language? Missionaries and Gikuyu Dictionaries, 1904 and 1914', *History in Africa* 27, 1997, pp. 257–72.

———, 'Of Mimicry's Making: "Religion" and Questions of Ambivalence in Early Colonial Encounters at Tumutumu, 1908–1918', Minneapolis, typescript, 1999.

———, 'Writing Gikuyu: Christian Literacy and Ethnic Debate in North Central Kenya 1908–1952', Ph.D. thesis, University of Minnesota, 2000.

Robertson, Claire C., *Trouble Showed the Way: Women, Men and Trade in the Nairobi Area, 1890–1990*, Bloomington and Indianapolis, Indiana University Press, 1997.

Ruel, Malcolm, *Belief, Ritual and the Securing of Life: Reflexive Essays on a Bantu Religion*, Leiden, Brill, 1996.

Sabar, Galia, *Church, State, and Society in Kenya: From Mediation to Opposition, 1963–1993*, London, Cass, 2000.

Sabar-Friedman, Galia, 'Church and State in Kenya, 1986–1992: The Churches' Involvement in the "Game of Change"', *African Affairs*, 96, 1997, pp. 25–52.

Sandgren, David P., 'Twentieth Century Religious and Political Divisions among the Kikuyu of Kenya', *African Studies Review*, 25–2/3, 1982, pp. 195–207.

———, *Christianity & the Kikuyu: Religious Divisions and Social Conflict*, New York, Bern, Frankfurt and Paris, Peter Lang, 1989.

Sanneh, Lamin, *Translating the Message: The Missionary Impact on Culture*, New York, Maryknoll, 1990.

Shaw, Carolyn Martin, *Colonial Inscriptions: Race, Sex, and Class in Kenya*, Minneapolis and London, University of Minnesota Press, 1995.

Shaw, Rosalind, 'The Invention of "African Traditional Religion"', *Religion*, 20, 1990, pp. 339–53.

Smoker, Dorothy (ed.), *Ambushed by Love: God's Triumph in Kenya's Terror*, Fort Washington, PA, Christian Literature Crusade, 1994.

Strayer, Robert W., *The Making of Mission Communities in East Africa*, London, Heinemann, 1978.

Tamarkin, Mordechai, 'Culture & Politics in Africa', *Nationalism and Ethnic Politics*, 2–3, 1996, pp. 360–80.

Taylor, John V., *The Growth of the Church in Buganda: An Attempt at Understanding*, London, SCM, 1958.

Thomas-Slayter, Barbara, and Rocheleau, Diana, *Gender, Environment and Development in Kenya: A Grassroots Perspective*, Boulder CO and London, Rienner, 1995.

Throup, David, '"Render to Caesar the Things that are Caesar's": The Politics of Church-State Conflict in Kenya 1978–1990', in Holger B. Hansen and Michael Twaddle (eds.), *Religion and Politics in East Africa*, London, James Currey/Nairobi, EAEP/Kampala, Fountain/Athens OH, Ohio University Press, 1995, pp. 143–76.

———, and Hornsby, Charles, *Multi-Party Politics in Kenya*, Oxford, James Currey/Nairobi, EAEP/Athens OH, Ohio University Press, 1998.

Thuku, Harry, *An Autobiography*, Nairobi, Oxford University Press, 1970.

Wa Kinyatti, Maina (ed.), *Thunder from the Mountains: Mau Mau Patriotic Songs*, London and Nairobi, Zed, 1980.

Walzer, Michael, *Exodus and Revolution*, New York, Basic Books, 1985.

Wamagatta, Evanson N., 'A Biography of Senior Chief Waruhiu wa Kung'u of Githunguri, Kiambu District, 1890–1952', MA thesis, Nairobi University, 1988.

Wanjohi, G.J., 'An African Conception of God: The Case of the Gikuyu', *Journal of Religion in Africa*, IX-2, 1978, pp. 136–46.

Wanyoike, E.N., *An African Pastor*, Nairobi, East African Publishing House, 1974.

Ward, Kevin, 'The Development of Protestant Christianity in Kenya, 1910–1940', Ph.D. thesis, University of Cambridge, 1976.

Wa Thiong'o, Ngugi, *Homecoming: Essays on African and Caribbean Literature, Culture and Politics*, London, Heinemann, 1972.

Weisner, Thomas S., Bradley, Candice, and Kilbride, Philip L. (eds.), *African Families and the Crisis of Social Change*, Westport, CT, and London, Bergin and Garvey, 1997.

Welbourn, F.B., *East African Rebels: A Study of Some Independent Churches*, London, SCM, 1961.

White, Luise, *The Comforts of Home: Prostitution in Colonial Nairobi*, Chicago and London, Chicago University Press, 1990.

Wiseman, E.M., *Kikuyu Martyrs*, London, Highway, 1958.

CHAPTER SEVEN

ARCHBISHOP JANANI LUWUM: THE DILEMMAS OF LOYALTY, OPPOSITION AND WITNESS IN AMIN'S UGANDA

Kevin Ward

On 16 February 1977 Janani Luwum, the Anglican Archbishop of Uganda, Rwanda, Burundi and Boga Zaire[1] was murdered on the orders of President Idi Amin of Uganda. Luwum, who was accused of complicity in a plot to overthrow the military regime, was one of a host of prominent public figures who were killed during the Amin regime. These included Benedicto Kiwanuka, a Catholic lawyer and the first Prime Minister of Uganda (1961), Fr Clement Kiggundu, editor of the Catholic newspaper *Munno*, and Lt. Col. Michael Ondoga, a Lugbara Anglican from West Nile and Amin's brother-in-law.[2] Muslims as well as Christians were victims.

Adrian Hastings ends his great history, *The Church in Africa 1450–1950*, with a chapter entitled 'Church, School, and State in the Age of Bishop Kiwanuka'.[3] Joseph Kiwanuka, ordained bishop in 1935, was the first Ugandan Catholic bishop, indeed the first black African diocesan bishop of recent times. His election was a mark of the extraordinary success and importance of Catholicism in Uganda and, in Hastings's words, a 'kind of landmark' for the church through-out Africa.[4] The Anglicans were some twenty years behind the Catholics in entrusting similar authority to a Ugandan, but, for both churches, the creation of fully autonomous hierarchies came just before Independence in 1962. In 1960 Kiwanuka became Archbishop of Kampala; in 1965 Erica Sabiiti succeeded Leslie Brown as Anglican

---

[1] From the creation of an ecclesiastical Province in 1961 until the early 1980s, the Anglican Church of Uganda was part of a larger unit including dioceses in Rwanda, Burundi and Zaire (the present Democratic Republic of the Congo).

[2] Ondoga was the brother of Kay, a wife of Amin, who was also murdered. They were the children of Archdeacon Sila Adroa.

[3] Adrian Hastings, *The Church in Africa 1450–1950*, Oxford, Clarendon Press, 1994, Chapter 12.

[4] Hastings, 1994, p. 573.

Archbishop of Uganda. Hastings writes, in one of his concluding remarks: 'A new age of the African Church was about to begin. An initial reaction would be that with political independence the Churches mattered less.' But, he continues, this did not turn out to be the case:

> Political independence helped liberate the Churches from their colo-
> nial links without in any way diminishing their usefulness or attrac-
> tiveness. Indeed the new states would come to find they needed the
> Churches and even the missions too, even more than had the old ones;
> moreover, the people would find that, when their governments grew
> tyrannical, the Churches might be the only institutions able to miti-
> gate or challenge the new bondage.[5]

In his earlier work, *A History of African Christianity 1950–1975*, Hastings had explored at some length this theme of the resilience of the churches in the early years of independence, their renewed impor-tance in the face of tyranny. In fact, he was engaged in writing this book precisely at the time of Luwum's murder, and he alludes to Archbishop Luwum as 'the Thomas of Canterbury of the twentieth century', a man who was able to face Amin with a 'divine calm' springing from a life of prayer and a wrestling of the soul which has characterized so many African Christians and has given them 'a secret strength which the historian cannot assess nor Caesar crush'.[6]

The present essay explores the theme of African leadership and martyrdom in the age following that of Kiwanuka and Sabiiti. It examines the social and political structures of independent Uganda and the continuing central role of the churches, to throw light on Archbishop Luwum's role as a Christian witness and martyr. It con-siders the disjunction between the international reception of Lu-wum as a 'martyr of the twentieth century' and the ambiguity of reaction to his death within Uganda itself, a reflection of the con-tentious nature of Ugandan political life, and its ethnic and religious divisions.

The ambiguity of martyrdom is not new in Uganda's history. In 1885 and 1886 a significant number of Christians, for the most part officials and pages of the Kabaka of Buganda, were executed for confessing their faith. Ten years earlier a similar 'holocaust' of Muslim

---

[5] Hastings, 1994, pp. 608–9.
[6] Adrian Hastings, *A History of African Christianity 1950–1975*, Cambridge, Cambridge University Press, 1979, p. 266.

converts had occurred. These events assumed considerable importance for the establishment and flourishing of Ugandan religious communities, defining their identity and channelling the zeal of their
members.[7] The assessment of their sacrifice again became contentious
at the end of the colonial era and in the early years of independence, a time when the place of religious institutions in Uganda's
life was being negotiated anew. The claim that the martyrs had been
'good Ugandans' was challenged by certain sections of the nationalist movement, who hailed the persecuting Kabaka Mwanga as a
proto-nationalist and opponent of colonialism. By contrast the martyrs were 'collaborators', stooges of colonialism, traitors to their
African heritage. Around the time of the canonization of the Catholic
martyrs by Pope Paul VI in 1964, a Ugandan resident in the United
States could write:

> We are required to believe that the martyrs died for the good of
> Uganda, for the advent of Christianity, for the civilization of Uganda. . . .
> Historians have written books in that tone, condemning Mwanga as
> a brutal murderer, murdering innocent people who had chosen the
> narrow path to heaven. It surprises me to see that our intelligent his-
> torians have not written any books praising Mwanga and Kabarega
> for trying to resist any foreign domination. . . . it is so annoying to see
> intelligent citizens spending their precious time canonizing a group of
> disloyal servants; these disloyal servants refused to obey the orders of
> the king and sided with a foreign master who had promised them
> thrones in heaven. The canonization of these disloyal pages and the
> condemnation of both Mwanga and Kabarega is a manifestation of
> the colonial mentality still rampant in our nation.[8]

But, as the independent state failed to promote unity, stability and
prosperity and to safeguard human rights, so the Uganda martyrs'
story took on renewed vigour and significance. To exalt the martyrs
of the past became an affirmation of local identity and local tradition against the pretensions of a state intent on creating new martyrs. In turn, these new martyrs, Luwum pre-eminent among them,
were to become the battleground of conflicting interpretations.

---

[7] J.F. Faupel, *African Holocaust: The Story of the Uganda Martyrs*, London, Geoffrey
Chapman, 1962.
[8] Nuwa Sentongo's letter to the President of Uganda is contained in NA,
Archbishops' Papers, Box 30 File 1. The letter is undated in this copy. It would
appear to date from around 1964. Kabarega was the Omukama (king) of Bunyoro,
the neighbour and rival of Buganda and contemporary of Mwanga.

Luwum's Reputation

Luwum belonged to Northern Uganda's Acholi people, who from the very first days of the military coup in January 1971 had been targets of Amin's vindictiveness. Acholi soldiers had previously constituted the backbone of the Ugandan army. Now they became chief victims of the state, along with an array of prominent Acholi civilians distinguished in the civil service and the professions.[9] The car whose 'crash' ostensibly ended Luwum's life in 1977 also contained two members of Amin's own cabinet. Erinayo Oryema, from Acholi, was a close friend of the Archbishop, and Charles Oboth-Ofumbi was from the Padhola of eastern Uganda, a people who share a common Lwo cultural and linguistic heritage with the Acholi.

Not since the days of Cranmer and Laud has an Anglican archbishop suffered the ultimate penalty for his faith, and Luwum has therefore a special place in the history of the whole Anglican communion. He has been remembered in a chapel dedicated to modern martyrs in Canterbury Cathedral. In 1998 ten statues commemorating Christian martyrs of the twentieth century were unveiled on the west face of Westminster Abbey in London. Archbishop Luwum and Archbishop Oscar Romero of El Salvador stand side by side with Maximilian Kolbe and Martin Luther King. There are three women, the Orthodox saint Elizabeth of Russia, killed by the Bolsheviks in 1918, Manche Masemola, a 15-year-old Anglican catechumen from South Africa, murdered in 1928, and Esther John, a Presbyterian evangelist from Pakistan, killed in 1960.[10] The two Africans commemorated, Luwum and Masemola, were both Anglican. A book of essays, *The Terrible Alternative: Christian Martyrdom in the Twentieth Century*, was produced to mark the completion of the project. Mandy Goedhals, in her contribution on Manche Masemola, noted that the circumstances of the young girl's murder were 'rooted

---

[9] Colin Leys, *Politicians and Policies: An Essay on Politics in Acholi, Uganda 1962–65*, Nairobi, East African Publishing House, 1967, p. 49. Leys notes the high rate of involvement in paid employment of Acholi, comprising 4.4 per cent of the population but 7.2 per cent of those in paid employment in Uganda as a whole.

[10] For a list of the martyrs commemorated and photographs of the ten statues, see *Christian Martyrs of the Twentieth Century: Ten New Statues on the West Front of Westminster Abbey*, text by Andrew Chandler, photography by John Carter Studios. Pamphlet of the Dean and Chapter of Westminster, 1998, p. 13.

in the struggle for political, economic and cultural autonomy in the northern Transvaal'.[11]

Janani Luwum's death, too, is inextricably bound up with the complex political and cultural history of Uganda's development as an independent state. John Sentamu, the Bishop of Stepney,[12] in his contribution on Luwum, rightly stresses that Janani Luwum was intimately involved in the defence of human rights, that he had an intense concern for the prisoner and the widow, both as Bishop of Northern Uganda and as Archbishop. He was 'a man intimately aware of the realities of a world of power'. There was a strong tradition in the Revival movement, to which Luwum belonged, of shunning the dirty world of politics. Luwum strongly resisted such a stance, regarding it as irresponsible and, for a bishop in Uganda, self-deceiving. He saw clearly the need for engagement, for struggle against dehumanizing forces.[13]

In his readiness to engage with political powers and dehumanizing forces, Luwum can be compared with another of the figures commemorated on the west front of Westminster Abbey, Dietrich Bonhoeffer, whose imprisonment and execution sprang from his opposition to Hitler and his involvement in a conspiracy to assassinate the Führer. Sentamu's essay avoids discussing whether, and to what extent, Luwum was involved in the equally abortive plot to get rid of Amin. In the light of the brutality of the Amin regime, it might seem immaterial to Luwum's status as a martyr whether he was an innocent victim or a conspirator. The inordinate German respect for authority that so frustrated Lenin (he spoke disdainfully of the difficulty of fomenting revolution in Berlin when protesters refused even to disobey signs not to step on the grass)[14] is almost unthinkable in

---

[11] Mandy Goedhals, 'Imperialism, Mission and Conversion: Manche Masemola of Sekhukhuneland', in Andrew Chandler (ed.), *The Terrible Alternative: Christian Martyrdom in the Twentieth Century*, London, Cassell, 1998, p. 28.

[12] Sentamu had first become acquainted with Luwum when, as a young man, Sentamu was appointed a magistrate in Gulu in 1973. He subsequently became a refugee. Ordained in the Church of England and eventually appointed bishop, Sentamu has himself been acutely aware of those realities of power in his work on the MacPherson enquiry into the murder of the black London teenager, Stephen Lawrence, and of the need to tackle 'institutional racism'.

[13] John Sentamu, 'Tribalism, Religion and Despotism in Uganda: Archbishop Janani Luwum' in Chandler, 1998, p. 146.

[14] Alexandra Richie, *Faust's Metropolis: A History of Berlin*, London, Harper Collins, 1998, p. xxxiii.

Uganda. Nevertheless, for Ugandans, colonial rule had inculcated a certain respect for constituted authority, not least among those Christians belonging to the Anglican Church, with its strong tradition of support for the state. Moreover, the circumstances of Luwum's death continue to be problematic for Ugandans, who remember both the divisive nature of the Obote regime (which had provoked the Amin coup in 1971) and the even more divisive political climate of Obote's second regime between 1980 and 1985. Evaluation of Luwum's death is coloured by the question of whether he was, in some measure, part of a plot to restore Obote and the Uganda People's Congress (UPC) to power, and whether such an outcome would have been desirable.

It is one of the unfortunate consequences of the chronic instability in Northern Uganda since 1986 that there has been no attempt to write an extended biography of Janani Luwum. Both his predecessor as Archbishop, Erica Sabiiti, and his successor, Silvanus Wani, have been the subjects of substantial and scholarly (though unpublished) biographies.[15] The desperate situation in Acholi, particularly since 1985, has made a similar enterprise impracticable for Luwum. In the immediate aftermath of his death, however, Margaret Ford wrote *Janani: The Making of a Martyr*.[16] Ford, of the Church Missionary Society (CMS), served as Luwum's personal secretary in both Gulu and Kampala. Her study, published in 1978, while Amin was still in power, had to be circumspect in its discussion of political issues. It was understandably concerned to portray the Archbishop as a Christian witness to truth, and to keep silent about direct political involvement. In her account of his last days, Ford emphasizes the parallels between Luwum's death and Christ's, in a long tradition of martyrology going back to Polycarp.[17] The book is still of considerable importance as an historical source, drawing as it does on the reminiscences of men and women who personally knew the Archbishop. It is to be hoped that a full biography of Luwum can eventually be published.

---

[15] Both Philemon Tinka's biography of Sabiiti, and the late Samuel Kermu's biography of Wani were written as dissertations for the ATIEA (Association of Theological Institutions of Eastern Africa) BD degree in 1987, and can be found in the library of the Uganda Christian University, Mukono.
[16] Margaret Ford, *Janani: The Making of a Martyr*, London, Marshall, Morgan and Scott, 1978.
[17] The second-century Bishop of Smyrna.

This essay utilizes written accounts of the church in Acholi, particularly from theological students.[18] It draws on the writer's own experience of living in Uganda, and from discussions with Acholi (ordinands, clergy and lay people), over twenty-five years.[19] Important documentary material comes from the Archives of the Church of Uganda at the Provincial Offices on Namirembe Hill, Kampala.[20]

Luwum's Acholi

Janani Luwum was born in 1922 in Mucwini, a village a few miles to the east of Kitgum, the main town of East Acholi. The Acholi are a Lwo people, with a language and culture distinct from the Bantu peoples of southern Uganda. The land of Acholi has a relatively sparse population, with farming and cattle-keeping as the basic means of livelihood. In colonial times cotton production was a major source of the revenue necessary to satisfy tax demands. Another important way in which Acholi became incorporated into the colonial state was the recruitment of young men into the security forces: the army, police and prison services. Luwum's father, Eliya Okello, and his mother were among the first Christians in East Acholi. Luwum attended Gulu High School (a Native Anglican Church school). From there he went to the Anglican teacher training college of Boroboro, near Lira, in the neighbouring district of Lango. By 1942 Luwum was serving as primary school teacher at Paranga, in his home district.[21] In 1948 he came in contact with the Revival, the *Balokole* (Luganda for the 'Saved People'). This movement had just been brought to Kitgum by the Muganda government medical

---

[18] In 1999 the author conducted fieldwork in Northern Uganda, with the collaboration and assistance of a number of friends and former students.

[19] The author was a tutor at Bishop Tucker Theological College, Mukono, the national seminary of the Anglican Church of Uganda (now part of the Uganda Christian University) from 1976 to 1990.

[20] I am grateful to Archbishop Livingstone Nkoyoyo and the Provincial Secretary, Canon George Tibeesigwa, for permission to consult the Namirembe Archives. Researchers are indebted to Mr Fred Mukungu, the librarian of the Uganda Christian University, for his fine work in ordering and cataloguing the archives and making them accessible for historical research.

[21] For basic biographical material in this section, see Ford, 1978, chapter 2. Materials on Luwum's conversion experience were given to Margaret Ford by John Sentamu himself, cf. Sentamu, in Chandler, pp. 146–8.

doctor, Eliya Lubulwa.[22] He introduced a local man, Yusto Otunnu,[23] to 'salvation' and Otunnu in turn became the driving force of the Revival throughout Northern Uganda. When Lubulwa arrived in the North he was already out of fellowship with the Brethren (as Balokole called themselves) in Buganda, and as a result Revival in the North developed a distinctive character. It acquired the name of 'Trumpeters', because Revivalists used megaphones to preach aggressive evange-listic sermons in market places and outside churches, disrupting the services taking place inside. Otunnu and Luwum were arrested for disturbing the peace in Kitgum in 1948. While always considering itself to be Anglican, the Revival developed an abrasively critical stance towards the church as an institution. The hostility was reci-procated by the CMS missionaries and the Acholi clergy, who for many years were deeply suspicious of the Revivalists.[24]

It is probably fair to say that at this period Christianity, in both its Protestant (Anglican) and Catholic manifestations, was marginal to most aspects of Acholi life. The army rather than the church was the primary point of reference for Acholi's interaction with the forces of colonial modernity. The 1959 census nevertheless records a sur-prisingly high percentage of Christian adherents in Acholi: 72 per cent of the population, with 39 per cent Catholics and 33 per cent Protestants. Only 0.6 per cent registered as Muslim. The figures for Christians may have something to do with the rise of sectarian pol-itics in the late 1950s, with recruitment to party membership and baptism being equated.[25] By contrast, contemporary observers of the religious life of Acholi were likely to stress, not the widespread pop-ularity of Christianity, but its lack of penetration into the culture, a phenomenon which required explanation.[26] It was the spiritual poverty

---

[22] Lubulwa's activities in various parts of Northern Uganda are recounted in Kefa Zodia, 'The History of the Revival Movement in West Nile', dissertation submit-ted for the Diploma in Theology, Makerere University, 1978. For references to Lubulwa as a medical doctor, see John Iliffe, *East African Doctors*, Cambridge, Cambridge University Press, 1998.

[23] Yusto Otunnu is the father of Olara Otunnu, a cabinet minister in the 1980s, and now a prominent official of the United Nations.

[24] See Kevin Ward '"Tukutendereza Jesu": The Balokole Revival Movement in Uganda', in Z. Nthamburi (ed.), *From Mission to Church: A Handbook of Christianity in East Africa*, Nairobi, Uzima Press, 1991.

[25] A process recorded by F.B. Welbourn in *Religion and Politics in Uganda 1952–62*, Nairobi, East African Publishing House, 1965. Welbourn also contains useful sum-maries of the 1959 census figures (Table 3).

[26] Most notably, Keith Russell (the first Anglican bishop of Northern Uganda),

of the church in Acholi, as the Revivalists saw it, which led Otunnu and the Brethren to encourage one of their number to train for the ministry of the Anglican Church, as a more positive alternative to unmitigated confrontation. Luwum was chosen by the Brethren, accepted by the church authorities, and in 1949 began his training at Buwalasi, the seminary of the Diocese of the Upper Nile (the second, less developed diocese of the Native Anglican Church in Uganda).[27] Luwum henceforth owed a dual loyalty, to church and to Revival fellowship, and when he became Bishop of Northern Uganda this led to conflicts with his former mentor, Otunnu, who was becoming progressively more detached from his Anglican affiliation.[28]

Luwum became a lay reader at the end of 1950, the first step on the slow ladder to the priesthood. He was eventually ordained in 1955, then spent time in parish work, alternating with two periods of study in England (1958 and 1963–65). He was appointed to the staff of the theological college at Buwalasi, and in 1966 became Provincial Secretary of the Church of Uganda, living for the first time in Kampala. As a Revivalist, he had his doubts about the enthusiasm for party politics, which seemed to dominate Ugandan life in the early years of independence. But any Acholi Anglican clergyman was bound to be associated in some way with the 'Protestant' party, the Uganda People's Congress (UPC). Party politics in the 1960s was much concerned with competition between and within local élites, especially over access to the limited and consequently highly contested largesse available from central government. In the North, where the educated élite was much smaller and more narrowly based than in the more prosperous societies of the South, clergy were more likely to be incorporated into that new élite. In neighbouring Lango, for example, it had been the Anglican professional workers (both the small number of ordained and the lay teachers) who had been active

---

in *Men without God?*, London, Highway Press, 1968, and the works of Okot p'Bitek, for example, *African Religions in Western Scholarship*, Nairobi, East African Publishing House, 1970.

[27] This was the official name for the Anglican Church in Uganda until it assumed the title Church of Uganda in 1961.

[28] Ford, p. 21. See also Kenneth Gong, 'The History of the Revival Movement in Kitgum Church of Uganda Parish, Northern Uganda Diocese', Makerere Diploma of Theology dissertation, November 1985, in Library of Uganda Christian University. Otunnu's 'Chosen Evangelical Revival' eventually broke with the Church of Uganda altogether and has become a separate church.

in fostering the first nationalist politics of the early 1950s. Milton
Obote, the first Prime Minister of independent Uganda, had established his political reputation in Lango, his home area.[29] As a result
of the rather exceptional character of the national movement in
Lango, UPC was seen (to a greater extent than almost anywhere in
Uganda) as an expression of local aspirations as a whole, rather than
the vehicle of a specifically Protestant political awareness, and the
Democratic Party (DP) remained weaker than in most other parts
of Uganda, even among Lango Catholics. Acholi was very different,
in that DP and UPC allegiance consistently followed denominational
lines, and this was exacerbated by bitter disputes over schools between
the two churches in the early years of independence.[30]

For much of this crucial period in the formation of local political identities, Luwum was absent from Acholi. But his position in
Kampala meant that he had to deal with many of the problems that
politics created for the life of the church as a national institution, at
a particularly important and fractious time. The Church of Uganda
was locked in a bitter internal wrangle about the respective merits
of a loose autonomous structure or a centralized one for the Province.[31]
Luwum was Provincial Secretary at the crucial period between 1966
and 1969 which saw the exile of the Kabaka, the abolition of the
monarchies, and the discussions about a constitution for the Church
of Uganda proposed in the 1969 Bikangaga Report. As the executive officer of the Province, Luwum was particularly identified in the
eyes of many Baganda Anglicans with Obote's attempts to smash
Buganda's autonomy. Bikangaga proposed a much stronger centralized structure for the church. It included a plan to create a diocese
of Kampala, carved out of Namirembe diocese (whose cathedral was
the 'mother church' of Buganda). This would become the see of the
archbishop. The plans were seen by many Baganda as autocratic
and centralizing measures, mirroring the state attacks on Buganda's
integrity. Equally controversial was the proposal to set up a department of Church Commissioners to administer church land. Since

[29] Interview with Canon Wilson Okaka, Lira, 5 March 1999.
[30] See Leys, 1967, for an illuminating account of the operation of politics at local
level in Acholi in the immediate post-independence period.
[31] For a discussion of this see K. Ward, 'The Church of Uganda amidst Conflict',
in H. Hansen and M. Twaddle (eds.), *Religion and Politics in East Africa*, London,
James Currey, 1995.

most of this was situated within Buganda, the proposal was interpreted as a stratagem for alienating land from the Kingdom of
Buganda. Land issues have always been extremely sensitive. As the
veteran Muganda churchman and politician E.M.K. Mulira put it,
this was a 'UPC mobilizing constitution'.[32] According to John Sentamu's
testimony, Luwum, while he was Provincial Secretary, was keen on
the idea of a separate diocese for Kampala.[33] There were many practical reasons for this view: the fact that Archbishop Sabiiti resided
in Fort Portal had caused considerable inconvenience and difficulties
for Luwum as Provincial Secretary, especially when political crises
needed attention. But it did not help his standing among his fellow
Anglicans in Buganda.

Luwum as Bishop of Northern Uganda 1969–1974

On 25 January 1969 Luwum was consecrated Bishop of Northern
Uganda in the Pece stadium in Gulu. President Obote and General
Amin both attended, along with the leading UPC politicians of Acholi.
For Obote this was an important opportunity to hold a rally. In an
increasingly divided and faction-ridden party, he needed to assert
central control over the regional élites, and to demonstrate to all in
Acholi, both supporters and detractors, the power of the ruling party,
its ability to get things done. The recently constructed stadium was
a good example of how a local community could gain from a positive relation to central government. Some church people were rather
upset by the highjacking of a religious ceremony for party political
ends. The veteran missionary Phoebe Cave Brown Cave wrote: 'It
seems to me that the church can serve the country best by truly
being the church, that is by putting God first and by making it clear
to the ordinary people of the land that they are doing so.'[34]

Luwum, with his Revivalist background, might be expected to
sympathize with that point of view. On the other hand, he could

---

[32] Such sentiments were well expressed to the author by Mulira on a number of
occasions, and are contained in his (unpublished) manuscript on the History of
Namirembe diocese. 'Mobilization' was a word much used by Obote, signifying the
utilization of manpower and resources for national rather than factional or purely
regional purposes.
[33] Sentamu, in Chandler, p. 151.
[34] Phoebe Cave Brown Cave to Archbishop Sabiiti, 2.12.69 in NA, Archbishops'
Papers, Box 10 File 141.

not ignore local political realities in the way that a veteran missionary was free to do. There was a strong body of prominent Acholi, not least in Kampala, who were determined to milk the event for all its political worth. Luwum's friend, Erinayo Oryema, Inspector General of Police in Kampala, was the chief organizer of the events in Pece stadium.[35]

Luwum was the third bishop of the diocese of Northern Uganda, which had been created out of the old Upper Nile diocese in 1961. His immediate predecessor was Silvanus Wani, who on the further division of the diocese chose to become bishop of Madi and West Nile. Northern Uganda diocese remained a large unit, lacking in cohesion, and bristling with organizational difficulties. Lango (which formed an archdeaconry) was very keen to have its own diocese, for which it campaigned vigorously throughout Luwum's episcopate. But this was resisted by Acholi. Lango was the more successful and prosperous part of the diocese, and its departure would leave an even weaker and more impoverished Acholi remnant. Lango Anglicans eventually did get their own diocese in 1976, but the financial arrangements for the division left a bitter taste, and Lango tended to blame Luwum for the niggardly settlement. Moreover, no sooner was Melchizedek Otim appointed bishop of the new diocese than he was forced into exile in the aftermath of Luwum's murder.[36] Even in Acholi proper, there were tensions between East and West Acholi (Kitgum and Gulu), and between the dominant clans of each area, Payira and Pajule. Luwum was an easterner from near Kitgum, but his diocesan centre was in Gulu. The apportionment of diocesan jobs between the two areas was always a delicate matter.[37] These tensions and divisions, while persistent, should not be exaggerated. The diocese was weak and under-resourced, in finance and personnel, and effective leadership was bound to be problematic. But Luwum was seen to possess good social and pastoral skills, enabling him to gain the respect of different people. As a moderate Revivalist, com-

---

[35] Ford, p. 37.

[36] See Michael Nyalo Opiyo 'The Formation of Lango Diocese and her Relationship to Northern Uganda (Acholi) Diocese', dissertation for Makerere University Diploma in Theology, 1978.

[37] The leader of the Mothers Union, from West Acholi, complained about Luwum giving jobs to relatives, but he received strong support from the rest of his diocesan council.

mitted to both church and fellowship, he was particularly sensitive
to the need to represent impartially all sections of the church.

The Church and the Amin Take-over 1971–4

On 25 January 1971, two years to the day after Luwum's consecration, Amin staged his coup, and immediately Acholi began to
suffer the consequences. Soldiers in the barracks around Kampala
were the first victims.[38] Obote had vastly expanded the army in the
1960s in response to the successive crises he faced. He came to rely
primarily on Acholi and Lango soldiers, and also promoted people
from these areas to high positions. This in turn created a climate of
resentment among the Nubi and West Nile section of the army, with
which Amin identified.[39] In addition, prominent Acholi businessmen
and intellectuals were soon at risk, especially after the failure of the
invasion of September 1972. Simply to be Acholi was dangerous, to
have been actively involved in the UPC even more so. Gulu gaol
began to swell with political prisoners. Both in Acholi and in Kampala,
Luwum became involved in tracing the whereabouts of prisoners,
bargaining for their release and comforting the relatives when bodies were discovered or people simply disappeared. A poignant letter
from a clergyman in Acholi, written to Amin (and copied to the
Bishop) illustrates this:

> I am deeply sorrowful following the arrest and disappearance of my
> son and I have had conflicting reports about him and this is adding
> more sorrow in my house. We would like your Government to tell us
> where our son might be and also who may have arrested him.[40]

Luwum was a key figure in alerting the church as a whole to this
situation and in persuading the Anglican Bishops to write confidentially
to the President about those who had disappeared. Three months
after Amin came to power, they wrote:

---

[38] Louise Pirouet, 'Religion in Uganda under Amin' in *Journal of Religion in Africa*,
XI.1, 1980, p. 17.
[39] H. Hansen, *Ethnicity and Military Rule in Uganda*, Uppsala, Scandinavian Institute
of African Studies, 1977.
[40] NA, Archbishops' Papers, Box 33 File 3. 'Northern Uganda Diocese'. Letter
of Archdeacon of Acholi, 31.1.1972.

... we want to pledge our loyalty and support in the government and
development of our country. It is the duty of the Church in every
country to be the right hand of Government, to pray for it, to cooperate with it in all things that are right in the sight of God, and to
advise it of anything that seems to be wrong in the sight of God.

We are writing at a time when many have been killed; many are
missing (including our two chaplains, the Revd. Captain Henry Ogwal
and the Revd. Captain Yosamu Olit); many are in fear of death; and
many others are in detention (including the head of our own Secretariat,
the Revd. Yona Okoth, who your secretary stated when the Archbishop
saw you had been released). Very humbly, and very conscious of our
own faults and weaknesses, we beg you to consider what is happening in the country and to use your authority to put a stop to what
we believe to be an evil in the sight of God. We beg you this for
three reasons:

1) for the sake of those who are suffering;

2) for the sake of Your Excellency yourself; and your Government,
whose popularity and good name are suffering as a result of these hap-
penings;

3) for the sake of the peace and prosperity and development of the
country as a whole, because whilst the land is in fear and trembling
it cannot go forward.

We realise that perhaps it may be necessary for a few people still
to be detained, but we ask Your Excellency to dispel the fear and
anxiety of so many of your people and to publish the names of such.[41]

A few months later a similar letter was sent by the bishops concerning the number of people fleeing into exile:

We submit that one of the big causes of this feeling of fear and insecurity is the fact that bands of indisciplined soldiers are roaming about
the country harassing and killing people, even including some of our
priests. Another of the causes ... is that people continue to remain in
detention for many months without trial, and even a list of their names
is not available.[42]

Dick Lythe, Bishop of Kigezi, wrote to Archbishop Sabiiti drawing
the parallel to the struggle of the German church against Nazism:
'When the Jews were persecuted in Germany before the War the
Christians failed to raise their voice in protest, and that failure has
gone in history to their shame'.[43]

---

[41] NA, Archbishops' Papers, Box 8, File 120 'Change of Govt.' Bishops to Amin
26.4.71.

[42] NA, Archbishops' Papers, Box 8, File 120, undated letter, possibly 22.10.71.

[43] NA, Archbishops' Papers, Box 10 File 138. 'Govt 1972'. Letter 9.8.1972. Lythe
was about to retire. His successor was Bishop Festo Kivengere.

Despite this early recognition of the evils of the new regime, one of the factors that tempered opposition was the fact that the coup brought tangible benefits to the Anglican Church in respect of its own severe ecclesiastical divisions. The two Buganda dioceses (Namirembe and West Buganda) were threatening to secede from the rest of the Province because of their unhappiness at attempts to impose the new centralized constitution.[44] There was a sense of gratitude when Amin's government brokered a reconciliation between the opposing groups. Even in western Uganda, the Bishop of Ankole, Amos Betungura, spoke of the relief from political bickering and infighting that the new regime had brought to his region.[45] But this was before the abortive invasion by Obote supporters in September 1972. Political killings, revenge attacks and disappearances then became a recurring feature of life in South West Uganda as they had been in the North from the beginning.

Luwum as Archbishop and the Plot against Amin

Luwum was elected archbishop in May 1974, on the retirement of Erica Sabiiti. Despite his Acholi origin, Luwum was probably more congenial to General Amin than Sabiiti had been. Sabiiti was the son of a prominent member of the traditional Ankole establishment, in stark contrast to Amin's marginal status. Amin and Luwum could speak together in Lwo, a language widely used in the army. Luwum went out of his way to establish and retain personal contacts with Amin. He also had access to government through his fellow Acholi, Lt. Col. Erinayo Oryema, a particular friend from school days. Oryema was appointed Minister of Land and Water Resources by Amin. Another cabinet minister was Charles Oboth-Ofumbi, from Eastern Uganda, a Japadhola. He had been the first post-independence District Commissioner of Acholi.[46] Luwum used these contacts assiduously, both on behalf of particular individuals in trouble and to attempt to restrain and, at times, to admonish Amin. When the

---

[44] Ward, 1995.

[45] NA, Archbishops' Papers, Box 19 File 213. 'Ankole'. Speech of welcome made during a visit of President Amin to Mbarara, August 1971.

[46] See letter of J.P. Twining, District Commissioner of Acholi District, to Archbishop Leslie Brown, 16.2.1963 in NA, Archbishops' Papers, Box 3 File 33 'Northern Uganda Diocese'.

young John Sentamu expressed some disquiet at the seeming close-
ness between the Bishop and the General, Luwum put it this way:

> My real concern is for the Church of Uganda to provide a guiding
> and steady hand on this erratic government. . . . Whenever I have the
> opportunity I have told the President the things the Church disap-
> proves of.[47]

The first year or so after Luwum's appointment as archbishop were
relatively quiet; the frenetic killings of the early years of the regime
had passed. But in 1976 a series of events raised the tensions again:
trouble at the university, including the killing of Esther Chesire and
Theresa Mukasa-Bukenya, conflicts between Muslims and Christians
in Ankole, the Entebbe raid by Israel and its aftermath. A meeting
of religious leaders of Catholic, Anglican and Muslim communities
was convened in August 1976 to explore ways of making joint representation about the state of the country. Amin was a Muslim, yet
Muslims were subject to disappearances and killings and Muslim religious leaders were also disquieted by the state terror. But it was the
churches and their increasingly vocal popular support that particularly alarmed Amin. When, early in 1976, Archbishop Emmanuel
Nsubuga returned from Rome after being made Cardinal, there had
been an outburst of popular enthusiasm. The Church of Uganda
was preparing for its centenary in June 1977, many foreign dignitaries were to be invited, and a project to build Church House, an
administrative centre in Kampala, was launched. Amin's animosity
to the churches grew in proportion to their renewed popularity.
Christmas was 'abolished' as a public holiday in 1976, and Archbishop
Luwum's Christmas sermon from All Saint's Cathedral, Kampala,
was cut off in mid-broadcast.

At the end of January 1977 the Anglican hierarchy went to Bushenyi
for the consecration of Yoramu Bamunoba as the first bishop of the
new diocese of West Ankole. Security men from the State Research
Bureau, conspicuous in their dark glasses, attended. Bushenyi was a
particularly sensitive place because it was the heartland of UPC support in western Uganda, strongly associated with Obote (he was to
choose Bushenyi to make his return by plane from exile in 1980).
Bishop Festo Kivengere preached a powerful sermon warning gov-

---

[17] John Sentamu, 'Archbishop Janani Luwum', p. 153.

ernment officials of their moral duties before God: 'How are you using your authority? . . . To crush men's faces into the dust?'[48]

Bamunoba's consecration occurred on 30 January, just a few days after the anniversary of Amin's coup. Around this time a conspiracy to overthrow Amin was uncovered by the security forces. It was thought to involve a number of Acholi and Lango in Kampala who had links with Obote, now in exile in Dar es Salaam. At 1.30 a.m. on Saturday 5 February the security forces raided the Archbishop's house on Namirembe Hill. A Langi businessman, Ben Ongom, badly beaten up, was forced to accompany them. Ongom had apparently confessed to receiving a large cache of arms from Obote, some of which had been found at his home, some of which he had distributed to others. The security forces were now looking for the other deposits. They searched the Archbishop's house and grounds without finding anything. In the morning, when the Archbishop tried to contact the President, using the special number he had, Amin was 'unavailable'.[49] The following day, the home of Bishop Yona Okoth in Bukedi, eastern Uganda, was also searched.

In this crisis the House of Bishops, hastily convened, sent an open letter to the President, with copies to other religious leaders, Christian and Muslim, and to government ministers. Couched in the respectful form of the earlier letters of 1971/72, this was nevertheless a hard-hitting indictment of the regime. The attack on the Archbishop's residence became a symbol for the invasion of property and human rights suffered by all Ugandans:

> The gun whose muzzle has been pressed against the Archbishop's stomach, the gun which has been used to search the Bishop of Bukedi's house is a gun which is being pointed at every Christian in the Church.

The use of 'Christian' rather than 'Ugandan' was not accidental, in that the next paragraph goes on to mention religious persecution of Christians specifically:

---

[48] Personal observation, based on my attendance at this occasion. For the quotation, see Anne Coomes, *Festo Kivengere*, Eastbourne, Monarch Publications, 1990, p. 356.

[49] AACC Newsletter, 'Special Edition: The Churches Mourn the Loss of Archbishop', a collection of documents produced as a Newsletter of the All Africa Conference Of Churches, 23 February 1977: Luwum's 'report of a very serious incident' in the early hours of Saturday 5th February 1977. Copy in the author's possession.

> While it is common in Uganda for members of one family to be mem-
> bers of different religious organizations there is an increasing feeling
> that one particular religious organization is being favoured more than
> any other. So much so that in some parts of Uganda members of
> Islam who are in leading positions are using these positions to coerce
> Christians into becoming Muslims.

While this was not simply an imaginary grievance, one wonders at
the advisability of bringing up the question of religious difference,
in the face of all the other injustices and insecurities endured by
every section of Uganda. The letter returned to these larger themes
in criticising the members of the Security Forces: 'When they begin
to use the gun in their hands to destroy instead of protecting the
civilian, then the relationship of mutual trust and respect is destroyed.
Instead of that relationship you have suspicion, fear and hidden
hatred.'[50]

Amin summoned Luwum to State House on Monday 14 February.
He went, accompanied by his wife. The President disclosed that
eleven boxes of arms had been discovered in Kampala, another cache
in Gulu, and yet another near the home of Bishop Okoth. Allegations
were made that arms were also found near the Archbishop's residence. According to the Uganda Radio report, Amin gave details of
an Obote-inspired conspiracy. It was, he claimed, directed specifically
against Catholics, and against all Ugandans who were not Lango or
Acholi. On the other hand, Obote was said not to target Muslims,
'because he had already managed to confuse them when he was still
in power', and did not regard them as a serious threat.

> For the Protestants, he aimed at killing all the Bishops except the
> Langis and Acholis, who he would put in all other dioceses. Other
> victims high on the list were the Baganda, because, according to the
> documents which the Archbishop himself agreed upon, they are the
> most difficult people, because they do not want people of other tribes
> to be bishops for Namirembe Cathedral.[51]

This was a caricature of Uganda's religious and ethnic divisions, but
sufficiently close to the mark to be highly explosive. The Bishops
again assembled and on the morning of Wednesday 16 February

---

[50] AACC Newsletter 23.2.77, Letter from the House of Bishops to President
Amin, 10 February 1977.
[51] AACC Newsletter 23.2.77, 'Amin Charges the Archbishop', transcript of Uganda
Broadcasting Corporation report of meeting between the President and the Archbishop.

prepared a response. They refuted all allegations of being involved in smuggling or hoarding arms as 'dangerous fabrications' and stressed the church's patriotism. 'Our Church carries no guilt for the damage of the name of Uganda.'[52] By then they had been summoned to the Lugogo stadium in Kampala, where Luwum and other conspirators were denounced. Luwum was separated from the other bishops and arrested. The next morning Uganda Radio announced his death 'in a car accident' in which the two Lwo ministers, Oryema and Oboth-Ofumbi, also died. 'The spokesman said the accident occurred when the three men were trying to overcome Major Moses in order to escape. Major Moses was taken to hospital where he is still unconscious.'[53] The story was received with universal disbelief.

The Burial

A grave was prepared in the grounds of Namirembe Cathedral. But the body was not released, nor was a memorial service allowed by the government. Thousands instead gathered for the main Sunday morning service on 20 February. The writer attended this extraordinary service. No mention was made of the Archbishop, apart from a brief factual announcement of his death during the notices. Bishop John Wasikye, who had been a student with Luwum at Buwalasi College, preached the sermon. He urged fortitude in difficult times but without referring to the events of the past few days. My recollection is of an unbearable tension in the cathedral. With no outlet for grief, the congregation filed out of the cathedral with a tremendous sense of unresolved emotion. The organist began to play the Martyrs' hymn *Bulijjo Tutendereza* (*Daily, daily sing the praises*), which, it is believed, the young Baganda Christian martyrs sang on their way to execution some ninety years before. The congregation began to sing the familiar words, and soon the whole church resounded with the hymn. People gathered around the empty tomb and the retired Archbishop addressed the crowd. For the first time the death

---

[52] AACC Newsletter 23.2.77, 'A Prepared Response of the House of Bishops of the C.O.U.-Rwanda—Burundi and Boga-Zaire to his Excellency on Wednesday 16th February 1977, in the Conference Centre in Kampala'.

[53] AACC Newsletter 23.2.77, 'Archbishop Luwum, Two Government Ministers Killed in "motor accident"—Radio Uganda says'.

of Luwum was openly acknowledged and proper tribute made. Pointing to the empty grave, Sabiiti proclaimed: '"He [Christ] is not here, he is risen." Janani also has gone to be with the risen Lord. We too should be willing to die for our faith.'[54]

John Sentamu states that the body has never been found and that Luwum never received a Christian burial. This is incorrect. Sentamu, a student at Cambridge at the time, is relying on his memory of the confused reports coming out of Uganda.[55] In fact, by the time Christians in Kampala were gathering for the Sunday service of 20 February and staring into the empty grave, Janani Luwum had already been buried, near the church in his home village of Mucwini. I visited Kitgum district in 1999 and Baker Ocholla, Bishop of Kitgum, took me to visit the grave. It was a doubly poignant experience. On the way, we passed the place where the bishop's wife had been killed in a landmine explosion in 1997. At Mucwini, we stood in front of the simple grave marked with the name of Janani Luwum. The bishop, and local people who had gathered at the graveside, told this story. The body was driven north to Mucwini in a government vehicle. Stopping at the family home, the soldiers instructed the people to bury the body there and then. But Janani's mother refused: 'he died for the church; take him to the church'. At the church, the soldiers repeated their demands for a quick burial. Several attempts were made to dig a grave. But in each case the ground proved too stony. As night began to fall the soldiers got impatient, and when at last an appropriate place had been found, but before the digging had been completed, they left the body in the church and drove away. Some mourners were thus able to open the coffin cautiously. They confirmed that it was indeed the Archbishop, that the body was wounded and mutilated (perhaps for ritual purposes, it was surmised) and that he had been shot in the head, mouth and stomach.[56]

The substance of this story is confirmed by an eye-witness report deposited in the Namirembe archives and written in the early 1980s (after Amin's fall) by Luwum's elder brother, Aloni Okecho. According to this account (original spellings), the body arrived at his home from

---

[54] These observations are based on the author's memory of the day, and also on a conversation with Stephen Tirwomwe.
[55] Sentamu, p. 156.
[56] Visit to Mucwini with Bishop Ocholla 24.3.1999.

Madi Opei barracks at 10 am. Okecho directed them to the church. There was a heavy military escort.

> This gave a frightening aspect all over Mucwini... They were hurrying us to bury the body as it was the order from the President. We told them we couldn't bury him until the widow of the late Archbishop and members of his family were all around.... It was very difficult to dig the grave. Three times when they tried it was so stonny. It was after we tried the 4th place when the grave was ready. He was buried on Saturday 19 February 1977 at 3.30 pm. Before he was buried, five of us secretly examined the cofin to prove the body and what caused his death.

They confirmed that it was the body of the late Archbishop. He had gunshots on abdomen, neck and chest. He had a knife-cut on the back and a bruise on the forehead. The groin area was bandaged up. The soldiers subsequently returned to ensure that the burial took place.

> Many songs of praises were sung, and many songs for funeral were sung. I was filled with the holy spirit and with my trumphet I preached to the soldiers and told them that it was common they kell but the words of God cannot be destroyed. I told them they had better turn away from their sinful way and beleive in the Lord so that their sins could be forgiven.

The 'trumpet' was the homemade megaphone with which the Revival brethren were accustomed to preach in their open air missions. In April, Okecho was visited by the local Commissioner of Police and some CID officials who took statements and asked if the government could assume financial responsibility for the family. Okecho could not speak for the immediate family, but, for himself, he refused: '[S]ince he [Luwum] was serving God for the rest of his life, and since he died a faithful servant and because the words of God could not be bought for money, I would not take any money from them.'[57]

The Penalty for Opposition

There was never any doubt that Luwum had been brutally murdered by a brutal regime. The Bishops, protesting the innocence of

---

[57] NA, Archbishops' Papers, Box 20, File 217. 'Bishop of Northern Uganda'.

the Archbishop, denied that the church had been involved in any plot to assassinate Amin. They lost little time in choosing a new Archbishop, elected in April 1977. He was Silvanus Wani, Luwum's predecessor in Gulu, a Kakwa from Koboko, Amin's own home area. Some six years older than Luwum, Wani was also a member of the moderate wing of the Revival movement that worked for co-operation with the institutional church. Wani had been a soldier in the King's African Rifles during the Second World War, and later, as Bishop, became chaplain-general to the Ugandan army. His popularity within the army may have been seen as a safeguard against another assault on the church leadership. Wani was felt to be someone who could talk to Amin in his own language (to an even greater extent than Luwum). It was hoped that Amin might respect Wani as an elder of the Kakwa people. Like Luwum, Wani was seen as having a pastoral sensitivity and big heartedness.[58] In June 1977 he led the Church of Uganda through its centenary celebrations, which Amin made a great show of supporting. Wani was Archbishop when Amin was overthrown, and endured some difficult years of innuendo and harassment: a victim of the anarchy and the political power struggle, which the fall of Amin created. He retired in 1983.[59]

Had Luwum become involved in a plot to overthrow Amin in 1976–7? There is general agreement that there was a plot: it was not simply concocted by Amin. It is unlikely that there will ever be documentary proof one way or the other of Luwum's complicity. The historian, Phares Mutibwa, feels that Luwum, with his intimate contacts in the Kampala Acholi community, would have had some knowledge of the conspiracy. Amin's own security service certainly did get to know of it through its extensive network of informers, which suggests that it was not a tightly guarded secret known only to a very small number. But it seems unlikely that Luwum was at the centre of the plot. Amin may have been incensed that Luwum,

---

[58] Samuel Kermu, 'The Life and Times of Bishop Silvanus G. Wani', ATIEA BD degree, 1987.

[59] Kermu, interestingly, basing his view on an interview with John Wani, the son of Silvanus, is of the opinion that Amin himself was not happy with Wani's appointment because of his popularity among the West Nile troops. Kermu also notes the severe difficulties that Wani faced in the aftermath of Amin's overthrow, by prominent members of the incoming UNLA army, who resented the fact that he was a West Niler.

with whom he had developed a close working relationship, had known about it and yet kept silent.[60]

In the mid 1990s, a researcher, Zak Niringiye, went to Lira in Lango, and interviewed Caroline Ongom, the widow of Ben Ongom, the man who had been forced to accompany the security forces to the Archbishop's house. Caroline told how her husband had been arrested several times when Amin came to power: he was imprisoned in Makindye barracks in March 1971, and re-arrested in September 1971 in the aftermath of the failed invasion. Released in 1973 he spent two years in hiding, before living openly at home in the Bukoto suburb of Kampala from 1975. He judged the tensions to have died down somewhat and the danger of being picked up to be less. Niringiye interviewed another of Ongom's relatives, who wished to remain anonymous. He confirmed that Ongom had been arrested on 1 February when arms were found at his home. A fellow Langi, Abdulla Anyuru (who had been chairman of the Public Service Commission) was arrested at the same time. According to this account, Ongom had been in regular contact with Obote in Dar, and Luwum had visited Ongom's home on a number of occasions in the weeks before the discovery of the plot.[61]

Ben Ongom remained under arrest after the death of the Archbishop and was shot by public firing squad in September 1977. His 28-year-old wife saw him in court shortly before he was killed. 'He told me that it was OK to die. They had burnt his fingers, all his toes, mouth and private parts. You could not recognise him. He said it was OK for him to die as he would not be useful if he lived. I had gone with my sister. This was the last time [I saw him]. Although I went to Kampala for the firing squad, I could not have courage to watch him.'[62]

Niringiye's evidence of Luwum's involvement is circumstantial and inconclusive. Luwum definitely had close relations with the Acholi and Lango community in Kampala. But it seems unlikely that the plotters would have wanted to implicate him directly by asking him

---

[60] Phares Mutibwa, *Uganda since Independence: A Story of Unfulfilled Hopes*, London, Hurst, 1993, p. 112.

[61] David Zak Niringiye, 'The Church in the World: A Historical-Ecclesiological Study of the COU with Particular Reference to Post-Independence Uganda 1962–1992', Edinburgh University, Ph.D. dissertation, December 1997.

[62] Niringiye, 1997.

to hide guns in his house. Such a situation would undoubtedly have been difficult for the Archbishop to reconcile with his position as leader of a church that had long traditions of loyalty to the state and the government of the day, or with his spiritual roots in the Balokole Revival movement. It is possible to justify a decision actively to participate in the violent overthrow of a regime as savage and oppressive as Amin's. On the other hand, within Uganda there remain decidedly ambivalent feelings about a plot that sought to bring back Milton Obote. This is eventually what did happen in 1980, after eighteen months of very messy political wrangling whose main purpose was precisely to pave the way for Obote's return. During this interim period, looting and killings were every bit as common as in Amin's time, and insecurity considerably worse. Under Obote II (1980–85), killings and disruption in the Luwero triangle (within Buganda and to the north and west of Kampala) were on an even greater scale. It is this outcome that makes the circumstances of Luwum's murder in 1977 acutely problematic.

Bishop Yona Okoth narrowly managed to escape Amin's assassins in 1977 and went into exile. He returned in 1979 and was appointed Archbishop in 1983. As an outspoken supporter of Obote and UPC, his election was seen, at least in Buganda, as politically motivated. His perceived failure to speak out against the Luwero situation further compromised him. In 1985 Obote was again overthrown, and Archbishop Okoth's position became extremely difficult. He was accused of being a leading agent of a putative organization called FOBA, whose aim was to 'Force Obote Back Again'! In this over-heated, conspiratorial atmosphere there was little understanding of, or patience with, attempts to commemorate the tenth anniversary of Luwum's death.[63]

On the other hand, the Acholi people equally felt let down. The defeat of an Acholi-dominated army (the Uganda National Liberation Army) by Museveni's National Resistance Army in 1986 was a profound blow to Acholi pride and self-esteem. There was a determination not to allow the situation of 1971 to recur, when Acholi had allowed themselves to become the helpless victims of Amin's murder machine. Unfortunately, the resistance inspired by Lakwena's

---

[63] I alluded to this occasion in Ward, 1995, p. 85.

Holy Spirit Movement and Joseph Kony's Lord's Resistance Army has proved even more catastrophic and devastating.[64]

A general consensus about the significance of Luwum's assassination thus continues to elude Ugandans. There have been suggestions that the Archbishop's body be brought from Mucwini and buried with fitting honours at Namirembe, the metropolitan cathedral of the Church of Uganda. But the family have been unwilling to grant this, partly because there is a sense that the church as an institution is failing to fulfil its responsibilities to the family of a man who died for his faith at the age of 54, defending the church and Uganda against tyranny. As long as the war goes on in the North it seems unlikely that Acholi generally would consent to removing his remains to the care of a South which seems so patently unable or unwilling to integrate Northern Uganda into the political and cultural life of the nation. There is an annual commemoration in London of Janani Luwum's death, which is an important focus for the Acholi community resident in Britain.[65]

Writing soon after Luwum's death, Adrian Hastings pointed out how so devout a prayer as the Revival hymn *Tukutendereza* 'could become in the circumstances of Amin's Uganda, by the empty grave of the archbishop outside Namirembe Cathedral, a timeless statement with unambiguously timely implications.'[66] However painful the memories and however contested the political terrain, Ugandans continue to be moved profoundly by the manner of Luwum's death and its character as Christian witness. On our visit to Mucwini in March 1999, Bishop Ocholla outlined his hopes for a great educational centre on the broad hill top where Janani Luwum is buried, a centre which, in a time of reconstruction, can potentially provide new hope and practical benefit for the people of Northern Uganda, and a fitting legacy for a great archbishop of the Church of Uganda as a whole.[67]

---

[64] Cf. Heike Behrend, *Alice Lakwena and the Holy Spirits: War in Northern Uganda 1986–97*, Oxford, James Currey, 1999.

[65] This was initiated by Revd. Modicum Okello, an Anglican clergyman in London. The author was present on Janani Luwum Day on 20 February 2000, when over 200 people attended a service in St John's Church, Stratford, in East London. Bishop John Sentamu was the preacher.

[66] Hastings, 1979, p. 266.

[67] Visit by the author to Mucwini, 24 March 1999.

Abbreviations

NA	The Namirembe Archives, the central archive collection of the Church of Uganda on Namirembe Hill, Kampala.
AACC	The All Africa Council of Churches, Nairobi.

CHAPTER EIGHT

PENTECOSTALISM AND NEO-TRADITIONALISM: THE RELIGIOUS POLARIZATION OF A RURAL DISTRICT IN SOUTHERN MALAWI*

Matthew Schoffeleers

'In the past traditionalists would worship peacefully, but nowadays they spit at Jesus!'
(An African church leader, Nsanje, 4.1.1982)

When Malawi gained its independence from Great Britain in 1964, its southernmost district, Nsanje, possessed a religious system famil-
iar in a great many rural areas in Black Africa. Most people still described themselves as adherents of the ancestral religion, and Christians by and large participated in both their own and the ancestral system without sensing much discrepancy. In the 1970s, how-
ever, that situation changed radically, as relations between Christianity and traditional religion polarized, even to the point of occasional physical violence. The immediate cause of this rather unexpected development was the introduction of two sharply antagonistic religious movements: on the one hand, a number of Pentecostalist bodies from outside Malawi, and on the other, a neo-traditionalist move-
ment, called the Church of the Ancestors, that had originated within the country.

This process of increasing sectionalism will be examined in this chapter against the background both of the major social and economic changes that took place in Nsanje during the twentieth cen-
tury, and of a widely disseminated nationalist ideology. It will be argued that these outbreaks of violent conflict are to be regarded as the most recent in a long series of attempts to re-define and re-
arrange relationships between old and young, men and women, and

---

* Editors' note: the research on which this chapter is based was undertaken in the early 1980s and references to the present indicate that period. The notes and bibliography have been updated in places.

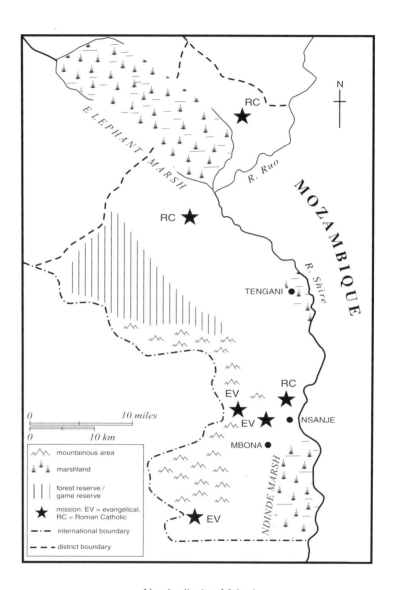

Nsanje district, Malawi

between the different economic strata in the district. National development policies have directly influenced this process: materially, by introducing or supporting measures which led to a sharp increase in differential access to goods, land and money; ideologically, by simultaneously promoting a traditional and a modern ethic, thus providing both sides in the conflict with what they considered an official legitimation of their doctrinal position.

The Economic and Religious Background

With the exception of its northern boundary, Nsanje is completely surrounded by Mozambique (see map). Its length from north to south is ninety kilometres; its width varies from ten to forty kilometres. It forms part of the Shire Valley, a hot, low-lying area, which itself is an extension of the Mozambican coastal plain. Most of the population, which in 1977 stood at 113,333, inhabits and cultivates the valley floor.

Until the late nineteenth century the population consisted mostly of Mang'anja, a matrilineally organized, Chewa-speaking people, whose forebears had lived there since the sixteenth century.[1] During the colonial era they were joined by large numbers of patrilineally organized immigrants from Mozambique who, though belonging to a variety of culturally different groups, are collectively known as 'Sena' after the town of that name on the south bank of the Zambezi. The Mang'anja have to a great extent adopted the Sena system of kinship and marriage, but the two groups have never entirely merged, mainly because the Mang'anja continued to consider themselves the rightful owners of the land (*eni dziko*) and sole claimants to a number of important religious and secular positions.[2]

The economic history of the district from 1900 onwards shows three distinct phases. In the first, which lasted from 1904 to the late 1930s, the economy was dominated by the commercial growing of cotton, mostly on a smallholder basis.[3] By the early 1930s Africans

---

[1] Tew 1950, pp. 30–50; Schoffeleers 1972.

[2] Thus, it is to be noted that of the six chieftaincies in the district none is held by an immigrant family. The same goes for senior headmanships and prestigious positions in the Mbona cult (section 2).

[3] Colman and Garbett 1973.

in the valley were cultivating approximately 8,000 hectares (20,000 acres), and by 1935 this had increased to 15,500 hectares (62,000 acres), most of it in Nsanje. The cotton-growing period ended when the sand bar at the mouth of Lake Malawi broke up in 1936, causing a sharp rise in the level of the Shire River, which continued to rise till 1939. The marshlands adjacent to the river, which had been prime cotton land, were permanently flooded, and some 48,000 hectares (120,000 acres) were lost to production. The flooding affected about 20,000 people, many of whom moved into the Chikwawa District in the northern part of the valley. Within a few years cotton production in Nsanje had virtually ceased, and the area became depressed and overpopulated in relation to the cultivable land remaining after the floods.[4]

The second phase, which lasted from the second world war to the early 1970s, was marked by a high increase in circulatory labour migration, particularly to Southern Rhodesia and South Africa. Historical data on labour migration from the Shire Valley are poor and unreliable, but research by the anthropologist Kingsley Garbett on the period 1966–1972 shows that the figures for Nsanje were relatively high and then still on the increase. In 1972 a total of 9,210 men aged between fifteen and forty-nine were estimated to be working elsewhere. The numbers were highest in the southern and central parts of the district, which had been the major cotton areas and the ones where the population pressure was greatest. In one case, the chiefdom of Tengani, it was reckoned that up to 53 per cent of males in that age category had found employment away from their homes. But although the numbers continued to rise, there was a change in the direction of the labour traffic from the 1960s onwards. The demand for foreign labour in the Zambian mines had ceased. Unilaterally Declared Independence (UDI) in Rhodesia ultimately brought a sharp fall in the recruitment of foreign labour and in early 1974 recruitment in Malawi for the South African mines was ended, following a fatal air crash involving Malawian mine workers. This latter decision affected an estimated total of 700 men from the district then still in South Africa. Others continued to go to Rhodesia, but the majority sought jobs within Malawi.

---

[4] Garbett 1977.

The third phase began formally in 1973, when Nsanje became part of a major development scheme, the Shire Valley Agricultural Development Project (SVADP), which had been set up with financial aid from the International Development Association (IDA). The project was designed to increase the production of a variety of crops, develop the livestock industry and improve fishing yields. In conjunction with this, market facilities were to be improved, roads developed and conservation measures undertaken.[5] As far as Nsanje is concerned, the project apparently met with a great many problems, particularly in regard to the anticipated increase in crop production.[6] Instead, emphasis was placed on the cattle industry, for which the district appeared to be eminently suitable. Even before the project was initiated, cattle had been a favourite form of investment for the wealthier members of the community, among whom were some ex-migrant labourers. From close to 3,000 in 1955 the number of cattle had risen to over 6,000 in 1965, and to 18,000 in 1973. This development has continued, and the present number appears to be about 23,800.[7] While a success in itself, the cattle industry has created problems for smallholders, who regularly see their crops trampled and can no longer open up dry-season gardens near the river, where the animals come to drink. In addition, food gardens near the cattle trails have to be fenced in, a time-consuming activity which had formerly been unnecessary.

Data from a survey of land holdings indicate that in the southern sector of Nsanje a reduction in cultivated acreage per person of four per cent per annum has been happening at least since 1968.[8] This has in all likelihood been one of the reasons for the migration of so many people to the northern part of the district and elsewhere as evidenced by the census figures of 1977.[9] Garbett notes as a

---

[5] Shire Valley Agricultural Development Project 1975.

[6] Informants (Dec. 1981) cited several reasons for this, among them fluctuations in the world market, but the main reason was held to be the unreliable rainfall which severely limits the range of cultivable crops as well as the average yield. Even the *guar* bean, from which a valued industrial oil is extracted and which fetched relatively high prices in the late 1970s, has since then lost much of its attraction.

[7] Figures obtained from district reports and national statistics. Information provided by the Ministry of Agriculture, Nsanje (3.1.1980) showed a total figure of 22,185 pertaining to a total of 1,845 larger and smaller herds.

[8] Garbett 1977.

[9] Comparison between the figures of the national census of 1966 and 1977 shows a population decrease in some of the southern chiefdoms ranging from twelve to

further consequence of this process of land reduction that a surprisingly large number of men have sought and developed new means
of earning an additional cash income, of which the trade in fish to
the urban centres in the southern region and rural crafts (carving,
wood turning, mat making, charcoal burning, fishing, for example)
were the most significant.

The historian E.C. Mandala, who has done extensive research on
the social history of the valley, holds the opinion that the rise in
labour migration had particularly severe consequences for the women.[10]
During the cotton era they had been able to maintain a certain
degree of equality with, if not independence from, the male world,
due on the one hand to their indispensability to the production
process and on the other to a set of unwritten regulations which
assured them a fair share of the proceeds. But the decline of cotton
and the shift to labour migration drastically altered this state of
affairs. It regularly happened that a single woman, probably deserted
by her husband and no longer able to pay tax, was forced to become
the second or third wife of a wealthier man, who would use her as
a form of cheap labour. More generally, women became fully dependent on remittances from their husbands, who also decided how the
money should be spent.[11] Control over this was generally exercised
by the husband's male kinsmen, thus once again emphasizing the
woman's dependency.

This situation improved with the gradual shift from external to
internal labour migration, and more especially with the development
of small entrepreneurship, whose success often depended on the
degree of co-operation between husband and wife. But while the
condition of the younger generation has tended to improve, that of
elderly people, and particularly of elderly men, has deteriorated.
These men, who at the height of the labour migration period often
acted as recipients and investors of their sons' remittances, became
increasingly dispensable and isolated from the cash economy. Furthermore, the recent extensive migrations of families, mainly younger

thirty per cent, while in the northern chiefdom of Mlolo there had been an increase
of over eighty per cent.
[10] Mandala 1982.
[11] Garbett 1977 has computed that only a third of the migrating men either sent
home some monthly remittances or brought money home at the end of their trip.
The actual figure may, however, have been considerably higher in view of the fact
that many used to transfer their savings through unofficial channels.

ones, to other parts of the district or outside it, have deprived many elders of regular support from their younger kinsmen.

It was the category of younger men that, as a whole, gained most upon the rise of labour migration and small entrepreneurship, since they were able to disengage themselves gradually from the control of the elders.[12] Although they still needed them as supervisors of their gardens and investors of their remittances, their interdependence was now of a different kind, based on mutual agreement rather than customary practice. But even this was to decline when internal labour migration and entrepreneurship became important and the younger men became more able to supervise their own affairs.

The Religious Pattern up to the 1960s

Until the turn of the century the main religious institutions in the district were the ancestor cult at lineage level, political cults at village and chiefdom level, and the Mbona cult at regional level. The latter is a rain and fertility cult to which people turn in times of drought, flooding, locust invasions and other forms of general disaster. After 1900 two other institutions were added to this complex: missionary Christianity and spirit possession. This section pays particular attention to the missions, the Mbona cult and spirit possession.

The First Christian Initiatives

Christianity made its entry with the founding of a station of the Evangelical Mission in 1901 in the extreme south of the district, followed by a second station in 1909, a few miles west of Nsanje Township (see map).[13] Due in part to the strict conditions imposed on prospective converts, advance was at first extremely slow, there being no more than 83 Christians by 1922.[14] But this was to change drastically when the Catholic mission started operating in the district. Founded in 1921, it could already boast 270 baptisms in 1925,

---

[12] This point is also made by Mandala, who considers the emancipation of the younger men as the single most important factor in the social history between 1940 and 1960 (personal communication, July 1982).

[13] The proper name of this mission at that time was South Africa(n) General Mission (SAGM). At some later date this was changed to Africa Evangelical Fellowship (AEF), and finally to United Evangelical Church of Malawi (UECM).

[14] Murray, 1922.

a number which by the time of its golden jubilee had risen to 12,919.[15] The rivalry between the two missions led to a veritable 'school war', both parties trying to establish as many small village schools as possible. The methods used were certainly doubtful, and so were the results. In 1940, one of the Catholic missionaries could complain that

> a serious mistake has been made by applying for too many schools, 150 in all, which nobody could possibly supervise. The teachers, most of whom have received little intellectual or religious education, have behaved so badly that there are no conversions among the people. Hence the fact that one finds no more than two or three Christians in the vicinity of schools that have been in existence virtually for decades.[16]

This internecine warfare slowed down somewhat in later years, but it never vanished completely until after independence, when the school system was brought under direct government control. Little of this hostility, however, seeped through to the population as a whole. The great majority of those baptized on either side lapsed after a while, becoming to all intents and purposes indistinguishable from those who had never formally entered the church.[17]

Yet it would be a mistake to measure the influence of the missions merely by the relatively small number of people who remained practising Christians for the rest of their lives. The very fact that thousands had for a longer or shorter period been exposed to Bible and catechism resulted in Christian ideas and symbols being directly or indirectly transmitted to practically the entire population, including those who had never gone to school or church.[18] Moreover, Christianity was not, or not generally, viewed as a hostile force. Missionaries might inveigh against 'pagan' or 'superstitious' practices,

---

[15] Nsanje Catholic Parish, Baptismal Register; Anon. Rev. G. Hautvast, 'Fifty Years Catholic Mission in Nsanje: A Historical Summary, 1921–1971', unpublished manuscript, 12 pp.

[16] Diary Catholic Mission, Nsanje, period February–September, 1940.

[17] This is my personal observation from twenty months' missionary work in the district (December 1958–September 1959), and from numerous subsequent visits to the various mission stations.

[18] This was brought home to me quite vividly when I visited a village that had not seen a missionary for twenty years and that had, religiously speaking, once again become fully traditional. Yet Christian texts, set to local tunes, had remained popular and were still being transmitted to the younger generation.

as indeed they regularly did, but in Nsanje, unlike some other places, this seldom if ever led to activities aimed at physically destroying shrines or other sacred objects. It is difficult to generalize about the feelings or mood of a population over a period of more than sixty years. However, as far as Nsanje is concerned that kind of exercise is perhaps a little less hazardous because of the presence of the Mbona cult, which for centuries has been an important vehicle for the expression of popular agreement and disagreement.

The Mbona Cult

Mbona is the name of a celebrated rain-maker who is generally believed to have migrated to the district long before the arrival of the British, and whose life story exists in several versions.[19] All agree that because of his growing influence over the population he aroused the envy of the political establishment of the time, which took its revenge by having him murdered by a band of hired assassins. But soon after his death Mbona revealed himself as a powerful spirit able to grant or withhold the rains. He therefore commanded that a shrine be dedicated to him where sacrifices were to be made, and that the king provide him with a woman who would live there permanently as his wife.

Historical research, based on sixteenth- and seventeenth-century Portuguese writings in combination with oral history, leads to the conclusion that the cult in its present form originated around 1600, although its real origin may go yet further back.[20] It features a complex ritual cycle, which, apart from the annual rain sacrifice, also includes the periodic rebuilding of the shrine, every five years on average (more or less synchronized with the minor drought cycle of the area), and the induction of a new spirit-wife, which may happen at intervals of twelve years or more, depending generally on the occurrence of a major drought.[21] The cult is formally organized by village and chiefdom, thereby duplicating the traditional political organization, but it also has a powerful informal element in the person of the cult medium, who is believed to personify Mbona himself,

---

[19] Schoffeleers 1980, 1992.

[20] Cf. Schoffeleers 1978. For a description and analysis of the political constellation in and around the district c. 1600, see also Alpers 1975.

[21] Details on the cult's ritual cycle in van Binsbergen and Schoffeleers 1985, and Schoffeleers 1992.

and whose orders may overrule those of the chiefs and headmen.[22] The medium, if he is to operate successfully, must have the support of the general population, which he gains only when he is prepared to put their grievances before the chiefs. The cult thus becomes a vehicle for venting protest and dissent, particularly on the occasion of major rituals.

With regard to the symbolic aspects of the cult, there are a number of obvious parallels between Mbona and Christ, which have led people to refer to him as their 'Black Jesus' (*Yesu wakuda*). The Catholic mission largely ignored the cult, but the Evangelicals tended to see it as a challenge that needed answering, and one of their first churches was therefore built in the immediate neighbourhood of the sacred grounds. Their conviction was not shared by their faithful, however, and in due time some of their converts came to hold positions in the shrine organization, a situation which has continued to this day.[23] In this way the Mbona cult has become the main area in which differences and similarities, agreements and disagreements between the local populace and the missionaries, and between Africans and whites, were routinely expressed. The point to be made at this stage is that for the whole of the colonial period that comparison was made and continued to be made in a generally positive fashion. Mbona was not primarily conceived as antithetical but as supplementary to Christ, much as traditional religion was to Christianity and traditional medicine to modern medicine. There have been periods in which the antithetical element was on the verge of becoming dominant, but those periods were too short to create any lasting state of disaffection.[24]

Spirit Possession
The one distinctive religious institution that the immigrants from Mozambique had brought with them was a possession ritual, almost entirely confined to women. There are two variations of this, depending on whether the intruding spirit is thought to be that of a witch

---

[22] Details on the medium's role and activities in Schoffeleers 1977 and 1992.

[23] Even today, several of the more important positions in the cult organization are still occupied by practising Catholics and Protestants, none of whom sees any discrepancy in that situation.

[24] Schoffeleers 1975.

or a more benevolent kind. In the former case, the patient has to be exorcized, but in the latter she has to 'marry' the spirit and accommodate him in a shrine inside her hut.[25] Both rituals are lengthy and elaborate and require the co-operation of a number of specialists, drummers, initiated women, and neighbours who assist with the provision of food and drink. The essence in both cases is that the 'spirit is made to speak', which means that the patient is to fall into a trance and, while in that condition, make the spirit's identity and wishes known. Only then can it be 'taken out', to be either exiled to the bush or accommodated in the patient's hut.

There is evidence that possession rituals showed a steep increase in the period 1940–1970, when commercial cotton growing had almost totally collapsed and labour migration was becoming one of the principal means of earning an income. As was seen earlier, this led to a serious deterioration in the position of many women who now, more than ever before, became dependent on and subservient to their husbands. It does not therefore seem unreasonable to assume some causal connection between this and the rise of spirit possession, and to interpret the latter as a form of female reaction to this situation.[26]

One remarkable aspect of spirit possession in Nsanje is that, for one reason or another, it does not seem compatible with other cult forms. Women who undergo this ritual, and who from then on wear special protective amulets and strings of beads, feel for instance that they cannot attend church, nor are they allowed to participate in the Mbona ritual. Officials at the shrine say that its guardians cannot marry a youngish woman for fear that she may become possessed. This suggests that until recently the major contrast was not between Christianity and traditional religion, as one would be inclined to think, but between male-focused religion (of which Christianity

---

[25] Spirits of the second type are always 'male'. Extensive descriptions in Schoffeleers 1967.

[26] This is also the point made by the anthropologist I.M. Lewis in connection with the so-called peripheral possession cults, the category to which the Nsanje cults belong (Lewis 1971). Lewis may have overstated his case somewhat and as far as Nsanje is concerned it would be incorrect to see male dominance as the sole source of possession. As I have shown elsewhere (Schoffeleers 1969), the exorcistic type in Nsanje has its source rather in the problematic relations of women with their families of origin. Even so, the husband-related type of possession during the period 1940–1970 was such that the conclusion we have arrived at seems to impose itself with some force. See also Maxwell 1999, p. 202.

and the Mbona cult were prime variants) and female-focused religion (of which spirit possession was the prime variant).

Something which needs emphasis in this overview of the main religious features of the district is the complete absence of religious sectarianism and the relatively slight impact of witch eradication movements during the colonial period.[27] The district records mention only one or two attempts by Tonga preachers from the north of the country to introduce the Watch Tower movement, but these remained unsuccessful. The single most important reason why these and similar movements affected the district only superficially has probably been the unusually strong position of the chiefs. This exceptional situation in comparison with most other districts of Malawi was a consequence both of a specific history of state formation from the late sixteenth century onwards[28] and of an unusually close linkage between the local chiefs and the colonial administration.

The New Christian Churches

This picture was changed in the post-colonial period, and particularly in the 1970s, by the more or less simultaneous appearance of a whole array of new, African-led churches, which will be collectively referred to as Spirit churches on account of their Pentecostalist character, and a powerful neo-traditionalist movement, which came to oppose both the missions and the new churches. The impact of this twin process, which at its peak directly involved several thousand adults, has been such that the religious landscape of Nsanje was profoundly altered. Limitations of space do not allow discussion of all these movements in detail, nor is this necessary. The more important spirit churches form the subject of the present section, while the Ancestor movement will be discussed separately.

---

[27] On the principal witch-eradication movements which swept Malawi and the surrounding countries in colonial days, see Richards 1935 and Marwick 1950.

[28] On the history of state formation in Nsanje and adjoining areas, see Alpers 1975 and Schoffeleers 1978.

Chart 1
Aspostolic Faith and Assembly of God Churches, Nsanje District

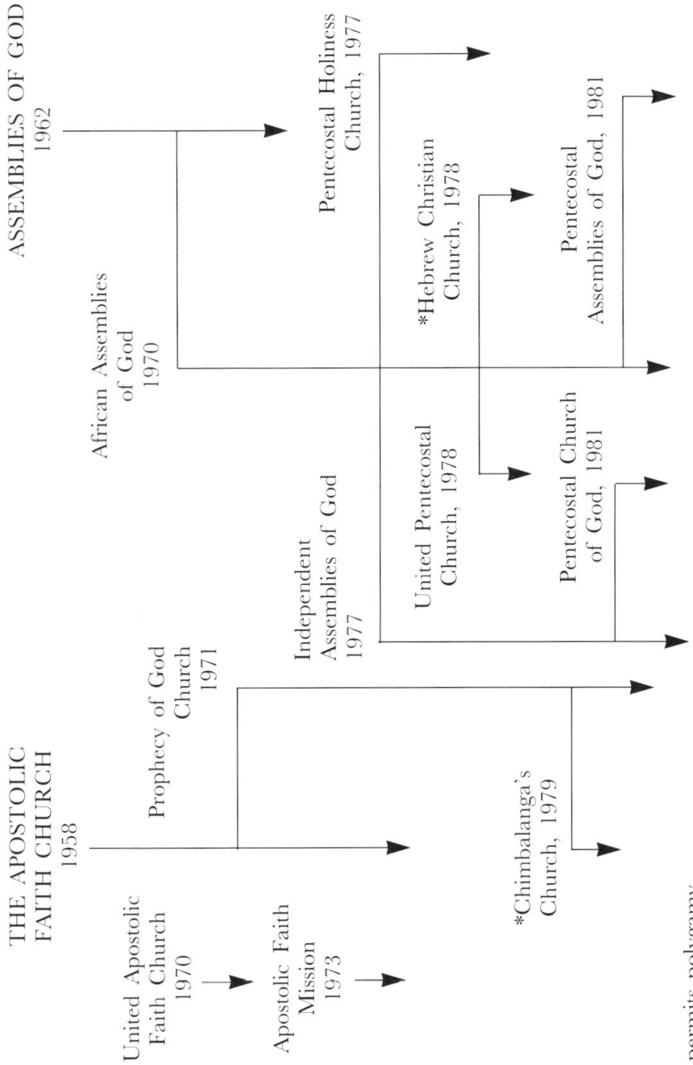

THE APOSTOLIC
FAITH CHURCH
1958

ASSEMBLIES OF GOD
1962

Prophecy of God
Church
1971

African Assemblies
of God
1970

Pentecostal Holiness
Church, 1977

United Apostolic
Faith Church
1970

Apostolic Faith
Mission
1973

Independent
Assemblies of God
1977

United Pentecostal
Church, 1978

*Hebrew Christian
Church, 1978

Pentecostal
Assemblies of God, 1981

*Chimbalanga's
Church, 1979

Pentecostal Church
of God, 1981

* = Church permits polygamy

The Apostolic Churches

The first church to be founded by Africans in the Nsanje District was the Apostolic Faith Church, which began in 1958, the year of Dr Banda's triumphant return to Malawi and of great nationalist effervescence. The church was introduced by three migrant workers, Millias Chimbalanga, J.P. Banda and W.J. Valera, who had converted to it in Bulawayo (Zimbabwe) and had subsequently been ordained ministers.[29] An offspring of Anglo-American Pentecostalism and originally brought to southern Africa by white missionaries, the Apostolic Faith Church is now fully under African leadership.

At the beginning of 1981 it claimed to have about 1,300 members of adolescent or adult age divided over thirty-four congregations, which makes it one of the largest among the new churches.[30] One of its major attractions is the reputation it has in the field of faith-healing. Therapeutic sessions are conducted both in public, as part of the church services, and in private at the home of a pastor. Those seeking to be cured must, however, be church members or persons seriously intending to join. Preachers in this church place much emphasis on man's basic sinfulness and the need to show public repentance. Those attending a service are invited openly to weep and sob, a habit which has made it popularly known as the 'weeping church' (*mpingo woliralira*).

Although only men can be pastors, the great majority of the members are women, most of whom claim to have been cured of spirit-caused diseases. The church maintains strict rules with regard to the use of tobacco and alcohol and the practice of polygamy; since social control is quite pronounced within its local congregations, serious trespassing seems to occur only rarely.

Most of the members have received at least a minimum of formal education, but few if any have gone beyond primary school, a typical example being the present leader, W.J. Valera, who left school after four years. Despite this they try to emulate the better educated with regard to housing, personal appearance and etiquette. Men

---

[29] Chakanza 1979; on Dr Banda, Malawi's first president (1964–1994), see Short 1974.

[30] Interview with Pastor M. Joglas and Mrs Valera, Chiphwembwe Village, 6.1.1980. See also Chakanza 1979, p. 91. These, however, are national figures. The number of adherents in Nsanje stood then at 242 divided over six congregations (J. Chakanza, personal communication).

make a point of appearing in church dressed in suit and tie, women come in ankle-length dresses, and children accompanying their parents to church service are well scrubbed and dressed in clean clothes. This, together with the prohibitions on drinking, smoking and polygamy, marks them out quite effectively from the mass of the population as an emergent lower middle class, intent on living up to the ideals its members have set for themselves. Many of the men are small shopkeepers, junior clerks and cash-crop farmers, who are all rather better off than mere subsistence farmers and who seem to feel attracted to a religious community which brings them into close contact with other members of their category; a community, moreover, whose ideology supports and legitimates their efforts to safeguard their economic and social positions.[31]

The second movement of this type was the United Apostolic Church, introduced in 1970 by one Nyakamera, a former teacher in the United Evangelical Church of Malawi and, at a later stage, in the Church of Central Africa Presbyterian (CCAP).[32] Like the Apostolic Faith Church, it has its roots in Anglo-American Pentecostalism, but in contrast it is still supervised by whites. Nyakamera was licensed by an American missionary to be its local supervisor, and its senior preacher, a former teacher in the Catholic mission, was given two years of theological training at the movement's regional headquarters in Pretoria. As far as was known at the time of research, he was the only preacher in the African churches at Nsanje with such a qualification.

Members of this church seem to be somewhat more prosperous than those of its counterpart. Nyakamera himself owns a medium-sized farm with some rice fields and a dozen head of cattle. Otherwise, the church, which has only a few congregations, is not very different. Its rules against alcohol and so forth are the same, and its congregation consists mostly of women. Nyakamera claims historical links

---

[31] I was not in a position, due to circumstances beyond my control, to conduct a proper statistical survey of the occupations of the men in this church, but I made a point of always enquiring after their occupations whenever I met with members of a congregation. There were none among those interviewed without a small but regular income besides subsistence farming, and only a few with a somewhat larger income. It is unlikely that this picture would have changed substantially had a more formal enquiry been undertaken.

[32] Chakanza 1979, p. 111. Interviews with Mr Nyakamera, founder, and Mr S. Zulu, senior preacher, Nsanje, 2.1.1982 and 3.1.1982.

with the Mbona cult, his ancestors having held a titled position in the shrine organization. This to him is a matter of some pride, since it identifies him as a descendant of an important autochthonous family and establishes him as an authority on traditional religion, but it is doubtful whether this attracts anybody in particular.[33]

The third church in this group is the Apostolic Faith Mission, established in 1973. Mazonda, its founder, supervises the largest African church in the district, with forty-five congregations and an adult membership of 1,460.[34] He regularly goes on tour, at one stage even into Mozambique, and seems to draw fairly large audiences. Like most other leaders he is a former member of the United Evangelical Church of Malawi, where he received a thorough grounding in the Bible. He introduced his church from Zimbabwe, where he went as a migrant worker, and he still holds himself responsible to the African leaders of its parent body. Mazonda ascribes the success of his church particularly to the appeal it has to women, who, he estimates, make up three-quarters of its total membership. Apparently these women, virtually all of whom had reportedly been afflicted by spirit-caused diseases, do much of the proselytizing work at village level.[35] Although Mazonda owns a decent house and church, his movement appears less directly tied to an emergent lower middle class than the others. Some of his followers at least appear to be people who derive their income mainly from subsistence farming. It is possible that the somewhat mixed character of his movement is due to its appearance at a time when the other movements had already absorbed a large part of the entrepreneurial establishment.

The history of the Apostolic churches in Nsanje since their inception in 1958 has generally been quiet. They expanded steadily without too many overt conflicts. The Apostolic Faith Church is an exception to this, although only to a degree. As already mentioned, this church was brought to the district by three labour migrants who had been ordained in Zimbabwe. One of these, Chimbalanga, accord-

---

[33] Nyakamera's church appears to be one of the few that do not condemn traditional religion outright, one of its maxims being that traditional religion contains a certain amount of good, but that in the past it failed to prevent witchcraft, village warfare and slavery (Interview 2.1.1982).

[34] Interview with Rev. Mazonda, Nsanje, 5.1.1982. Figures were supplied by him and refer to a church count in April 1981.

[35] This apparently is also the reason why many women from Mozambique regularly join Mazonda's congregations in Malawi.

ing to local observers the most talented of the three, was entrusted with the overall leadership of the movement, while the others were to serve under him. After a while, however, it was discovered that he had secretly married three wives, which led to his immediate dismissal.[36] Another, J.P. Banda, who may have been disappointed because of his minor position, returned to Zimbabwe, where he converted to the Prophecy of God Church. In 1971 he established this church in Nsanje in the very same village as the headquarters of his former church.[37] His new church was American-sponsored which enabled him to put up a brick prayer house with permanent roofing, earning him a good deal of prestige. 'How wonderful', as one informant said, 'to get support from America. Everyone envies you for having friends in such a rich country.'

Despite this, and despite the support provided by Chimbalanga, who in the meantime had come to join him, the movement expanded at a rather slow pace compared with some of the others. By the end of 1979, after eight years of work, there were only 386 members organized in a dozen congregations. Before then, however, both Banda and Chimbalanga had already been expelled for disciplinary reasons, but Chimbalanga got his revenge when he subsequently founded a new church, which explicitly permitted polygamy and which reportedly weaned away some members from the Prophecy Church.[38]

In conclusion we can say that two of the Apostolic churches described here have been able to build up a sizeable and stable following. People joining them tend to remain, and large scale secessions have not yet occurred. The one direct secession that took place did not pose a serious challenge to the parent body. Not only have these two bodies remained relatively free of internal conflict; they have also managed to keep rivalry down to a minimum.

---

[36] Details about Chimbalanga's career were obtained from Ms I. Lind of the United Evangelical Church of Malawi to which he had formerly belonged (Interview 4.1.1980), and from members of his present church (Int 7.1.1980, Chiphwembwe Village).

[37] Chakanza 1979, p. 98.

[38] This new church was founded in December 1979 and reportedly attracted quite a few people (Interview with Lind 4.1.1981). The reasons for the expulsions are not known to me, but it is likely that they had something to do with the two men condoning polygamous unions among the church members. This is at least suggested by Chimbalanga's subsequent actions.

Leaving out the latest secession, about which only a few details
were available at the time of our research, we note that out of the
four remaining churches two are small, attracting no more than a
few hundred followers. Both of these are controlled and supervised
by whites, which gives their local leaders a measure of prestige, but
which otherwise seems to have had a limiting effect on their growth.
A final observation to be made is that polygamy was already an
issue from the very beginning, leading to the expulsion of the most
talented leader in the oldest movement, and finally to the founding
by the same person of a religious body which legitimated polygamous unions. Although this may seem to be no more than a minor
event, it reflects, as we shall see, a fundamental issue in the second
Christianization of the district.

The Assembly Churches

The second most important group of churches enters the history of
the district with the founding, in 1962, of the white-controlled
Assemblies of God.[39] This church, like its Apostolic counterparts,
puts much emphasis on faith-healing, but its services tend to be more
ecstatic, speaking in tongues being a frequent phenomenon. Its first
pastor was N. Useni, who led the church until about 1970, when
he transferred his allegiance together with most of his followers to
the African Assemblies of God, which has its headquarters near the
township of Nsanje.[40] The shift from a white-controlled to an African-
controlled church proved to be timely, because the church then
began to expand until, in 1977, it had seventeen congregations with
an estimated membership of around 600.[41] Due to some disagreement with the founder of the church, Useni and most other leaders
were relieved of their posts in 1977, an event which led to a spate
of secessions reducing the parent body virtually to insignificance.

The first two secessions, which had already happened in 1977,
were the most successful in terms of numbers. I. Kanyuchi, a former colleague of Useni, introduced the Independent Assemblies of

[39] Details in Wishlade 1965, p. 36 and *passim*.
[40] The Assemblies of God Church was founded in Blantyre in 1969 by J.P.
Chitaka, a native of Nsanje, who had been a migrant worker in South Africa and
Zimbabwe (Chakanza 1979, p. 82).
[41] Interview with Pastor Useni, Nsanje, 6.1.1980. Useni claims to have had many
followers. The present estimate is computed on the average membership in the district, which stands at about 34.

God, which has its headquarters in Blantyre and is under joint white and African control. By early 1980 it claimed ten congregations in Nsanje with probably over 300 followers.[42] Ph. Forty, who earns a living as a tailor at the local government hospital, and who is also one of Useni's former colleagues, introduced the Pentecostal Holiness Church, which by January 1980 claimed 242 members.[43] Useni himself followed in 1978 with the United Pentecostal Church, which by early 1980 had six congregations with possibly over 200 members.[44] In the same year E. Tengani, scion of a famous line of chiefs, founded the Hebrew Christian Church which, as its name suggests, focuses on the Old Testament and allows polygamy.[45]

The most recent secessions are J. Potifar's Pentecostal Church of God, which began operating in 1981 with just over fifty adherents, and I. Kanyuchi's second church, the Pentecostal Assemblies of God, which began in the same year with thirty-five members.[46] Potifar's church is controlled by an African minister from Blantyre; Kanyuchi's by American missionaries stationed at Lilongwe, the national capital. The difference between these two congregations, both of which I had a chance of visiting while they were at worship, was most striking. Potifar's group consisted of poorly dressed, illiterate villagers, most of whom were the founder's neighbours and relatives. Kanyuchi's was composed of well-dressed, mostly middle-aged men and women, who had already managed to put up a neat little church building, and who in every respect looked the lower-middle-class congregation they aspired to be.

Comparing the Apostolic and the Assembly churches one can see a number of parallels. In both cases the leaders are men, despite the fact that the great majority of the members are women. Faith-healing plays an important role in both groups, and most of the

---

[42] Interview with Pastor J. Jack, Nsanje, 8.1.1980. Also Chakanza 1979, p. 102.

[43] Interview with Pastor Ph. Forty, Nsanje, 5.1.1980. The Pentecostal Holiness Church was founded in 1940 in the Central Region of Malawi by N. Phiri (Chakanza 1979, p. 107).

[44] This church has its headquarters in the neighbouring Thyolo District and is one of the few supervised by a woman, its head at the time of my research being a Mrs Sitima.

[45] Interview with Y. Manthando, Emmanuel Gospel Mission, Nsanje, 10.1.1980. Chakanza, 1979, p. 89 renders its name as Aheberi African Church. Details on the Tengani family in Schoffeleers 1975, pp. 24–25.

[46] Interview with J. Potifar, Nsanje, 1.1.1982, and I. Kanyuchi, Nsanje, 5.1.1982. The reasons why Kanyuchi left the Independent Assemblies, which he himself had founded in the district four years earlier, are not known.

women members have joined after being cured of spirit-caused diseases. Again, in both cases secessions are led by former leaders, one
of whom founds a small church which allows polygamy. Both groups
have at least one church under white supervision. Finally, both appear
to recruit among the lower middle class and to some extent also
among the poorer section of the population, but not, or hardly ever,
among the wealthier or more highly educated.

But the differences are equally obvious. The Assembly group has
remained much smaller, counting perhaps 900 adherents against three
times that number in the Apostolic churches. In the Assembly group
separatism is apparently also much more of a threat, and when it
occurs it tends to leave the parent group severely weakened. There
are also signs that the new divisions have a tendency to form along
class lines, separating the poor from the more privileged.

The career of the Assembly churches appears to confirm the observation made earlier that African-controlled churches are more
successful than those controlled by white missionaries, the most telling
case being Useni's switch to the African Assemblies in 1970. But it
also suggests another regularity: that churches led by African agencies outside Malawi tend to fare better than those led by African
agencies inside the country. It seems more than just coincidental that
the Apostolic group, which is by far the largest and most successful, is being supervised from Zimbabwe, whereas the Assembly group,
with its history of rampant sectionalism, is entirely supervised from
within Malawi.[47]

---

[47] This suggests, with regard to the churches under consideration, that control
by national agencies is likely to be influenced by tensions and conflicts inherent in
the national political situation, while control by an external agency might be a
means of transcending these. To test the validity of this hypothesis comparison with
the religious situation in other districts is needed, but due to lack of reliable data
this has proved impossible.

<table>
<tr><td colspan="2" align="center">*Chart 2*
*New Churches in Nsanje, 1958–1981**</td></tr>
<tr><td>1958</td><td>The Apostolic Faith Church</td></tr>
<tr><td>?</td><td>The African Apostolic Church of Yohane Maranke</td></tr>
<tr><td>1962</td><td>The Assemblies of God</td></tr>
<tr><td>1970</td><td>The United Apostolic Faith Church</td></tr>
<tr><td>1970</td><td>African Assemblies of God</td></tr>
<tr><td>1971</td><td>The Prophecy of God Church</td></tr>
<tr><td>1971</td><td>Church of the Black Ancestors</td></tr>
<tr><td>?</td><td>Full Gospel Church</td></tr>
<tr><td>1973</td><td>The Apostolic Faith Mission</td></tr>
<tr><td>?</td><td>The Disciples of Christ Church</td></tr>
<tr><td>1976</td><td>The Emmanuel Gospel Mission</td></tr>
<tr><td>1977</td><td>The Church of the Nazarene</td></tr>
<tr><td>1977</td><td>The Baptist Mission</td></tr>
<tr><td>?</td><td>The African Church</td></tr>
<tr><td>?</td><td>The Topia Church (Abraham Church)</td></tr>
<tr><td>1977</td><td>The Independent Assemblies of God</td></tr>
<tr><td>1977</td><td>The Pentecostal Holiness Church</td></tr>
<tr><td>1978</td><td>The United Pentecostal Church</td></tr>
<tr><td>1978</td><td>The Hebrew Christian Church</td></tr>
<tr><td>1979</td><td>Chimbalanga's Church</td></tr>
<tr><td>1981</td><td>The Pentecostal Church of God</td></tr>
<tr><td>1981</td><td>The Pentecostal Assemblies of God</td></tr>
<tr><td>1981</td><td>The Bible Deliverance Fellowship</td></tr>
<tr><td>1981</td><td>The Gospel Message Church</td></tr>
<tr><td>1981</td><td>Zion Apostolic Church</td></tr>
<tr><td colspan="2">* Not all are discussed in this chapter
? Precise date unknown</td></tr>
</table>

The Effects of the Second Christianization

The second christianization wave had not yet come to a standstill at the time of my last visit to the area in January 1982. The churches I have just described and others, mostly smaller ones (see Chart 2), continue their recruiting efforts, and it seems likely that their number will keep growing. Although it was impossible to obtain precise figures about the total membership of these movements, it is not impossible that it stood then at well over 3,000, the larger part of whom would belong to one or other of the Apostolic churches.[48] Many of their members have transferred from the older mission

---

[48] According to my estimates, the Apostolic churches' membership stands in the neighbourhood of 2,000; that of the Assembly churches at around 600, and that of the residual category at slightly over 500. At any rate, it is clear that the Apostolic churches are by far the most influential group.

churches, the hardest hit being undoubtedly the United Evangelical Church of Malawi, whose main centre near Nsanje Township has dwindled almost to insignificance. Where formerly its vast church building was filled to capacity twice every Sunday, it now stands virtually empty. Indeed, most of the founders of the new churches have come from the Evangelical community.[49] Although the Catholic mission was less dramatically affected, it too sustained significant losses, and its baptismal classes have been so greatly reduced that the number of new converts is hardly sufficient to make up for the losses caused by deaths and conversions to other religious groups.

Despite this, the number of Christians and, more importantly, the number of actively engaged Christians, has increased considerably since the introduction of the new churches. Moreover the type of Christianity now dominant is quite different from that of either of the two older churches. It is fully African-led, intensively localized, and entirely dependent on local resources. Pastorally, it directs itself at problems of immediate relevance to the faithful, such as spirit afflictions amongst the women and drunkenness amongst the men.[50] It is this therapeutic function which seems to constitute the major attraction of the new churches.

Turning to their impact on traditional religion, one can say that this is most visible in the area of spirit possession. Traditional ceremonies meant either to appease or exorcize intruding spirits have largely disappeared, and a great many women now seek to be exorcized in the new churches. Where formerly one heard the sound of possession drums almost every night, this has become a rarity.[51] It

---

[49] Interview with Ms Lind, Nsanje, 4.1.1980. According to Ms Lind most of these men were persons who had been disciplined or whose ambitions for leadership found no outlet in the Evangelical Church. She pointed out further that conflicts within the missionary establishment had also been a contributing factor. One disaffected evangelical missionary, for instance, became a Baptist and founded a Baptist congregation in the immediate neighbourhood of his former mission.

[50] I met a strikingly large number of men who stated they had joined one or other of these churches to be cured of alcoholism. Several church leaders confirmed that this was indeed a not infrequent phenomenon.

[51] This was confirmed by several knowledgeable informants. Some, however, believed that it had gone underground, the women being ashamed of what rather suddenly had come to be looked upon as old-fashioned and backward. Investigations among local shopkeepers, who sell strings of beads and other paraphernalia worn in possession ceremonies, tended to confirm this. Although trade in these articles was said to have dropped sharply over a number of years, it has not completely died out. One must therefore conclude that traditional possession has survived to a certain extent but in a strictly privatized form.

is not claimed here that this dramatic decline in possession ceremonies is directly or exclusively due to the emergence of the new
churches. Rather, it would seem that both processes, the decline of
one form of spirit therapy and the rise of another, were provoked
by a number of converging factors outside the field of religion. More
specifically, they seem to be related to the changing position of
women in the domestic as well as the public sphere. The national
government at that time put great stress on the political and cultural emancipation of women through the medium of the Malawi
Women's League, which used to be represented in most villages and
which wielded considerable influence at various levels of public life.[52]
I have no evidence that the League explicitly expressed disapproval
of the traditional possession ceremonies, although the possibility cannot be excluded. But, even without any direct action, it is clear that
the League's very presence in a village was bound to have a limiting effect on the practice.

Apart from spirit possession the new movements also turned against
traditional medicine and its practitioners as a whole,[53] the only true
medicine-man being Christ, as shown by the following hymn:

Yesu sing'anga;	Jesus, the medicine-man;
Halleluya, bwerani!	Halleluja, come!
Yesu sing'anga	Jesus, the medicine-man
Amachiza matenda	Cures diseases
Yesu sing'anga	Jesus, the medicine-man
Amachotsa ziwanda	Drives out evil spirits
Halleluya, bwerani!	Halleluja, come!

It is certainly not an overstatement to say that the new churches
disengaged themselves and their followers from traditional religion
to a greater degree than the mission churches were able to do. The
point, however, is not so much that the leaders commanded it, but
that the faithful demanded it. It is this latter aspect which is the
most relevant and which constitutes the most basic difference from
the mission churches.

---

[52] The Malawi Women's League has never been professionally studied. My assessment of its influence in Nsanje is based on personal observations.

[53] Several informants maintained that in the beginning most of the new churches
also forbade use of modern medicine, but that this had been changed under pressure from their congregations. Whatever the case, most now allow their members
to visit the local hospital.

The Ancestor Church

The Church of the Black Ancestors (*Mpingo wa Makolo Achikuda*) was brought to the district in 1971 by a local man, who had joined it as a migrant labourer in Blantyre, where the headquarters of the movement is located.[54] The movement itself was reportedly founded some thirty years earlier by Peter Nyambo, a Ngoni from the present Central Region of Malawi, who when younger had been known as an active critic of the colonial order.[55] It is one of several neo-traditionalist movements in the district,[56] the others being the Ethiopian Church (also known as 'Topia' or Abraham Church) and the African Church, which have however remained relatively small in comparison with the Ancestor Church.[57] But even the latter did not make much headway at first, as it was not until the mid-seventies that it began to develop into something resembling a mass movement.

The main points of its doctrine are set forth in an official circular issued by the headquarters of the movement in Blantyre, which

---

[54] Interview with D.D. Forty, secretary of the Nsanje division of the Church of the Black Ancestors, Mbeta Village, 31.7.1978. The local founder was one Zuze J. Alufinali from the village of Mphomba, which lies a short distance from the Mbona shrine. Dr Chakanza informs me that some members translate the Chewa name of their church as 'African Ancestors Religion'.

[55] Peter Nyambo was born about 1884 and became a Christian when still a young boy. He travelled extensively through Europe and parts of Africa in the service of the Seventh Day Adventist mission. Later he went to South Africa, where he became actively engaged in a small movement which wanted to draw the British Government's attention to the abuses of the colonial administrations in the Rhodesias and Nyasaland. In this function he sailed to England in May 1914 to present a petition to the king, returning to South Africa in 1917. The Church of the Black Ancestors was reportedly founded soon after his definitive return to his native district around 1942 (Shepperson and Price 1958, pp. 203–209; Wishlade 1965, pp. 20–21). Bishop Makauli, a former leader of Peter Nyambo's church, maintains, however, that Nyambo was the founder of the Ethiopian Universal Church (J. Chakanza, personal communication).

[56] The term 'neo-traditionalist' is used here in the same sense as Linton's 'nativistic movement', meaning 'any conscious attempt on the part of a society's members to revive or perpetuate selected aspects of its culture' (Linton 1943, pp. 230–240).

[57] There is some confusion as to the use of the phrase 'Ethiopian Church'. Wishlade, who studied sectarianism in the highlands area to the north-east of the valley, uses it throughout as an alternative name for the Church of the Black Ancestors (Wishlade 1965), but in Nsanje the two names definitely refer to two different bodies. The African Church was founded in 1932 by Jordan Njirayafa, like Peter Nyambo a Ngoni from the Ntcheu District. It came to Nsanje only recently and is there under the leadership of the Rev Moses Samu (Chakanza 1979, p. 83).

carries the title 'The truth about Jesus, the Saviour of the Israelites and the Whites'.[58] The general tenor of the circular is that Christianity is an alien religion, which has no relevance for Africa except that it has been used as an instrument of subjection. There is no mistaking the sometimes bitter tone, as when it states that under the Europeans 'we were but fourth-class citizens, human filth in the country which was ours by birth'. It is the same sort of language that is being used in their recruiting drives throughout the district, particularly when they are dealing with Christians among their audience.

The strategy used in the circular is not that of proving that the Bible is wrong, but that it is a book of the whites which nevertheless contains stories and references which parallel the Black condition. Thus it starts by noting that if Christ was called the Lion of Judah, the Life-President of the Republic, Dr H. Kamuzu Banda, is hailed as the Lion of Malawi, because he freed his people from the foreign oppressor. Again, if the Apostle Paul could say that under the new dispensation there was to be no Greek and no Hebrew, no circumcised and no uncircumcised person, the same can be said for Malawi, where Dr Banda emphasizes that under the new order there can be no persons belonging to this or that tribe, but only Malawians. Finally, if the Israelites had become divided because of worshipping foreign gods, so the people of Malawi had become divided because of their acceptance of the religion of the whites. The latter is obviously the main point, for it leads directly to the exhortation that, if the population of Malawi wishes to regain its unity and self-esteem, it will have to return to the religion of its ancestors which has everything that Christianity has and is therefore its equal.

Thus the Bible, though ostensibly rejected, nevertheless provides the movement with its major unifying symbol. This is hardly surprising in view of the cultural diversity with which the movement has to deal, even in a relatively small country like Malawi, and which it actually emphasizes by its attempts to revive local forms of worship instead of promoting some generalized form of African religion.[59]

---

[58] 'Zoonadi zacheza Mpulwnutsi wa alsraeli—Azungu. Yesu' (3pp.; no date).

[59] This at least is what one might have expected in view of their stated rejection of tribalism, but the movement has as yet not produced any literature which points in that direction apart from a brief guideline for adapting the church's central tenets to different cultural environments.

Within Nsanje, this local emphasis has come to be centred on Mbona, whose life and death provide an immediate analogy with Christ. A number of hymns have been composed in honour of Mbona, which are now part of the movement's services, and it is developing a rudimentary catechesis which sets forth the main points of his salvific work.[60] These services are held on Sundays, preferably under a tree, trees being considered the dwelling place of the spirits. They begin with praises of the *Ngwazi* (literally 'conqueror'), which is the principal honorific title of the Life-President: 'He it was who delivered us from the slavery of the whites, and thanks to him we are now free to spread the message of the ancestral religion to our fellow citizens. No longer are we forced to embrace a foreign religion; no longer is there any need to, for we now have our own religion given back to us'.[61] This is followed by hymns, like the following, in honour of the ancestors:

Sindipempha mzimu wina	I ask for no other spirit
Koma wamakolo anga	Than that of my ancestors
Uli pafupi	You are near;
Uli pafupi ndi ine!	You are near me!
Poyenda ulendo wanga,	When I am travelling
Mzimuwe ukhale nane!	You my spirit, stay by me![62]

The central and by far the longest part of the service consists of a series of hortatory sermons, each dealing with a particular theme, and each preceded by the recitation of a number of biblical texts considered relevant to the theme in question. There being but a few members who can read, this task usually falls to the leader of the congregation, but, as far as the exhortations are concerned, every-

---

[60] Both the hymns and the elementary Mbona catechesis are contained in a notebook kept by the church's District Secretary, which he kindly allowed me to quote.

[61] Quotation translated from notebook of D.D. Forty, the District Secretary. It seems, however, that the Ancestor people have been warned several times by government officials not to draw too explicit parallels between Dr Banda and certain biblical figures.

[62] These hymns are a new phenomenon and directly borrowed from Christian practice, there being no ancestral praise songs in traditional culture. Wishlade mentions that the two congregations of the Ancestor Church which he visited in the Mulanje District in April 1959 used the hymnbook published by the Nyasaland Federation of Missions, apparently with little or no regard for the doctrinal implications of the words. This I find rather difficult to accept, and it seems more likely that they selected only those hymns which were doctrinally acceptable or which could be made so by slight changes in the text.

one may join in by supplying evidence about the negative effects of Christianity and by stressing the advantages to be gained from a restoration of the old cultural and religious code. At this point the themes which receive particular emphasis are the need to restore the old sacrificial rites at district, village and lineage level, and the need to instruct the young again in the traditional mores and more especially sexual mores. With regard to the latter the leaders of the Ancestor Church maintain that it is the ignorance of the young in these matters which has been the cause of much sexually transmitted disease.[63] The Nsanje services may end with a Mbona hymn such as the one reproduced here:

Mbonaye, m'Khulubvimo,	Mbona, yonder in Khulubvi,
Tinakuiwala ife lero	We today, have forgotten you,
Tabwelera, Mbuya!	We have returned to you, (our) Lord!
Oh, tayimba m'rnanja.	Oh, we have clapped hands.
Mbonaye, Mbonaye,	Mbona, Mbona, you,
M'Khulubvimo.	Yonder in Khulubvi
Oh, tayimba m'manja.	Oh, we have clapped hands!

Membership and Organization

The great majority of the members of the Ancestor Church are traditionalists who have never been Christians, but the movement also contains a considerable number of lapsed Christians, who are indispensable because of their familiarity with the Bible. It would seem, though, that Catholics are more inclined to join the Ancestor Church than Protestants.[64] The reason for this may be twofold. First, Catholics have always remained closer to traditional customs and culture. They are for instance allowed to take beer and liquor, which most Protestants are not, on pain of disciplinary action, and although they are not allowed to drink beer in ritual settings such as the ceremonies for the dead, the dividing line between ritual and non-ritual settings is not always clearly discernible and may easily be transgressed without leading to sanctions by the church.[65] More importantly, Catholics

---

[63] Cf. Wishlade 1965, who makes the same point, quoting a church member as stating during a service that this type of disease (or this ignorance on the part of the young) was caused by wanting to be like whites.

[64] This is the impression I gained from a number of random encounters with ex-Christians in the movement.

[65] Catholics who have participated in ancestral rituals routinely confess this with usually no more than an admonition and a slight penance to follow.

on the whole tend to belong to the poorer strata of society, to which
the overwhelming majority in the Ancestor Church, with the partial
exception of some of their leaders, also belong, for, compared with
its Christian counterparts, the Church of the Ancestors is first and
foremost the religious home of the illiterates and the economically
disadvantaged.

Another important characteristic of the Ancestor Church is that
it is the only religious body or movement in the district in which
men are noticeably more numerous than women, a fact also observed
by Wishlade in a neighbouring district.[66] Local Christians ascribe this
to the fact that the Ancestor Church allows or even encourages
polygamy.[67] It is difficult to say how far the Ancestor leaders explicitly encourage the practice, but it is not improbable that their failure to discourage it keeps a significant number of women from joining
the movement, since women tend to take a rather negative view of
this custom.[68]

The church is organized on the principle of a dual hierarchy: one
bureaucratic, the other ritual. The bureaucratic hierarchy consists of
offices such as that of local chairman, vice-chairman, secretary, trea-
surer, district chairman and so forth, which are directly copied from
the Malawi Congress Party. The ritual hierarchy consists in principle of all traditional chiefs, headmen, shrine officers and territorial
mediums in the district.[69] The qualification 'in principle' is required
since not all of these functionaries actually belong to the Ancestor
Church. Indeed, quite a few among them are opposed to it, as we
shall see, but this does not prevent the Ancestor people from view-
ing these men as potentially forming part of their organization.

The two hierarchies are similar in that both are almost exclusively
dominated by men, women occupying only secondary and minor
positions.[70] They are different in that the bureaucratic hierarchy is

---

[66] Wishlade 1965, p. 132.

[67] Interview with Y. Manthando et al., 10.1.1980. This opinion is quite general
in other districts also, where the Ancestor Church is often nicknamed *Zoipa Chitani*,
the 'Do-bad-things-church'.

[68] The reason most frequently cited for this view is that polygamy leads to many
conflicts between co-wives, which in their turn often lead to witchcraft accusations.

[69] The phrase 'territorial spirit mediums' (*ndoswa*) refers to chiefdom mediums and
Mbona mediums, all of whom have jurisdiction over a land area and its population as a whole in contrast to private spirit mediums (*nyahana*) who deal with their
clients on an individual basis (Schoffeleers 1967; Mandala 1982).

[70] This has not always been the case, however, with the ritual hierarchy, which

largely manned by the immigrant Sena, whereas the ritual hierarchy, particularly its higher echelons, is the preserve of the autochthonous Mang'anja. This is not particularly surprising, as it represents the continuation of an age-old principle, known to many parts of Africa, according to which in situations of conquest or massive immigration the autochthonous section retains ritual power over the land and its population, whereas the immigrant section tends to strive after secular power.[71] The resulting arrangement leads to a situation of interdependence and co-operation, but on the other hand, it is also a source of antagonism and conflict, instances of which will be discussed presently.

Spatially, the Church of the Ancestors is organized on a village basis. Individuals who are familiar with its teachings and who want to establish a local congregation first try to win over the village headman. If the latter is sympathetic, the movement stands a good chance of succeeding, since the headman's influence is still such among the older inhabitants that a number of them may join. The next step is to formalize the existence of the new congregation by having it and its leaders recognized at district level, and the final step is a recruiting drive involving the entire village and neighbouring settlements.

Entry requirements are few and easy to fulfil, consisting mainly in having one's name entered in the local register and paying a small fee, different for men and for women.[72] Once fully established, the new congregation establishes relations of co-operation with other congregations in the same area regarding public preaching, the organization of propagandist meetings at various central places, and the visiting of chiefs, headmen and other traditional office holders, who do not yet belong to the movement, in an attempt to win them over.

---

for centuries has been dominated by women. This began to change only in the second half of the nineteenth century and was more or less finalized in the 1960s, when the last female territorial medium gave up her post with the remark that it had become 'too dangerous for women on account of all the politics involved' (interview with Chief Nyachikadza, 12.7.1972). The ongoing absorption of these posts by the male-oriented Ancestor organization can only be seen as a further consolidation of this trend.

[71] For evidence on the operation of this principle in a number of African societies, see especially Mitchell 1961 and Schoffeleers 1979, 'Introduction'.

[72] Fees tend to differ from place to place according to the activities engaged in by the different congregations, but the entrance fee rarely goes beyond fifty *tambala* (about twenty-five pence) for men and ten *tambala* for women.

The Expansionist Strategies of the Movement

Until about 1976 the Ancestor Church had remained a fairly insignificant body with only a few congregations, mainly in the southern
and central part of the district. From 1976 onwards, however, the
movement gradually gained speed, and three years later it claimed
a membership of over 5,000 adults, affiliated to more than sixty congregations in six chiefdoms. In the same period there was also a
sharp increase in clashes with the Christian churches and in cases
of physical harassment of Christians, leading to occasional police
intervention and court cases. Some of these events will now be
described, with particular attention to the strategies that were employed.

In retrospect one can discern three phases, each marked by its
own expansionist strategy. During the first phase, which covers all
of 1976 and part of 1977, the Ancestor people were particularly
intent on gaining a foothold in the southern part of the district,
where the Mbona shrine is located. In the second phase, in the latter half of 1977, their activities concentrated particularly on the central part of the district, and in the third and final phase they shifted
their activities to the north.

In 1976 rumours circulated to the effect that the Mbona shrine
was in such bad shape that it was on the point of collapsing. As
usual, these rumours led to others purporting that some calamity
was about to take place unless action was quickly taken.[73] For the
leaders of the Ancestor Church, whose most important congregation
was then located in the village of Mbeta, only a few kilometres from
the shrine, this seemed an excellent opportunity to offer their services and thereby gain perhaps some measure of influence in the
shrine organization. They therefore paid a visit to the two principal
officers of the cult, both of whom were also recognized chiefs, but
they forbade the church leaders to set foot inside the shrine grounds,
and one even warned them to stay out of his chiefdom altogether.[74]
Following this, they decided to approach the principal guardian of
the shrine, a senior headman whose village borders directly on the

---

[73] The usual rumour is that Mbona will send a drought or some pest affecting
the crops; see Schoffeleers 1977, pp. 232–33, for a more detailed account.
[74] Interview with B.A. Phiri, councillor to the shrine-chief Malemia, Nsanje,
3.1.1979; D.D. Forty, leader of the delegation, Nsanje, 6.1.1979; Headman Mbangu,
chief guardian of the shrine, Mbangu Village, 5.1.1980; on the position of the two
principal cult officers, see Schoffeleers 1977, pp. 223–227.

sacred grounds, but once again they met with firm opposition.[75]

Some months later, they made a third attempt by trying to get the cult's medium on their side. This was a particularly clever move, because the medium had for years been living in extreme conflict with the rest of the cult's officialdom and had even tried to get a counter-shrine going.[76] But once again they were unsuccessful. Three reasons may account for this. First, the medium was in ill health at the time and was actually to die a year later. Second, he may have been afraid of yet another serious fray with the two chiefs. Third, and perhaps more important, he disagreed openly with the political character of the Ancestor Church, ordering his visitors even to remove their nationalist badges; a daring act indeed, which might have landed a lesser person in prison. The point here is not so much that he disagreed as an individual, but that he disagreed as the immediate representative of Mbona, who is supposed to be superior to any secular power and above secular politics.[77]

Realizing that resistance in the southern part of the district was too strong, the Ancestor people now turned to Tengani, the principal chief in the central area, who apparently showed himself considerably more friendly and even made a small contribution to their fund.[78] Among the various topics discussed was the Tengani's

---

[75] The reference is to Headman Mbangu (cf. n. 32), who is directly responsible to the two authorities just mentioned, and who is not allowed to let anyone enter the shrine grounds without their permission.

[76] The medium in question was Joseph Thom, who died in May 1978. The nature of his disagreement with the other members of the cult establishment is described in Schoffeleers 1977, pp. 230–231.

[77] Mbona's superior position in relation to any worldly ruler is a theme constantly reiterated in the cult's ritual and oral history. It is to be noted that, despite appearances to the contrary, the Mbona cult retained a certain amount of power to express political discontent, even under the Banda regime. Thus during a severe famine in 1972–3 Mbona was rumoured to have descended from the clouds in the form of a pangolin to save his people from destruction. This caused two outbreaks of general unrest which could be quelled only by a combined intervention of the traditional chiefs and senior officers of Banda's Malawi Congress Party (Chikwawa District Monthly Report, December 1972 and April 1973). I owe these references to Prof E.C. Mandala of Rochester University, USA.

[78] Interview with D.D. Forty and other Ancestor leaders, Nsanje, 6.1.1979, and notebook of D.D. Forty. Apparently the reception granted them by Tengani, the first chief to do so, was extensively exploited by the leaders for propagandist purposes. Two stories in particular, both dealing with the duplicity of white missionaries, and reportedly communicated to them by the chief, were regularly repeated to village audiences.

historical position in the Mbona cult, which the present incumbent's immediate predecessor had abdicated, but which the Ancestor people wanted to see restored with a view to gaining entry into the cult along a different route. Tengani's relations with the present shrine chiefs, however, were such that it was impossible for him to bring any pressure to bear upon them. Other means had to be used, and it is in this light that one should see two extraordinary events which took place in the months following. The first was the emergence of a new Mbona medium near Tengani's own headquarters, the second an attempt by three enterprising individuals to create a new cult centre to replace the existing one.

Kingy Butao, the new medium, about 65 years of age, is said to have become possessed for the first time on 25 September 1977. The event was preceded, as usual in the case of territorial mediums, by pains in the head, the legs and the abdomen.[79] When Mbona had entered him, he stumbled, hands outstretched, towards a tree, all the while shouting 'I am Mbona!' People gave him a mat to sit on and squatted around him to hear what he had to say. Kingy then told them that Chief Tengani must inform the Mbona officers that the shrine should be rebuilt forthwith and that a sacrifice must be made to remove the locusts, which were then ravaging the district. Kingy further insisted on Mbona's behalf that Tengani himself had to participate in both these activities as in the days of old.[80]

In the context of this paper it is important to note that Kingy was a Mang'anja, who had previously been a healing medium, and whose forebears had had long-standing connections with the Mbona cult. He was also a member of the Ancestor Church. It is therefore more than likely that his possession was provoked partly by the unsuccessful negotiations just described. The event of his possession had, however, few tangible results, partly because the official medium was still alive. The shrine was provisionally repaired one or two months later and a simple sacrifice made, but Tengani took no part in it, nor would the other officers have allowed him to. Meanwhile

[79] Interview with D.D. Forty, Nsanje, 31.12.1978; K. Butao, the medium, Tengani Village, 13.1.1979; A. Kambula, catholic catechist, Tengani Village, 13.1.1979; notebook of D.D. Forty.
[80] The Tenganis played a central role in these rituals until 1936, when the first Christian incumbent of the title decided to discontinue this tradition (cf. Schoffeleers, 1975, pp. 24–25).

Kingy maintained his claims and has, because of his celibate life and visionary experiences, become some sort of sacred figure to the Ancestor movement.[81]

Soon after Kingy's possession, in November 1977, there appeared on the scene a man called Armando who was also a Mang'anja and a traditional healer. He claimed to have received a revelation from Mbona to the effect that the cult centre had to be removed from its old place to a forest patch near Tengani's headquarters.[82] This project, much more radical than the first, also looked more realistic, as it bypassed the existing organization and particularly the two shrine chiefs, who had no jurisdiction over Tengani's area. Tengani himself kept a guarded distance, but he did not prevent one of his councillors, nor one of his senior headmen, Lukwa by name, from teaming up with Armando, whose authority and prestige were thereby considerably increased.

The villagers built a hut for Armando close by the forest path known as Mtayira ('place of the thrown-aways'), where in former times the corpses of those who had succumbed to the poison ordeal had been left to the hyenas. A space was cleared in the forest and a shrine built in the form of a small circular hut, about 1.3m high. The entrance to the clearing was marked by a length of dark-blue cloth (a symbol of rain clouds), which had been fashioned into some kind of archway, through which the worshippers were to pass. Armando had also ordered some ritual implements to be placed in the shrine next to three large clay pots which had been sunk into the floor to receive the beer offerings.[83]

The dedication of the shrine was accompanied by much singing and dancing, but no rain fell. Armando then ordered fresh beer brewed for a second attempt, but this, too, was unsuccessful. People

---

[81] Territorial mediums usually lead a normal married life as indeed Kingy himself did until he was possessed by Mbona. He maintains that it was Mbona who commanded him to live in celibacy from then on.

[82] Interview with P. Thom, Catholic church elder; A. Kambula, Catholic catechist; D.D. Forty, Ancestor leader, Tengani Village, 13.1.1979; Nsanje police, civil case no. 121/77. The three interviewees maintained that the incident took place in the month of November, which is a normal month for rain rituals, but the police reports state that it happened 'between August and September'. This is very unlikely and should be considered an error.

[83] When I visited Armando's place on 3.1.1979, the 'shrine' was still partly intact, but his hut, which stood at a little distance from the forest patch, had been razed to the ground by the villagers.

then began to doubt his calling, and a meeting was convened at
which the councillor and the senior headmen were to answer charges
of misleading the population, Armando having fled in the meantime
to Mozambique. The two remaining men were arrested and taken
to court, where they were charged with withholding the rain under
section 471 of the Penal Code as read with section 2 of the Witchcraft
Act. Both pleaded not guilty, but they were detained till March 1978.[84]

It is not easy to assess the direct or indirect role which the Ancestor
Church played in this project, but it can hardly be coincidental that
the event took place at a time when the Ancestor people were con-
centrating their activities on precisely this part of the district. It is
ironic to say the least that, while the Mbona cult was rapidly declining in its traditional form, it was at the same time being revived in
a sectarian form by the Ancestor Church. About the decline of the
old shrine there can be no doubt. In 1977 the district administration had discontinued its long established practice of making gifts to
the shrine on the occasion of the annual rain prayers.[85] In May 1978
the medium died after having held that position for thirty-four years.
Although he was not precisely bemoaned by the other shrine per-
sonalities, they nevertheless paid their respects to him by sending
official representatives to the funeral, which attracted a large group
of mourners.[86] Although it is impossible to predict whether or not a

---

[84] Nsanje police, civil case no. 121/77. Section 2 of the Witchcraft Act (12th
May, 1911) reads: 'Trial by ordeal of muabvi or other poison, fire, boiling water,
or by any ordeal which is likely directly or indirectly to result in the death or bodily injury to any person shall be and is hereby prohibited' (*Laws of Nyasaland* 1934,
p. 76). How this section came to be applied to Armando's case I am unable to
explain, except that the forest patch in which his shrine was erected had a long
historical link with the poison ordeal. During the interrogation, Lukwa stated that
he and Armando were descendants of Mbona and that it had been their intention
to travel by night to the place where Mbona is believed to be (i.e. the old shrine)
and take him (sic) to their own place so that people at Tengani would enjoy a regular supply of rain.
[85] Interview with B.A. Phiri, former member of Nsanje District Council, 8.1.1979.
These gifts usually consisted of a black umbrella (for Mbona's 'wife') and several
lengths of black cloth, to be placed on Mbona's 'bed' in the shrine and worn by
the shrine guardians as loin cloths. This practice, which had already began in colonial days, was continued after independence. The official reason for its discontinuation was that the District Council no longer made provision for occasional gifts
to deserving causes, but it no doubt also reflects the cult's declining importance in
the life of the district.
[86] Interview with Jimu Thom, the late medium's brother, Nsanje, 1.1.1979; B.A.
Phiri, cult deputy at the funeral, Nsanje, 2.1.1979.

successor will in time emerge, it is unlikely that this will happen soon, since the cult itself has virtually disappeared and the medium's position has become politically impossible. In 1981 the shrine lay in total ruins, but the sacred grounds were still guarded by a few elderly custodians.[87]

The new strategy of the Ancestor Church, which took shape from the beginning of 1978 onwards, had a double focus, one geographical, the other institutional. Geographically, the main thrust was now towards the northern part of the district, which is not only by far the most populous but also the area least influenced by the Protestant churches, the major Christian influence there being the Catholic mission. Institutionally, the movement from then on focused its attention on religious cults at the village level, and more particularly on the revival of the rain and fertility ceremonies in honour of the village headman's ancestors. It was this twin focus which was to give the movement its main impetus.

The reasons are not difficult to find. In the first place, the northern part of the district was, on account of the rather marginal Protestant influence, culturally more attuned to the Ancestor doctrine. Although it would be an exaggeration to say that the Ancestor Church has become the dominant religious body in the area, it has nevertheless been able for a while to attract a large following. Thus a rally, organized in October 1978 near the Catholic Mission at Muona, seems to have drawn well over 900, most of whom are said to have joined the movement.[88] That this rally was more than a passing event is clear from the increasing frequency with which the Ancestor people began to disrupt Catholic Sunday services.[89] This sometimes caused panic among the worshippers, as when a frenzied mob surrounded the small church at Tsanya Village, yelling and

---

[87] Interview with L. Rice, Nsanje, 31 December 1981. Mr Rice, a catechist at Nsanje Catholic Mission, who had been allowed to visit the place together with three companions on 29th September 1981, observed that little remained of the shrine except a few poles stuck in the ground. The roof had caved in and, like the reed walls, been eaten by white ants. However, when at my request the place was visited on two occasions in the course of 1997 by Mr Menno Welling, then a student of Leiden University, he found the cult and shrine once again functioning normally.

[88] Interview with District Secretary Ancestor Church, Nsanje, 31.12.1978.

[89] Interview with M. Kanaventi, Catholic Catechist, Tsanya Village, 30.12.1978; Rt Rev F. Mkhori, Bishop of Chikwawa Diocese, 30.12.1978; Rev T. Cronin, parish priest, Nsanje 31.12.1978.

shouting that Christ was for the whites, but Mbona was the only
Saviour of the Blacks. The fact that similar incidents also began to
take place elsewhere suggests that the successes of the Ancestor
Church in the northern section of the district had a stimulating effect
on the movement as a whole. Ancestor preachers were found daily
at the central market in the township of Nsanje, where they harangued
the public about Christianity in such a manner that they had to be
officially warned by the authorities.[90]

But it was not only the Catholics who were the butt of the Ancestor
attacks, although they were the most obvious target, being both the
largest denomination and the one with the largest white missionary
presence. Other churches were also attacked, and in some of the
Ancestor strongholds Pentecostalist leaders were even prevented from
preaching or visiting their faithful.[91] There were also cases where
attempts were made to force Christians to participate in village
sacrifices, a practice which had already died out in most places, but
which was now being revived.

Towards the end of 1978 the headman of Chadzuka village in
the chiefdom of Tengani ordered his people to contribute a basket
of millet per family for the brewing of beer in honour of the spirits of the locality. All complied except an elder of the Apostolic Faith
Church who, upon being challenged by the headman's deputy,
answered that his church organized its own prayers for the well-
being of the community. The headman then ordered the elder to
be brought in by a messenger who treated him rather roughly. The
elder, however, took the matter to the police, and subsequent investigations led to the headman's being warned by the Chairman of
the District Council.[92]

---

[90] The Ancestor preachers have an extensive repertoire of invectives, abusive dit-
ties and lurid insinuations in relation to Christ, churches and ministers. Christ is
routinely referred to as *mbava* (thief); scriptural passages such as the conversation
between Christ and the Samaritan woman (Jn. 4 1–30) are given a sexual twist;
men such as Maranke's Apostles, who wear long robes at their prayer meetings,
are called transvestites, and so forth. I know of no other instance of such patent
and sustained collective hatred in the entire colonial and post-colonial history of
the district as that of the Ancestor Church against Christians.
[91] Interview with Y. Manthando, former leader of the Emmanuel Gospel Mission,
Nsanje, 10.1.1980; M. Nyakemera and S. Zulu, leaders of the United Apostolic
Faith Church, Nsanje, 4.1.1982; B. Zuze, Catholic Mission, Nsanje, 4.1.1982.
[92] Interview with P. Thom, Catholic church elder, Tengani Village, 3.1.1979.

Similar incidents were apparently reported from other villages, but although the Ancestor people had become more careful to avoid excesses of the kind just mentioned, their drive to revive village sacrifices was continued and had some degree of success. This was not without its importance, because it gave the Ancestor Church a hold over an annual ritual which still attracted people and which could be exploited for propagandist purposes.

It is impossible to predict what the future of the Ancestor Church in Nsanje will be. Some local observers thought that the movement was already losing some of its drive in 1981 on account of internal conflicts and numerous defections, but the Ancestor leaders deny this. Whatever the case, there is no denying that it has been, and to a certain extent still is, an influential movement whose strongly anti-Christian stand sets it apart from all other religious bodies in the district.

The Development of the New Religious Movements

Looking back on the religious history of Nsanje in the twentieth century, one can perceive a series of shifts and changes, which in a broad and general way appear to coincide with those that occurred in the economic sector. During the cotton period, which signalled the effective incorporation of the local economy into a metropolitan trade system, we witness the introduction of the missions, the dissemination of Christian symbolism through large sections of the population, and the emergence of what looks like a folk religion combining significant elements of the Christian and ancestral tradition. This is most clearly visible in the Mbona organization, which is increasingly penetrated by Christians, who apparently refuse to dichotomize between the two.

With the collapse of cotton on the eve of the second world war and the growing importance of labour migration, there is a steep rise in possession cults which remain a dominant feature till the early 1970s. Although the phenomenon itself was not directly generated by these changes, since possession was already in evidence long before they took place, it is nevertheless more than likely that there was a causal connection between the deteriorating situation of many women in the district and the unusually high frequency of possession rituals in this period. At the very least, these rituals created a bond of friendship and co-operation between women of the same neighbourhood. In this connection it is also important to note the apparent incompatibility between these cults on the one hand and missionary Christianity and the Mbona cult on the other, suggesting that the polarizing process of the 1970s already had its parallel and part of its roots here.

Finally, the decline of long distance labour migration, the growth of the cattle industry and the development of small-scale entrepreneurship coincide on the one hand with the emergence of a new type of Christianity, which to all intents and purposes absorbs the possession cults, and on the other with a massive neo-traditionalist movement. One of the characteristics of this emerging complex is that it shows a certain degree of statistical correlation between religion and social class. Thus we find the wealthier and better educated particularly in the mission churches, the emergent lower middle class in the Spirit churches, and those lowest on the social and economic scale in the neo-traditionalist movement. But this pattern, though clearly visible, appears to be intersected by a number of other variables, such as gender and age, suggesting that it would be too simplistic to view the present religious pluralism as primarily or exclusively reflecting social stratification. If a more adequate picture is to be obtained, it will be necessary to look more closely at the different processes that, together, led to the present situation.

Analysis of Processes

The year 1958, when the first Spirit church was established, was also the year in which the nationalist movement finally got off the ground, due to Dr Banda's assuming its overall leadership. The three founders of this church, all of them labour migrants just returned from Zimbabwe, introduced a novel religious formula (novel, that is, to the inhabitants of the district) which possessed three distinct qualities not generally present in missionary Christianity: it was fully under African leadership; it offered an alternative to spirit possession; and it provided small entrepreneurs, such as the founders themselves had become, with an ethic and a set of behavioural rules geared to safeguard their newly won position vis-à-vis their kinsmen and neighbours. The formula proved successful, and was repeated with certain variations by other Spirit churches, with the result that by 1975 this new wave of christianization had already affected the entire southern section of the district as well as a number of places beyond.

While it does not seem too difficult to account for the attraction it held for small traders, shopkeepers, junior clerks, and the like, all of whom stood to gain from a religion relieving them of the duty to participate in the traditional commensality circuit,[93] it seems less easy to account for the presence of so many women. Part of the answer may be provided by an issue which appears to have played an important role from the outset, namely polygamy. The problem had already arisen in the very first church to be introduced, when its chief leader was discovered to have three wives, and it continued to crop up till the late 1970s, when each of the two groups of Spirit churches produced a minor secession accommodating those who wished to legitimize the practice. The movement as a whole continued to emphasize monogamy as the sole permissible form of marriage, and there are strong indications that this has in large part been due to the collective pressure exercised by its women members.[94]

This potential for collective pressure and, if need be, concerted action, constitutes one of the crucial differences between these churches and the traditional possession cults, which are organized in small local groups without much inter-linkage. The transition from one to the other, from possession cults to Spirit churches, may have been attractive for this reason, but it was facilitated largely by the gradual breaking up of local possession groups in the southern part of the district under the influence of the extensive population movements which took place from 1966 onwards.

The type of Christianity which resulted was, by comparison with the missions, much more explicitly opposed to traditional religious and cultural practices, and much more female-oriented despite its male leadership, which in itself forms another major difference from

---

[93] Parkin 1972.

[94] Catherine Robins (1979, p. 201) notes in a study of the East African Revival movement in Rwanda and Uganda that analysts of indigenous churches in Africa have greatly emphasized the selective adaptation of local movements to such strongly rooted customs as polygamy and ancestor veneration, but that the conversion accounts in the Revival movement suggest that women come into the movement seeking religious legitimation for the rejection of polygamous unions rather than a religious accommodation with polygamy.

the possession cults. It would, however, be too easy to view this simply as a sign that the women have been co-opted into the dominant male culture.[95] Rather, it would seem that both parties are
intricately dependent on each other. In the more successful churches,
men provide the organizational skills and the international contacts
which they acquired when working in the south. Moreover, men
have generally received more formal education (an important asset
in organizations which value such things as registers and accounts)
and, not being hampered by children and household chores, they
can move about more widely and freely, which is important both
for the movement's expansion and the maintenance of contact with
outlying congregations.

Women in their turn provide the numbers necessary for the success of the church, and they probably also contribute most of its
funds. They are also separately organized within the movement to
some extent, having their own committees and, in a number of cases,
their own mid-week services. Beyond and on account of this, it is
more than likely, as suggested before, that they wield considerable
influence as a pressure group in matters of church policy and conduct. In the final analysis there is every reason to view these organizations as an instance of class alliance.[96] In sum, the Spirit churches
provide the women with a cultural environment congruent with the
norms and values of the national state, and with a social environment which as a group (but less so as individuals) gives them parity
with men.

The success of the Spirit churches among women and small entrepreneurs led to the gradual isolation of the mass of subsistence farmers and, more particularly, of the elderly among them. This isolating
process had religious as well as social and economic effects. In the
religious sphere, these elders were affected by a decline in lineage
worship over which they customarily presided. Socially, it was the
erosion of their authority in kinship affairs that counted most, and
economically they had to forego income derived for ritual services
for kinsmen and other villagers. The economic strain was particularly felt by headmen, herbalists and diviners, but it extended to
family heads also, who on the occasion of ancestor rites were wont
to receive gifts of food and drink from their juniors. Taken in com-

---

[95] Mandala 1982.
[96] Rey 1973.

bination with the continuing decline of small-holder farming and the ongoing migration of younger households, which were actually far more critical factors in this process of impoverishment, the conditions were set for the type of massive reaction represented by the Ancestor movement.

It is not at all surprising that the Ancestor movement started in the southern section of the district where impoverishment and isolation were greatest, nor that it aimed at the restoration of sacrificial rites from district level down to kinship level, since these had traditionally been the central symbol of hierarchical authority. Finally, it was to be expected also that headmen, herbalists and diviners would be prominent in the movement, as illustrated by the abortive attempts to establish an alternative Mbona shrine in which all three categories were explicitly involved. But while the restoration of the sacrificial system was aimed at the population as a whole, the movement also made and still makes attempts to involve the younger generation. This it did, perhaps somewhat unexpectedly but nevertheless logically, by seizing on a real or imagined high incidence of venereal disease, citing cohabitation during the menstrual period as a particular cause. The point involved was a double one. First, it meant to establish the indispensability of traditional mores and of the old as the natural authorities in this matter. Second, and less explicit, it re-emphasized the need for proper separation between male and female, cohabitation during the menstrual period being at one and the same time the prime symbol of boundary transgression and of its inevitable consequences.

The implications, however, are somewhat subtler than the example, for sexual separation in this case also refers to social separation and the necessity of a hierarchical order in which men are superior to women (who after all are the supposed source of the disease). Both contrasts, old/young and male/female, are focal contrasts in the movement, but while the former contrast is emphasized in its preaching and teaching, the latter is particularly manifest in its organization, which is dominated and directed by men, without much counterpoise being exercised by women as in the Spirit churches. The immediate cause of this lack of female influence is mainly of a statistical nature. In the Spirit churches women heavily outnumber men, whereas in the Ancestor movement the opposite is the case. The more remote cause, on the other hand, is connected with a difference in gender orientation. The Spirit churches, though male-led,

are to a great extent female-oriented, while the Ancestor movement
is both male-led and male-oriented.

The Ancestor movement's model with regard to ethical values,
norms and symbols is an idealized version of the hierarchical order,
based on commercial cotton cultivation, which came into being in
the period between the two world wars. What the Ancestor movement reacts to is not primarily the difference between the more and
the less economically privileged (indeed, their support of chiefs and
headmen suggests the opposite) but the erosion of the kinship hierarchy of which the traditional political hierarchy is seen as both symbol and safeguard. More directly stated, the basis of the movement
is formed by people who in their younger years had to obey and
work for their elders but who, now that they themselves have reached
elderhood, see themselves deprived of authority as well as support,
and who want that situation reversed. While the movement had no
dearth of actual and potential followers, it did lack the type of religious entrepreneurs and their aides who had become founders and
leaders of Spirit churches. There were of course some, the present
District Secretary of the movement being one example, but they
were too few to organize efficiently a movement of this magnitude.
There may have been several reasons for this. One appears to have
been the very neo-traditionalism embodied by the movement, which
carried the seeds of serious conflict with the Christian population
and possibly the national state, and which on that account was reason for caution. The situation might have been different, had the
state organization itself, as in Zaire's *authenticity* campaign, initiated
or supported an ideology of this kind, but the Malawian government
did so only in a remote and non-committal fashion. Yet it is significant
that the Ancestor movement made every effort not only to show its
loyalty to the state, but also to adopt nationalist symbols and part
of the nationalist rhetoric to propagate and legitimize its aims. Despite
this, and partly because of this, it repeatedly fell foul of state agencies like the district administration and the police. A further reason
for its lack of appeal to potential religious entrepreneurs was probably the hostility of the chiefs, the supposed kingpins of the new
society, who were decidedly unwilling to become associated with a
movement overtly opposed to Christianity and thus liable to create
disturbances in the areas under their jurisdiction. But underlying
everything was a patent lack of congruence between the social and
economic system that prevailed in the 1970s and the kind of system

the Ancestor movement envisaged. It was, and still is, essentially out of touch with reality as shaped and dictated by national policies, and on those grounds alone it could hardly attract an efficient leadership.

It has thus become the kind of loose organization that it is, consisting of a core of committed men—headmen, diviners and so forth, who direct its activities—and a large penumbra of villagers, who drift in and out and are with greater or lesser regularity mobilized for action. Left with few feasible goals and even fewer demonstrable gains—the restoration of the sacrificial system was only partly successful, and there is as yet little evidence of a conversion of the young to the ancestral mores—the movement has increasingly turned to desperate actions such as harassing Christian congregations, which made the process of religious polarization complete.

Conclusion

Summarizing the process as a whole, we can say that the religious complex that emerged between the turn of the twentieth century and the second world war was largely male/elder oriented, the central legitimizing agencies being the missions and the Mbona cult. After the war the younger men were able to redefine their relationships with the elders by making them their financial partners. This blurring of the age contrast has had the effect of sharpening the gender contrast. Women reacted in a way which alienated them from the central religious agencies. Economic and demographic developments in the 1960s and after led to the gradual discontinuation of the partnership between the young and their elders, and to the isolation of the latter. At the same time local possession circles crumbled and several thousands of women became available for recruitment into more centrally organized religious movements. This materialized by means of an alliance with young entrepreneurs, the outcome being religious groupings which showed a fair degree of power balance between male and female, but which isolated the elderly still further, leading to an almost total reversal of their erstwhile dominant position. Their present situation shows striking parallels with that of the women at an earlier stage. Like the women, they have found themselves at the bottom of the economic scale; like them, they have reacted by adopting a religious ideology which is incompatible with the dominant one; and, finally, like them they were weakly organized and thus unable to act efficiently as a pressure group. All that remained was 'to spit at Jesus'.

A final conclusion to be drawn is that the religious history of Nsanje shows that the notion of 'folk religion', which has gained wide acceptance among Africanist historians and anthropologists[97] to describe situations of religious plurality in rural communities, has its limits and should be handled with care. People from different religious persuasions may indeed make use of each other's services and specialists; they may even simultaneously occupy positions in cult systems which are, or seem to be, doctrinally opposed to each other, but, as has been illustrated here, cults which appear to integrate a community at one stage may act as agents of division at another. Looked at merely synchronically, the impression of unity and integration does indeed often impose itself with some force. Looked at diachronically the impression becomes quite different. Thus, to the uninformed outsider, the Mbona cult prior to the second world war might have appeared as a textbook example of religious integration. Yet it was then already a religious organization in which the young had no place and from which the women had more recently absconded. With the benefit of hindsight we are now able to understand why later movements reacted to it the way they did: possessed women avoiding it, founders and leaders of Spirit churches condemning it, and the Ancestor adherents trying in vain to restore it. Collectively, these various movements brought into the open tensions that hitherto had been acute, but had remained hidden.

ACKNOWLEDGEMENTS

The research on which this paper is based has at various stages been funded by the Nuffield Foundation, London, the University of Malawi, and the Free University, Amsterdam. I wish to acknowledge my indebtedness to these institutions. An earlier version was published in 1985 by the Free University Press in Amsterdam, but is now out of print. I thank Dr J. Chakanza of the University of Malawi for his stimulating comments. I also owe a debt of gratitude to the various missionaries and church leaders in Nsanje for their hospitality and co-operation.

---

[97] Murphree 1969; Kuper 1979; Ranger 1979.

BIBLIOGRAPHY

Alpers, Edward A., *Ivory and Slaves in East Central Africa*, London, Heinemann, 1975.
Chakanza, Joseph E., *A General Survey of Independent Churches in Malawi*, MA Dissertation, Aberdeen, 1979.
Colman, D.R. and Garbett, G.K., *Economic and Sociological Issues in the Development in the Lower Shire Valley; First report*, Zomba, Government of Malawi, 1973.
Garbett, G. Kingsley, 'Labour Migration and Development in the Lower Shire Valley, Malawi, in Historical Perspective', Leiden, International Seminar on Migration and Rural Development in Africa, 1977.
Jules-Rosette, B., (ed.) *The New Religions of Africa*, Norwood, NJ, Ablex Publishing Corporation, 1979.
Kuper, Adam, 'The Magician and the Missionary', in P.L. van den Berghe (ed.), *The Liberal Dilemma in South Africa*, London, Croom Helm, 1979.
Laws of Nyasaland, Crown Agents for the Colonies, London, 1934.
Lewis, I.M., *Ecstatic Religion*, Harmondsworth, Penguin, 1971.
Linton, R., 'Nativistic Movements', *American Anthropologist* vol. 45, 3, 1943, pp. 230–240.
Mandala, Elias C., 'Kinship and Capitalism: A Historical Survey of Women in the Lower Tchiri (Shire) Valley of Malawi, 1860–1960', Workshop on Kinship and Capitalism, Cambridge, Massachusetts, 1982.
Marwick, Max, 'Another Modern Anti-Witchcraft Movement in East Central Africa', *Africa*, XX, 2, 1950, pp. 100–112.
Maxwell, David, *Christians and Chiefs in Zimbabwe: A Social History of the Hwesa People c. 1870s–1990s*, Edinburgh, Edinburgh University Press, 1999.
Mitchell, J.C., 'Chidzere's Tree: A Note on a Shona Land Shrine and Its Significance', *NADA*, no. 38, 1961, pp. 28–35.
Murphree, Marshall W., *Christianity and the Shona*, London, Athlone Press, 1969.
Murray, S.S., (ed.), *A Handbook of Nyasaland*, London, Crown Agents for the Colonies, 1922.
Parkin, D.J., *Palms, Wine and Witnesses: Public Spirit and Private Gain in an African Farming Community*, London, Intertext, 1972.
Ranger, Terence O., 'The Churches, the Nationalist State and African Religion', in E. Fasholé-Luke et al. (eds.), *Christianity in Independent Africa*, London, Rex Collings, 1979, pp. 479–502.
Rey, P.P., *Les alliances de classe*, Paris, F. Maspero, 1973.
Richards, Audrey, 'A Modern Movement of Witch-Finders', *Africa*, VIII, 4, 1935, pp. 448–461.
Robins, Catherine, 'Conversion, Life Crises and Stability among Women in the East African Revival', in Jules-Rosette 1979.
Schoffeleers, J.M, *Evil Spirits and Rites of Exorcism in the Lower Shire Valley of Malawi*, Limbe, Montfort Press, 1967.
———, 'Evil Spirits and Problems of Human Reproduction', *Malawi Medical Bulletin*, vol. 2, no. 1, 1968, pp. 12–17.
———, 'Social Functional Aspects of Spirit Possession in the Lower Shire Valley of Malawi', *University of East Africa Social Science Conference, Religious Studies Papers*, Kampala, 1969, pp. 51–63.
———, 'The History and Political Role of the M'Bona Cult among the Mang'anja', in T.O. Ranger & I. Kimambo (eds.), *The Historical Study of African Religion*, London, Heinemann, 1972, pp. 73–94.
———, 'The Interaction between the M'Bona Cult and Christianity', in T.O. Ranger & J. Weller (eds.), *Themes in the Christian History of Central Africa*, London, Heinemann, 1975, pp. 14–29.

————, 'Cult Idioms and the Dialectics of a Region', in R.P. Werbner (ed.), *Regional Cults*, ASA Monograph no. 16, London, Academic Press, 1977, pp. 219–239.

————, 'A Martyr Cult as a Reflection on Changes in Production: The Case of the Lower Shire Valley, 1590–1622 A.D.', *African Perspectives*, 2, 1978, Leiden, African Studies Centre, pp. 19–33.

————. (ed.), *Guardians of the Land: Essays on Central African Territorial Cults*, Gwelo, Mambo Press for the University of Salisbury, 1979.

————, 'The Story of Mbona the Martyr', in R. Schefold et al. (eds.), *Man, Meaning and History*, The Hague, M. Nijhoff, 1980.

————, *River of Blood. The Genesis of a Martyr Cult in Southern Malawi, c. A.D. 1600*; Madison, University of Wisconsin Press, 1992.

Shepperson, G., and Price, T., *Independent African*, Edinburgh, University Press, 1958.

Shire Valley Agricultural Development Project, *An Atlas of the Lower Shire Valley, Malawi*, Blantyre, Department of Surveys, 1975.

Short, Philip, *Banda*, London, Routledge and Kegan Paul, 1974.

Tew, M., *Peoples of the Lake Nyasa Region*, London, Oxford University Press, 1950.

Van Binsbergen, W.M.J., and Schoffeleers, J.M., (eds.), *Theoretical Explorations in African Religion*, London, Kegan Paul International, 1985.

Wishlade, R.L., *Sectarianism in Southern Nyasaland*, London, Oxford University Press, 1965.

CHAPTER NINE

A TRADITIONAL RELIGION REFORMED: VINCENT KWABENA DAMUAH AND THE AFRIKANIA MOVEMENT, 1982–2000[1]

Samuel Gyanfosu

Background

The Afrikania Movement emerged during the political era in Ghana which has come to be known as the 'Second Coming' of Flight-Lieutenant Jerry John Rawlings, and is marked in the annals of the nation as the 31st December Revolution. As a 'new' indigenous religious movement, Afrikania was founded at a rather auspicious time, when there was a renewed suspicion, distrust and even antagonism on the part of the state towards 'foreign' importations, especially from the west. Foreign religions in general, and Christianity in particular, specifically of the 'historic' or 'missionary' variety, could not escape the onslaught.

Afrikania became an attractive and significant player, at least in its early days, in the contemporary drama of events unfolding in the country. This was, however, not so much for its religious position or theological content, but for its strong element of cultural renaissance, its reassertion of Black and African identity and dignity, and for wholeheartedly throwing in its lot with the Revolution, as a religio-cultural corollary. For the ideology of the Revolution and its leaders, at least at the outset, was hardly sympathetic to religion in any form. Nevertheless, Afrikania remained basically a religious movement, and vigorously paraded itself as a viable spiritual alternative for Ghana, Africa and humanity as a whole.

---

[1] This chapter is an edited and shortened version of Chapter 7 of Samuel Gyanfosu, 'The Development of Christian-Related Religious Movements in Ghana, with Special Reference to the Afrikania Movement', Ph.D. thesis, University of Leeds, 1995, with two final additional sections, bringing the story of Afrikania up to date.

The socio-economic conditions at the time were, to say the least, dismal. The new administration was still grappling with the legacy of a society characterized by widespread poverty and riddled with economic malpractices and other forms of anti-social behaviour. There was, on the other hand, a continuing religious ferment and fervour, as new religious movements, mainly of the Christian variety, thrived and proliferated, in the face of all odds.

Afrikania claims to represent a re-birth, re-activation, re-organization or re-structuring and updating of African Traditional Religion, 'to make it relevant to our times' and enable it to 'regain its pre-eminent position among the major religions of the world'.[2] In short, Afrikania represents a *reformation* of African Traditional Religion, which, according to Damuah, Afrikania's founder, is 'mankind's first recorded religion and the mother of all religions',[3] and which is traceable to 'thousands and thousands of years before Christ, along the banks of the River Nile, from East Africa down to Egypt',[4] producing 'great spiritual leaders such as IMHOTEP, Black Egyptian, born 2700 BC, priest-politician, adviser to King Zoser of Egypt, architect, scientist, the world's first medical doctor, and the greatest genius of the ancient world.'[5]

Despite this ancient connection, however, Afrikania, as a distinct and identifiable Ghanaian religious movement or organization, is traceable only to the 1980s. It was first called 'Afrikanianism' and quickly changed to 'Afrikania Religion or Mission' or 'Reformed African Traditional Religion', before eventually adopting, or rather adding on, the alternative name 'Godianism' or 'Godian Religion'. In addition, Afrikania is also known as 'Sankofa' ('a return to our roots'), and 'Amen-Ra', a supposedly ancient African word meaning 'God-centred' or 'Almighty God'.

Osofo-Okomfo Damuah proclaimed the founding of Afrikania and inaugurated it at the Arts Centre (now Centre for National Culture)

---

[2] See Osofo-Okomfo Damuah, 'Why I Resigned', in the *Afrikania Voice*, Vol. 1, No. 1, Aug. 1–15, 1983, p. 3. This stated aim is found in several of the documents on Afrikania. See again, for example, 'Osofo-Okomfo Damuah Hits Back', in the *Christian Messenger*, Vol. 4, Nos. 2–3, Jan.-Mar. 1984, pp. 2–3.

[3] See Osofo-Okomfo Damuah, *Miracle at the Shrine (Religious and Revolutionary Miracle in Ghana)*, Accra, Damess Paper Products Ltd., 1990, p. 54. Here Damuah seems to be echoing Casely Hayford (*Ethiopia Unbound*, 1911, p. 194), writing some eighty years earlier.

[4] 'Osofo-Okomfo Damuah Hits Back'.

[5] Ibid.

in Accra on Wednesday 22 December 1982, simultaneously with his historic resignation from the Catholic priesthood. The message that Afrikania and its leaders and adherents wished to communicate to the whole world on that day was that 'God speaks to every race and culture, and as Africans the best way to serve God and our society productively is through our cultural perspective.'[6] Afrikania was 'spiritually outdoored' the following Sunday, 26 December, with its first worship service at the same venue. At this service, on the day after Christmas, the founder called on Ghanaians to embrace the new Movement, to assist and enable it to spread the 'message of true liberation throughout the country and the world at large.'

Following the inauguration and 'outdooring' of the Movement, the founder and his team of helpers embarked on a nation-wide 'crusade' to open branches and spread the message of Afrikania. From Asankragwa and Accra, the main starting points, branches were established at Apowa, Barde, Bawdia, Bremen, Enchi, Hiawa, Samreboi, Sekondi-Takoradi, Wassa Akropong and Yakasi, all in the Western Region, as well as at Agona Swedru, Cape Coast, Saltpond and Winneba in the Central Region. Other branches were opened at Asamankese and Koforidua in the Eastern Region, Ho, Keta and Kpandu in the Volta Region, and Domiabra, Ejisu and Kumasi in Ashanti Region. The remainder were in Dormaa-Ahenkro and Sunyani in the Brong-Ahafo Region, Tamale in the Northern Region, Bolgatanga, Navrongo and Pusiga in the Upper East and Wa in the Upper West Regions, respectively. This planting endeavour was supposedly so vigorous that by August 1983, barely eight months after its inception, Damuah had this to say about the progress of the Mission with regard to its outreach and extension programme:

> We have branches of Afrikania in all the regions of Ghana. We are in four African countries, two countries in Europe and two branches in the USA. We are growing slowly but surely. We get letters from all parts of the world inviting us to start branches accordingly.[7]

---

[6] 'Afrikania Crusade', in *Afrikania Voice*, p. 2 (see note 2).

[7] See Damuah, 'Why I Resigned', p. 4. See also 'New Religion, "Truly African"', in *African Christian*, Nairobi, African Church Information Service, Vol. 3, No. 9, Mar. 7, 1983, pp. 2–3. In that interview Damuah is reported to have declared with regard to the membership of his Movement: 'We are legion. We also have branches in Greater Accra and Western Region, especially at Wassa Akropong, Barde, Hiawa and Domiabra', adding that he had received invitations to open branches in many parts of Africa, which he proposed to do the following year. See also, 'Osofo Damuah Defends Afrikania Religion' in the *Christian Messenger*, Jan. 1983, p. 5.

Barely seven months later, in March 1984, still in buoyant mood, Damuah backed this up with the further claim that Afrikania had branches not only in all the regions of Ghana but also 'in all the five continents'.[8] However, what were regarded as 'branches' of the Movement probably consisted of small groups of people, some of them traditional ritual attendants and specialists, and in some places only a token representative or two. In any case, subsequent developments seem to indicate that many of these so-called branches, if they existed at all, must have had a very short lifespan. It seems reasonable to suggest that Damuah's claims of expansion were exaggerated.

The Founder

Vincent Kwabena Damuah was born in April 1930 (the exact date is not known, but his name, Kwabena, suggests that he was born on a Tuesday), at Asankrangwa, in the Wasa Amanfi District of the Western Region of Ghana. His father, Kwasi Appong, and his mother, Ama Nsowah, had worked as farmers. Damuah started his formal education at the Local Government Primary and Middle Schools, after which, in 1947, he gained admission to St Theresa's Seminary at Amisano, near Elmina in the Central Region, to begin his training for the Roman Catholic priesthood. During the ten years of training, Damuah proved to be a hardworking student who won the admiration of tutors and fellow students alike. He was ordained at Cape Coast in December 1957 at the age of twenty-seven. His first station was Agona Swedru, also in the Central Region, where he served under the supervision of Archbishop John Kodwo Amissah and Father Paul Louis. Damuah acquitted himself creditably in the discharge of his first parish assignment, organizing literacy classes, youth movements and community self-help groups, activities which he had already enjoyed in Asankrangwa during his days as a seminarian.

In 1960 he was sent to London by the Catholic Church for further studies in Social Action, Community Development, Economics and the Lay Apostolate, at the Claver House Institute. On his return

---

[8] See the introductory parts of Damuah, *Afrikania: Reformed African Traditional Religion—Answer to Critics—Common Sense Series 7*, Accra, Afrikania Mission, Mar. 31, 1984, and *Common Sense Series 8*.

home the following year, Damuah was posted to Saltpond (again in the Central Region) where he was appointed Rector of St Theresa's Preparatory Minor Seminary, and Moderator of Lay Apostolate and Catholic Action in the archdiocese of Cape Coast, which at the time consisted of the Western and Central Regions. It was during this period in Saltpond that he reactivated the Catholic Youth Organization (CYO), serving as its first National Director.

He now started writing articles in the Catholic Church's mouth-piece, the *Catholic Standard*, in which he dealt with such issues as youth movements, credit unions and social questions. Some of the articles were critical of the government of the day and soon got him into trouble with the Nkrumah administration. As a result of his crit-icism of certain aspects of the Ghana Young Pioneer Movement (a government youth structure for ideological indoctrination or 'con-scientization'), Damuah was detained on 13 January 1963 at Saltpond Police Station, and transferred the next day to Elmina Police Station. At both Saltpond and Elmina, large numbers of people gathered to demonstrate their support for the detained priest, turning him into something of a hero overnight.

At Elmina Police Station there was a non-stop, sit-in protest, with the crowds growing day after day, which compelled the authorities to release Damuah on the sixth day of his detention. His Archbishop (Amissah) also lent his support and demanded his release. There are some reports of what was perceived as a spectacular manifestation of divine intervention and support for Damuah, and of divine dis-approval of the action of the authorities: it was claimed that on the last day of Damuah's detention at Saltpond there was a heavy down-pour lasting seven minutes, only at the Police Station![9]

In any case, Father Damuah remained undaunted by his arrest and detention and continued to discharge his priestly duties with devotion, zeal and courage until 1964, when he was awarded a schol-arship to study at Canisius College, New York State, USA. He obtained a BA in Sociology there in 1965 and an MSc in Education in 1966. In 1967 he proceeded to Duquesne University, Pittsburgh, to study Economic Development, earning another master's degree

---

[9] See *Funeral Programme*, p. 2. For a fuller description of the sequence of events and a discussion of some implications and issues involved see John S. Pobee, *Kwame Nkrumah and the Church in Ghana 1949–1966*, Accra, Asempa Publishers, Christian Council of Ghana 1988, pp. 171–173 and 176.

in 1968, followed by a Ph.D. in Theology at Howard University, Washington, DC (1971). In his thesis, 'The Changing Perspective of Wasa Amanfi Traditional Religion in Contemporary Africa', he argued that '"Nanaism", the solidarity with our ancestors, compares very favourably with the Christian concept of the mystical body of Christ' and that 'even though there is only one theology Africans must approach it not from a colonial perspective but Afro-centrically, that is, from an African dimension'.

In the summer of 1972, Damuah began post-doctoral studies on Pan-Africanism at the University of the West Indies in Kingston, Jamaica. He returned to the USA later that year to serve as Director of Black Studies at Delaware State University and Visiting Professor of Ancient History and African Politics at Wesley College, Dover, Delaware, appointments which he held between 1972 and 1976. During this period he delivered public lectures at high schools, on college campuses and in both Black and white communities, speaking of issues relating to the primacy and importance of the African or Black experience, including the African (hence Black) contribution to world civilization, Black Power, identity and dignity, and the religious insights and awareness of African people.

While in the USA, Damuah maintained a hostel in Washington, DC, known as Africa(n) House or Africa Centre, to offer free accommodation to students from Africa, in particular from Ghana, on their first entry into the country. He also founded the African Students Organization of the Washington Metropolitan area and was President of the Association of Chaplains in the same area. In addition he served as Consultant on Afro-American affairs in the Diocese of Pittsburgh, which was then under the supervision of Cardinal John Wright.

After such an eventful stay in the USA, lasting twelve years, Father Damuah returned to Ghana in 1976 and took the next three years as a kind of sabbatical leave from regular parish work (apparently against the wishes of the church authorities), and spent the time at Asankrangwa, trying to organize an Agricultural Institute aimed at developing the agricultural resources and potential of his home district. The venture, however, proved a fiasco, due largely to the activities of certain 'negative local elements', much to Damuah's disappointment.

Following this failure, Damuah returned to normal parish work in 1979, in the Sekondi-Takoradi Diocese. He was appointed to the Star of the Sea Cathedral at Takoradi as parish priest, and put in charge of religious instruction in the parish. In 1980 he became President of the National Union of the Ghanaian Catholic Diocesan Priests Association, a position which he held for two years.

Damuah's activities as parish priest soon brought him into conflict with his bishop, particularly on 'matters of spiritual renewal and inculturization [inculturation]'[10] The worsening situation and the strain, division and confusion that ensued forced Father Damuah to leave for Nigeria in 1981 to take up a lectureship in the University of Jos. After a rather brief stay there, he was recalled home after the 31 December 1981 coup and made a member of the ruling Provisional National Defence Council (PNDC). He accepted the appointment against the strong opposition of his colleagues in the Christian clergy, especially the Catholic bishops, and was consequently suspended by his own bishop. However, his membership of the PNDC was also short-lived, lasting only a few months. By August 1982 he had resigned from the government, though he still maintained links with it.

On 22 December 1982, the twenty-fifth anniversary of his ordination to the priesthood, Father Damuah resigned from the Catholic Church, and indeed from the Christian communion, effectively renouncing his faith completely, to found and lead the Afrikania Mission, or Reformed African Traditional Religion. In his resignation letter he declared:

> . . . after much prayer, thoughtful deliberation and counsel, and by the Grace and mysterious plan of Divine Providence, I resign from the Roman Catholic Church in order to commit myself to total spiritual and human development of mankind, especially the plight of the suffering masses, without restraint.

> . . . through God's inspiration and guidance, I have undertaken a completely new challenge, to reform, update and organise the African Traditional Religion, so that it can take its rightful place among the major religions of the world. . . . its main thrust will be
> (a) to make religion really and truthfully a way of life
> (b) to make it relevant and sensitive to human issues
> (c) bring God down to earth, as it were.

According to Damuah, Afrikania religion is not new but 'is the ancient religion of Africa that is now reformed and born again for

---

[10] *Funeral Programme*, p. 4.

our benefit. It takes the best of the old Africa and blends it with
the best of the new Africa, to form a synthesis for the mutual benefit
of mankind'.[11] Henceforth he was known as Osofo-Okomfo (Dr)
Kwabena Damuah, the 'First Servant' of Afrikania Mission.

During his life, Damuah wrote and published a number of booklets, tracts and articles, both as a Catholic priest and as the spiritual head of Afrikania Mission. In the latter capacity he founded his
own newspaper, *Afrikania Voice*, which became the official mouthpiece
of his mission. Publication, however, was irregular and ceased altogether after January 1988, apparently for lack of funds. Ghana radio
gave him airtime to broadcast religious programmes, which provided
him and the movement with an important forum and a high profile.
In all his writings and public utterances, Damuah sought to project
the African personality and identity and particularly to portray the
African traditional religious heritage and world-view as a viable,
authentic and legitimate alternative, especially to Christianity and
Islam.

He travelled extensively, at home and abroad. While his overseas
travels were mainly for lecturing and research, his tours in Ghana,
especially after the founding of Afrikania, were to spread the movement's message, establish new branches and strengthen existing ones.
Around 1988, Damuah married Akua Tano (also known as Margaret
Owusu), a woman thirty years his junior who, like Damuah himself,
came from Asankrangwa. Within a year, Damuah's first and only
child, a son named Kwame Ampong Damuah, was born.

In 1990, Osofo-Okomfo Damuah led his Afrikania Mission into
a kind of union or partnership with Godianism,[12] which was based
in Nigeria and founded and led by His Holiness Prophet (Chief)
K.O.K. Onyioha, Spiritual Head of the Godian Religion and chairman of the Organisation of Traditional Religions of Africa (OTRA).
Damuah was subsequently appointed as 'the Chief High Priest of
the Godian Religion in Ghana, as the Continental Envoy of Godianism

---

[11] Damuah, *Common Sense Series, No. 7: Answer to Critics*, p. 1. See also the *Daily Graphic*, Tuesday 28 December 1982, p. 5.
[12] The Godian religion, basically African Traditional Religion, was founded in Nigeria by Chief Onyioha, in the 1960s. Turner links it with the earlier National Church of Nigeria and the Edo National Church and places its date of inception at around 1963–64. See H.W. Turner, *History of an African Independent Church*. Vol. 1, *The Church of the Lord (Aladura)*, Oxford, OUP, 1967, p. 6, fn. 3.

for all the continent of Ghana [*sic*] and as the All-Africa Secretary-General of the Organisation of Traditional Religions of Africa'.[13] In May 1990 Afrikania Mission officially renamed itself Godian Religion, or Godianism, albeit without forfeiting its original title, by which it is better known, and is still called in Ghana.

Osofo-Okomfo Kwabena Damuah died on Thursday 13 August 1992 at the Nyaho Clinic in Accra after a short illness, at the age of 62. After being laid in state at the Arts Centre (Centre for National Culture), Accra, on 1 October he was buried in his home town on 3 October 1992.

Why Afrikania?

There is no easy answer to the question why Damuah, after so many years in the Catholic priesthood, left his church and founded Afrikania. According to an article in the *People's Daily Graphic* after his death,

> His breakaway from the Catholic Church was historic. . . . the Christian tradition and the Church of Christ . . . has not been functioning properly in Ghana as it had been in the past. . . . the Christian Church in Ghana has become so weakened that it could not carry on its ecumenical and prophetic duties well.[14]

A similar comment appeared shortly after the founding of Afrikania:

> Osofo Damuah's resignation from the Catholic Church is by all accounts a great loss to the church. But the commercialization of Christianity and all the harm it has caused to the moral and social health of the nation weighed on Father Damuah's conscience and he felt he could not take it any longer.[15]

Damuah himself expressed it thus:

> The Catholic Church preaches democracy but it is more dogmatic, authoritarian, paternalistic and doctrinaire than any other worldwide institution. Its claim as the sole custodian of revealed religious truth is tantamount to spiritual imperialism that keeps many in outmoded religious bondage. The greatest mistake of the Catholic Church and Christianity in general, is their blanket condemnation of the gods about

---

[13] Letter of appointment, dated 7 June 1990.

[14] Larweh Therson-Cofie, 'Tribute to Osofo Okomfo Damuah', *People's Daily Graphic*, 10 October 1992, p. 5.

[15] Editorial Comment, *The Ghanaian Times*, 4 January 1983, p. 2.

which they know very little or next to nothing. According to Jewish and Christian biblical mythology, the angels who joined Lucifer in a coup attempt against God, were dumped here on earth where they became devils or gods. This is just a myth, but no wonder George Bernard Shaw described the bible as the most dangerous book on earth. I think it should be kept out of the reach of children.[16]

He identifies the turning point as follows:

The final challenge came, when at an international religious conference in Moscow in 1982 I discovered that all the major religions of the world were represented except the African traditional religion. Behold a voice whispered into my ears saying 'The Time Is Now', so by the power of God I decided prophetically and instantly to represent Africa from that time onwards.[17]

Having taken that prophetic and instantaneous decision, there was no turning back for Damuah, who appeared absolutely convinced about his new role and mission, and grew impatient with anyone who questioned it. When he was asked to comment on the report that his bishop, on hearing of his resignation, had 'expressed surprise and . . . prayed that Dr Damuah would change his mind', Damuah threw back the challenge with poignancy and passion:

I am also praying for the bishop and his flock to come and join the *Afrikania* religion, which I consider the best. Tell those church leaders and Christians that we are all under mental bondage and colonialisation and we have to unchain ourselves. I have released myself from the 'chain' and I want to release those still in chains. Believe me, I have been called by God to introduce this *Afrikania* religion to my people and I shall not disappoint them.[18]

What shines through Damuah's words is his disillusionment with Christian doctrine in general and Catholic dogma and administration in particular, his intense desire for the recognition of African identity and values, as well as his perception of himself as a divinely ordained apostle, with a message to proclaim and a mission to accomplish. Another point worth stressing is his twelve years' stay in the United States, most of the time not in Catholic institutions. It cer-

---

[16] Interview with Damuah by Kwesi Pratt, 'The Rebel Priest', in *West Africa*, 25 Sept.–1 Oct. 1989, p. 1598.
[17] Ibid.
[18] 'New Religion, "Truly African"', *African Christian*, 'Osofo Damuah Defends Afrikania Religion', *Christian Messenger* (see note 7).

tainly looks as if he had become alienated from the Catholic Church during his years there, and found it impossible to re-acclimatize, as it were, on his return to Ghana. The intellectual 'conversion' was not, therefore, really in 1982 but much earlier.

The question that remains to be answered is whether Damuah's situation was the case of an extreme crisis of faith, the confusion of an earnest and determined seeker after truth, a radicalism and rebellion run riot, an unbridled quest for recognition and fulfilled ambition, or the zealous and faithful receipt of a divine charge. Or was it perhaps a combination of all?

Damuah undoubtedly saw himself as appointed by divine providence to carry out a specific assignment:

> The Almighty and Merciful God, by His divine providence chose His servant KWABENA DAMUAH to proclaim HIS message to mankind from an African perspective. He was assisted in no small measure by his Chief Spokesman, Osofo KWADWO OPOKU-POKU who is general secretary of the Afrikania Mission. As a religion, it is the language of Africa and therefore has no founder. It is a gift of God, and we must polish it up, refine it, animate it and live it. It is God's revelation to Africa that Osofo Damuah and his people the 'AFRIKAN-IANS' are preaching. They are messengers of God not 'founders'. They are merely putting the pieces together.[19]

Damuah stopped short of presenting himself as a Messiah, but was content to compare himself and his role to that of John the Baptist, preparing the way for the coming Messiah, though he failed to identify who this was to be. To Damuah, therefore, Afrikania was a prophecy still in the process of fulfilment.

Despite the strong emphasis on African *particularism* in his message, Damuah seems careful not to create the impression of preaching a message of African *exclusivism*. He thus declares that Afrikania '. . . . is open to all men and women, irrespective of race, colour, creed, or national origin. Religion is first and foremost a matter of conscience. All are invited to the oldest religion on earth that is now 'born again' and again.[20]

---

[19] Damuah, *Afrikania Handbook*, Section 35 and Appendix 4. On his belief in the divine inspiration behind Afrikania, see also Damuah, *Afrikania in Brief*, p. 7, section 8, and *Common Sense Series No. 8*, p. 9, section 14.

[20] See Damuah, *Afrikania Handbook*, Sections 39, 60, and 71.

As a notable Ghanaian scholar put it

> What we had in Afrikania was more than another new religious move-
> ment; indeed, perhaps even more than a revitalisation of traditional
> religion. Rather, what we had was a deliberate universalising of the
> traditional religion into an alternative to Christianity and Islam. Thus
> in Ghana it amounted to a fundamental challenge to Christianity, in
> particular, to offer an adequate interpretation of reality to provide a
> credible framework for African life.[21]

Damuah's vision, actions and writings all carried a significant ring
of cultural nationalism, of a distinctively African variety, and this
was an integral part of his movement. Asare Opoku observes that

> The cultural nationalism which comes through Damuah placed him
> in the line of other nationalists who preceded him . . . such as Edward
> Wilmot Blyden, Casely Hayford, etc. . . . But Damuah differed from
> them in the extent to which he went pushing for African particular-
> ism and making a complete break with Christianity. For the leaders
> of the churches inspired by nationalist feeling, such as Rev. Dr Mark
> Christian Hayford and his National Baptist Church, founded in 1898,
> and Rev. J.B. Anaman and his Nigritian Church, founded in 1907,
> stayed within the fold of Christianity.[22]

It could be argued that Damuah saw himself above all as a religious
reformer rather than a cultural nationalist, but to him nationalism,
politics and the rest were all 'religious' (or 'holy') and worthwhile
endeavours, even duties, which come under the umbrella of religious
life and living. True to African Traditional Religious life, thought
and practice, Damuah preached the integration of everything in life,
the material and the spiritual, the secular with the sacred.

After the founding of Afrikania, Damuah abandoned the title of
Reverend Father for that of *Osofo-Okomfo*, which created confusion
because of the conventional identification in Ghanaian society in
general and Akan society in particular of the title *Osofo* with a Christian priest and of *Okomfo* with a traditional religious priest. To com-
bine them could seem ludicrous, even sacrilegious. However, as Asare
Opoku explains

---

[21] Kofi Asare Opoku, p. 55, citing Kwame Bediako in his William Ofori Atta
Memorial Lectures 1992, Lecture II, 'Ghana's Legitimate Quest for Cultural Identity—
A Christian Response and Contribution.'
[22] Ibid., pp. 55–6.

The Akan word 'Osofo', which Christian ministers have applied to themselves since the introduction of Christianity into the Akan world, originally referred to the official who interpreted the utterances of possessed priests and priestesses at the shrines ... The word 'Okomfo' also refers to a priest or priestess who is the servant and mouthpiece of a god or goddess. The 'Okomfo' is possessed by a deity and usually receives a call after which he or she undergoes a period of training before assuming office.[23]

However, from the evidence available it seems that Damuah did not play the role of '*Osofo*' in the traditional religious sense, nor was he known to have been possessed by any deity. Asare Opoku surmises that Damuah chose the titles to give himself respectability and identity to further his cause, and in fact he stuck to them, characteristically dismissive of objection and ridicule.

It is clear that Damuah felt called by God to establish Afrikania for cultural and, especially, religious reasons. More specifically, he sets out in some detail what he considers the rationale for the coming into being of his Movement. Concerning the choice of name, he writes, 'The name Afrikania is an invitation to all of us to return to our roots, to the original and pure sense of love, truth and justice that is not adulterated, not commercialized and not polluted.'[24]

In his *Afrikania Handbook*, Damuah enumerates and explains the reason for Afrikania as follows:

a) We must remember that God speaks to every race and culture and the message communicated must be adapted according to the mode of the receiver.

b) Religion is the real essential commodity meant to be shared not hoarded. It is more essential than sugar, soap, sardines and all material things put together.

c) We want to make *AFRIKANIA* a living reality centrally relevant to the world in general and Africa in particular.

d) It is our duty to resuscitate the *AFRIKANIAN* religion. We can't '*stay put*', merely to preside over the death of the African Traditional Religion in these days of African Redemption and pride in African religious culture.

e) It is better to risk abuses in our genuine attempt at re-structuring the AFRIKAN faith rather than not making the attempt. It is better to light one candle than to curse the darkness.

---

[23] Ibid., p. 57.
[24] Damuah, *Common Sense Series No. 8*, p. 2.

f) We take great consolation in the teaching of Vatican II, that the moral good in non-Christian traditions be acknowledged, preserved and promoted.

g) We live in Africa and the best way to serve God effectively and productively is through the expression of our unique identity. God is our Father, not a stranger. We must serve HIM, the way we know Him and understand Him. We should not be carbon copies of other people's experiments and styles. We should be ourselves and create our own forms of worship from our own perspective.

h) Many Africans are turned off by so-called foreign religions and are in dearth [*sic*: probably 'dire' was intended] need of something 'traditional' which is based on their roots. All they need is the opportunity to worship in an African way. We have to win converts by personal good example.

i) We are committed to restructuring this 'born again' faith (AFRIKAN-IAN) so that it can take its pre-eminent role as the source of organised religions.

j) In order to succeed, the African Revolution must have a strong spiritual base, stretch her hand to God, the true and living God of Africa, the God of the whole universe. (Ethiopia shall stretch forth her hand unto God.)

k) The Afrikanian has the responsibility to take a stand in stewardship to rid our. . . . [incomplete in the document]

l) Conversion to AFRIKANIA is a kind of spiritual and mental liberation. It is actually *being born again and again*. 'Mental bondage is invisible violence'. Spiritual bondage is a form of colonial bondage. The time to follow our own conscience is overdue. . . . It means, accepting new challenges, making new social relationships and breaking old ways.

Finally, Damuah laments

The Chinese are proud of their spiritual heritage. They pray to God according to their tradition and God hears them. The Japanese are proud of their spiritual heritage, and the same applies to the Arabs, Jews, Indians, etc. Why is it that many Africans are ashamed of their rich spiritual tradition? Because they have not studied it properly, and they do not understand it.[25]

In short, Damuah's answer to the question 'Why Afrikania?' would seem to be 'Why not? It is culturally appropriate for Africa to have its own religion.'

[25] See Damuah's works *Common Sense Series No. 8*, Preface, *Common Sense Series No. 7*, *Answer to Critics*, Preface, *Afrikania in Brief*, Introduction, *Introduction to Traditional Religion*, pp. 1 and 16–17, *Gye Nyame Series No. 1: Fundamental Notions of Afrikania*, p. 1, *Afrikania Mission*, Preface.

Theology, Doctrine and Practice of Afrikania

The theological and doctrinal content of Afrikania religion basically reflects an African traditional religious worldview, coupled with a Christian orientation, mediated through the language, background and outlook of the founder. Damuah sets out his understanding of theology as follows:

> Theology literally means 'the science about God'. In the African context, religion permeates our entire way of life and everything we do has a religious dimension. Indeed, we see God as the force and power in everything that exists. Theology is about 'why' and 'how' God plays a role in our life.[26]

He follows this with his definitions of Liberation and Black Theology, and theologies of marriage, time, sex and sexual politics,[27] as well as practical theology:

> In order to obtain SALVATION we must put into action the following:
> 1. Practical Theology of LOVE and LIBERATION
> 2. Practical Theology of REPENTANCE and CORRECTION
> 3. Practical Theology of SELF-RELIANCE and GOOD WORKS.[28]

Damuah asserts that the Afrikania Movement is 'much more than doctrine', and describes it rather as

> A way of life and not a matter of believing in certain abstract propositions and practising some rituals. It is the treasury of the best from our culture and the collective experience of our people. In brief, it is a family with God as our Grandfather; a co-operative, that believes in winning by example, with special emphasis on *cleanliness, human values*, and all aspects of *farming*, fish, crop and animal husbandry. Projects such as spiritual and traditional healing clinics, museums, libraries, digging wells, writing local history, cultural workshops, are very important in our programme.[29]

He did, however, provide more conventional guidelines as to what Afrikania required its members to believe and live by. The basic beliefs are contained in different versions of a 'Statement of Declaration' known as 'OUR LIVING FAITH':[30]

---

[26] *Afrikania Handbook*, section 82.
[27] *Afrikania Handbook*, sections 83, 84, 96, 97, 98.
[28] 'Why I Resigned—Damuah', p. 3.
[29] *Afrikania Handbook*, section 38.
[30] What follows is a compilation of different versions from the following sources:

1. We believe in one God the Creator of the Universe whose nature is LOVE, and that the best way to serve Him is to serve mankind, and to use His creatures for His glory. . . . God is the Mystery of Mysteries, Supreme Spirit, Creator of the universe, perfect in Himself, without beginning and without end.

2. We believe that He is the CENTRE of our life. He is everywhere by His power, presence and essence and He knows, sees and hears everything. (This is) Theo-centrism, or God-Centred approach to life.

3. We believe in the spirituality and immortality of the human SOUL and the possibility of re-incarnation for all.

4. We believe that after DEATH, the separated soul enters a new state of 'Happiness' or 'Unhappiness' in the spirit world (*asamando*) in accordance with GOD'S JUDGEMENT and our belief that 'we shall reap what we sow.' . . .

5. We believe that the human race is ONE FAMILY, with God as our Grandfather and First Ancestor. This implies love (concern) and fellowship for all, not hate. The rich must help the poor, who must, in turn, make an honest effort to uplift themselves . . .

6. We believe in LIBATION as the climax of our COMMUNITY WORSHIP in which we pray to God directly, and also through our ancestors and other intermediaries . . .

7. We believe in commitment to total human development through CREATIVE EDUCATION with special emphasis on the mental, moral and manual aspects.

8. We believe that in order to obtain SALVATION (for both soul and body) we must serve (worship) God according to our conscience and conviction, and how God is revealed in our culture. This implies
    a) A Positive implementation of the basic meaning of LOVE and REDEMPTION (LIBERATION).
    b) A Life of REPENTANCE and RECONCILIATION (COR-RECTION).
    c) A Commitment to SELF-RELIANCE and GOOD WORKS (DEVELOPMENT).
    d) A Revolution in the meaning of Religion and Salvation.
    e) A Theology of Action and Liberation.

9. We believe that PRAYER means basically living righteously and creatively for the benefit of society. It is a way of life that implies constructive and positive thinking, meditation, doing one's duty well, attending meetings for a good cause, development projects, agricultural evangelism, and all kinds of good works.

'Why I Resigned—Damuah', *Afrikania in Brief*, pp. 2–4, *Afrikania Mission*, p. 2, *Common Sense Series No. 7*, pp. 15–17, and *No. 8*, pp. 3–6, *Introduction to Traditional Religion*, pp. 4–5.

10. We believe that SERVICE to our country, mankind, the community, neighbour and all God's creatures is a prayer and service
to God. Amen-Ra (Amen).

An Afrikania Worship Service

Damuah prepared an order for worship services, variants of which
appear in a number of his writings. The proceedings observed by
the author over several months in 1993 follow this closely. The services were held at a temporary 'shrine' at the Centre for National
Culture (Arts Centre) in Accra, and the membership largely represented the Accra Branch of the Mission. Worship usually began
around 11 am and lasted for approximately two hours. There was
an average attendance of thirty or so, mostly male, with a handful
of women[31] and children. The main languages used were English
and Akan.

Preparation

An 'Altar' is prepared, represented by a couple of simple tables joined
together, and covered with a piece of cloth, designed in black traditional 'Adinkra' symbols, against a blue background. Alternatively,
the 'altar' table is covered with a piece of the Afrikania special com-
memorative cloth. This has designs consisting of a male horn-blower
dressed in traditional cloth, and surrounded by a number of 'Adinkra'
symbols, with the inscription 'Afrikania' printed at the base of the
horn-blower. It comes in two main colour combinations: one has
the symbols and inscriptions printed in green over a yellow background, while the other has blackish designs and lettering over a
greyish background. At the centre of the table is placed a fairly large
wooden 'Gye Nyame' symbol and here again there are two types,
one in black and brown colours and the other white. It is flanked
on one side by a miniature hoisted national flag (or a miniature wood

---

[31] While Afrikania affirmed its belief in sexual equality, particularly with reference to women priests, the role and participation of women was limited. It must
be one of very few religious movements in Ghana with women members in the
minority. In 1993 there was only one woman with any real authority, Madam Aba
Baffoe, who held the office of 'National President' and was the sole female member of the National Executive Committee of the Movement. Damuah's widow,
Madam Akua Tano, played the role of a kind of 'mother' or 'first lady', but her
position was more ceremonial than executive.

flagstaff to which are attached both the national and Afrikania flags, the latter consisting of a 'Gye Nyame' insignia), and on the other by a 'Sankofa' symbol. Other things on the table include a couple of whisks made of horsetails, known as 'bodua' in Akan.

Another (single) table is prepared to the left of the 'altar', also covered with a piece of the Afrikania cloth. On the table are placed the accessories needed for the libation prayer, consisting of a bottle of water, schnapps or other drink, two calabashes, and a small locally woven basket, which serves as a collection bowl. There are also about four drums standing ready to be used by the Youth (Musical) Wing, as well as a beaded rattle, a castanet, an ivory horn ('abentia') and one or two other local instruments. The linguist is also ready with his staff.

Commencement

There are introductory songs or chants, as the functionaries and congregation take their places: the Main Officiant (or Master of Ceremonies), accompanied by two or three other elders or leaders, behind the altar table; the Linguist, usually in the company of one elder, to the right of the altar facing the congregation; the Musical Group to the right of the rest of the congregation, facing the altar.

Procedure

The service proper begins with a couple of Afrikania chants or 'Asafo Songs'. The Leader or Officiant greets and welcomes the congregation. This is followed by the opening prayers by the Officiant, or an invited member of the congregation. These prayers are usually confession of sins against God and neighbour and commitment to the service of God and fellow human beings. The Officiant then leads the congregation in making the circular symbol of God's protection on their foreheads, before a reading of an extract from one of Afrikania's publications or one of its favourite books,[32] followed by a short explanation or comment, punctuated by shouts of approval and encouragement from the congregation.

---

[32] Damuah's intention was that Afrikanians should develop their own body of scriptures, including *The Book of Truth* (never completed), but in fact they drew freely from books about Ghanaian and African cultural and traditional values, those depicting Egyptian civilization as being African in identity and orientation, as well as ancient Egyptian spiritual writings, including *The Book of the Dead*. Favourites included Kofi Antubam, *Ghana's Heritage of Culture* (1963), J.B. Danquah, *The Akan Doctrine of*

After a song or responsorial chant, there are 'cultural lessons' from two or three members, which may include current news relevant to the Movement. More singing and drumming precedes the main message, delivered by an Afrikanian priest, leader or 'guest messenger', then comes the offertory, accompanied by singing and filing past the altar, and the libation prayer. Newcomers and visitors, if any, are introduced and announcements made. Members of the congregation, amidst singing, then file past the altar once again, dip their fingers in the libation drink and smear their foreheads with it, while forming a circle. All join hands for the final prayers and benediction, during which the officiant sprinkles the libation liquid on them.

Damuah wrote at length about the importance of libation in Afrikania worship, explaining

> Libation in general is a prayer which consists in the pouring of some liquid (for example, water, beer, wine, schnapps, other beverages), or the sprinkling of some food (mashed corn or yam) and the invocation of the Supreme Being, intermediary gods and the spirits of our ancestors. In Libation we pray to God directly and also through the god spirits or mini-gods, our ancestors (dead, but alive in spirit) and other intermediaries of our choice, and ask for God's blessings for our country and the world.[33]

Afrikania: The Political Connection

Despite its stated religious objectives, in its early days Afrikania was perceived by many as a wing of the 31st December Revolution., partly because of Damuah's (brief) membership of the ruling PNDC, and partly because of his public pronouncements in support of the Revolution. The Movement also received infra-structural, logistic and other support from the government, notably its headquarters building, located in an 'exclusive' residential part of Accra. Damuah's strong support for the leader of the Revolution is seen in the following reply from his interview in the *Afrikania Voice*:

God (1968), Cheikh Anta Diop, *African Origin of Civilization: Myth or Reality* (1974), *Precolonial Black Africa* (1987), *Civilization or Barbarism* (1990), G.M. James, *Stolen Legacy* (first edn. 1954), R.S. Rattray, *Religion and Art in Ashanti* (1927).

[33] *Afrikania Handbook*, section 6.5, *Afrikania in Brief*, p. 8, 'Why I Resigned—Damuah', *Gye Nyame Series No. 1*, p. 6, *Common Sense Series No. 7*, pp. 7ff. and *No. 8*, p. 11, *Introduction to Traditional Religion*, pp. 3 and 13ff., *Miracle at the Shrine*, p. 65.

I am not sure whether I was the first to use the beautiful expression 'Junior Jesus' as the title for Flt.-Lt. J.J. Rawlings, Head of State of Ghana. It seems to me that the expression sprang up spontaneously from the masses during the first week after June 4th, 1979 . . . At any rate I endorse the idea as a genuine assessment of the masses. It is a credit to Jesus and a challenge to J.J. Rawlings to live up to his commitment which is basically LIBERATION, LOVE, TRUTH, FREE-DOM and JUSTICE. The message Christ preached and the aims of the Ghana Revolution or Holy War are the same.[34]

Further, in his *Let Your Light Shine*, Damuah devotes a whole section to Rawlings and his Revolution, and writes,

That name [Rawlings] rings like a bell. Now, whether we accept it or not, he was sent by God to deliver a message to Ghanaians. And he did it. *As a prophet, he is Ghana's John the Baptist; as a leader, he is a brave Moses.* He confirms the lesson that: 'You can fool all the people for some of the time. You can fool some of the people all the time. But you can't fool all the people all the time.' Before the June 4th Revolution we had all given up hope for a better Ghana, but now through Rawlings and the AFRC [Armed Forces Revolutionary Council], we realise that the time for our salvation is now.[35]

The reasons for Damuah's leaving the PNDC are unclear, and his own statements on the matter are ambiguous, though he did declare that he still supported the revolution wholeheartedly.[36] However, the alliance between the Movement and the government did not last long, at least not in the way it began: Damuah and his Afrikania, the weaker party, had more to lose as resources dwindled and importance and influence plummeted.

The Decline of the Movement

For a time Afrikania enjoyed support not only from those who saw it as an interesting and useful religio-cultural dimension of the political revolution, but also from leaders and practitioners of traditional religion, who naturally saw in it an opportunity to reassert their

[34] 'Why I Resigned—Damuah', interview in the *Afrikania Voice*, see note 2.
[35] *Let Your Light Shine*, 1980, pp. 13–14. For comment on this, see Max Assimeng, *Religion and Social Change in West Africa: An Introduction to the Sociology of Religion*, Accra: Ghana Universities Press, 1989, p. 242. See also John S. Pobee, *Religion and Politics in Ghana*, Accra: Asempa Publishers, Christian Council of Ghana, 1991, p. 63.
[36] 'Osofo Damuah Defends Afrikania Religion', *Christian Messenger*, see note 7.

belief and practice. There was another category of supporters in a small core of well-educated, mainly young people, who constituted a type of elite membership, vigorously promoting the Movement's image via the media and organizing symposia and lectures on African issues. However, Afrikania did not succeed in effectively reaching out to or truly representing the majority of traditional religious practitioners, many of whom are illiterate or barely literate working-class people. This is probably because many of the core of well-educated leaders, including the founder himself, in fact had no real traditional religious background or experience. They could therefore easily be perceived as representing a kind of club for the traditional religious elite, mostly resident in Accra and other big cities, appearing to be preoccupied with gaining social respectability and recognition for the Movement, and in the process carving out an image for themselves.

Afrikania also had its 'natural enemies', mostly Christians, especially from the evangelical and fundamentalist streams, who saw the Movement as nothing short of a 'demonic assault' on the nation and used the Christian newspaper *The Watchman* to attack it, even after Damuah's death. He was also challenged at a more intellectual and theological level by other opponents, notably the Revd Dr S. Asante-Antwi (currently Presiding Bishop of the Methodist Church of Ghana).

But a crucial factor in the Movement's decline was the emergence from the 1970s of Christian Neo-Pentecostalist or Charismatic Churches,[37] which draw their membership largely (though not exclusively) from the country's educated youth. The appeal of these churches derives from their persuasive message and presentation, as well as the apparent concrete physical and material indicators, acting as a forceful witness to their teaching and claims. Also attractive are their vibrant, modern and sophisticated worship services, as well as the personal participation of members, coupled with the concern of the church for almost every aspect of members' lives. They have efficient evangelistic strategies, and one or two even have an overt and specific *African* cultural agenda and emphasis, thus further counteracting Afrikania's appeal and undermining its distinctiveness.

---

[37] See Elom Dovlo, 'A Comparative Overview of Independent Churches and Charismatic Ministries in Ghana', *Trinity Journal of Church and Theology*, Vol. 2, No. 2, 1992, pp. 55–73, and Paul Gifford, 'Ghana's Charismatic Churches', *Journal of Religion in Africa*, XXIV.3, 1994, pp. 241–265.

It soon became obvious that, despite Afrikania's initial appeal, which in any case would soon wear off, it would stand no chance of competing with these new churches or, indeed, with Christianity in general. Though Ghanaians as a people may be proud of their ethnic affiliations, nationality and racial identity, many prefer to identify above all with the Christian faith. The Movement was, furthermore, lacking in resources, nor did it have good overall administrative and organizational machinery.

Damuah's death brought more problems, including a leadership struggle, exacerbated by ethnic factors, which were continuing at the time the author concluded his main period of fieldwork in 1993. Ten years after its foundation, Afrikania was still far from being a major player in Ghanaian religion, though its few members naturally hoped that it had a bright and promising future. Visits from researchers may have given the Movement a boost, but Afrikania faced a precarious future. At that time, its significance was becoming increasingly a matter of insignificance.

Afrikania in Crisis: Conflict, Confrontation and Confusion

By 2000, the struggle over Osofo-Okomfo Damuah's mantle, eight years after his death, had eventually resulted not only in conflict and apparent schism, but also in legal wrangling. In summary, from the Afrikania Mission emerged a distinct body known as Afrikan Renaissance Mission (ARM), or the Sankofa Faith, founded in 1997 by one of the first priests ordained by Damuah, a building contractor in secular life who now wishes to be addressed as His Holiness Osofo Kofi Ameve.

ARM traces its origins to the Afrikania Mission, but seeks to present itself as 'reorganized' Afrikania, while using the two names synonymously. This potentially confusing position is sharply contested by an opposing faction led by another of Damuah's ordained priests, Osofo Kwasi Dankama Quarm, a former Acting Deputy Director for the Co-ordination of Herbal Medicine at Ghana's Ministry of Health, who calls himself '(Acting) Head of Afrikania Mission' and 'Osofo-Okomfo II'.

This faction insists that the ARM is not identical to Damuah's Afrikania Mission since, among other things, it is registered as a sep-

arate and distinct body, and that it should not claim to be the genuine Afrikania. The two sides have played out much of this drama,
with claims and counter-claims, in the media, especially in newspapers. Two other functionaries now found in opposite camps who
have been contributing to the press battle are Ameve's supporter,
Osofo Yaw Boakye, designated National Organizer for Afrikania
Mission, and Okofo Bessebrow Bray, who uses the title Press Secretary
of Afrikania Mission, and is sympathetic to Quarm's cause.

Meanwhile, Ameve's ARM seems to be asserting itself as an
influential mouthpiece of Ghanaian African Traditional Religion,
though this has not been without further controversy and conflict
with some traditional religious authorities in the country. It therefore appears that the whole drama of the Afrikania Movement, in
whatever form, is still unfolding.

Conclusion

This essay has centred on one of the most interesting developments
in Ghanaian religio-cultural history and spirituality. The founder of
the Afrikania Movement was as radical and controversial as the
movement itself, as was the socio-political period in which Afrikania
was established. However it is clear that whatever influence the socio-
political context may have had on Afrikania, it was essentially and
ultimately a *religious* movement, with a strong cultural content and
agenda, 'Afrocentrism' as Damuah might term it. Equally interesting is the apparent rapid decline of the Movement and the further
controversy into which it was plunged after the founder's death.
Contrary to earlier expectations, in view of these unfolding events
its real significance may yet lie in the future.

Select Bibliography

A. *Books and Pamphlets by Osofo-Okomfo Kwabena Damuah*

Let Your Light Shine (Father Damuah Series 1), Takoradi, Ghana Humanitarian Association for National Advancement (G.H.A.N.A.), 1980, with an Introduction by Revd John Baptist Kobina Baidoo (parish priest of Shama).

Afrikania Handbook, Accra, Afrikania Mission, n.d. (c. 1983).

Fundamental Notions on Afrikania—Reformed African Traditional Religion—Gye Nyame Series No. 1, n.d.

Afrikania Mission: Basic Teachings; and The Fourteen Pillars of Life (Fundamental Rules of Life for Afrikanians, compiled by Okofo ['Warrior'] Bessebrow Bray, Press Secretary, n.d.

Afrikania in Brief (Reformed African Traditional Religion), Accra, Afrikania Mission, December 1983.

Afrikania (Reformed Traditional Religion)—Common Sense Series No. 7: Answer to Critics, Accra, Afrikania Mission, March 1984.

Afrikania (Reformed Traditional Religion)—Common Sense Series No. 8, Accra, Afrikania Mission, March 1984.

African Contribution to Civilization—African Heritage Series No. 1, Accra, Afrikania Mission, January 1985.

Introduction to Traditional Religion, Reformed African Traditional Religion (2nd edn.), Accra, Afrikania Mission, 1988.

Miracle at the Shrine. Religious and Revolutionary Miracle in Ghana, Accra, Damess Paper Products Ltd., 1990.

Constitution of the Afrikania Mission (Godian Religion) Re-activation of African Traditional Religion, n.d. (c. 1990).

B. *Afrikania Newspapers*

Afrikania Voice, Vol. 1, No. 1, August 1–15, 1983.
Afrikania Voice, Vol. 1, No. 2, September, 1983.
Afrikania Voice, Vol. 1, No. 3, January 16–30, 1987.
Afrikania Voice, Vol. 1, No. 4, February/March, 1987.
Afrikania Voice, Special Edition, January 1988.

CHAPTER TEN

CHRISTIANITY WITHOUT FRONTIERS: SHONA MISSIONARIES AND TRANSNATIONAL PENTECOSTALISM IN AFRICA

David Maxwell

Introduction: Religious Transnationalism[1] in Central and Southern Africa

The religious map of central and southern Africa has long been coloured by great regional religious identities. Before Christianity established itself, the territorial cults of Mbona in Malawi and Mwari in Zimbabwe received streams of pilgrims from polities hundreds of miles away.[2] Pioneering missionaries had an equally broad African vision, locating their mission stations on highways or natural frontiers with little concern for the region's eventual political landscape. The Universities' Mission to Central Africa station on Likoma Island, Lake Malawi, is a prime example. Other regional Christian identities, like the Anglican Archbishopric of Central Africa, were made possible by the existence of empire. Expanded Christian identities were not only created organizationally but also arose from movements of Africans taking their religion with them. Some predated empire. Refugees fleeing the early nineteenth-century *Mfecane* took their faith as far as Lake Malawi. Labour gangs from Pedi and further north in the Transvaal encountered Christianity as they moved in search of work and spread it into Botswana and Ovambo.[3] But

---

[1] The term 'transnational' refers to a movement that operates at supra-national or regional level. While such movements transcend state boundaries they are not 'global' in the sense of having an effect which is 'world-wide' (Giddens, 1990, p. 64, cited in Nederveen Pieterse, 1995, p. 48). Neither can such movements claim to be 'international' 'in the strict sense of involving nations as corporate actors' (Hannerz, 1996, p. 6.). Often key actors are economic migrants, traders, diaspora and refugees. For more general literature on globalization see Featherstone *et al.*, 1995.

[2] Ranger, 1985 and 1999. Schoffeleers, 1992.

[3] Sundkler and Steed, 2000, chapter 7.

the coming of empire increased the frequency and intensity of such
encounters. Communication was aided by English as a *lingua franca*,
although it was certainly not the only language in which religious
encounter took place. Adrian Hastings sets the scene well in his
magnificent *The Church in Africa 1450–1950*:

> There had always been more travelling than many an outsider had
> imagined . . . Railways helped to make it possible, so did the bicycle,
> which by the 1930s was becoming the cherished possession of the
> slightly better-off, but improvement in the roads helped the basic busi-
> ness of walking and many people walked extraordinary distances. As
> labourers travelled they carried religion with them . . . The pull of edu-
> cation took many on to the road. The pull of employment and the
> earning of money in mine or plantation drew still more. Catechists
> might abandon their almost unpaid work to find money on the
> Copperbelt for a bicycle, yet the pull of religion could also lead to
> remarkable journeys . . . By the 1930s countless ordinary Africans took
> books, trains, and bicycles very much for granted as part of their own
> lives. They could have homes in northern Nyasaland and work on the
> Rand, or in Tanganyika and work in Uganda or Kenya. They spoke
> more languages than most missionaries. The very uniformity of the
> colonial order, the lack of manned frontiers, passports, or a clear sense
> of citizenship, all helped the emergence of an almost continent-wide
> new society.[4]

The openness of colonial frontiers had unexpected consequences for
demographics and subsequently for Christianization. Before the late
1950s Nyasa and Portuguese East African migrants in Salisbury,
Southern Rhodesia, outnumbered local Shona.[5] These migrant groups
dominated urban life, and the Nyasas in particular had a profound
influence on religious culture, bringing with them Presbyterianism
and strengthening the city's Dutch Reformed contingent.[6] But religious traffic moved in many directions, and it was not always the
historical mission churches and their 'unplanned people movements'
that were most mobile. The so-called African independent churches
had a great propensity to movement, often to the point of its being

---

[4] Hastings, 1994, pp. 544–5.
[5] In 1956 only 40 per cent of workers were Southern Rhodesian in origin while
20 per cent were from Nyasaland and 40 per cent from Portuguese East Africa.
Report, Director of African Administration, Salisbury, 1956, National Archives of
Zimbabwe (NAZ).
[6] Yoshikuni, 1989. Hallencreutz, 1998, chapter 3.

a defining characteristic.[7] Initially unencumbered by large bureau-cratic infrastructures and developmentalist goals, these churches could acquire a huge transnational reach. Two Shona movements appear-ing in the 1930s are pertinent to this case study, the Apostolic Church of Johana Maranke and the Apostolic Church of Johana Masowe, popularly known as the *Vapostori*. By 1973 the *Vapostori* of Johana Maranke had spread from eastern Zimbabwe along migrant labour routes into Botswana, Rhodesia, Zambia, Malawi, Tanzania, Angola and Zaire,[8] and Johana Masowe had witnessed the spread of his Apostolic or Korsten Basketmakers Church into eastern and central Africa as well as South Africa. While propelled by the same mix of migrancy and evangelistic zeal,[9] the Basketmakers' journey north, toward Jerusalem, was also motivated by a sense of pilgrimage, and exodus from a succession of hostile colonial governments.[10]

Since 1957 another Shona religious movement, which eventually became Zimbabwe Assemblies of God Africa/Forward in Faith Inter-national (ZAOGA/FIFMI) has slowly developed a transnational reach. In the 1960s and 70s, under the humbler name of Assemblies of God African (AOGA), it spread just beyond its borders into neigh-bouring countries, but after independence it expanded into Central, East and West Africa and even beyond the continent.[11] Its early methods of growth had paralleled those of the *Vapostori* but by the 1980s it appeared at times more like an electronic church in the global born-again movement.

---

[7] Werbner, 1989, chapter 8.
[8] Jules-Rosette, 1975, p. 229 and chapter 7.
[9] Dillon-Malone, 1978, pp. 106, 116 and 117.
[10] Hastings, 1979, pp. 248–50.
[11] Until 1967 the movement operated informally as a small band known as the Ezekiel Guti Evangelistic Association (EGEA), see 'A Brief History of Ezekiel "All Nations Evangelistic Crusade"' by R.M.G. Kupara, c. 1980, file, 'Histories', ZAOGA Archives, Waterfalls (ZAW). Then, for less than a year, from March 1967, it was officially known as the Pentecost African Assemblies of God, see Constitution in the possession of David Choto. In 1968 it became the Assemblies of God, African (AOGA), see J. Choto, 'To Whom it May Concern', July 1968, file, AOGA Correspondence 1964–80. From 1972 onwards much of its transnational work has happened under the banner Forward in Faith Mission International (FIFMI), see *The Macedonian Call*, 20 May 1972, vol. 1, no. 1, published by FIFMI. In 1977 it evolved into the Assemblies of God Africa (still AOGA). And finally, after inde-pendence it became the Zimbabwe Assemblies of God, Africa (ZAOGA). Executive Committee Minute Book, 6 December 1977 and 26 May 1981, ZAW.

Pentecostalism, Labour Migrancy and the Origins of AOGA

The flux of people and ideas in which ZAOGA was forged was
given added stimulus by Southern Rhodesia's post-war boom.[12] As
Salisbury's manufacturing base expanded, more labour migrants
flooded in from Nyasaland and Portuguese East Africa. Turnover
was high. Analysis of the 348,000 Africans working in the city between 1953 and 1957 revealed that 70 per cent were employed for
only 5.3 months before leaving.[13] Such mobility rapidly expanded
the horizons of the migrants. In 1952 the Director of African Administration, Salisbury, commented on the recent experience of thousands of migrants who had been transported to Witwatersrand's mines
by air:

> . . . [T]he African of Southern Rhodesia, led by men who have trav-
> elled, is no longer to be regarded as a simple minded rustic whose
> ideas extend no further than a dilapidated kraal in a Native reserve,
> [but he is] growing into a man of the world whose views, while not
> necessarily the product of personal experience, will doubtless be coloured
> by a wide and probably cosmopolitan circle.[14]

ZAOGA had a dual pedigree of transnational Pentecostalism: the
Apostolic Faith Mission of South Africa (AFM) and the Assemblies
of God of South Africa (AOGSA). The Apostolic Faith Mission was
one of Africa's earliest Pentecostal movements. It was founded in
South Africa in 1908 by American missionaries only two years after
the Azusa Street Revival in California, usually regarded as the beginning of the Pentecostal phenomenon. In 1915 an AFM evangelist,
Zacharias Manamela, entered Gwanda reserve in Southern Rhodesia
and established a church of some 400 adherents. Two years later
the first two white missionary couples arrived. The manner in which
the AFM was founded here characterized its subsequent development. It was a dynamic proselytizing movement led by zealous African
evangelists, and followed by a handful of overstretched, but no less
zealous, missionaries, who tried to bring it under their centralizing
control. By the 1930s the AFM was very active in the reserves around
Salisbury and in the east. Left to their own devices the movement's

---

[12] Phimister, 1988, chapter 5, Phimister and Raftopoulos, (2000).
[13] Annual Report, Director of African Administration, Salisbury, 1957, NAZ.
[14] Ibid. 1951–52 (NAZ).

evangelists and pastors created their own version of Pentecostalism, drawing particularly on the purity laws in Leviticus. AFM prophets, with shaven heads, long beards, and wearing white robes, roamed the reserves with a message of repentance, divine healing and exorcism. The movement contributed directly and significantly to the rich composite of ideologies and ritual practices in the *Vapostori* movements of Masowe and Maranke, the former of which is the subject of Terence Ranger's essay in this volume.

The AFM prophets' exotic appearance, their rejection of bio-medicine, their propensity to rebaptize mission church converts, their mountain-top meetings in which adherents could fall into ecstatic 'whitefire' trances, and their association with the *Vapostori* movements all caused the colonial state considerable discomfort. In 1934 AFM missionaries were banned from the reserves, which only served to increase the African section's sense of autonomy. The black section of the AFM, viewed by the state as a subversive 'pseudo-religious movement', had at its core the desire to proselytize unfettered by either missionaries or the state. This imperative was exemplified by one of the AFM's leading evangelists and later head minister, Enoch Gwanzura. Having 'stolen' the missionary's and administrator's hat, Gwanzura roamed rural areas in his white pith helmet proclaiming a message of salvation which revolutionized social relations: burning fetishes, overturning beer pots, breaking up traditional ceremonies, and challenging the authority of elders.[15]

The immediate circumstances of ZAOGA's birth lay in two further metamorphoses in the black AFM. The first was its establishment in the city. From the late 1930s a small church existed in Harare (later Mbare), Salisbury's first African township.[16] The second was the arrival in 1938 of more hard-nosed AFM missionaries, willing to curb the spontaneous activities of their black brothers in return for state recognition. As attempts were made to halt the more exotic activities of white-robed prophets and to control proselytizing by lay evangelists, a wave of schisms occurred.[17] In 1959, a later, and at the time apparently insignificant, schism led to the emergence of AOGA.

---

[15] See Hastings, 1994, p. 456.
[16] Hallencreutz, 1998, p. 198.
[17] Maxwell, 1999(a), pp. 191–92 and 1999(b) pp. 260–63.

By the 1950s the activities of the AFM had spread from Harare to the newer township of Highfields. A group of artisans and entrepreneurs from both locations came together as a youth choir: Joseph Choto, Raphael Kupara, Lazarus Mamvura, James Muhwati, Priscilla Ngoma, Caleb Ngorima and Abel Sande. They retained connections with rural Pentecostalism, gathering in the mountains and reserves around Salisbury for night meetings, and they looked to Enoch Gwanzura for inspiration. Increasingly they came under the influence of a carpenter and lay evangelist, Ezekiel Guti, forming a prayer band to support his semi-autonomous evangelistic activities. The prayer band proved extremely loyal. Meetings were held in Priscilla Ngoma's house and Abel Sande cared for Guti's family while Ezekiel, aided by Caleb Ngorima, ran his own campaign in Manicaland in 1957 under the guise of the Ezekiel Guti Evangelistic Association (EGEA).[18] Guti's local evangelistic activities were given a considerable boost when he won a new bicycle in a race sponsored by his employer, Fisons Fertilizer Company. A chapter in Guti's hagiography was devoted to the bike and its acquisition, such was its significance.[19]

Guti established a significant following. Black AFM ministers would invite him to preach,[20] and when he was at home a stream of clients would come to his cottage in Highfields in search of healing. He had a particular gift for curing infertility.[21] His unofficial activities soon attracted the attention of missionaries and elder African pastors, irked by his attitude and unnerved by his success. Missionary attempts to curtail Guti's activities proved fruitless, and in 1959 he left the AFM, followed by his prayer band.

This secession from the AFM coincided with the arrival of a new dynamic Christian force in the black city: the Zulu evangelist, Nicholas Bhengu and the Assemblies of God, South Africa. The AOGSA's missionary origins coincided with those of the AFM, c. 1908. It also had direct links with the Pentecostal outpourings in Azusa Street in 1906. But the two movements differed in organizational style. While the AFM evolved into a unitary body, the AOGSA was an umbrella for a variety of assemblies run by missionaries and by black and

[18] 'A Brief History', file, Histories, ZAW.
[19] Erwin (n.d.), pp. 55–56.
[20] Interview, Pastor Jeries Mvenge, AFM, Mutare, 19 July 1996.
[21] On the importance of child-bearing for female status and permanence within the city see Scarnecchia, 1997.

white South Africans. Bhengu's connection with it dated from 1938, when the previously independent Pentecostal Emmanuel Assemblies came under the umbrella. He rose to prominence from 1945 through his revival campaigns in Port Elizabeth and East London. His vision expanded both geographically and conceptually and in 1950 he launched his Back to God Campaign, preaching a message of social and personal renewal.[22]

When Bhengu pitched his crusade tent in Highfields, Guti and his choir offered their services. At the end of the campaign they became part of the AOG configuration which was principally an alliance of Bhengu's Back to God team from South Africa and the Pentecostal Assemblies of Canada (PAOC). Bhengu sent Guti to establish a new church in the Rhodesian mining town of Bindura in 1960,[23] but his desire to keep in contact with his own following and to control Pentecostal activities in Highfields meant that he remained an active presence in the township. Over the next seven years his faction acted as a church within a church, as it had done in the AFM. The Ezekiel Guti Evangelistic Association organized its own activities in Highfields, undermining Bhengu's appointed leadership. The Guti faction drew upon Canadian and South African resources to enhance its own following, while rejecting all external authority. In early 1967 an exasperated Bhengu expelled the Guti faction from his movement.[24] By that stage the faction was already operating as the Pentecost African Assemblies of God with Guti as Chairman, Sande as Vice-Chairman and Choto as Secretary. In January 1968 they rechristened themselves Assemblies of God, African (AOGA).

AOGA's transnational character derived from both of its Pentecostal progenitors. Both were driven by the same adventist zeal, but there were differences. The AFM strand had strong links with a predominantly rural independency. It was vigorously autonomous; schisms resulted from personal revelations and in response to overbearing missionary interference. Its prime directive was evangelism and the

---

[22] Watt, 1992, chapters 1–3.

[23] Guti did take a credential from Bhengu, 'How ZAOGA Began', c. 1988, file, Mashonaland East, ZAW.

[24] N. Bhengu, Johannesburg, to Rev. G.R. Upton, PAOC, Canada, 5 Oct 1966. John Bond, Pretoria, General Secretary, AOGSA, to Township Manager, Highfield African Township, 28 March 1967, file, Bhengu, Pentecostal Assemblies of Zimbabwe (formerly Canada) (PAOZ).

manifestation of the gifts of the Spirit. Borders were ignored as evangelists carried out campaigns across them and migrants returned
home with their faith.

The AOGSA strand was more modernizing and more openly international. Bhengu had expanded his movement through crusades in
urban locations; his converts were taught domesticity and social ethics
as well as the basics of the faith. By 1964 he had preached in
Southern Rhodesia and Zambia and had developed a vision for all
of Africa, as well as preaching at Pentecostal conventions in Europe.[25]
Schism in the AOGSA was less significant because factionalism was
institutionalized. The 1938 constitution drew together a diverse collection of assemblies and leaders. There were two factions working
amongst the whites, each led by one of the Mullen brothers. Fred
Mullen headed a strand associated with American and Canadian
missionary activity, while James Mullen led a more indigenous section. A similar pattern was repeated in the black churches. There
was a 'black work' led by AOG missionaries and an indigenous
strand under Bhengu's leadership.[26]

The intention of the constitution was to create a congregational
type of government giving individual assemblies as much autonomy as possible. But the assemblies tended to coalesce around strong
leaders. Bhengu and James Mullen evolved an 'apostolic' system of
leadership. Each sought to train by example rather than through
Bible Schools, gathering around themselves groups of ministers whom
they knew and instructed personally. Apostleship created a permanence amongst the leaders and, for the sake of group cohesion, left
ordinary ministers with little influence.[27] This led self-styled apostles,
like Guti, to resent the authoritarianism of their elders and break
away to found their own followings. The potential for schism was
also increased by the abundance of Pentecostal mission organizations
and maverick missionaries willing to ally with and fund breakaway
movements.

There were other more secular ideological sources underlying
AOGA's transnationalism. The first was a pan-African vision of black
autonomy and self-reliance. Much of this derived from Bhengu. In
his Back to God Campaign of the 1950s and early 1960s he con-

---

[25] Mayer, 1961, pp. 198–203. Watt, 1992, pp. 52–54.
[26] Watt, 1992, p. 38.
[27] Watt, 1992, p. 93.

ceived of a post-colonial Africa, Christian from Cape to Cairo. The continent was a 'sleeping giant' and its people must awake to claim their own destiny. To do so they needed to learn the virtues of cleanliness, industry and self-reliance. Bhengu disliked American missionaries and would accept external money only if no strings were attached.[28] Guti's auto-hagiography dates his own prayer for Africa from 1957.[29] Fixing the prayer to that moment may well have been retrospective, like much of ZAOGA's *Sacred History*, but he and his prayer band were certainly praying for Africa, and beyond, in the 1950s. Abel Sande was even sending donations to Gordon Lindsay's Voice of Healing Crusade for the Christian renewal of the USA.[30] Guti's revelation/realization in 1963 that he should learn to preach in English is given prominence in both his official and unofficial hagiographies: 'The Lord spoke to my heart "Learn to preach in English; because you will go to many countries with my word."'[31]

The Guti faction was inevitably affected by nationalism, since Highfields was the birthplace of the nationalist movement. It is clear that nationalism fired the prayer band in their struggle with AFM missionaries in the 1950s and coloured Guti's relations with all missionaries whom he subsequently encountered.[32] It also created tensions with Bhengu's South African lieutenants in Highfields in the 1960s. But, like Bhengu,[33] the prayer band, and later AOGA, eschewed formal politics and preached an alternative message of moral and material advancement.[34]

Bhengu was a powerful embodiment of his own message. There had been earlier Pentecostal and evangelical crusades in Salisbury: William Branham in 1952; Oral Roberts in 1956; Frederick Bosworth and Lorne Fox, also in the 1950s. Billy Graham's 1960 Crusade happened just after Bhengu.[35] Some of these evangelists had captured the imaginations of the prayer band. Sande talked of Branham leaving a 'fire burning' in his heart.[36] But they were white, and some

---

[28] Watt, 1992, p. 40.
[29] Guti, 1989, Erwin (n.d.).
[30] Interview, Abel Sande, Waterfalls, 30 April 1996.
[31] Guti, 1989, p. 10. See also Erwin (n.d.), p. 91.
[32] Erwin (n.d.), p. 142.
[33] Watt, 1992, p. 180.
[34] Maxwell, 2000.
[35] Hallencreutz, 1998, pp. 292–97. Interview, Sande, Waterfalls 30 April 1996 and 30 August 1999.
[36] Ibid.

of their meetings had been segregated. As a black man, Bhengu had
an inspirational effect which was unparalleled. He arrived in Highfields
attended by whites and supported by an impressive infrastructure: a
vast tent, public address systems and generators, trucks and Land
Rovers.[37] Zimbabweans had never seen an African preacher with
such authority. In unpublished reminiscences Guti (or one of his
ghost writers) described the impact:

> My mind can still vividly remember Rev. Bengu [sic]—a giant among
> men. . . . He was a great intellect and yet had a simple childlike faith
> in the Saviour. . . . He was a strange . . . a South African, a foreigner,
> yet he was not a stranger to me after he had proclaimed the Gospel.
> His seriousness was clearly impressed on my mind. From the begin-
> ning of the service until the end, I gave the most respectful attention
> to the preacher.[38]

AOGA's final transnational impetus lay both in the social networks
created by rural and urban Pentecostalism and in the political economy that underpinned them. Here Philip Mayer's study of Bhengu's
movement in East London, South Africa, is most useful. From his
research in the 1950s and 1960s Mayer contended that, prior to
leaving the countryside, Xhosa migrants lived in integrated, 'loose
knit' networks of relations with kin and neighbours. But once in
town the migrant was given more agency in constructing his network.[39] Bhenguists chose to construct 'close knit' networks centred
upon the church, in which most of the people they knew were
acquainted with one another. This resulted in a 'strong corporate
feeling' and subsequently a 'cultural reformation' as the new community erected boundaries between itself and the world. In part, this
took the form of rejecting 'traditional' medicine and ancestor veneration. But barriers were also erected through the rejection of popular culture: the consumption of alcohol, gambling, dancing and the
bio-scope. Bhenguists redirected their social and recreational activities to the church, participating in a continuous round of nightly
prayer meetings and Sunday services.[40]

---

[37] J. Bond to Controller of Customs and Excise, Salisbury, 1967, file, Bhengu,
PAOZ.
[38] 'Not I But Christ' unpublished ms., c. 1977, file, Histories, ZAW. The prose
style is not Guti's.
[39] Mayer, 1961, p. 13 and 14.
[40] Ibid. pp. 200–201.

Mayer does not appear to have followed Bhenguists back to rural areas, though he does note that many were reluctant to leave the safe confines of the urban church for fear of being drawn back into rural networks and compromised through participation in traditional rituals and acts of commensality. But he does describe a strong missionary zeal amongst other Bhenguists, a desire to hold revival meetings in rural areas and to found rural branches. This mission is motivated not only by the evangelistic impulse, but by the desire to remain in a state of Pentecostal purity. Village Pentecostalism created new communities which sustained the returning migrant.[41]

Remade in an urban milieu, the Bhenguist convert, and members of comparable movements, could, then, survive the return home. Indeed, as this chapter and, more particularly, Matthew Schoffeleers's essay have demonstrated, rural Pentecostalism has always been a viable option. Boundaries between the believer and the world are simply constructed with other markers. Occasionally they have been spatial. A homestead or village of believers will gather around a returned migrant, or believers will relocate in the vicinity of a Pentecostal mission.[42] Sometimes the difference is marked out by dress (white robes in the case of the *Vapostori*) but more significantly by abstention. Boundaries are created between the believer and the world by abstinence from 'traditional' rituals and practices, and through participation in Christian alternatives. Possession rituals, rain-making and first-fruits ceremonies, sessions of divination and beer parties are seen as wasteful, and the spirits involved are believed to be demonic. A Pentecostal counter-community exists alongside a more integrated rural society. While Pentecostals will visit neighbours or kin to express condolences over a death they will not participate in accompanying rituals.

AOGA's Evangelistic Zeal

The desire to create a Pentecostal home from home, evangelistic zeal and a tendency to fission combined to propel AOGA from its Salisbury birthplace into the rest of Southern Rhodesia and beyond.

---

[41] Ibid. pp. 203–05. See also Werbner, 1989, pp. 313–15.
[42] Maxwell, 1999(a), chapters 2, 3, and 7.

In the late 1950s Guti's prayer band lived like their Bhenguist
cousins in East London. They held noisy cottage meetings where
there were public heartfelt confessions of sin. There were also powerful manifestations of the Holy Spirit. Sande recalled 'we would
preach and pray. People were filled with the spirit and fell over.
People did not understand and thought it was magic. Some ran
away.'[43] The sheer numbers of people in townships facilitated evangelism as church members turned first to their kin and then to their
neighbours. Those who missed services were followed up and encouraged back into the fold.[44] But while relatives were targets for evangelism they were also viewed with suspicion as a potential 'door to
the devil'.[45] As the faction grew in the 1960s and 1970s so its sectarian character developed. As well as avoiding nationalist politics,
members shunned the flourishing popular culture of music, cinema
and dance which was taking off amongst the townships' richer inhabitants. Bonds with kin and one's ethnic group were being replaced
by those with Christian 'brothers and sisters'. Secular networks for
welfare provision, such as burial societies, were avoided. Instead the
church cared for the sick and buried the dead. Elder informants
reflecting on early days spoke of the strong bond of intimacy and
mutuality that was part of church life: 'It was like you could forget
your own relatives because of the love'.[46] And this new society was
very attractive to outsiders in search of a place to belong to: 'Because
of the oneness of love in these people and their great prayer lives,
souls were just magnetised [to the] church'.[47] And when AOGA
members returned home they took this world with them, converting
their immediate and extended family and then inviting an evangelist
in to help found an assembly.[48] Others had the burning desire to
proselytize. For instance, in 1969 Appiah Manjoro was healed of a
long sickness by Guti and henceforth had an incurable urge to preach,
often gathering an audience under the tower lights in Highfields.[49]

---

[43] Interview, Sande, 30 August 1999.
[44] Interview, Mateus Simau, Waterfalls, 12 December 1995. Reminiscences, Ida
Chikono, Anniversary celebrations, Mt Pleasant, 12 May 1996.
[45] Deeper Life Meeting, 13 November 1974, file, Deeper Life, 1974–1996, ZAW.
[46] Mrs Chesa, Anniversary celebrations, Mt Pleasant, 12 May 1996.
[47] Report on Highfields 1977, file, AOGA correspondence 1964–80, ZAW.
[48] Guti, 1989, pp. 12–13. Short descriptions of the crusades are given for the
Christ for the Nations Native Church Project, file, CFNI, 1970s and 1980s, ZAW.
[49] Interview, Bartholomew and Appiah Manjoro, Belvedere, 27 April 1996.

AOGA members were poor at the start. They had no church buildings in the city until 1968, pastors went unpaid, few members owned motor vehicles, and the only musical instruments were accordions and tambourines. Any spare resources were pooled for evangelism. Highfields itself was first subjected to a considerable amount of proselytism, followed by new adjacent townships such as Dzivarasekwa, Tafara and Kambazuma.[50] Next came surrounding towns and cities and finally the rural areas. The strategy was clearly to reach the biggest concentrations of people first.[51] This made sense in the 1970s when the rural areas were torn by the liberation war. Evangelistic methods were simple and straightforward. The Crusade Team often consisted of no more than an evangelist, usher and song leader, who would together erect the tent and distribute handbills.[52] The leading evangelist was Abel Sande, a man with a remarkable gift for moving his audience to tearful repentance. Sande had an impressive pedigree in the more autonomous forms of Zimbabwean Christianity. Born in Urungwe, he had grown up in what Terence Ranger has called the 'Lomagundi Watch Tower movement', another Malawian-derived church with strong millennial credentials.[53] His father had been arrested three times for preaching that 'whites would be washed away and blacks would rule'. But Sande's Pentecostal conversion in the AFM in 1949 had brought him the gift of the Holy Spirit, which made him one of the most prolific evangelists in Zimbabwe's history.[54]

The endeavours of AOGA's leaders and ordinary members bore great fruit. The movement's ministry of healing and evangelism, its teaching of sobriety and industry and self-reliance, proved relevant and attractive. Guti himself was an emblem of the movement's success. In 1971 he went to the Christ for the Nations Institute (CNFI), Dallas, USA to study for a year. He returned with higher status but also new ideas and access to a vast pool of resources and international

---

[50] Permission for meetings had first to be obtained from the police. File, BSA Police, 1960s and 1970s, ZAW.

[51] Executive Meeting 1979, Executive Committee Minute Book, 1977–1984, ZAW.

[52] Minutes of Workers Meeting, Nyanyadze, 8 July 1968, file, AOGA Correspondence 1964–1980, ZAW.

[53] Ranger, 1970, pp. 202–215.

[54] Interview, Sande, 30 April 1996. In the 1970s he, for example, pitched his crusade tent in locations as diverse as Chinoyi, Kadoma, Triangle, Mhangula, Dangamvura, Beit Bridge, Karoi, Trojan Mine and Gwanda, file, CNFI 1970s and 1980s, ZAW.

contacts. By 1977 AOGA had over 40,000 members in Rhodesia, 185 branches (with thirty-four in Salisbury), fifteen church buildings, and six in progress. With the title Forward in Faith Mission International (FIFMI) it had also grown considerably elsewhere. There were over 50 branches in Mozambique, thirty-two in Malawi, five in Botswana and four in Zambia.[55]

AOGA and Transnational Expansion Prior to Independence

The initial link with Malawi came through J.P. Chitakata, a Malawian labour migrant working for the Rhodesian window-manufacturing company Springer and Aimis. Chitakata had joined the AFM Harare branch in the 1950s and was an original member of the prayer band which left in 1959 to join Bhengu. In 1961 he returned to Malawi and founded an Assemblies of God group in Nsanje district[56] (thus becoming a footnote in Matthew Schoffeleers's chapter). Guti also travelled to Nsanje in 1961, and it is clear that he believed that Chitakata was working under his authority and that the Malawi assemblies were his. Indeed a typical hagiographical piece even claims Guti was the founder: 'In 1961, the Lord led Ezekiel to go to Nsanje in Malawi. He was able to build a mud church there. Many people were healed from their diseases, many were delivered from their sins . . .'[57] But Chitakata was Guti's kindred spirit only in the sense that he exhibited the same traits of opportunism, entrepreneurship and autonomy. He played the same game of manipulating external resources to build up a following,[58] and this time Guti was the victim.

In 1964 Chitakata joined with another Malawian, Lyton Kalam-bule, and Magnus Udd, a maverick American Assemblies of God missionary, to form the Assemblies of God, Southern and Central Africa (AOGSCA), in collaboration with Bhengu. (After complaints from the 'official' Assemblies of God in Malawi, the three group-ings re-christened themselves the Independent Assemblies of God

---

[55] 'Not I But Christ', chapter 16.
[56] Chakanza, 1983, p. 6.
[57] 'Biography of Rev. E.H. Guti', n.d., file, Histories, ZAW. Another earlier unpublished history reports that Guti went as part of a team stationed at Port Herald on the Shores of the Lake, 'Not I But Christ', file, Histories, c. 1977, ZAW.
[58] Interview, Bartholomew Manjoro, Belvedere, 26 April 1996.

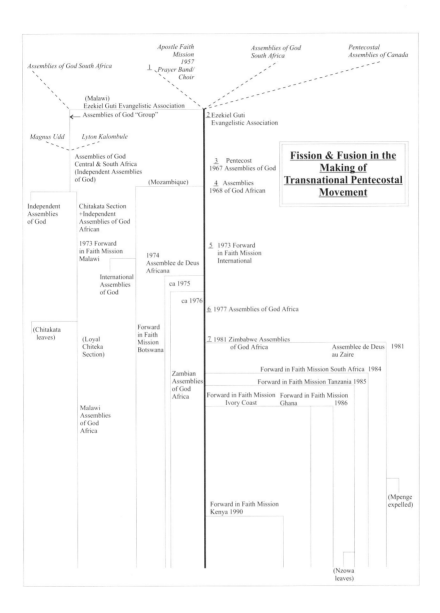

Fission & Fusion in the Making of Transnational Pentecostal Movement

(IAOG)).[59] This new Pentecostal constellation was a threat to Guti's denominational dreams. Udd's independence from the USA meant that he was more easily controlled by Bhengu and the two appeared close. Malawian delegates would travel to Bhengu's Conventions in East London, South Africa.[60] Around 1967 Bhengu mooted the idea of Udd's mopping up the Rhodesian 'Assemblies' work after the South Africans had withdrawn.[61] Fearing for his fledgling organization, Guti wrote to warn his pastors in 1969:

> We must be very careful, because the South Africans are looking to destroy our work, also the Malawi missionaries and even our residents. As the Lord reveals to us all the time by His spirit, I want to warn you that the big snake is coming to fight and to destroy many souls in our congregations, but we will win through the name of Jesus.[62]

A month later he wrote, with remarkable self-confidence, to Udd himself, warning him to keep away, throwing in the threat of God's curse for good measure:

> I have heard that you have agreed to work against me and all the work in Rhodesia which God has called me to do.
> ... what I know is that God has called me to preach the gospel to my own people and others also. . . .
> if you are coming to Rhodesia to work against me to please the South African people, (Numbers 22:6) . . . it is better for me to warn you that if you do that you will damage your own work in Malawi for a long time.[63]

In 1969, after a power struggle, Chitakata split from the Independent Assemblies and founded his own African Assemblies of God, re-affiliating to Guti's AOGA.[64] But fission and fusion continued, stimulated by missionary and African ambition and a broader political culture of Malawian nationalism. One Malawian assembly appealed

[59] Chakanza, 1983, pp. 6–7, 14–15, 30–31, 48. Udd left the AOG Springfield USA in 1958 when their missionaries accepted polygamists into the church.
[60] J. Bush, Salisbury, to G. Upton, Canada, 1 December 1966. G. Upton, Canada, to J. Bush, Salisbury, 12 December 1966, file, Bhengu, PAOZ.
[61] Nicholas Bhengu, 'Suggestions for Rhodesia', c. 1968, file, AOGA correspondence 1964–80, ZAW.
[62] E. Guti, 'Ku Vafundisi Vese', 11 January 1969, file, AOGA correspondence 1964–80, ZAW.
[63] E. Guti to M. Udd, 27 February 1969, file, AOGA correspondence 1964–80, ZAW.
[64] Chakanza, 1983, pp. 6–7. Special meeting of the Chiloni Church, Blantyre, 1969, file, Malawi: Missions, ZAW.

unilaterally to Rhodesia against Chitakata, another affiliated to escape missionary authoritarianism. Between 1973 and 1974 AOGA reinvented itself as Forward In Faith International in Malawi, claiming only *affiliation* with the Assemblies there. Relations with Chitakata deteriorated when he established connections with one of Guti's former white patrons, F. Warrilow, a Rhodesian businessman. Links were finally severed in 1977; loyal assemblies coalesced around D. Chiteka, a Malawian with strong Rhodesian connections, who was faithful to Guti.[65] Alongside the transnational realpolitik local evangelism continued. Chiteka founded assemblies in Ndirande, and F.S. Phiri returned to Blantyre from Rhodesia to found churches in Ntcheu and Chikwawa.[66] Other Malawian assemblies moved under the control of AOGA's Mozambican arm in 1977.[67]

The early Mozambican story provides a contrast to the Malawian one. Here faction and ambition were far less prominent. The dominant themes were sacrifice and loyalty in the face of adversity. Portuguese East Africa was a settler state like Rhodesia, and movement of migrant labour between the two was relatively easy. English was not the *lingua franca* but ChiShona sufficed in the central Manica Province. AOGA's Mozambican story began with a brief campaign by Guti in 1969. He drove from Umtali in Rhodesia into Machipanda and from there preached in Tete and Gaza provinces. He visited churches in Beira, Chimoio and Maputo and 'many people who were crippled, blind and those who had suffered from body diseases were healed in Jesus' name'.[68] The following year he sent Mateus Simau back to found a church in Chimoio. Simau had come to Salisbury as a labour migrant in 1960, found accommodation in Dzivarasekwa and worked as a carpenter. In 1963 he was converted by a relative and joined an assembly led by Joseph Choto. Choto encouraged him and soon he was spotted by Guti who eventually ordained him as a pastor.

[65] Correspondence, 2 February 1972, 31 December 1972, 31 December 1972, 4 January 1973, Minutes of Meeting, Blantyre 6 January 1973, correspondence 12 July 1973 and 16 May 1974, file, Malawi: Missions. Executive Minutes, 23 June 1973, file, AOGA correspondence 1964–1980, ZAW. Interview, Ezekiel Guti, Glen Lorne, 8 February 1996.
[66] 'Mozambique (and Malawi)' c. 1978, file, Mozambique: Missions, ZAW.
[67] Executive Committee Minutes, 6 September 1977, ZAW.
[68] 'Not I But Christ', chapter 13.

Once back in Portuguese East Africa, Simau worked in much the same manner as his Zimbabwean brethren. Towns and cities were targeted first, rural areas later. Congregations in Chimoio were built through a combination of door-to-door work and small-scale open-air meetings. As with AOGA's inception, and numerous other nascent Pentecostal movements before it, converts were attracted by powerful manifestations of the Holy Spirit. Prayer for the sick and deliverance for the demon-possessed was vital. By 1972 a number of local pastors had joined Simau. But with them came pressure to re-affiliate to the better resourced International Assemblies of God. Some left, taking their churches with them. In 1974, Raphael Kupara, AOGA's administrative genius, entered Mozambique to register the movement as the Assemblee De Deus Africana (ADDA). By 1978 it had spread along the two main arteries into Rhodesia: the Beira and Tete corridors.[69] But evangelism was never straightforward in Mozambique. Under the Portuguese, Catholicism had a near monopoly, while the Marxist Frelimo Government, coming to power in 1975, was hostile to all religions. Simau was imprisoned three times between 1978 and 1981. Reflecting on this period he revealed how his faith had sustained him: 'I was strengthened by the struggle of [King] David who fought the bear, then the lion and then Goliath'.[70]

Other Mozambican pastors were more fortunate. In Vila Fontes, on the Tete corridor, Pastor Nyakanyanza came to an understanding with local chiefs and party workers, perhaps because his mission against 'witch doctors' was in line with Frelimo's attack on 'obscurantism'.[71] Low-key, localized evangelism, done mostly on foot, was crucial to the movement's success. Its public profile remained low as it gradually expanded its cell-like structure across townships and villages. As in Zimbabwe, its independence from missionary control saved it from the Marxist slur of association with 'capitalist imperialism' and made it difficult to dislodge.

The two other pre-independence transnational outgrowths, although much smaller, arose through the same processes. Zambia's linchpin was Pastor Mwanza. He had grown up in AOGA, Salisbury, in the 1960s and 1970s, while his father worked for the Rhodesian rail-

---

[69] 'Mozambique (and Malawi)' c. 1978, file, Mozambique: Missions, ZAW.
[70] Interview, Mateus Simau, Waterfalls, 12 December 1995. Sermon, Deeper Life Conference, 6 February 1996.
[71] 'Mozambique (and Malawi)' c. 1970, file, Mozambique: Missions, ZAW.

ways. Guti sent him back to Zambia and work began, getting a small boost in 1977. While on a tour through Central and East Africa, Guti persuaded two Zambians working with other Pentecostal movements to join AOGA's Zambian team. Another impressed Zambian promised a house. By the end of the year, however, the house had not materialized and one of the pastors had not joined. Guti sent a prominent elder from Rhodesian AOGA to help organize the work, but it remained small until after independence.[72]

In 1974 Appiah Manjoro felt called to preach in Botswana. Her spell in Gaborone laid the foundations for a small number of assemblies. Later in the same year Abel Sande was sent there to stir them up.[73] Botswana's poor relations with the white minority regime in Rhodesia made movement between the two states difficult. The work there remained small but well organized, led by a local businessman-cum-pastor, Last Fundira.

Independence and Religious Globalization

After a costly liberation struggle, independence came to Zimbabwe in March 1980. AOGA continued to expand through tried and tested means. Low-level, face-to-face evangelism proceeded, as did the crusading activities of evangelists like Abel Sande. War and social unrest remained an important force, shaping the Mozambican work and limiting expansion into South Africa. But independence did herald a new era. With an end to sanctions, and to restrictions on movement of people and information across borders, the possibilities for transnational expansion greatly increased.

The 1980s also saw the rapid growth of the global born-again movement, reaching out from the USA and Latin America to Africa and Asia. It influenced AOGA's growth and evolution in a number of ways. First, it had a strong association with media technologies. Audio and video tapes, produced locally and internationally, supplemented Gospel tracts, Bible study guides and Christian monthlies as tools of teaching and proselytism. Religious broadcasting and

---

[72] Executive Meetings 6 August and 2 December 1977, Executive Minute Book, ZAW.

[73] Interview Bartholomew and Appiah Manjoro, Belvedere, 27 April 1996. E. Guti, To Whom it May Concern, 7 September 1974, file, AOGA correspondence, 1964–80, ZAW.

gospel music became key media for propagating the Christian message. Secondly, inter-denominationalism was fostered by parachurch bodies like Woman's Aglow, the Full Gospel Business Men's Fellowship, International Scripture Union, and the Haggai Institute. Inter-denominationalism and media technologies together contributed to another characteristic: apparent homogeneity. This was created by large American Bible Colleges, such as Gordon Lindsay's Christ for the Nations Institute, Dallas, and the Oral Roberts University, Tulsa, and by the movement of born-again leaders around conventions and conferences across the globe.[74]

Africa's born-again explosion also coincided with, and was stimulated by, the beginning of its socio-economic malaise: crippling external debt; state contraction; dramatic population rise and food scarcity.[75] The retreat of states from welfare provision forced by structural adjustment programmes both prompted a flood of secular NGOs and provided opportunities for new types of mission work and church involvement, much of it originating from North America. In the 1980s, Zimbabwe, like many other African countries, experienced an increase of almost 250 per cent in the number of Protestant missionaries, many of them American and born-again.[76] Because of its impressive resource base, the external born-again movement posed a threat and an opportunity to ZAOGA. The threat was two fold: sheep-stealing by well endowed missionary organizations, and loss of identity in a broad monochrome inter-denominational movement. The opportunity lay in fleecing the well-meaning but naive foreign shepherds for their resources.

To mark the new era AOGA became ZAOGA in 1981. But the movement went through more profound changes than this. It drew much in terms of style, presentation and resources from the global born-again movement. New expanded crusade teams appeared, led by Paul Saungweme and Bill John Chigwenembe. These men had been tutored by Sande and Guti, but their operations were slicker. Gospel music was now essential to draw crowds, and the teams developed impressive musical line-ups: male vocalists with sharp hair cuts and smooth voices, and backing groups of pretty girls in sleek satin dresses, accompanied by musicians on electric guitars and the ubi-

[74] For useful introductions see Gifford, 1998, and Maxwell 2001(a).
[75] Iliffe, 1995, pp. 243 270.
[76] Gifford, 1994, p. 519.

quitous Hammond organ. Vocalists such as Lawrence Haisa, Biggie Tembo and Xechs Manatsa won much popular acclaim. Zimbabwean Pentecostals learnt from Reinhard Bonnke's Christ for All Nations Crusades, held in the country in 1980, 1984 and 1986.[77] But the younger evangelists also drew stylistically from preachers like Jimmy Swaggart, Jimmy Bakker, Benny Hinn and John Avanzini, whose video and audio tapes were now locally available.[78]

Guti also made direct use of his connections with the American Bible Belt, and beyond, to expand the Zimbabwean movement. The CFNI Native Churches Project provided generous sums of money to roof simple church buildings, giving ZAOGA both permanence and a higher profile in the regions. His travels throughout the USA and Europe developed a host of sympathetic contacts with small semi-independent churches operating in a congregational AOG-type framework. Such churches were looking for a 'mission' connection but were unwilling or unable to meet the expense of a missionary. Instead they made donations in the range of US$500–$1,000 towards ZAOGA's work, and in return received personalized or circular letters offering Christian greetings and news of crusading activities, with conversion figures and stories of repentance and deliverance. These letters, along with personal contacts, did much to stimulate a shared sense of mission, made more urgent by reminders of Christ's imminent return.[79]

As ZAOGA grew it developed a rich associational life of 'ministries' and 'fellowships' for wives, husbands, youth, students, postgraduates and businessmen. Such associations not only served to mitigate the potential dullness and alienation of institutional church life[80] but again, by their 'born-again' style, facilitated the movement of people and resources. Names and styles were lifted directly from other denominations encountered by Guti and his wife, Eunor, on their travels. Another point of connection with the global born-again movement was the annual Deeper Life Conference for deacons and elders to which international speakers and dignitaries were invited. ZAOGA's leaders had drawn on the west for resources since the

---

[77] For background see Gifford, 1987.
[78] Interviews, Paul Saungweme, Glenorah, 11 October 1995 and Bill John Chigwenembe, Arcadia, 8 November 1995.
[79] Files, CNFI 1973–1996, US Correspondence 1991–1995, Sponsors 1994–95, ZAW.
[80] Hastings, 1994, pp. 592–593.

1960s, and more so after Guti's year in Dallas in 1971. But from the 1980s there was a dramatic increase in foreign contact, which made ZAOGA more globally orientated.[81] One connection could lead to another. Money raised by Forward in Faith Mission International, London, England funded the first crusade in Tanzania. White born-agains in Cape Town, outside the movement, helped bankroll FIFMI South Africa in its early stages.[82]

Although the Zimbabwean movement took on a standard born-again hue, the content of its teachings and its style of management remained specific and attuned to local and regional contexts. The personality cult around Guti made the church distinctive. He was referred to as the Apostle and the Servant of God, celebrated in song and an annual recital of his life story. Adherents were taught to pray to the 'God of Ezekiel'. Those in search of security or prosperity wrote in their hundreds asking for his prayers for jobs, health, fertility, and exam success.[83] Guti himself wrote numerous tracts on a range of domestic and leadership issues, behaving like an heir to the urban community leaders of the 1940s and 1950s.[84]

The movement also developed its own doctrines on wealth and poverty. International connections with donors were strictly controlled by Guti and his immediate family. Gifts of money were accepted without popular knowledge and put to specific uses. Drawing on Bhengu's teachings on self-reliance and on more recent teachings on black pride and self-actualization by black American born-agains, Guti preached strongly against missionary paternalism and neo-colonialism, asserting that ZAOGA had to raise its own money. Africans had to escape from their 'Third World Mentality' of dependency on foreign churches and NGOs, and from a culture of waste and corruption which sapped self-respect. Specific teachings evolved on the causes of poverty, explaining it in terms of ancestral curse, a destructive mindset inherited from one's progenitors. Wealth and personal security would come through being delivered from this 'spirit of poverty', and also by the working of Talents—penny capitalism—

---

[81] Hannerz, 1996, pp. 17–18.
[82] FIFMI, Edgeware, Middlesex, Financial Report, April–June 1989 (FIFMI England, or indeed Australia, is beyond the scope of this chapter). Letter 7 September 1987, files, England and South Africa: Missions, ZAW.
[83] File, Locals, 1989–1997, ZAW.
[84] For example, Guti, 1993, 1994, 1995(b).

particularly by women. At key times the fruits of this female entre-preneurship went into church finances, and vast amounts of money were raised locally, far more than was donated externally.[85]

ZAOGA's actual foreign connections were cautious and low key. The movement's own evolution had been shaped by continual struggle for autonomy from external agents and its leaders were all too aware of the force of cultural nationalism and of the damage neo-colonial associations could do to their image.[86] Apart from policing foreign connections the leadership took advantage of a growing tendency amongst international agencies to preserve and promote 'images of local specificity', and sought out international organizations which participated in this globally constructed localism.[87] Donors and visiting missionaries were told that the movement was 'indigenous', run by 'indigenous workers who know how to handle the situation in their country'.[88] Thus while Southern African Pentecostals have an existential and ideological aversion to 'tradition', they nevertheless foster specific notions of authenticity in specific contexts to gain resources and political capital.[89]

ZAOGA had its own experience of schisms. The most severe ruptures were the departure of Cuthbert Makoni and Raphael Kupara in 1984, of Joseph Choto and Abel Sande in 1988 and of Bartholomew Manjoro in 1992. As the movement prospered, Guti's former colleagues grew increasingly frustrated that they did not benefit personally. Guti used external resources as a form of extraversion.[90] Gifts received were given away strategically to boost his status and create loyal followers. ZAOGA had a neo-patriarchal form of government. Although it developed a complex bureaucracy of provinces and overseers to control its expansion it was nevertheless a personalized one in which Guti intervened on behalf of clients. Increasingly, he elevated his kin, 'tribe', and successful businessmen, at the expense of his co-founders.

---

[85] Maxwell, 1998.
[86] Maxwell, 2000.
[87] Miller, 1995, p. 9. Robertson calls this process 'glocalization', 1995.
[88] For example, Friends International Christian University, which validates ZAOGA's Bible courses. Circular letter to donors, FIFM, Mutare, file, 'Sponsors 1984–85', ZAW.
[89] This seems to run counter to Latin American Pentecostals. Lehmann, 1998, pp. 608–615
[90] Bayart, 1993, pp. 20–32.

But despite its problems the movement grew. By 1994 the Zimbabwean arm had approximately 125,000 members paying tithes, but probably about 400,000 regular adherents. It owned 140 church buildings and 186 houses with thirty-five new buildings under construction. It had approximately 2,500 assemblies and 2,000 pastors, including part-time assistant pastors.[91] It had also expanded geographically throughout Africa, and beyond. The 1990 Deeper Life Conference drew members from thirteen countries beyond Zimbabwe: Mozambique, Zambia, Tanzania, South Africa, Ghana, Botswana, Rwanda, Zaire, Ivory Coast, Kenya, Uganda, Malawi and England.[92]

The Post-Colonial Dispensation

Throughout the 1980s ZAOGA's pan-Africanist vision was sharpened into an ideological critique of dependency and western Christianity and a powerful assertion of Africa's mission. Western churches, once the cradle of Christianity, were now apostate. Africans had become the bearers of Christian truth. In 1988 Guti instructed a large gathering at Zimbabwe's National Stadium:

> One of the problems we have in the third world is that of copying what backslidden western people are doing instead of copying the good things they were doing before they backslid. These nations used to have many churches and many of their leaders were Christians . . . but when they prospered they forsook God . . . I believe this is our time. It is time for black people and their nations to rise up. Don't go to Europe and learn their ungodly things. Learn what they used to do before . . .[93]

Although missionaries were to be praised for bringing the gospel, they nevertheless acted as unwitting 'agents of colonialism' which used Christianity as a 'tool for the western domination of Africa'. After independence missionaries 'spoiled Africans, who got to depend on the leadership and hand outs from abroad. They despised their own skin and sunk into apathy'.[94]

---

[91] Central Statistics, 30 November 1994. Target 2000 form 1995, file, Statistics, 1995, ZAW.
[92] Deeper Life Programme 1990, file, Deeper Life, 1974–1996, ZAW.
[93] Guti, 1989, pp. 23–27.
[94] Ibid. Unpublished Interview with Ezekiel Guti, *Africa Arise*, c. 1993.

Like many European churches before it, ZAOGA promoted its own 'tin mission fund' for Sunday School children, encouraging them to give a few cents from their pocket-money for the work of the gospel. This was helped enormously by the environment created by independence in 1980. Freedom to enter and leave Zimbabwe provided an immense boost to ZAOGA's transnational expansion, bringing its leaders into contact with ambitious and entrepreneurial Pentecostals beyond its borders. Many of the initial connections were made by Bartholomew Manjoro whose rise to prominence as the movement's key administrator was speeded by Kupara's departure in 1984. Like Guti, he went for a period of study at CNFI, Dallas, which boosted his status and expanded his horizons beyond Zimbabwe. Links with Zaire came in 1981 while he was visiting the Zambian work. While on the Copper Belt he met Francis Penge, a Zairian, who subsequently invited a ZAOGA team back into his country to form the Assemblée de Dieu au Zaïre, Afrique (ADAZA). Manjoro was also responsible for the beginnings of the Tanzanian work. While in Zambia again in 1985, Manjoro met an energetic Tanzanian, Stephen Nzowa, who was on a preaching tour. Nzowa invited him to visit his church in Mbozi, Tanzania, and the work was integrated into ZAOGA's empire.[95] The Kenyan churches came via the Tanzanian connection. They were founded by a Kikuyu named Paul Kimaruh, who learnt of FIFMI from Nzowa while participating in a Tanzanian crusade and was invited to the 1990 Deeper Life Conference in Zimbabwe. Henceforth he decided to put his work under the oversight of a 'Spiritual Father' and 'Apostle', Ezekiel Guti.[96] Work in West Africa began after Manjoro had a chance meeting with some Ghanaian pastors at the Bonnke Harare Fire Conference in 1986, and contacts with Rwanda were first made through Central African Pentecostals who got hold of Manjoro's business card.

The South African link was forged by Joseph Choto in 1984 who came across the name of a Pastor, Wilson Mabasa, working for the Pentecostal Full Gospel Church in Soshanguve. Mabasa was invited to ZAOGA's Pastors' Conference and encouraged to join the

[95] Interview, Manjoro.
[96] Interview, Paul Kimaruh, Glenorah, 8 February 1996.

movement. Choto had helped to found the Bulawayo assemblies, and the initial negotiations were conducted in Sindebele.[97]

Once links had been established, Zimbabwean evangelists, teachers, administrators, and Guti himself went to help locals expand their embryonic movements. Both Saungweme and Chigwenembe made extensive visits outside Zimbabwe with their crusade teams. Saungweme took groups to Swaziland and Zambia in 1991, and Mozambique in 1995. He was also part of a smaller contingent led by Manjoro to Zaire in 1986. Chigwenembe led teams to South Africa in 1992 and 1995 and also to Botswana, Zambia and Malawi. Both evangelists were part of a large teaching and preaching team led by Overseer Elson Makanda to Tanzania in 1988.[98] Their reports detailed numbers of conversions and powerful manifestations of the Holy Spirit such as healing miracles or victories of deliverance over local spirits. Apart from Manjoro's visit to West Africa, the journeys were all made by road. Chigwenembe was eventually to lose his life in a car accident while returning from a crusade in Harare. In interview the Zimbabweans recounted in detail the travails they experienced on their journeys: breakdowns, accidents and near misses, shortage of foreign exchange, the trials of border controls, the search for accommodation.[99] Their accounts of transnational encounters resembled those of pioneer Victorian missionaries. Faced by difficulties, they were making conquests in the wilderness beyond, in the name of civilization.[100]

Transnational crusades demanded great sacrifices from those involved. While the Zimbabwean movement prospered, members of the crusade teams felt marginalized in a church that had moved from mission to maintenance. In 1995 they were paid just Z$300 a month. Their lifestyles could not be further removed from those of American tele-evangelists, and their satisfaction was derived from a deep sense of Christian service.[101] Saungweme, like his mentors, had

---

[97] Interviews, Choto and Mabasa.

[98] Interviews, Saungweme and Chigwenembe and file, Missions, ZAW.

[99] Interviews, Chigwenembe, Manjoro, Saungweme.

[100] Jean and John Comaroff, 1991, p. 172. Both sets of missionaries were borrowing from St Paul but they embellished their accounts with a civilizing rhetoric.

[101] Interview, Innocent Makwarimba, Glenorah, 6 February 1996. Makwarimba joined a crusade team in order to work alongside Saungweme and use his gift of deliverance.

that 'burning desire to preach'. Soon after his conversion in the late 1970s he went out on his own in eastern Zimbabwe armed with a gas lamp, a sleeping bag and a Bible.[102]

In spite of all the costs ZAOGA did make transnational strides. Zimbabwean leaders offered technical expertise on bureaucratic matters and advice on strategies for church growth. Crusade teams brought encouragement and inspiration, often helping to kick-start a local church. But as with ZAOGA itself, much of the real work was done by local agents. To begin with, Wilson Mabasa stayed in his job with the South African railways, preaching on trains on his way to work. At the weekends, in Soshanguve, he concentrated on a Sunday School for young people, sending them home to evangelize their parents, then following them up with his own visits, praying for the sick and needy. The church spread to Mamelodi and Soweto. In Mozambique, other remarkable men and women helped Simau propel the church forward. Jorge Joachim Matus joined the church in Nampula in 1983 after his wife was healed. In 1987 he left his profession as a tailor and became a full-time pastor. After a vision he moved to the far north of the country to start the church in Cabo Delgado Province. Settling in Pemba, he moved from house to house preaching and healing the sick, slowly building a church. One of his elders, Fernado Sumunitato, felt called to evangelize the Makonde on the plateau. Wycliffe Bible Translators working there testified that the ADDA spread like wildfire, offering deliverance and protection against demonic possession and restoring families riven by domestic violence and alcoholism.[103] Violence and social dislocation continued to shape the ADDA. By 1980 the counter-revolutionary movement, RENAMO, was wrecking the hopes of independence. Simau was abducted by RENAMO in December 1981 and only escaped by hiding in a pit-latrine. On the plateau on Cabo Delgado, Catholics, fearful of the Pentecostal challenge to their monopoly, conspired to have Sumunitato arrested as a RENAMO agent. Yet, throughout the 1980s the Mozambican movement grew steadily. By 1986 it was present in eight provinces, with 52 pastors and 94 buildings. The take-off came in 1988 with the construction of a Bible

---

[102] Interview, Saungweme.
[103] Interviews, Jorge Joaquim Matus, Pemba, Mozambique, 28 June 1996, Fernado Sumunitato, Pemba, Mozambique, 28 June 1996, Benjamin Leach, Resthaven, Harare, 31 May 1996.

School. By 1995 the movement claimed 120 pastors, 300 buildings and 100,000 adherents.[104]

While increase was less spectacular in other countries, patterns of growth were similar to the Zimbabwean movement's evolution. Having established itself in the city the Malawian church turned rural areas into a mission field. Thus work started on Chikwawa District in 1987, producing three assemblies and 380 adherents by the following year.[105] By 1991, Lusaka Province had twenty-five assemblies and seven trained pastors. The Copper Belt had three assemblies. In Petuke, a witch doctor of great renown converted, abandoning his 'mashabe' dance and numerous Mozambican clients to found three assemblies. Guti had advised the movement that a strong urban membership would put the church's finances on a surer footing and aid rural expansion.[106] Having rapidly established the movement in Dar es Salaam from its base in Mbozi, Nzowa founded churches in Mbeya District.[107]

But some of the Zimbabwean movement's more worldly characteristics were also replicated, sometimes to a greater degree. In 1981 Guti told a Zambian audience of his frustrations with their Malawian brethren:

> In Malawi people were in trouble because of what they use[d] to say or do when someone comes from America. They went to join him because of money. Now if the money is finished they left him and join someone else whom they know had bring [sic] another bag of money. They were not after God but after money.[108]

This pattern of fission and fusion continued in Malawi and elsewhere. Six Malawian pastors left to found their own ministries but were welcomed back into the movement in 1989.[109] After receiving an exceptional amount of resources from Zimbabwe and England

---

[104] 'All Pastors and Buildings 1986', file, Mozambique, Missions, ZAW. Interview, Simau.
[105] Correspondence, Isaac Phiri, Blantyre, 6 Dec 1988 and Mabviko Phiri, Chikwawa, 29 Dec 1988, file, Malawi, Missions, ZAW.
[106] Report Zambia Assemblies of God, c. 1991, file, Zambia, Missions.
[107] B. Manjoro, ZAOGA to Ministry of Home Affairs, Registry of Societies, Dar es Salaam, 29 May 1985, file, Tanzania, Missions, ZAW.
[108] AOGA Zambia Committee Meeting, 22 August 1981, file, Zambia, Missions, ZAW.
[109] Ezekiel Guti to Pastor and Mrs Owiti, Kisumu, Kenya, 19 July 1989, file, Kenya, Missions. Correspondence to Pastor J. Mabviko Phiri and Pastor BM Pondamali, 26 August 1988, file, Malawi, Missions, ZAW.

and training at the Zimbabwean Bible College, Nzowa decided to go his own way in 1995.[110] The Zambian church seemed to reproduce the character of the dominant socio-political culture. In 1990 an irate pastor wrote to Zimbabwe complaining of nepotism and favouritism. Only a select few preached at the richer churches where the rewards were great. Church positions were bought with bribes and pastors preferred to conduct their own business rather than care for their flocks. Other reports alluded to the misuse of church funds and tribalism in the distribution of scholarships to the Zimbabwean Bible College.[111]

When it came to corruption, Zaire was in a league of its own. It appeared that Francis Penge was using his church identity and transnational connections to further his own business interests. Unlike Muslim traders in West Africa, Penge did not use his Christian networks as a guarantee providing strict rules of conduct to boost the confidence of those he dealt with.[112] Instead he plundered them for resources. Soon another Zairian, Simon Monde, educated in Zimbabwe and more loyal to ZAOGA, was petitioning the Harare Headquarters for Penge's removal. His letters claimed that Penge had committed numerous crimes: not paying pastors' salaries; hiding the bank book, correspondence, the church stamp, headed letters, post-office keys; selling invitations to Zimbabwe to Nigerians; falsely promising bales of clothes in return for cement for church buildings. Before he was removed, Penge wrote a damaging letter to the Zimbabwean Ministry of Foreign Affairs claiming that Monde was secretly involved in the arms trade.[113]

To counter the fissile and destructive tendencies within both the Zimbabwean movement and its transnational plants, ZAOGA's leaders resorted to a combination of bureaucratic control and promotion of its own distinctive brand of Pentecostalism. The leadership actively went out to export its message and mechanisms but also

---

[110] Tanzania Forward in Faith Ministries Church Board with its Financial Committee, 23 October 1988, file, Tanzania, Missions, ZAW.

[111] Correspondence and reports 1989–1992, file Zambia, Missions, ZAW.

[112] MacGaffey and Bazenguissa–Ganga, 2000, pp. 14–15.

[113] Letters from Simon Monde to Harare, 5 March 1987, 28 March 1987, April 1993, file, Zaire, Missions. Chimpaka Lawanda (Francis) Penge, Lusaka, to the Minister for Foreign Affairs, Zimbabwe, 13 February 1987, file, Relations with Government, ZAW. Interviews, Ezekiel Guti, Glen Lorne, 8 February 1996; Simon Monde, Glenorah, 7 February 1996.

drew newcomers into its centre so that they could experience these things at first hand.[114] Soon after a transnational connection had been made, or, in Mozambique's case, when it was safe enough, flying squads, often accompanied by crusade teams, would visit the country. Leaders like Makanda, Manjoro, and occasionally Guti himself would instruct local members on how to achieve self-reliance through tithing and penny capitalism. Leaders of the Gracious Women and Gracious Single Women Associations, Liniah Rusere for example, would advise on money-making activities like sewing and cooking and more generally teach domesticity, leadership skills and ways of strengthening marriage. Once local money was being generated, direction was given on its appropriate management. Tithes were to be receipted and the money deposited in bank accounts controlled by properly constituted boards. Pastors were to be paid regularly to stop them from 'running away due to lack of food'.[115] Once the women's movements were functioning, the youth work and men's work was encouraged. As in Zimbabwe's case, this proliferation of associations created a multiplicity of cross-cutting bonds of fellowship which ran across ethnicities and regions, reinforcing the movement's cohesion. They also provided fora for its key teachings on the family.

In the case of the Zambian, Malawian and Zairian assemblies, Manjoro or Makanda were called in as trouble shooters to sort out financial misdemeanours, sexual improprieties and general mismanagement. Zimbabwean 'missionaries' were also sent out to help 'kick-start' new foreign works. In 1991 Pastor Mpanduki went to South Africa and Pastor Christmas to Botswana. These missionaries were sent to establish bureaucracies and administrative procedures. Others like Maggie Ndlouvu, also sent to South Africa, had specific gifts in evangelism and youth work and, more importantly, the local language. Crusade teams also demonstrated Zimbabwean capabilities. They were sent to Lusaka and Pretoria in 1990, after defections of assemblies, as a show of force.

Finally, the Zimbabwean leaders would also instruct surrounding nations on the movement's *Sacred History*, a canonized narrative of the spiritual autobiography of Ezekiel Guti. Copies of this history in

---

[114] File, Missions, ZAW, particularly years 1988–97.
[115] Minutes of Makambako Committee Meeting, 7 October 1988, file, Tanzania, Missions, ZAW.

short tract form were distributed and for Zaire it was translated into French. New assemblies were encouraged to participate in its synchronized annual recital, bringing about the imagination and embodiment of the transnational community in text and performance.[116] Foreign leaders were taken on pilgrimages to memorials in Zimbabwe which marked key moments in Guti's life. Simon Monde argued that Guti would ultimately prove more successful than the great Zairian prophet, Simon Kimbangu, because 'he wrote things down'.[117]

Schisms often resulted directly from sheep- and shepherd-stealing. Foreign pastors and their flocks transplanted into the movement came with different mentalities and sometimes found ZAOGA's doctrines and practices too exacting. While the leaders of ZAOGA's transnational branches could not be 'home-grown' they could at least be drawn into the movement's Zimbabwean core for re-formation. Thus the favoured Zairian leader, Monde, and the South African leader, Mabasa, were brought in for a year's training at the Zimbabwean Bible School and in placements at the headquarters and Harare churches. Once established in Zaire in 1988, Monde set about founding fresh assemblies by convening small worship meetings in homes. 'Now we have started the real ZAOGA', he wrote to Manjoro.[118] Many other foreign leaders and pastors experienced this formation process. The Bible School with its rigorous diet of doctrine, prayer and worship, general work and placements in pastoral or evangelistic teams was a powerful homogenizing force. In 1989 it was reported that three Zambian pastors who had defected would be allowed back into the movement if they first consented to go to the Bible School for the 'refreshing of their minds'.[119]

More temporary, but no less vivid, experiences of the Zimbabwean movement were offered through the annual Pastors and Deeper Life Conferences which drew hundreds of foreign delegates to the movement's impressive 3,000-seat conference centre complete with television relay to over-spill tents. The Deeper Life Conference combined the traditions of the Vapostori *pasca*, the Methodist Camp Meeting and the born-again convention, offering visitors a week of teaching

---

[116] See Maxwell, 2001(b) and Connerton, 1989.
[117] Interview, Simon Monde.
[118] Simon Monde to B. Manjoro, 4 January 1988, file, Zaire, Missions, ZAW.
[119] Report, Zambia Assemblies of God, Africa to Ezekiel Guti, 21 November 1989, file, Zambia, Missions, ZAW.

from Zimbabwean and trusted international speakers, and high quality music and worship, climaxing in a final communion service. Core
ZAOGAn doctrines were continually expounded by Zimbabwean
speakers, while high-profile African and American guests emphasized
links with the global born-again movement. National and ethnic cultures were celebrated with flags, dress, and evening festivities: thigh-
slapping Zulu dancing; Tanzanian drumming; the award-winning
Zimbabwean Kambazuma and Marlborough choirs; and a host of
other rich traditions. It was at once an affirmation of global and
African Christian identities and an assertion of the movement's
Zimbabwean design.

Other homogenizing forces were the locally produced audio-visual
and print media. Key sermons and events were recorded for circulation within the movement. Those unable to afford electronic media
could buy ZAOGA's cheap and widely circulated tracts on doctrine
and history. Thus a flying squad visiting assemblies in Accra in 1995
showed new Ghanaian members video recordings of an Ezekiel Guti
sermon on repentance, and of ZAOGA style worship.[120]

ZAOGA's appeal in surrounding African countries, and beyond,
lay in its general Pentecostal practice and its own specific doctrines.
Its pioneers, both Zimbabwean and non-Zimbabwean, all stressed
the importance of 'signs and wonders' in founding moments. Public
confession of sin, the destruction of polluted objects, deliverance,
divine healing and possession by the Holy Spirit animated fledgling
assemblies and drew adherents. In Mozambique, where growth was
most rapid, the context of violence and dislocation was also important. Pentecostalism's attraction lay in its cell-like organization which
made it difficult to dislodge. It also lay in its tendencies towards
peace and social reconstruction. Its message of sobriety and industry, its taboos on alcohol, marijuana and tobacco, its focus on stable married life offered a powerful contrast to the 'Kalashnikov
culture', so prevalent amongst young men.[121] In many respects the
ADDA's growth replicated ZAOGA's trajectory in the 1970s. A similar, though less pronounced, pattern was discernable in South African
townships in the late 1980s and early 1990s.[122]

---

[120] Isaac Frimpong Mintah, Forward in Faith Ministries International, report,
Ghana, 25 January 1995, file, Ghana, Missions, ZAW.
[121] See Martin, 1996, chapter 2.
[122] Interview, Wilson Mabasa, Mamelodi, South Africa, 20 May 1996. R. Mabasa
to Ezekiel Guti, c. 1991, file, South Africa, Mission, ZAW.

The prevalence of other well established Pentecostal movements in South Africa was always going to limit ZAOGA's 'take-off' there.[123] And the existence of competing Pentecostal movements throughout Africa meant that the distinctiveness of ZAOGA's own brand was also the key to its appeal. ZAOGA/FIFMI was an impressive operation: fleets of trucks, lorries and cars all monographed with the ZAOGA logo; well-dressed dynamic young pastors; gifted evangelists and musical soloists with a national, even international, reputation; hundreds of church buildings; a Bible School and conference centre; conventions held at international hotels; an Armani-dressed Apostle, Ezekiel Guti, chauffeured in a silver Mercedes; international connections which facilitated the movement of people and resources. Its success struck Africans and missionaries alike, and seemed to bear out the logic of its own teachings on self-reliance and black autonomy. Many new adherents, used to missionary largesse, confessed to being enchanted by a movement of black missionaries.[124]

ZAOGA's expatriate workers were indeed missionaries. In one sense they were the heirs of the Shona missionaries of the Masowe and Maranke movements but with the sophistication of the global born-again movement. In another sense they replicated the missionaries of the imperial age. Not only did their accounts resemble the narratives of Victorian pioneers, their histories likewise stripped their subjects of any agency in the mission process. And Guti's self-confidence was the match of any nineteenth-century missionary. In 1982 he told a Zairian assembly: 'I know how to work with all tribes in the world. I cannot make a mistake.'[125]

Moreover, like Victorian missionaries before them, the Zimbabweans' endeavours had economic backing. Their relative economic strength gave them an advantage in the informal hierarchy of nations which operated in Southern and Central Africa. Up to the late 1990s, the Zimbabweans could boast a stronger economy, better infrastructure and a more valuable currency than most of their neighbours. Some nineteenth-century missionaries preached a gospel inseparable from capitalist imperialism; ZAOGA's was inseparable from the language of development. Orthodox Pentecostal doctrines and ZAOGA's more idiosyncratic ones were interspersed with references to 'upgrading'.

---

[123] Allan Anderson, 1992.
[124] Interviews, Simon Monde and Mateus Simau.
[125] Report of meeting, 4 August 1982, file, Zaire, Missions, ZAW.

Sermons and meetings were littered with references to cars, lorries, houses and bank accounts. For those beneath Zimbabwe in the hierarchy of nations the ideology could create dependency. Malawians, Zambians and Zairians asked repeatedly for Zimbabwean leaders to help sort out their problems. Monde of Zaire wrote: 'I am not in the state of looking to the east or the west but to our lovely JERU-SALEM, HARARE'. 'May you clear the Bishop of Macedonia to come to us. Rev. B. Manjoro'.[126]

Those above or equal to Zimbabwe in the hierarchy presented other problems. Those in Botswana resented the repatriation to Zimbabwe of tithes and offerings and openly criticized the leadership cult and continued reference back to Harare. The South Africans proved even less deferential, demanding an updated version of the *Sacred History* which would celebrate their own agency. While the Zimbabweans' crusading capabilities impressed many, South Africans, brought up on a diet of born-again megastars like Bonnke and Pretorius, offered only a muted response, struggling with messages poorly translated into Afrikaans.[127] Others spoke out against the activities of Zimbabwean missionaries who seemed to prefer exporting knitting machines to curing souls.

Finally, there was a limit to the extent to which the Zimbabwean centre could dominate distant mission fields. Travel beyond the country's borders was perilous, not just for Zimbabweans. In 1985 Monde wrote 'It was war with the Devil to enter Zaire. We arrived in Lubumbashi with not a cent left.'[128] The most effective form of communication with Zaire was via a white lorry driver who transported eggs into the Copper Belt. In Cabo Delgado Province, Mozambique, ADDA members organized their own local anniversary to celebrate the life of their own local founder, Joaquim Matus, and appeared only vaguely aware of the distant figure of Ezekiel 'Goot' (*sic*).[129]

---

[126] S. Monde to E. Guti and Bishop Nduna, 30 April 1991 and 25 April 1992, file, Zaire, Missions, ZAW.
[127] Interview, Mabasa.
[128] Simon Monde to Ezekiel Guti, 24 March 1985, file, Zaire, ZAW.
[129] Field work, Pemba, Mozambique, June 1996.

Conclusion

This chapter has analyzed the specific, contingent and changing shape of a transnational Pentecostal movement as it expanded from its Zimbabwean base into the rest of Africa. As such it provides a powerful counter to externality theories about contemporary Pentecostalism, and highlights the heterogeneous and multi-stranded nature of the global born-again movement with which ZAOGA/FIFMI interacts. In its early stages of growth the movement was propelled forwards by the relentless proselytism of young men and women, driven by the urgency of Christ's imminent return. Others came home to found new assemblies and construct simple mud buildings as places of worship. These labour migrants were driven by the desire to maintain their Pentecostal society within a society, a world constructed out of networks of multi-stranded relationships which were frequent and intense but by no means durable.[130] Later, from the early 1970s onwards, but particularly after independence, the movement expanded and modernized by making connections with global born-again Christianity, drawing resources from the American Bible Belt and reappropriating western Pentecostal signs and practices. Its distinctive identity was maintained through its authoritarian government and the circulation of its printed sacred history and locally produced audio-visual media. Although exploiting, even flaunting, its connections with American Christianity, ZAOGA nevertheless resisted neo-colonial influences by centrally controlling American missionary activity, mobilizing its own resources, and making a vigorous critique of western Christianity couched in the language of indigenous authenticity. While its early growth was driven by ordinary labour migrants, humble pastors and evangelists, the movement's recent direction and governance has been an elite affair controlled by religious executives who are 'frequent flyers and faxers'.[131]

More generally, ZAOGA/FIFMI has evolved from a religious movement with strong links to Christian independency into a 'territorial' organization with a hierarchy of ordered centres resembling that of historic mission churches.[132] Or as Hastings has put it 'a small *communauté de base* with some intense shared religious insights and

---

[130] Mitchell, 1969, chapter 1.
[131] Hannerz, 1996, p. 29.
[132] Werbner, 1989, pp. 315–17.

fellowship' has become 'a "church"—an ongoing network of congregations held together by an "objective" order of name, ministry,
[and] stabilised particular tradition.'[133] As ZAOGA evolved, so the
strong adventism which drove the movement in the early stages of
growth has shifted from a motive force to a point of doctrine, and
the leadership has grown ever more concerned with maintenance
and memorialization. Nevertheless, the familiar sociological story of
the transition of sect to church has not been as neat or as complete
as the theory. As long as Guti lives, charisma remains a force to be
reckoned with. Attempts at bureaucratization are often thwarted by
the leader's idiosyncrasies and personal revelations. Moreover, in the
margins the movement relives its sectarian beginnings.

Apart from its own specific brand of Pentecostalism, ZAOGA's
success also lay in its control of the key centre, Highfields, known
in the 1960s as the 'black capital' of Rhodesia. Dominating the centre was also crucial to Guti's victory over his co-founders. While
they went out to do the work of evangelism and pastoring he remained
at the heart of the movement, playing them off against each other,
and building up his network of patronage. In January 1996 he
returned to Highfields Revival Centre, the movement's first building
in the city, to bless his son-in-law, recently appointed as regional
pastor. With a little hyperbole he declared 'This is the mother church.
From here we have spread all over the world'.

BIBLIOGRAPHY

Anderson, Allan, *Bazalwane: African Pentecostals in South Africa*, Pretoria, UNISA, 1992.
Anderson, Benedict, *Imagined Communities: Reflections on the Origin and Spread of Nationalism*,
  London, Verso (revised edition), 1991.
Bayart, J.F., *The State in Africa: The Politics of the Belly*, London, Longmans, 1993.
Chakanza, J.C., *An Annotated List of Independent Churches in Malawi 1900–1981*, University
  of Malawi, Department of Religious Studies, 1983.
Comaroff, J. and J., *Of Revelation and Revolution: Christianity, Colonialism and Consciousness
  in South Africa*, vol. 1, Chicago, University of Chicago, 1991.
Connerton, Paul, *How Societies Remember*, Cambridge, Cambridge University Press,
  1989.
Dillon-Malone, C., *The Korsten Basketmakers: A Study of the Masowe Apostles, An Indigenous
  African Religious Movement*, Manchester, Manchester University Press, 1978.
Erwin, Gayle, D., *The African Apostle: The Life of Ezekiel Guti*, Waterfalls, ZAOGA,
  (n.d.).

---

[133] Hastings, 1979, p. 268.

Featherstone, Mike, Lash, Scott, and Robertson, Roland, (eds.), *Global Modernities*, London, SAGE, 1995.
Giddens, A., *The Consequences of Modernity*, Stanford, Stanford University Press, 1990.
Gifford, Paul, '"Africa Shall be Saved": An Appraisal of Reinhard Bonnke's Pan-African Crusade', *Journal of Religion in Africa*, XVII.1, 1987.
———, *The New Crusaders: Christianity and the New Right in Southern Africa*, London, Pluto, 1991.
———, 'Some Recent Developments in African Christianity', *African Affairs*, 93, 373, 1994.
———, *African Christianity: Its Public Role*, London, Hurst, 1998.
Guti, Ezekiel, *The Sacred Book of ZAOGA Forward in Faith to the Leaders and the Saints*, pt. 1, Waterfalls, ZAOGA, 1989.
———, *Hearing and Listening is a Problem Even in the Home*, Waterfalls, EGEA Publications, 1993.
———, *Does Your Marriage Look Like This?*, Harare, EGEA Publications, 1994.
———, *The Sacred Book of ZAOGA Forward in Faith to the Leaders and the Saints*, pt. 2, Waterfalls, ZAOGA, 1995(a).
———, *SH-hh Shut Your Mouth: Marriage and Young Couples Character*, Harare, EGEA Publications, 1995(b).
Hallencreutz, C., *Religion and Politics in Harare, 1890–1980*, Uppsala, Swedish Institute of Missionary Research, 1998.
Hannerz, Ulf, *Transnational Connections: Culture, People, Places*, London, Routledge, 1996.
Hastings, Adrian, *A History of African Christianity 1950–1975*, Cambridge, Cambridge University Press, 1979.
———, *The Church in Africa 1450–1950*, Oxford, Clarendon Press, 1994.
Iliffe, John, *Africans: The History of a Continent*, Cambridge, CUP, 1995.
Isichei, Elizabeth, *A History of Christianity in Africa: From Antiquity to the Present*, London, SPCK, 1995.
Jules-Rosette, Bennetta, *African Apostles: Ritual and Conversion in the Church of John Maranke*, Ithaca and London, Cornell University Press, 1975.
Lehmann, D., 'Fundamentalism and Globalism', *Third World Quarterly*, 19, 4, 1998.
MacGaffey, Janet, and Bazenguissa-Ganga, Remy, *Congo-Paris: Transnational Traders on the Margins of the Law*, London, James Currey, 2000.
Martin, David, *Tongues of Fire: The Explosion of Protestantism in Latin America*, Oxford, Blackwell, 1990.
———, *Forbidden Revolutions: Pentecostalism in Latin America and Catholicism in Eastern Europe*, London, SPCK, 1996.
Maxwell, David, '"Delivered from the Spirit of Poverty": Pentecostalism, Prosperity and Modernity in Zimbabwe', *Journal of Religion in Africa*, XXVIII.3, 1998.
———, *Christians and Chiefs in Zimbabwe: A Social History of the Hwesa People c. 1870s–1990s*, Edinburgh University Press, Edinburgh, 1999(a).
———, 'Historicizing Christian Independency: The Southern African Pentecostal Movement 1908–1950', *Journal of African History*, 40, 1999(b).
———, '"Catch the Cockerel Before Dawn": Pentecostalism and Politics in Post-Colonial Zimbabwe', *Africa*, 70. 2, 2000.
———, '"African Gifts of the Spirit": Fundamentalism and the Rise of the Born-Again Movement in Africa', in Martyn Percy (ed.), *Fundamentalism, Church and Society*, London, SPCK, 2001(a).
———, '"Sacred History, Social History": Traditions and Texts in the Making of a Southern African Transnational Religious Movement', *Comparative Studies in Society and History*, 43,3, 2001(b).
Mayer, Philip, *Townsmen or Tribesmen: Conservatism and the Process of Urbanisation in a South African City*, Cape Town, Oxford University Press, 1961.
Miller, Daniel, 'Introduction: Anthropology, Modernity and Consumption' in Daniel

Miller (ed.), *Worlds Apart: Modernity Through the Prism of the Local*, London, Routledge, 1995.
Mitchell, J. Clyde, 'The Concept and Use of Social Networks' in Clyde Mitchell
(ed.), *Social Networks in Urban Situations*, Manchester, Manchester University Press,
1969.
Nederveen Pieterse, Jan, 'Globalization as Hybridization', in Mike Featherstone, Scott
Lash and Roland Robertson (eds.), *Global Modernities*, London, SAGE, 1995.
Phimister, I., *The Economic and Social History of Zimbabwe 1890–1948: Capital Accumulation
and Class Struggle*, London, Longmans, 1988.
———, and Raftopoulos, Brian, '"Kana sora ratswa ngaritswe". African Nationalists
and Black Workers: The 1948 General Strike in Colonial Zimbabwe', *Journal
of Historical Sociology*, 13.3, September 2000.
Ranger, T.O., *The African Voice in Southern Rhodesia 1898–1930*, London, Heinemann,
1970.
———, 'Concluding Summary', in K. Holst-Peterson (ed.), *Religion, Development and
African Identity*, Uppsala, Scandinavian Institute of African Studies, 1985.
———, *Voices from the Rocks: Nature, Culture and History in the Matopos Hills of Zimbabwe*,
Oxford, James Currey, 1999.
Robertson, Roland, 'Glocalization: Time-Space and Homogeneity-Heterogeneity',
in Mike Featherstone, Scott Lash and Roland Robertson (eds.), *Global Modernities*,
London, SAGE, 1995.
Scarnecchia, T., 'Mai Chaza's *Guta re Jehova* (City of God): Gender, Healing and
Urban Identity in an African Independent Church', *Journal of Southern African
Studies*, 23, 1, 1997.
Schoffeleers, J. Matthew, *River of Blood: The Genesis of a Martyr Cult in Southern Malawi,
ca. A.D. 1600*, Wisconsin, University of Wisconsin Press, 1992.
Sundkler, Bengt, and Christopher Steed, *A History of the Church in Africa*, Cambridge,
Cambridge University Press, 2000.
Watt, P., *From Africa's Soil: The Story of the Assemblies of God in Southern Africa*, Cape
Town, Struik, 1992.
Werbner, R.P., *Ritual Passage, Sacred Journey: The Process and Organization of Religious
Movement*, Manchester, Manchester University Press, 1989.
Yoshikuni, T., 'Black Migrant in a Black City: A Social History of Harare 1890–1925',
Ph.D. Thesis, University of Zimbabwe, 1989.

CHAPTER ELEVEN

THE SHAPING OF A PROPHET: THE AFRICAN CAREER AND WRITINGS OF ADRIAN HASTINGS[1]

Ingrid Lawrie

The Shaping of Prophecy: Passion, Perception and Practicality[2] is a collection of articles by Adrian Hastings, published in 1995. As one reviewer, who describes the book as magnificent, remarks: 'The author has recently retired as Professor of Theology in the University of Leeds, but no one can take from him the mantle of a prophet.'[3] All his other personae—writer, talker, campaigner, ecumenist, scholar and teacher, journalist, historian, editor, theologian, priest—at times have a prophetic voice. His bibliography (chapter 12 of this volume), covering more than fifty years, includes everything traceable that he has published:[4] not only the usual books, articles and reviews, but newspaper articles and letters, since these are often where his prophetic role is most evident.

Education and Training: 'The Most Difficult, the Most Completely Sacrificial Thing'

At the age of six, Adrian Hastings made up his mind to be a priest. It was his own decision, not influenced by his family, staunchly Catholic as they were, or indeed by any individual at all, so far as he can remember. Should he become a secular priest of the Birmingham diocese, in which the Hastings family was living at that time,

---

[1] I am very grateful to Cecily Bennett, Kevin Ward, Alistair Mason and to David Maxwell for their help and encouragement with this chapter. The largest debt, however, is to Adrian himself, who gave me hours of interviews, and allowed me extended use of his books and archive materials.

[2] London, Geoffrey Chapman, 1995.

[3] Eric James, review in *Theology*, March/April 1996, p. 138.

[4] Special thanks are due to Paul Gifford, who with great tact persuaded me that the bibliography should include everything published by AH, from books to letters. He was absolutely right, though a careful reading of the full list would almost make this chapter superfluous.

or a religious? If the latter, of which order? There was never any
desire to be a Benedictine (it would not be sufficiently challenging),
though his family had very close links with Stanbrook Abbey, where
his grandmother had become a nun after she was widowed in 1901,
and where his mother had been brought up:

> Hazel, at little more than five, found her home to be the tiny school
> of no more than twelve girls, a relic of former ages, inside the monas-
> tic enclosure. It was a strangely medieval education. The girls wore a
> black habit and a veil for much of the time, shared in the liturgy and
> became expert in plainsong, Latin, calligraphy, heraldry, and astron-
> omy, but not much else.[5]

AH himself was educated at a Benedictine School, Douai Abbey,
though his strongest influence there was a lay teacher, Oliver Welch,
who inspired him and guided his passion for history.[6] After his family moved to Oxford in 1938 and became part of the Blackfriars
community, they grew very close to the priests there and it was expected, after AH left school and went up to Worcester College, Oxford, in October 1946 (aged 17), that he would become a Dominican.

In his first long vacation, he spent a month at the Cistercian
monastery on Caldey Island, alone in the guesthouse, reading a great
deal. He was attracted to the life, but somehow felt compelled to
do 'the most difficult, the most completely sacrificial thing',[7] and neither Caldey nor Blackfriars would be sacrificial enough. 'It seemed
to me that I should be willing to offer myself for something a great
deal more exacting and unpleasant . . . the life of a missionary
in Africa',[8] in spite of being a rather weak, impractical intellectual,
'a little Englander, wholly uninterested in the Empire, or in non-
European cultures.'[9] Not surprisingly, some doubts appeared during
his final year at Oxford, and he oscillated again between being a
diocesan priest and a missionary. To resolve matters, he consulted
the Headmaster of Douai, Fr Ignatius Rice, putting to him in strong
terms the disadvantages of both courses, not least those of the African

---

[5] Typescript of article, 'Hazel Hastings', for the *New Dictionary of National Biography*,
Oxford, Oxford University Press, forthcoming (2004). See also *In Filial Disobedience*,
Great Wakering, Mayhew-McCrimmon, 1978, pp. 27–28.

[6] See 'Pre-Vatican II English Catholicism: The Case of Oliver Welch', *Downside
Review*, Vol. 119, No. 414, January 2001, pp. 11–34.

[7] Interview with AH, July 1999.

[8] *In Filial Disobedience*, p. 34.

[9] Ibid.

way is displayed in the exchange of letters with the Father Provincial of the Order, Bishop Durrieu, and Bishop Kiwanuka among others in the summer and early autumn of 1953. It is worth quoting several paragraphs from a very long letter to Bishop Durrieu, because they explain, in a clear and maturely considered way, what he wanted and why.

> My interests and aptitudes both draw me to missionary work in one of the more developed parts of Africa; in fact I have long had a particular interest in Uganda. My desire has been and is to work for and with the African évolués—both lay and clerical. I realise very well that White Fathers can and do do similar work, but in fact they will do that work chiefly in dioceses not yet sufficiently ripe for handing over to the indigenous clergy. . . . This of course is natural and right enough; but my desire is precisely to work in a territory which has been handed over, where in fact the work is no more the basic establishment of the Church but rather the enriching of its organism—the passing (if I may so describe it) from a 'utility' church to a 'fully-fashioned' one. I think that there is an intermediate period between the handing over of a territory and the full growth of its new Christian community, in which there is great need for the help of foreign auxiliaries of the kind I envisage. I believe that . . . it is the native clergy alone who can really represent the Church in Africa adequately, they alone who can give the requisite Catholic leadership and take an effective positive attitude in matters of social, political and educational development. But to do this they need at the beginning full-time encouragement and assistance; this I think can best be given by one within their ranks and sharing their life.
>
> At the present time, the colour conflict is threatening to ruin British Africa; as an Englishman I feel perhaps a particular responsibility in this matter. Fundamentally it is not a question of colour but of man's attitude to colour and the basing of social distinctions on colour; thus in British W. Africa there is no colour question. The only way to overcome the evils and injustices of the colour-bar is to react strongly in the opposite direction. It is that that I wish to do by living in permanent community with Africans under an African superior; I cannot think that this can have other than a good influence, however small, on the stormy society of modern Africa.
>
> . . . . It is just this that I desire to do—to be a member of an African community not a European one; a priest belonging to an African diocese, not to the English province of an international society; and, if necessary, even a citizen of Uganda and not one of Great Britain. These may be in part formalities but they are symbols of something more.

The battle was finally won: it was agreed that he might approach Bishop Kiwanuka, who accepted him and arranged for him to go

to the College of Propaganda Fide in Rome, where a number of
Ugandan students were among those training for ordination. He
arrived in the first week of November 1953, and, although he had
not been unhappy at 's Heerenberg, he found Rome wonderfully
liberating: open, interesting, cosmopolitan, with students not only
from Africa, but from Australia, India, China, Japan, Korea, Vietnam,
a few from the USA, Norway and two others from England. One
of his earliest ventures into journalism is an article about the College,
'"Go and Teach All Nations"', published in the *Catholic Worker*[18] in
the autumn of 1955. He writes proudly of the fact that one of his
great heroes, Newman, studied there: 'It was here that he celebrated
his first Mass, on an altar still treasured in the college.'[19] But he is
also proud of the college's internationalism, the 'unity which tri-
umphs over diversity', and the fact that it trains men who will go
back to their own countries as missionaries, who 'having learnt to
wed national character and Catholic religion in their own personal
lives can now return to their own lands to bring about this marriage in the hearts of their people.'

What he does not mention is the freedom given to the students,
which enabled him to make close friends not only within his own
Camerata (the groups of around 20 into which the students were
divided in the College) but at the Beda and the English College.
This freedom also meant the opportunity to indulge again in intellectual interests. He wrote his first substantial African piece, the
pamphlet *White Domination or Racial Peace?*, several years before reaching the continent. It was published in 1954 by the Africa Bureau in
London, mostly staffed by Protestants who were pleased to dissem-
inate a Catholic viewpoint for the first time. *White Domination* is
about politics, not religion, and many missionaries were horrified by
its radical nature. Looked at from the distance of almost half a
century, the author's conclusion might seem idealistic, but hardly
contentious:

---

[18] A newspaper in financial difficulties, whose survival until then had been aided
by 'the generosity of Mr Hastings of the Newman Bookshop, Oxford' (AH's brother
Peter). The struggle to keep going is perhaps reflected in the fact that the issue
from which these quotations are taken nowhere carries the year (though it is possible to work it out). It is simply 'Overseas Edition No. 11, September-October'.
[19] AH celebrated his own first mass at the same altar later that year.

The lines that British policy must take in Africa, if it is to do nothing else than avoid disaster, are clear: the ending of the colour bar
not only in social relationships but also in the division of land; strong
encouragement of a peasant, as opposed to an estate economy; the
recognition not only of the plural but also of the primarily African
character of these territories; and, finally, the tactful adaptation of
African political institutions so as to meet the new needs of a developing society. But such a policy, if genuinely and courageously adopted,
will do far more than avoid disaster: it will build up British Africa on
a basis as sound politically as it may well be prosperous economically, and it will secure for the free world the friendship of half a
continent.[20]

The new freedom in Rome also enabled AH to mount his first newspaper campaign, taking issue, not for the last time, with the Portuguese
government. In articles and letters in the *Catholic Herald* and *The
Tablet*, he supported the cause of Goan independence from Portugal
and inclusion within India, pointing out that the matter was a political one, *not* 'a religious question in which all good Catholics must
take up their stand by praying for the continuance of Portuguese
rule.'[21]

As with his Oxford BA, he did not allow the completion of his
licentiate and his doctorate (begun in 1956) to interfere with other
activities. During this time he wrote his first book, *Prophet and Witness
in Jerusalem: A Study of the Teaching of St Luke*,[22] encouraged by his
New Testament teacher, Mgr Garofalo, to pursue some personal
research on the Gospels. It was published in 1958, the same year
as his first edited collection, *The Church and the Nations*. He remains
especially proud of the Introduction to the latter, composed during
his term of teaching practice at St John Fisher School, Purley. At
Bishop Kiwanuka's request he was taking a Postgraduate Diploma
of Education, and had chosen to do so at Cambridge, where he
lived for the first time at St Edmund's House. In the autumn of

---

[20] *White Domination or Racial Peace?*, London, The Africa Bureau, 1956, p. 16.
[21] Letter, *Catholic Herald*, 3 September 1954.
[22] London and New York, Longmans, Green and Co. Ltd., 1958, 200 pp. As
we see in the Preface, 'my sister Cecily [now Dr Cecily Bennett], who ... carried
through a careful revision of the whole work' was even then making her contribution to publications by her younger brother, a collaboration renewed most recently
for *The Oxford Companion to Christian Thought*. Her editing work on *Christianity and the
African Imagination* has been invaluable.

Adrian Hastings in Masaka, Uganda, early 1960s

1958 he returned to Rome to defend his doctorate, and then, at last, set forth for Uganda.

Mission: Uganda, Tanzania, Zambia, Birmingham

AH's own description ('an essay of reminiscence') of the parish of Villa Maria where he arrived in October 1958 is too good to summarize or paraphrase. The opening paragraphs give the flavour of the whole:

> The church of Villa Maria is very old, the oldest building in all its countryside. It stands amid the green hills and the banana plantations and above the papyrus swamps of the *ssaza* or 'county' of Buddu in Uganda. It is a dark place—dark at least in comparison with the bright equatorial sun outside—but vast and well able to accommodate beneath its interlacing roof beams some thousands of the Bannabuddu. It stands unchanging in its great cross form with twenty massive white pillars, its little round-headed windows and the smell of countless bats inhabiting the inaccessible rafters.
>
> Besides its age and size, the church possesses a great holiness, for it goes back almost to the age of the martyrs and it was there that so many had to come from afar, before the modern parishes were set up, for baptism and catechism and confirmation. It was here that the priests have been made year after year since 1913, hallowed, respected men who mastered Latin when learning was still something rare and wonderful. . . . It was Munsenyere Stensera [Monsignor Streicher] who founded the mission and built the church and ordained the first priests. It was he, with simple faith, iron determination and effective planning, who made of all this land a Catholic countryside and impressed on it his own ideas and enthusiasm, the strength and the narrowness of the Catholicism of his own homeland far away in Alsace . . . He himself is still here, buried close below the main altar, awe-inspiring still in his presence, a shrine where the people come to pray.[23]

But his skills were needed elsewhere, and after fifteen months of curacy he was moved to the minor seminary[24] of Bukalasa, to be

---

[23] Published in different forms elsewhere, but having its final incarnation as the opening of 'Ganda Catholic Spirituality' in *African Catholicism*, London, SCM, 1989, pp. 69–70. For a description of the building of the Villa Maria mission, see chapter four.

[24] Minor seminaries, for boys in their teens, were theoretically the first stage in training for the priesthood, but, since there was no obligation to go on to the major seminary, they functioned in practice as somewhat privileged boys' secondary schools.

'an apostle of the British examination system as applied to the training of priests.'[25] The move was not entirely unwelcome: he was certainly committed to providing the African church with the best-educated priests possible, and gave all his energies to this for the next five years, but he foresaw that conflicts would arise because he would inevitably need to challenge the system.

There were great pleasures to be gained from teaching: the development of GCE A Level courses for the more able students and the excitement of Shakespearian productions. The quality of his students' acting was staggering, and he was grateful to John Waliggo not only for his Laertes and Mark Antony but also for help in organising rehearsals, an early indication of leadership qualities. However, the Bukalasa years were rather barren as regards writing, and rather bleak ones for AH. As he explained in an article written more than thirty years after his arrival in Uganda,

> Little by little I came to question whether we were really on the right track and found it necessary to try to rethink theologically the nature and appropriate shape of the ordained ministry. The whole concept of a minor seminary was something I found uncongenial . . . Quite inevitably, the clergy of Masaka were a great deal more conservative theologically than I was and very little in touch with ideas which were by then elsewhere sweeping through the world church. My very concern to take seriously the job I had been given drew me increasingly into a collision course with those I had come to serve and to obey.[26]

The writing that was achieved during this time was mostly in the form of articles for *AFER* (*African Ecclesiastical Review*), with a few non-African pieces for British periodicals, including the delightful 'Justice for Umbria: On a Walk in Central Italy'.[27] He also completed the revision of his doctoral thesis on ecclesiology, which appeared in 1963 under the title *One and Apostolic*. For all its strongly ecumenical approach, in the preface he states firmly that 'controversial writing is very necessary', thus setting his own agenda for the future.[28]

From December 1964 to December 1965 he was back in England for a year, at first feeling 'broken' and out of touch with British intellectual life, but used the time to write the greater part of *Church*

---

[25] *In Filial Disobedience*, p. 69.
[26] 'My Pilgrimage in Mission', *International Bulletin of Missionary Research*, Vol. 16, No. 2, April 1992, pp. 62–63.
[27] *The Month*, August 1960, pp. 106–110.
[28] *One and Apostolic*, London, Darton, Longman and Todd, p. xi.

and Mission in Modern Africa, which helped to bring him back into the swim theologically. On his return from leave in December 1965, the earlier conflicts, the 'collision course', meant that he was not allowed to return to Bukalasa, being now judged a bad influence on the students. He was placed instead in the remote parish of Bigada, where he was surprisingly happy, but his health, never robust, deteriorated and he suffered a very serious bout of malaria. He would probably have been obliged to return to England, perhaps for good, had he not been saved by a new enterprise. Bishop Blomjous of Mwanza, one of the founders of *AFER*, had acquired funding for a major programme of post-Vatican II education for the whole of East Africa, and AH was appointed to work on it. The organizational structure did not develop as planned, his very appointment was in doubt at one point, but in 1966 he moved to Kipalapala in Tanzania, a White Fathers seminary, to begin a totally revolutionized life after the years of isolation at Bukalasa.

One of his frustrations at the seminary had been his complete lack of involvement with the Second Vatican Council. Now, belatedly, he could immerse himself in it. For two years, twice a month, he produced eight pages of commentary on the Council's documents. These were distributed to about fifty dioceses, and were well received. At that point they were not identified as his work, but went out over the name AMECEA, the Association of the Members of Episcopal Conferences in Eastern Africa, which made them more authoritative. (The anonymity did not persist, because they were later published in England as a two-volume commentary, and his name was allowed to appear.[29]) He also led seminars in a variety of places, including a month-long course at Gaba Pastoral Institute (Uganda). He was revitalized by this 'profoundly missionary experience', which constituted 'a new theological, pastoral and ecumenical education', moving him 'from being a preconciliar liberal to being a postconciliar radical.'[30]

Another crucial contribution to the revolutionary new life was the Anglican-Roman Catholic Preparatory Commission, which Cardinal Bea, Head of the Secretariat of Unity, invited him to join in 1966. The presence of non-Catholic Observers at Vatican II and a visit

---

[29] *A Concise Guide to the Documents of the Second Vatican Council*, London, Darton, Longman and Todd, Vol. 1, 1968, Vol. 2, 1969.
[30] 'My Pilgrimage in Mission', p. 63.

by Archbishop Michael Ramsey to Rome in March 1966 had effectively changed the nature of relations between the Roman Catholic Church and the Anglican Communion.[31] The Archbishop's visit was quickly followed by the creation of the Commission. Its initial session at Gazzada in the Italian Alps was an almost unprecedented official, public meeting between Catholics and Protestants and aroused great excitement. There was strong theological and episcopal representation on both sides, and AH felt that at first he was regarded not only as a junior member with idiosyncratic views but perhaps also as a token African presence. However, he soon established himself, and in the end had a very influential role, contributing significantly to the final Malta Report (January 1968).[32]

The higher public profile resulting from his membership of the Commission was reinforced by the publication in 1967 of *Church and Mission in Modern Africa*, one of his most important books not only for its contents but because of its impact and success. It was 'a tentative personal assessment of a vast reality: the Catholic Church in modern Africa and the missionary effort that goes with it', an attempt recognized by the author as 'wildly rash ... The subject is so enormous, the work so diverse that no one can possibly be expert, or near-expert, in the whole.'[33]

The appearance of this book confirmed him as an international figure and a voice on Africa, and incidentally inaugurated one of his great Africanist friendships, that with Terry Ranger.[34] Terry was then Professor of History in University College, Dar es Salaam, and their first contact came when he wrote to AH with the draft of a review article on *Church and Mission*[35] to ask if he was interpreting

---

[31] '... Archbishop Ramsey went to Rome in a blaze of publicity. The Vatican Council was over. Ecumenical reconciliation was now the order of the day. Pope Paul placed his own ring on Michael Ramsey's finger and was soon to declare Canterbury a "sister Church". The subsequent growth in a shared collegiality is obvious.' Edward Carpenter, *Cantuar*, London, Mowbray, 1997, new introduction by Adrian Hastings, p. XXIII.

[32] See *A History of English Christianity 1920–2000*, chapter 34, 'The Second Vatican Council' and chapter 36, 'Roman Catholicism', especially pp. 569–571.

[33] *Church and Mission in Modern Africa*, Introduction, p. 11.

[34] Though in one of those fascinating connections that often seem to link expatriates, Professor Ranger had taught AH's wife, then Ann Spence, at the University College of Rhodesia and Nyasaland, where he lectured from 1957 to 1963.

[35] This appeared as 'The Church in the Age of African Revolution' in *East Africa Journal*, August 1968, pp. 11–17.

him aright. The answer was yes, they later met when AH visited Dar, and have been interpreting one another in the subsequent thirty or so years. The first interpretation by Terry was, perhaps, the most enthusiastic:

> There have been painstaking studies of the Catholic church in Africa by experienced missionary priests before now which have contained almost nothing of interest to revolutionaries and which have touched at no point the revolutionary dynamic of modern Africa. But Father Adrian Hastings's book is very different. Of all the books relating to East Africa which I have read in the past year, his discussion of the predicament and potential of the Catholic church displays the acutest sense of what the African revolution is and will be about, the most impressive powers of analysis and recommendation, and the most radical challenge to the thinking of those in control of a major institution. It seems to me not only an essential book for East African Christians of all denominations but also a very important book for everyone concerned with the development of East African society.[36]

Another major change was now imminent. After the post-Vatican II work ended, AH spent fifteen months as theological consultant for the Mindolo Ecumenical Foundation in Zambia. He did not find this entirely satisfactory, though it resulted in another book, *Mission and Ministry*, published in 1971, which dealt with social and political matters in a quite radical way, offering solutions to the problem of maintaining the vigour of the church's missionary function in new circumstances. He had, for some time, been thinking about the issue of marriage, including polygamy, and this had now become a central concern. The request from the Anglican Archbishops of Cape Town, Central Africa, Kenya, Tanzania and Uganda to compile a report on marriage came at exactly the right moment. The report, for which he surveyed nine countries of the Anglican communion, in eastern and southern Africa, covered indissolubility and church (as opposed to customary) marriage, but a substantial part was devoted to a re-examination of polygamy, from historical, sociological and theological viewpoints. His recommendation to the Archbishops was that, while monogamy is the ideal, 'polygamous marriage is most certainly to be classified as marriage and not as adultery; that the New Testament does not explicitly reject it while it does strongly condemn the breaking of a marriage; that Christians have frequently

---

[36] Ibid, p. 11.

to put up with socio-moral situations that are not theoretically ideal . . .'.[37] He returned to this argument in *The Church in Africa 1450–1950*, in a thematic chapter, 'Kings, Marriage, Ancestors, and God', and most recently in a booklet entitled *Love and Law: The Nature of Christian Morality*. Here, while acknowledging again the great complexity of the issue,[38] he reiterates a central principle:

> . . . it still seems extraordinary to claim that where wives have already fully accepted a polygamous marriage according to the custom of their society, their marriages must be dissolved, with all the damage to both them and their children, before they or their husband can be baptized. Can that be an expression of love? What has happened here is that a general implication that love is best served by a monogamous relationship has been turned into a law with consequences which, in such cases, seem decidedly unloving.[39]

The lectures on which *Love and Law* is based were given in Lincoln, and it was in Lincoln that AH completed his report, *Christian Marriage in Africa*,[40] during a term as ecumenical lecturer in the Theological College in 1972. When the book was finished, he was in effect unemployed and homeless, though St Edmund's in Cambridge provided lodging and fellowship when needed. After he had left Mindolo and returned to England in early 1970, he had no base in Africa, though he did spend a considerable amount of time there during the next two years on a variety of activities: external examining for Makerere University, teaching at Gaba Pastoral Institute for a month each year, carrying out the marriage survey, and, at the invitation of Archbishop Hurley of Durban, giving Winter School lectures in five different venues in South Africa.[41]

While the Catholic Church in England continued to show no interest in employing him, the Anglican Church stepped in again, this

---

[37] 'A Report on Marriage', *New Blackfriars*, June 1973, p. 254.

[38] See *Christian Marriage in Africa*, p. 5, 'Missionaries were for the most part simple men, at times perhaps too simple, yet they were quickly forced to struggle with complexity, but in no field has the complexity and indeed the perplexity been greater than in that of marriage.'

[39] *Love and Law: The Nature of Christian Morality. Lincoln Lectures in Theology 2000*, Lincoln Cathedral Publications, 2001, p. 38.

[40] London, SPCK, 1973.

[41] For several months in 1971 he was on crutches, having broken his leg very badly by slipping on a highly polished floor at St Edmund's. For the next ten years he suffered a great deal of pain, which was relieved only by a hip replacement operation in Aberdeen in 1981.

time with a tutorship at the USPG College of the Ascension at Selly Oak, Birmingham. This tided him over until another great turning point, a 'hinge moment', to use one of his own phrases, his appointment as Research Officer at the School of Oriental and African Studies, University of London, to work on a Leverhulme-funded project on Christianity in independent Africa. But before this began, he had been for a few months at the centre of a national and international drama, when he made known to the world a massacre of 400 people, mostly women and children, by Portuguese troops in a group of villages in Mozambique. We shall return to the story of Wiriyamu later.

It was at Selly Oak too that he met Ann Spence, whom he married in 1979, amidst the inevitable publicity resulting from the decision of a Catholic priest to take such a step. The greater part of *In Filial Disobedience* constitutes his *apologia* and his own words cannot be improved. As always in his writings on the subject, he stresses that he does not reject celibacy itself, but the imposition of it on all priests. He concludes the first chapter: 'May the flowers of celibacy bloom beside the flowers of marriage, and may they both be the flowers of the priesthood as they are both the flowers of the unordained.'[42]

Academia: SOAS, Aberdeen, Harare, Leeds

The project which took AH to SOAS was devised by Richard Gray, one of the two scholars (the other being Andrew Walls) 'who, between them, salvaged my career and guided it into academic waters when— the years in Africa over—it seemed to have lost its way.'[43] The three-year project, consisting of a series of seminars in London and a hugely successful conference at Jos in September 1975, resulted in three books and a solid reputation for AH as *a historian of* Africa, whereas hitherto he had written mainly as a theologian and *interpreter for* Africa. The first book, *African Christianity*,[44] was written in a matter of weeks after the Conference, remarkable even for someone whose speed and facility of writing is inclined to arouse envy in his

[42] *In Filial Disobedience*, p. 12.
[43] Preface to *African Catholicism*, p. xiv.
[44] London, Geoffrey Chapman, 1976.

fellow academics. But there is no indication of rushed production, and the first chapter, 'A Century of Growth', is an expert summary of the hundred years, 1875–1975, in which Christianity was fully established on the African continent, a lively and compelling account, fitting into sixteen pages half the subject matter of *The Church in Africa*, with vivid introductions to prophets and martyrs, kings and prime ministers, missionary societies and independent churches. As he himself says of the story he has to tell, 'what riches and complexity are to be found here!'[45]

Next came his contribution to the writing and editing of *Christianity in Independent Africa*, the collection of papers from the Jos Conference, followed by *A History of African Christianity 1950–1975*[46] as the conclusion of the project. As the author lays down in his introduction, this is a 'fairly straight history', and he even eschews the role of the prophet, as well as that of the moralist (while stressing that a history without morality can only be produced by dehumanized scholarship). He continues:

> Certainly, this is a story which includes its measure of folly, of mediocrity, of insignificant ventures, but it is also a record of faith and hope and fellowship and subtle imagination and striking courage and hard endeavour, and of all these things as being inalienable and significant elements within the total history of a society and its culture.[47]

The book was completed in Aberdeen, where AH obtained his first permanent university post in 1976, at the age of 47. He joined the staff of the Department of Religious Studies, which was trying to develop its African side, an ideal situation for him. He was fortunate to be there at 'a wonderful time', with Andrew Walls (Head of Department), Lamin Sanneh, Rosalind Shaw and Elizabeth Sirriyeh as colleagues, and Kwame Bediako, Rosalind Hackett and David Shank among the research students.[48] He described the department as 'a shining light in the field of the interpretation of African reli-

---

[45] *African Christianity*, p. 2.
[46] Cambridge, Cambridge University Press, 1979.
[47] *A History of African Christianity 1950–1975*, p. 3. See also David Maxwell's introduction to this volume.
[48] 'African Christian Studies, 1967–1999: Reflections of an Editor', *Journal of Religion in Africa* XXX.1, 1999, pp. 36–37, 38.

gious and missionary experience'.[49] It was in Aberdeen that he taught Donald Mackay, one of his best students ever, whose career he guided first to the University of Zimbabwe, then to Leeds as a British Academy Research Fellow. AH pays an entertaining and affectionate tribute to his Head of Department in Aberdeen and predecessor at the *Journal of Religion in Africa* in 'AFW as Editor', part of a collection marking Professor Walls's move to Edinburgh.[50] One paragraph describes AFW's wider contribution to the life of Aberdeen, giving a picture not only of the man but of the town, in what now sounds like a long-gone age, when academics had time to be human beings.

> Historians of the north-east may in future be perplexed over the exact relationship between Andrew Walls, the academic we have been discussing, and another Andrew Walls, a formidably active local Labour politician and Aberdeen City Councillor. The striking visual likeness between the two must add to the problem, given the old story that when Councillor Walls occasionally encountered Professor Walls hurrying down Union Street, they passed one another with but a nod of recognition. And then there is that third character, Finlay Anderson, whose humorous luncheon hour recitals at the Art Gallery, with their extraordinary range of Scottish, and even Sassenach, culture, popular and literary, delighted audiences week after week. It is whispered that Finlay Anderson was really Councillor Walls impersonating his more academic namesake, while there is another opinion that it was just the other way round.

Aberdeen was an extremely important stage in AH's career, turning him into an academic. He had no experience of university teaching, had never lectured in religious studies, but was soon deeply involved in undergraduate courses and Ph.D. supervision. In 1980, after the publication of *A History of African Christianity*, he was given a Readership. He learnt an enormous amount in Aberdeen, one of its valuable assets being Harold Turner with his collection of material on New Religious Movements, which provided sources for both the 1979 *History* and later for *The Church in Africa 1450–1950*. However,

---

[49] Review of *New Testament Christianity for Africa and the World: Essays in Honour of Harry Sawyer*, Mark E. Glasswell and Edward W. Fasholé-Luke (eds.), *The Tablet*, 22 February 1975.

[50] James Thrower (ed.), *Essays in Religious Studies for Andrew Walls*, University of Aberdeen, Department of Religious Studies, 1986, pp. 5–9. See also the Editorial in *JRA* XXVII.1, 1997, a special issue in honour of Andrew Walls to mark the *Journal's* thirtieth birthday.

AH's life had been one of movement, and it is in his nature continually to seek fresh challenges. While taking up the Chair of Religious
Studies in the University of Zimbabwe (on secondment from Aberdeen)
in 1982 was far from being 'the most difficult, the most completely
sacrificial thing', it was certainly very demanding, not least for someone half way through a history of twentieth-century *English* church
history.

Thinking that he would not go back to Africa, he had looked for
a new direction in his research and writing and had turned to modern English Christianity. With the encouragement of David Edwards,
the Provost of Southwark (who was later to describe him as 'the best
historian of Christianity in Africa, and in England after 1920'[51]), he
had negotiated a contract with Collins for what proved to be his
most successful book, now in its fourth edition, updated to the end
of the millennium.[52] Reviews of the first edition were enthusiastic,
and contain many memorable words of praise. The *Crucible* review
is quoted, partly because it is representative of the rest, mainly because
it was written by Oliver Tomkins, the subject of the last item in the
books section of AH's bibliography:

> This is a richly rewarding book . . . Its rewards lie not only in the emi-
> nently readable style—its 700 pages flow smoothly by—but in the
> unusual combination of factual information over a wide field with inci-
> sive comment and wise judgements, as well as brilliant little character
> sketches of the main actors. . . . Again and again this book exhilarates
> by showing familiar facts from unfamiliar angles. The diligence of the
> research involved is formidable.

We can regret, with Terry Ranger, that the three years in Harare
did not result in a book on local religious history,[53] and sympathize
with AH's feelings of guilt that he was writing about England in the
1950s and 1960s instead of Zimbabwe in the 1980s, but we cannot
wish that *A History of English Christianity* had not been written: it
remains a great achievement.

In Harare, as elsewhere, writing was only one of many activities.
AH learned how to run a university department, one which, after
his arrival, expanded in several ways, with the introduction of both

---

[51] Review of *Cantuar: The Archbishops in their Office*, *The Tablet*, 18 October 1977.
[52] *A History of English Christianity 1920–1985*, London, Collins, 1986; fourth edition, *A History of English Christianity 1920–2000*, London, SCM Press, 2001.
[53] See chapter four of this volume.

Honours BA and MA courses and the addition of Classics to Religious Studies and Philosophy. He established links with the Catholic Theological College, enabling its students to take degrees of the University of Zimbabwe. In the early 1980s, Zimbabwe was an exciting place to be, prosperous and peaceful, and AH greatly enjoyed his time there. He had no hesitation in persuading others to come, including Donald Mackay from Aberdeen, and was pleased to be on the interviewing panel that appointed his successor, Carl Fredrik Hallencreutz from Uppsala.[54]

Just as Aberdeen made of AH a university teacher, UZ made of him a Head of Department, putting him in a strong position to apply for the Chair of Theology at Leeds. The name of the Chair was tied to an endowment, but the department was very much one of Theology *and* Religious Studies and AH was particularly effective in linking the two areas. In 1985 he brought to Leeds a legacy of his Aberdeen days, the *Journal of Religion in Africa*, whose editorship Andrew Walls had handed on. Both the department and the *JRA* were in a somewhat depleted and depressed state; his energy and determination turned both around and left them increased in size and reputation on his retirement.

AH introduced African studies and African students to the department, enriching the postgraduate community. John Karanja, who later completed a Ph.D. with John Lonsdale and is now a member of the *JRA*'s editorial advisory board, was one of the first African MAs. Later, in 1993, came Tomaida Milingo, niece of the Archbishop whose healing ministry AH had analysed so sympathetically in 'Emmanuel Milingo as Christian Healer'.[55] His research students included Jerome (Yoramu) Bamunoba, Bishop of West Ankole, who makes an appearance in Kevin Ward's essay in this volume, and Sam Gyanfosu, who has his own chapter. Andrew Walls was Sam's external examiner, insisting on travelling to Leeds for the *viva voce* examination in spite of illness. The supervisor, however, was not in Leeds, as required by university regulations, but stranded in a besieged Sarajevo, where the airport had just been closed. Eventually he made

---

[54] See AH's appreciation, 'Carl Fredrik Hallencreutz, 1934–2001', *Journal of Religion in Africa*, XXXI.2, 2001. AH's lecture at the IAMS Harare Conference referred to in that piece is published as 'Mission, Church and State in Southern Africa: The First 150 Years', in *African Catholicism*, pp. 156–183.

[55] In *African Catholicism*, pp. 138–155.

his way out by a dangerous journey through the tunnel under the airport, and up Mount Igmen, accompanied and helped, he was at pains to make clear, by Bosnian *Serbs*.[56] This was probably the only occasion on which he was not at hand to give his support, which was unstinting, both academically and pastorally. During those years, many postgraduates, not just those from Africa, benefited from the generous hospitality of Professor and Mrs Hastings, and their practical help when the inevitable problems arose.

AH was fortunate in many ways during his Leeds period, not only because he was Head of Department at a time when the administrative burdens, while onerous, were not all-consuming, but also because of the quality of the students. In addition to Africans and Africanists, there were many other very talented postgraduates, and, as finalists in his last year before retirement, an exceptionally lively, interesting and clever group of undergraduates, many of whom he taught and guided to success. One measure of a first-class student is how much the teacher learns from her or him: among the sources for AH's chapter on 'Latin America' in his own *World History of Christianity* is an undergraduate dissertation he supervised in that golden year.[57]

This part of the story would not be complete without mention of two extraordinary students, even though this involves further digression from our African theme. Christopher Gray was one of the ordinands of the College of the Resurrection, Mirfield, who at that time came to the department to take a second BA degree. Chris already had an outstanding first-class BA and a B.Phil. from Oxford, and AH described him as

> quite the most brilliant student I have had the pleasure of teaching, and all the more pleasurable because, despite his politeness, he clearly made no concessions even to lack of omniscience on the part of his professor. He transformed my seminars on the first two questions of the *Summa Theologica* of Aquinas by turning them almost into a dialogue, ensuring that I could never get away with less than complete clarity of exposition.[58]

---

[56] He had been invited to a meeting of the Serb Civic Forum, which he saw as an ideal opportunity to disprove the accusation that he was anti-Serb. See 'Serbs Against Fascism', *The Tablet*, 6 May 1995.

[57] Daniella Klein, 'Canudos and the Language of Liberation', *A World History of Christianity*, London, Cassell, 1999, p. 368, note 12.

[58] Obituary, *The Guardian*, 15 August 1996.

His commitment to an inner-city parish led to his murder. He was 32. 'Christopher died when an unbalanced criminal, whom he was trying to help, drove a knife into his heart just outside his Liverpool parish church. The loss for the church and for British society is a huge one.'[59] AH converted grief into prose, in a moving obituary for the *Guardian* and later in a short (unpublished) address for Christopher's memorial service in Liverpool Cathedral.

Constance Millington's first contact with the Department of Theology and Religious Studies[60] was a telephone call lasting forty-five minutes, centring on whether she was mad to consider applying to do a doctorate on the Anglican Church in South India ('the awkward little diocese of Nandyal'[61]) at the age of 70. Assured that she was not mad, she applied, was accepted, became AH's student and devoted admirer, completed her Ph.D., and under his academic and editorial direction wrote three books, completing the third shortly before she died at the age of 85 in January 2000. The admiration was reciprocated, as is clear in his obituary,[62] which omits to mention the crucial part he played in her late-developing research career.

When he retired in 1994, he could be proud of many successes. One of the most pleasurable was a conference that both looked back to his Leverhulme Fellowship at SOAS and, as it proved, looked forward to future collaboration, particularly over the *JRA*. When in autumn 1991 he received a letter from Richard Gray reminding him that there was a cache of £5,000 remaining from his 1970s Fellowship, his first reaction (after asking whether the money had been earning interest[63]) was to suggest a project for Paul Gifford, with whom he had worked at UZ. The result was another Leverhulme Fellowship, shared with SOAS, and directed there by John Peel (Professor Gray's successor). Paul's recent work for the All Africa Council of Churches (Nairobi), and his excellent relations with many church people and academics across the continent, made him the ideal co-organizer of a conference on 'The Christian Churches and the Democratisation

---

[59] Ibid.
[60] She had a Leeds degree, but in Geography and Botany (1937).
[61] Obituary, *The Independent*, 4 February 2000.
[62] Ibid.
[63] AH's flair for financial management may be one of his lesser-known talents. While not a mathematician, he has an unnerving ability to spot immediately an error or implausibility within dense columns of figures, whether financial accounts or examination marks.

Adrian Hastings with Cardinal Tumi and Archbishop Tutu, Leeds,
September 1993

of Africa'.[64] This meeting, which AH modelled specifically on his Jos conference of 1975,[65] was held in Leeds in September 1993, and it was a tribute both to Paul Gifford's powers of persuasion and to the respect and affection inspired by AH that it was attended by Cardinal Tumi, Archbishop of Douala, Cameroon, and Archbishop Tutu of Cape Town, as well as other leading African churchmen. John Waliggo was there, as were John Peel and Terence Ranger, with David Maxwell and other younger scholars who have since made valuable contributions to the *JRA*. The meeting was a great success, not least in terms of friendly relations between academics and clerics, and its papers were published by Brill in the *Studies of Religion in Africa* series.[66]

The Church in Africa 1450–1950, published shortly after AH's retirement, must stand as a huge achievement of the Leeds years. Other contributors to this volume have offered praise, but it is worth quoting one review which points to our concerns in this *Festschrift*:

> ... Hastings skilfully tells the various 'stories' in a way that gives due place to the foreign missionaries as well as to the indigenous Christians, clerical and lay, upon whom the ultimate success of Christianity depended ... this book [is not] a 'great man' history for Hastings tries very hard to bring out, as far as the sources allow, the nature and character of popular piety, whether of the courtly Catholicism of the Kongo kingdom of the seventeenth century or of the twentieth century evangelical East African Revival movement.[67]

Chapters and Articles: Out of and into Africa

It has proved impossible to tell the story of AH's career without devoting a good deal of space to his books, for the two have been closely intertwined at many points. But an attempt can be made to deal separately with some other sections of his bibliography that do not fit so neatly into the chronological narrative.

---

[64] Additional funding was obtained from the Pew Trusts and the British Academy.

[65] The proceedings were published as *Christianity in Independent Africa*, edited by Edward Fasholé-Luke, Richard Gray, Adrian Hastings and Godwin Tasie, London, Rex Collings, 1978.

[66] Paul Gifford (ed.), *The Christian Churches and Africa's Democratisation*, Leiden, E.J. Brill, 1995.

[67] Andrew Ross, *New Blackfriars*, Vol. 76, No. 897, October 1995, p. 465.

He did not write creatively as a child, surprisingly for someone who has never stopped writing as an adult, and it is not clear how he developed his characteristic style, which appears in his earliest work. To say that something is beautifully written is easy, to explain how is rather difficult. AH's language is clear and concise without being terse, is rarely forced or overblown, has a pleasing rhythm, is often passionate and always informed by an intense concern for his subject. While his writing is supported by careful research and when necessary packed with statistics (see, for example, much of his writing on the Balkan conflicts), he does not distract the reader with excessive referencing. Indeed it could almost be said of him, as it was of another great historian whom he much admired, Sir Richard Southern, 'His work is even shockingly short of the industrial footnotes often thought inseparable from high scholarship'.[68] He writes quickly and with great facility, and one can almost imagine that some pieces have simply sprung from his head, fully armed. This impression is supported by his account of drafting the article on 'Theology' for the *Oxford Companion to Christian Thought*: 'I had no intention of writing it when I set out [on holiday], but it jumped to the top of the queue and would admit no refusal . . . I had no idea all this was going to come into it, until it all insisted on being included.'[69]

Both before and after his positive decision to move away from African research and writing, it has been almost impossible for him to keep Africa out of his work.[70] For example, a fascinating article on 'Holy Lands and their Political Consequences'[71] begins with references to Schoffeleers's Mbona cult, Ranger's Matopos Hills, Gray's Kingdom of Kongo and Lienhardt's rain-making shrine, Luak Deng— then moves quickly to describe Syrian Muslim cosmonauts who served on the Mir space-station, praying at an Orthodox shrine of Our Lady. Again, in 'The Twentieth Century',[72] originally a most suc-

---

[68] Martin Brett, obituary of Sir Richard Southern, *The Independent*, 9 February 2001.

[69] Letter to the author, 9 September 1998.

[70] See Ingrid Lawrie, 'Adrian Hastings: An African Bibliography, 1950–1999', *Journal of Religion in Africa*, XXIX.2, 1999, pp. 230–233.

[71] Originally a lecture given at a conference at the LSE, March 2001. Publication in *Nations and Nationalism* forthcoming.

[72] Published in *Christianity: Two Thousand Years*, Richard Harries and Henry Mayr-Harting (eds.), Oxford, Oxford University Press, 2001. AH was the only non-Oxford academic invited to speak in the series.

cessful lecture[73] in the Oxford millennium series on Christian history, AH ensnares his listeners with the engaging story of the prophet William Wadé Harris:[74]

> In 1910 a Glebo Episcopalian mission teacher in Liberia, William Wadé Harris, had a vision while in prison of the Angel Gabriel. Harris was there for his part in an attempted coup whose aim was to establish British rule in this one nominally independent part of West Africa. He had even raised the Union Jack near his home in Cape Palmas. The coup failed and Harris, who had long prided himself on being a civilized Christian Glebo, wearing western clothes and teaching western ideas, was now disillusioned and in prison, ripe for a religious conversion which made of him the most effective Christian evangelist Africa ever experienced.... The Angel Gabriel had ordered him both to burn the pagan 'fetishes' he had hitherto never given up and to abandon his western clothes, including his shoes, and wear instead a single piece of white cloth with a hole for his head. So dressed and armed with cross, bible and calabash, and accompanied by two wives, he became a prophet of Christ proclaiming God. The shoes had a special poignancy. The Episcopalian clergy were recognized to be the best-dressed body of coloured ministers in Liberia, and Harris had surely been anxious to fit that image. Almost the only thing we have written in his hand is an order in October 1907 for various items from an American catalogue, including a sewing machine and two pairs of 'men's stylish shoes'. How much those shoes must have mattered to him. And how perceptive was the Angel Gabriel to insist that they above all must be abandoned. The prophet of Africa must walk free of all such westernisms.

If his audience remembers nothing else of that evening, they will surely remember the Prophet Harris and his stylish shoes.

But there is cross-fertilization, and AH brings to his African writing a bold and illuminating (and probably unfashionable) variety of western references: biblical, historical, literary, political, contemporary. His inaugural lecture at UZ, 'Mediums, Martyrs and Morals'[75] is a good example of this, as is a 1974 *Tablet* review article, in which he confesses that he finds Idi Amin curiously like Henry VIII:

---

[73] So much so that, in addition to praise heaped on AH himself, a few people felt compelled to e-mail his assistant (who had, after all, only typed the lecture) to report on its enthusiastic reception.

[74] See David A. Shank, *Prophet Harris: The 'Black Elijah' of West Africa*, Leiden, E.J. Brill, 1994. His Aberdeen Ph.D. thesis (1980), *A Prophet of Modern Times: The Thought of William Wadé Harris*, on which the book was based, includes the order for the shoes in the Appendices.

[75] Published in *African Catholicism*, pp. 52–68.

The king was a much better educated man, but apart from that they
have much in common. Both are heavy and athletic, very proud of
their athletic achievement, which goes with a bluff, jovial friendliness,
but also a quick willingness to appeal to religion, conscience and love.
Behind these traits, each has combined a very shrewd eye to political
survival with ruthless cruelty, the speedy annihilation of enemies, including ministers and relatives, from the most distinguished judge down.
Both have made a politic use of public execution, and both have
relieved a state of near bankruptcy brought on through heavy military
expenditure by the systematic expropriation of a wealthy minority
group: the monasteries in Henry's career played the part of the Asians
in Amin's. And each has had a fair number of wives.[76]

John Lonsdale picks this up in his splendid *JRA* review of *The
Construction of Nationhood*,[77] written when AH had ostensibly given up
African scholarship, but containing a strong chapter of African case
studies: 'Only Adrian Hastings could have compared Alfred's trans-
lation of Bede with Nyerere's translations of Shakespeare, or the
Yoruba cleric Samuel Johnson with Bede himself.'[78]

Editing: How to Make Enemies?

Adrian Hastings's entry in *Who's Who* lists cutting hedges among his
interests and the literal cutting back of excess growth to precisely
the right size and shape is a valuable transferable skill for an editor. His own writings show the same application of the shears: they
are never over-long, nor are they too dense.

His first two edited works were rather personal enterprises, in contrast to the commissioned books that came later. *The Church and the
Nations* was part of his Propaganda Fide experience, with suggestions
for contributors coming from friends in the College, and is

> an attempt to describe, on a small scale, some of the richness and
> diversity to be found within the Catholic Church, and to give some
> idea, too, of the difficulties that Catholics have to face in countries
> other than our own. It has been written by men and women from a
> variety of nations and their aim has been to show how far Catholicism

---

[76] 'An African Dictator', a consideration of *General Amin* by David Martin, *The
Tablet*, 6 July 1974.
[77] *The Construction of Nationhood: Ethnicity, Religion and Nationalism*, Cambridge, Cambridge University Press, 1997.
[78] *Journal of Religion in Africa* XXX.1, 2000, pp. 129–133.

is integrated with the national character and national life of their countries and what this integration feels like to them personally.[79]

Bishops and Writers is, on the other hand, a particularly English collection,[80] a *Festschrift* for Garrett Sweeney, Master of St Edmund's
House,[81] where AH had more than once found a home. It appeared
in 1977, followed the next year by *Christianity in Independent Africa*, the
fruits of the Jos Conference, of which, as we have seen, AH was a
co-editor, and to which he contributed a chapter on 'The Ministry
of the Catholic Church in Africa, 1960–1975'.

There is then a gap before we come to the three major edited
works published in the last ten years. First is *Modern Catholicism* (1991),
'an authoritative one-volume guide to the Catholic Church and its
developing life in the quarter-century since the close of the Second
Vatican Council in December 1965'.[82] This was masterminded by
AH from the beginning, but the second of these editorial enterprises,
A World History of Christianity, came to him after the death of Peter
Hinchliff, so the plan was already laid out and authors (including
AH himself) commissioned. However, the work did not proceed
smoothly, and no fewer than four contributors (of the original thirteen) withdrew because of ill health. The final loss the editor decided
to make good himself, with the result that the book contains two
very different chapters by him, one on the early church, the other
on Latin America. He had refused Professor Hinchliff's original invitation to write the African chapter, suggesting instead Kevin Ward,
and chose the more difficult task of writing on a part of the world
outside his specialism. There is no indication of either of these chapters being written under pressure, that on the early church beginning *in medias res*, in typically attention-grabbing fashion: 'In July of
the year 180 a number of very insignificant people, led by a man
named Speratus, coming from the small, now unidentifiable townlet
of Scillium, were brought before the proconsul Saturnius in Carthage
and charged with the practice of an illicit religion.'[83] As always, the
people who make the history, however insignificant in themselves,
are in the forefront.

---

[79] *The Church and the Nations*, Introduction.
[80] AH's own chapter, reprinted in *The Shaping of Prophecy*, is entitled 'Some
Reflexions on the English Catholicism of the late 1930s'.
[81] It gained the status of a College in 1975.
[82] Preface to *Modern Catholicism: Vatican II and After*, London, SPCK, 1991.
[83] *A World History of Christianity*, Chapter 2 '150–550', p. 25.

To meet the deadline for a volume of this size and scope after so many changes of personnel, without allowing one's exacting standards of editorship to waver, while carrying out the many other activities that retirement brings, would seem a formidable task in itself, but all this was happening at the same time as AH's third and greatest editorial project of that decade, *The Oxford Companion to Christian Thought*. Oxford University Press never had reason to regret pressing him to accept the commission for a book of 850,000 words, which was described most generously by David Edwards as 'a feast of knowledge and wisdom and an amazing feat both of organization and of writing by the main editor, Adrian Hastings'.[84] That accolade is particularly gratifying in that AH wrote over 70 (a total of over 100,000 words) of the 600 plus articles, including not only 'Theology', 'History', 'God', 'Political Theology' and the major 'Twentieth Century: An Overview', but also 'Bread', 'Fire', 'Sheep and Shepherds', as well as 'Shakespeare' and 'Teresa of Calcutta'. The fine article on 'African Christian Thought' was written by Kwame Bediako, but AH assigned 'Ethiopian Theology' to himself. Readers of *The Church in Africa 1450–1950* will be aware of his enthusiasm for that country's history.

From 1985 until the end of 1999, whatever his other commitments—writing, editing, running a university department, campaigning on behalf of Bosnians and Kosovars—AH never neglected the *Journal of Religion in Africa*. Although he described the requirement to produce four issues annually as a 'treadmill', he greatly enjoyed the whole process, and devoted an enormous amount of time to getting the best out of authors. Some were deterred by his long, detailed suggestions for revision, but others responded willingly, perhaps to surprise themselves by the quality of the finished paper. The same dedication was given to the *JRA*'s companion monograph series, *Studies of Religion in Africa*, whose editorship AH has now handed on to Paul Gifford, with not a little relief.

When he became editor of the *JRA*, it had not appeared for some time, because of Andrew Walls's illness, but he soon brought it back into production, after an initial near-disaster when one of the articles in his first issue was found to be plagiarized. It also grew in size, from 240 pages per year in 1985 to 512 by the time it was

---

[84] David Edwards, in 'Books of the Year', *The Tablet*, 23/30 December 2000.

entrusted to David Maxwell. Its style changed somewhat too, with more regular special issues on a particular theme or country, sometimes with a guest editor. The reviews side was expanded considerably, particularly during Rosalind Shaw's ten years of service as Reviews Editor.

The Editor had a strict rule of not writing articles for his own journal, and he did not break this until 1998[85] with 'The Christianity of Pedro IV of the Kongo, "The Pacific" (1695–1718)', in a special Lusophone issue, containing articles by two of his former research students, Teresa Cruz e Silva and Jim Grenfell. In the editorial[86] he points out that Portuguese-speaking Africa 'has been excessively marginalised in modern history, religious history especially', in spite of the great wealth of the archival resources ('five hundred years of documents'). He himself made good use of these resources in *The Church in Africa 1450–1950*, especially in a substantial chapter on 'The Kongo, Warri, Mutapa and the Portuguese'. Fortunately for the *JRA*'s Reviews Editors, his self-imposed ban applied only to articles, and, as his bibliography shows, he was generous in providing reviews, sometimes of major works and publications by friends like Matthew Schoffeleers, but sometimes of books he felt might otherwise be overlooked, particularly those by African writers. The ban on articles was lifted on 31 December 1999 and the first issue of the new editorship contained an entertaining synthesis of the *JRA*'s history and place in scholarship.[87] This was originally given as a paper at the memorable Leiden Colloquium, hosted most generously by Brill, our publishers, in June 1999 to mark AH's seventieth birthday and his retirement from the journal.

AH is fond of pointing out that, as he was told by a distinguished scholar, editing is a good way to make enemies. But it is also a good way to make friends, and in his case the balance is very much on the positive side. Over his editorial career there has been much appreciation and gratitude and surprisingly little acrimony, particularly in view of his sometimes impossibly high standards, his very wide knowledge of the subjects on which the writers are meant to

---

[85] Until then his only *JRA* article had been 'Ganda Catholic Spirituality' in VIII.2, 1976, reprinted in *African Catholicism*, pp. 69–81.

[86] *Journal of Religion in Africa*, XXVIII.2, 1998, pp. 129–130.

[87] 'African Christian Studies, 1967–1999: The Reflections of an Editor', *JRA* XXX.1, 2000, pp. 30–44.

be the experts, his outrage at factual errors—a manifestation of the passion which inspires everything he does—and the inevitable biases of an upper-class liberal Catholic.

Journalism: Great Campaigns and Short Letters

Only someone who writes easily and quickly could produce scholarly publications in such quantity as well as a substantial number of newspaper articles, particularly for *The Tablet*, which, as David Maxwell has pointed out, he sees as his pulpit in the Catholic Church.[88] He has been describing and explaining events in Africa and elsewhere for its readers for most of his literary career. From September 1972 to November 1973, he was responsible for a bi-weekly column, 'In the Margin', on whatever subject was to the forefront of his mind.

His two major campaigns, one African, one European,[89] were fought largely with letters and articles in newspapers. The details of the massacres at Wiriyamu and Chawola in Portuguese-occupied Mozambique, their disclosure to the world in July 1973 and the reaction (mostly disbelieving at first) to that disclosure are set out in his book, *Wiriyamu*,[90] written very shortly after the events described. What follows can be no more than an outline.

As we have seen, the young Hastings had criticized Portuguese colonial policy in Goa in the 1950s, and twenty years later he was deeply concerned about what was happening in Mozambique. In the spring of 1973, colleagues at the Catholic Institute for International Relations (CIIR) were planning an anti-Portuguese meeting, with AH as one of the speakers, at Chatham House in London to coincide with a visit by the Prime Minister, Marcelo Caetano. This meeting would no doubt have taken place with a decent minimum of publicity had it not been for a providential combination of circumstances. First, AH was lecturing in Rhodesia in April and May, and happened to meet there members of a Spanish missionary society, the Burgos Fathers, whose priests were also working in Mozambique.

---

[88] Editorial, *Journal of Religion in Africa*, XXIX.2, 1999, p. 136.
[89] An interesting and depressing element of the reaction to these campaigns is that when he writes about Africa, opponents criticize him for not taking up causes closer to home, when he writes about the Balkans, they (perhaps even the same people) ask why he ignores the genocide in Rwanda.
[90] *Wiriyamu*, London, Search Press, 1974.

From them he heard the first claims of recent Portuguese atrocities, though without details or documentation. Second, he had been invited to an ecumenical conference in Salamanca in June, and this gave him the opportunity to visit the Generalate of the Burgos Fathers in Madrid and discover that they possessed the essential detailed documentation, which they mailed to him in England.

The report of the massacre at the village of Wiriyamu on 16 December 1972 was crucial, and he had no doubt about its accuracy:

> The report itself, in its simplicity, its straight forward statement of fact, its precision in naming place, date and individuals, bore the hall-mark of truth. If much of the detail was horrifying, that was unfortunately no reason whatsoever for thinking it not true.... But if it was true, and still more if being true the Portuguese Government had done nothing whatsoever to investigate its charges or punish the culprits, then its significance was immense. It had got to be published.[91]

It was published, in *The Times* on 10 July.

> By 8 a.m. the BBC was on the phone. The storm had begun and for the next ten days it did not stop ... I had not foreseen how vast the reaction would be and how largely everything would depend on me—my credibility, clarity and the firmness with which I held to my position.[92]

Amidst the reaction there was strong support, including very positive meetings at the United Nations in a rapid visit lasting thirty-six hours, but also a great deal of opposition and disbelief, even denials from the Portuguese Embassy and the *Daily Telegraph* that the village of Wiriyamu existed. Of course it had existed, but no longer. In April 1974, Caetano's government fell, for reasons not entirely clear, but it is possible to argue that the disclosure of the massacre at Wiriyamu by an English Catholic priest was one of them.[93]

The first letter in the Balkan campaign was published on 27 November 1991, when most people were just becoming aware that Yugoslavia was no longer a rather pleasant place for a package holiday. The barrage of letters and articles continued throughout the Bosnian war, and was resumed in support of the Albanian majority

---

[91] Ibid., p. 87.
[92] Ibid., p. 88.
[93] AH's continuing involvement in Portuguese politics is described in 'Wiriyamu and its Aftermath', in *The Shaping of Prophecy*, pp. 136–144.

in Kosovo in 1998, alongside appearances on radio and television and participation in public meetings and conferences. For a time, AH partly withdrew from his duties as Head of Department at Leeds, but it was only a nominal withdrawal, and he drove himself hard enough to risk his health. Some friends and colleagues found it difficult to understand (as he did himself) quite why he espoused the Bosnian cause with such extreme passion, since he had hitherto had no particular interest in and no connections with that part of the world. But he very soon became something of an expert on Balkan history, as well as having the latest information about the conflict always at his fingertips, though when asked why he has not written a book about these wars, he claims not to know enough. His commitment to the Balkans continues.

Not all AH's letters have been about war and the destruction of life. They cover a great range, from the metric system to the closure of the Newman-Mowbray bookshop in Oxford, from doctrinal matters to the reform of the House of Lords. Whatever their subject, they display scholarship, passion and the prophetic voice.

> 'Some people write letters, some don't. While most of the great letter-writers have been men of leisure, people who otherwise composed little but used their correspondence as a chief and deliberate vehicle of self-expression, the busy scribblers of books and articles—finding in these more than sufficient outlet for their ideas—have shown little desire to carry the same activity into private life. To this Belloc was a striking exception.'[94]

And Adrian Hastings too. One could almost imagine him composing this passage to supply a future biographer with an apposite quotation, but he was not yet thirty and could not have anticipated that a bibliography of his writings forty years later would include a substantial section of published letters. In private life too, he may be one of the last regular letter writers. He does not use a computer (though he is a fast, and, when necessary, accurate, typist[95]) and is both rather scornful of e-mail and worried for future generations of

---

[94] 'Belloc's Letters', *The Dublin Review*, Summer 1958, p. 169.
[95] His normal practice is to prepare a first draft in longhand, then type this himself, editing as he goes, before handing over this corrected typescript for word-processing. The handwritten additions may wander between lines, fill the margins, shoot off at odd angles, and cross to the back of the page, but the train of thought and the sentence construction never falter for a moment.

historians that such an ephemeral means of communication will result in the disappearance of permanent records. But he is no Luddite, and is very eager to use electronic communication, via an intermediary, when it serves his purpose. E-mail certainly has the great benefit, for someone of his rather impatient nature, of eliciting a quick response.

Conclusion

While AH's pace has gradually slowed in retirement, he continues to be active and productive. In 2000, at the age of seventy, he paid his first visit to Australia, giving lectures, including the keynote address at the annual conference of the Australian Historical Association. This trip was also significant for a number of reunions with fellow students from Propaganda Fide, fulfilling his own prediction of 'a common purpose which will continue to link Propagandists long after they have left the college and returned to their home countries.'[96] In November of the same year he went back to Uganda for the first time since 1972, and his impressions of the country after a twenty-eight-year absence are given in a moving and optimistic article in the *Tablet*.[97] When describing his joyful meetings with his former Bukalasa students, many of whom (including John Waliggo) are now in influential positions in Uganda, he introduces them by their roles in his Shakespearian productions, which remain vividly happy memories for him and for the players.

This chapter, and AH's bibliography, must end somewhere, though it is difficult to draw the line when his writing goes on, when invitations to lecture, now often on nationhood and nationalism,[98] are regularly received, and when at any moment a turn in events in Africa or the Balkans or the Catholic Church can result in a telephone call from the editor of *The Tablet*, requesting another commentary. Some of his subjects are enduring ones: thus we find him first writing about Albania in a *Tablet* article in 1955[99] while the last

---

[96] '"Go and Teach all Nations"', *The Catholic Worker*, Overseas Edition No. 11, September-October, see note 18.

[97] 'Good News from Uganda', 6 January 2001, pp. 6–7.

[98] Resulting from interest in *The Construction of Nationhood*.

[99] 'Albanian Fastness: Where the Curtain is Most Tightly Drawn', *The Tablet*, 7 December 1955, pp. 602–603.

such article in the bibliography, at the end of March 2001, is 'The Albanians: Rebels with a Cause',[100] in response to a new outbreak of fighting in the Balkans. Some subjects, like the ecological crisis, are quite new. 'Beware Apocalypse', published in the first issue of *The Tablet* of 2000, is a devastating and unusually pessimistic prophecy that by the middle of the twenty-first century the effects of global warming will have changed the whole ecological balance of the world, and he calls on those who can see the danger to 'bring the world's leadership to its senses while something can still be done to limit the scale of the disaster'.[101]

One wonders, however, if the despair would have been quite so profound had he been writing at the end of 2000, instead of the beginning. Somewhat to his surprise, he found hope on his return to East Africa, in Uganda, not least in the boys he had taught so many years before who are now 'grappling quite unassumingly with the public needs of today. . . . part of a warm-hearted, effective pro-fessional class, something which simply did not exist thirty years ago.' He concludes: 'It seems to me important that people elsewhere in the world should sense something of the profoundly encouraging transformation of African society and its church in the last few decades, to set against an often unmitigated picture of gloom and doom.'[102]

---

[100] *The Tablet*, 31 March 2001, pp. 440–441.
[101] *The Tablet*, 8 January 2000, pp. 8–9.
[102] 'Good News from Uganda'.

CHAPTER TWELVE

ADRIAN HASTINGS'S BIBLIOGRAPHY, 1950–2002

Ingrid Lawrie

Introduction

This is an unusual bibliography, particularly for an academic historian and theologian, because it contains almost everything published
by Adrian Hastings, African and non-African, from authored books
to correspondence. It was the view of Paul Gifford, editor of Brill's
Studies of Religion in Africa, that to give a rounded picture of AH's
writings it was necessary to include his articles for *The Tablet*, a fascinating collection, as well as pieces written for other newspapers
and his published letters. There is also a section of reviews, demon-
strating a great range of interest and expertise, not to mention an
impressive rate of production. While he has always been a careful
record-keeper, there are inevitably some incomplete entries, particularly dating from times of great activity, like the Bosnian war. There
will certainly be some omissions.[1] In spite of these faults, it is hoped
that the bibliography as a whole shows every facet of Adrian Hastings,
from editor of a major reference work to journalist to outraged
citizen.

Books

Prophet and Witness in Jerusalem: A Study in the Teaching of St Luke,
Longmans, Green and Co. Ltd., London and New York, 1958, 200 pp.

The Church and the Nations, edited with Introduction, pp. xi–xxii, Sheed
and Ward, New York and London, 1958, 260 pp.

One and Apostolic, Darton, Longman and Todd, London/Sheed and
Ward, New York, 1963, 200 pp.

---

[1] After AH fell in March 2001, a planned final check was impossible.

Church and Mission in Modern Africa, Burns and Oates, London/Fordham University Press, New York, 1967, 260 pp.; German translation *Das schwarze Experiment*, Verlag Styria, Graz, 1969; Polish translation *Kosciol I Misje W Afryce*, Pax, Warsaw, 1971.

A Concise Guide to the Documents of the Second Vatican Council, Darton, Longman and Todd, London, Vol. 1, 1968, 246 pp., Vol. 2, 1969, 264 pp.

Mission and Ministry, Sheed and Ward, London, 1971, 214 pp.

Christian Marriage in Africa, SPCK, London, 1973, 185 pp.

Wiriyamu, Search Press, London, 1974, 158 pp.; other editions published in the USA, Kenya, the Netherlands, Germany, Sweden, Poland and Portugal.

The Faces of God, Geoffrey Chapman, London/Orbis, New York, 1975, 165 pp.

African Christianity, Geoffrey Chapman, London/Seabury Press, New York, 1976, 105 pp.; Japanese translation, Kyo Bun Kwan, Tokyo, 1988, 190 pp.

Bishops and Writers, edited with Preface and one chapter, Anthony Clarke, Wheathampstead, 1977, 263 pp.

Christianity in Independent Africa, jointly edited with E. Fasholé-Luke, Richard Gray and Godwin Tasie, and with one chapter, Rex Collings, London, 1978, 630 pp.

In Filial Disobedience, Mayhew-McCrimmon, Great Wakering, 1978, 180 pp.

A History of African Christianity 1950–1975, Cambridge University Press, Cambridge, 1979, 335 pp.

A History of English Christianity 1920–1985, Collins, London, 1986, 720 pp.; 3rd edition, with an additional chapter and the title *A History of English Christianity 1920–1990*, SCM Press, London, 1991; fourth edition, with additional chapters and the title *A History of English Christianity 1920–2000*, SCM Press, London, 2001, 720 pp.

In the Hurricane, Collins, London, 1986, 124 pp.

African Catholicism, SCM Press, London/TPI, Philadelphia, 1989, 208 pp.

The Theology of a Protestant Catholic, SCM Press, London/TPI, Philadelphia, 1990, 213 pp.

Modern Catholicism: Vatican II and After, edited with 2 chapters, SPCK, London/Oxford University Press, New York, 1991, 473 pp.

Church and State: The English Experience (The Prideaux Lectures for 1990), University of Exeter Press, Exeter, 1991, 84 pp.

Robert Runcie, Mowbray, London, 1991, 221 pp.

The Church in Africa 1450–1950, Clarendon Press, Oxford, 1994, 702 pp.

The Shaping of Prophecy: Passion, Perception and Practicality, Geoffrey Chapman, London, 1995, 182 pp.

The Beatitude of Truth: Reflections of a Lifetime by Donald Nicholl, edited with Introduction, pp. xi–xviii, Darton, Longman and Todd, London, 1997, 236 pp.

The Construction of Nationhood: Ethnicity, Religion and Nationalism (The Wiles Lectures for 1996), Cambridge University Press, Cambridge, 1997, 235 pp. Spanish translation, *La construcción de las nacionalidades*, Cambridge University Press, Madrid, 2000.

The Testing of Hearts by Donald Nicholl, edited with Foreword, pp. ix–xvii, Darton, Longman and Todd, London, 1998, 270 pp.

A World History of Christianity, edited with Introduction and two chapters, Cassells, London/Eerdmans, Grand Rapids, 1999, 594 pp.

The Oxford Companion to Christian Thought, edited with 76 entries, Oxford University Press, Oxford and New York, 2000, 777 pp.

Oliver Tomkins: The Ecumenical Enterprise, SPCK, London, 2001, 184 pp.

Booklets

White Domination or Racial Peace?, Africa Bureau, London, 1954, 16 pp.

The World Mission of the Church, Darton, Longman and Todd, London, 1964, 61 pp.; American edition entitled *The Church's Number 1 Problem. Mission*, Paulist Press, New Jersey.

The Church as Mission, Pretoria, 1971, 76 pp.

Church and Ministry, Pastoral Papers 25, Gaba Publications, Uganda, 1972, 52 pp. (a revision of *The Church as Mission*, above).

Christian Marriage in Africa, abridged edition, CLAIM Press, Malawi, 1974, 44 pp. (also published in Swahili and Chewa).

Southern Africa and the Christian Conscience, CIIR, 1975, 16 pp.

The African Church of the 80s, *Mission Today* No. 9, Catholic Missionary Education Centre, London, 1981, 20 pp.

Should Women be Ordained?, Southwell and Oxford Papers on Contemporary Society, 1987, 8 pp.

Gospel and Culture in Africa, *Mission Today* No. 43, Catholic Missionary Education Centre, London 1988, 15 pp.

Where does the Ecumenical Movement Stand Now?, Southwell and Oxford Papers on Contemporary Society, 1988, 12 pp.

SOS Bosnia, Action for Bosnia, London, three editions, 1992, 1993, 1994, 54 pp.

Elias of Dereham: Architect of Salisbury Cathedral, R.J.L. Smith and Associates, Much Wenlock, 1997, 29 pp.

Walter Hilton (Eighth Southwell Lecture, October 1996), Diocese of Southwell 1997, 12 pp.

Nationalism, Genocide and Justice (Las Casas Lecture, November 1998), Blackfriars Publications, Oxford, 1999, 11 pp.

Love and Law: The Nature of Christian Morality. Lincoln Lectures in Theology 2000, Lincoln Cathedral Publications, 2001, 44 pp.

Entries in Encyclopedias and Dictionaries

Encyclopedia of Theology, Karl Rahner (ed.), Burns and Oates, London, 1975.
'Mission', pp. 967–969.

The New Catholic Encyclopedia, Vol. 17, Catholic University of America, Washington, and Publishers Guild, New York, 1979.
'African Christianity', pp. 11–13.

Penguin Dictionary of Religions, John R. Hinnells (ed.), Penguin, 1984.

'African Religions', 'Ancester Veneration (African)', 'Akan Religion', 'Bagre', 'Bantu Religion', 'Chisungu', 'Dinka Religion', 'Divination (African)', 'Divine Kingship (African)', 'Dogon Religion', 'Fon Religion', 'Ganda Religion', 'Ifa', 'Iruva', 'Jok', 'Katonda', 'Leza', 'Lovedu Religion', 'Mbona', 'Mende Religion', 'Mizimu', 'Modimo', 'Mulungu', 'Mwari', 'Ncwala', 'Nganga', 'Nilotic Religion', 'Nkisi', 'Nuer Religion', 'Nyau', 'Nzambi', 'Orisha', 'Rain-Making (African)', 'Shilluk Religion', 'Shona Religion', 'Spirit Possession', 'Witchcraft Eradication (African)', 'Yoruba Religion', 'Zande Religion', 'Zulu Religion'.
New edition, Blackwell 1995, with additional article, 'Igbo Religion'.

The Encyclopedia of Religion, Vol. 3, Mircea Eliade (ed.), Macmillan, New York, 1987.
'Christianity in Sub-Saharan Africa', pp. 411–418.

The New Catholic Encyclopedia, Vol. 18, Catholic University of America, Washington, with Jack Heraty and Associates, Palatine, Illinois, 1989.
'The Catholic Church in England and Wales', pp. 66–72.

The Blackwell Biographical Dictionary of British Political Life in the Twentieth Century, K.G. Robbins (ed.), Blackwell Reference, Oxford, 1990.
'Davidson, Randall', 'Heenan, John', 'Hume, Basil', pp. 121–122, 198–199, 219–220.

Contemporary Religions: A World Guide, I. Harris et al. (eds.), Longman, London, 1992.
'Christianity', pp. 12–20.

Encyclopedia of Language and Linguistics, Vol. 2, R.E. Asher (ed.), Pergamon Press, Oxford, 1994.
'Christianity in Africa', pp. 542–544.

The HarperCollins Encyclopedia of Catholicism, Richard P. McBrien (ed.), HarperCollins, New York, 1995.
'England, Catholicism in', pp. 466–467.

Encyclopedia of Africa South of the Sahara, John Middleton (ed.), Charles Scribner's Sons, New York, 1998.
'Christianity: Overview', 'Equiano, Olaudah', 'Fasiladas', 'Galawdewos', 'Kimbangu, Simon', 'Kiwanuka, Joseph', 'Susenyos', 'Zara Ya'iqob'.

Biographical Dictionary of Christian Missions, Gerald H. Anderson (ed.), Simon and Schuster, New York, 1998.

'Bessieux, Jean Rémi', 'Cardoso, Mattheus', 'Cripps, Arthur Shearly', 'Ezana', 'Hanlon, Henry', 'Hinsley, Arthur', 'Jacobis, Justin de', 'Julian', 'Kitagana, Yohana', 'Kiwanuka, Joseph', 'Kobès, Aloÿs', 'Lavigerie, Charles Martial Allemande', 'Massaja, Guglielmo', 'Mendez, Alphonsus', 'Scott, Michael', 'Vaughan, Herbert'.

Encyclopedia of Politics and Religion, Robert Wuthnow (ed.), Congressional Quarterly Books, Washington DC, 1998.
'Christianity', pp. 131–142, 'Jesus', pp. 424–425.

Religion in Geschichte und Gegenwart, 4th edition, Mohr Siebeck, Tübingen.
Vol. I, 1998: 'Afonso I', 137–138, 'Afrika III Christentumsgeschichte', 148–158, 'Angola', 494–495.
Vol. II, 1999: 'Cardoso, Matteus', 63–64.

The Oxford Companion to Christian Thought, Adrian Hastings (ed.), Oxford University Press, Oxford and New York, 2000.
'Abhisiktananda', 'Anger', 'Antisemitism', 'Apostolicity', 'Blood', 'Body', 'Bread', 'Cathedrals', 'Catholicism', 'Christianity', 'Communion', 'Conciliarism', 'Conscience', 'Constantine', 'Councils', 'de Foucauld, Charles', 'Devil', 'Dialogue', 'Dionysius the Pseudo-Areopagite', 'Discipleship', 'Dualism', 'Episcopate', 'Ethiopian Theology', 'Fire', 'Freedom', 'Freire, Paolo', 'God', 'Hell', 'History', 'Incarnation', 'Introduction', 'Jesus', 'John XXIII', 'Kingship', 'Laity', 'Language', 'Law', 'Lewis, C.S.', 'Light and Darkness', 'Limbo', 'MacKinnon, Donald', 'Maritain, Jacques', 'Modernity', 'Morality', 'More, Thomas', 'Nationalism', 'Natural Law', 'Newman, J.H.', 'Orthodoxy', 'Papacy', 'Patriarchates ', 'Play', 'Political Theology', 'Prayer', 'Prophecy', 'Reason', 'Reconciliation', 'Religion and Religions', 'Rome', 'Salvation', 'Schism', 'Shakespeare, William', 'Sheep and Shepherds', 'Subsidiarity', 'Temple, William', 'Teresa of Calcutta', 'Theology', 'Transubstantiation', 'Truth', 'Twentieth Century: An Overview', 'Ultramontanism', 'Vatican II, Council of', 'Ward, Mary', 'Water', 'Wine', 'Witchcraft'.

International Encyclopedia of the Social & Behavioral Sciences, Neil J. Smelser and Paul B. Baltes (editors-in-chief), Pergamon, Oxford, 2001.
'Catholicism'.

Chapters in Books

'Il nazionalismo e la chiesa in Africa oggi' and 'Una nota di conclusione' in *Il nazionalismo e la chiesa in Africa oggi: Atti della XII Giornata Missionaria per gli studenti ecclesiastici degli Atenei Romani*, Rome, 1955, pp. 22–35 and 44–46.

'Nazionalismo e nazionalismo' in *Il destino dell'Africa*, Vittorino Dellagiacoma (ed.), EMI, Bologna, 1956, pp. 39–53 (a reprint of the above).

'The Teaching of the Faith and the Lay Apostolate' in *Proceedings, East African Lay Apostolate Meeting*, Nyegezi, Tanganyika, 21–27 August 1961, Rome, 1962, pp. 43–53.

'The Theology of Race' in *Race: A Christian Symposium*, Clifford S. Hill and David Mathews (eds.), Victor Gollancz, London, 1968, pp. 135–150.

'From Aramis to Afro-Asia' in *The Experience of Priesthood*, Brian Passman (ed.), Darton, Longman and Todd, London, 1968, pp. 24–36.

'The Papacy and the Church' in *On Human Life*, Peter Harris et al. (eds.), Burns and Oates, London, 1968, pp. 72–85.

'Christian Faith and Social Commitment' in *The Arusha Declaration and Christian Socialism*, Tanzania Publishing House, Dar es Salaam, 1969, pp. 1–10.

'In the Field' in *The Church is Mission*, Geoffrey Chapman, London, 1969, pp. 80–98.

'Factors Relating to Ordinations to the Priesthood in the Roman Catholic Church in Eastern Africa' in *African Initiatives in Religion*, D. Barrett (ed.), East African Publishing House, Nairobi, 1971, pp. 188–197.

'The Ministry of the Catechist Considered Theologically' in *Missionaries to Yourselves*, A. Shorter and E. Kataza (eds.), Geoffrey Chapman, London, 1972, pp. 103–118.

'Ventos de separação' in *O 25 de Abril na Imprensa Estrangeira*, Publicações Dom Quixote, Lisbon, 1974, pp. 99–103.

'Poder Militar em Portugal' in *Portugal na Imprensa Estrangeira—um ano depois*, Publicações Dom Quixote, Lisbon, 1975, pp. 63–64.

'John Lester Membe' in *Themes in the Christian History of Central Africa*, T. Ranger and J. Weller (eds.), Heinemann, London, 1975, pp. 175–194.

'Intermarriage and the Wider Society' in *Beyond Tolerance*, Michael Hurley (ed.), Geoffrey Chapman, London, 1975, pp. 1–8.

'Recent Developments in the Roman Catholic Church' in *The Oxford Conference*, Church Bookroom Press Ltd., London, 1975, pp. 25–36.

'Church-State Relations in Black Africa, 1959–1966' in *The Church in a Changing Society*, CIHEC Conference in Uppsala, August 17–21, 1997, University of Uppsala, pp. 402–407.

'Some Reflexions on the English Catholicism of the late 1930s' in *Bishops and Writers*, Adrian Hastings (ed.), Anthony Clarke, Wheathampstead, 1977, pp. 107–125.

'The Ministry of the Catholic Church in Africa, 1960–1975' in *Christianity in Independent Africa*, E. Fasholé-Luke, R. Gray, A. Hastings, G. Tasie (eds.), Rex Collings, London, 1978, pp. 26–43.

'The Bible, Evangelisation and the World' in *The Bible Now*, Paul Burns and John Cumming (eds.), Gill and Macmillan, Dublin, 1981, pp. 188–199.

'Who Can Prophesy Today?' in *The Burden of Prophecy*, Neil McIlwraith (ed.), SCM Publications, London, 1982, pp. 39–50.

'Why the Church in South Africa Matters' in *Catholics in an Apartheid Society*, Andrew Prior (ed.), David Philip, Cape Town, 1982, pp. 154–166.

'The Theology of Race' in *A Textbook of Christian Ethics*, Robin Gill (ed.), T & T Clark, Edinburgh, 1985, pp. 526–531 (an abbreviation of 'The Theology of Race', 1968).

'The Council Came to Africa' in *Vatican II by those who were there*, Alberic Stacpoole (ed.), 1986, Geoffrey Chapman, London, pp. 315–323.

'AFW as Editor' in *Essays in Religious Studies for Andrew Walls*, James Thrower (ed.), Aberdeen University, 1986, pp. 5–9.

'The Authority of the Church, Universal and Local' in *By What Authority*, Robert Jeffrey (ed.), Mowbray, London, 1987, pp. 51–64.

'Emmanuel Milingo as Christian Healer' in *African Medicine in the Modern World*, Christopher Fyfe and Una Maclean (eds.), African Studies Centre, University of Edinburgh, 1987, pp. 145–171.

'East, Central and Southern Africa' in *World Catholicism in Transition*, Thomas M. Gannon SJ (ed.), Macmillan, New York, 1988, pp. 308–319.

'The Church of the Future' in *Wakefield Cathedral Centenary Lectures 1988*, J. Allen (ed.), Diocese of Wakefield, 1988, pp. 78–90.

'British Academic Journals in Religious Studies: *The Journal of Religion in Africa*' pp. 70–71, and 'Christianity in Africa', pp. 201–210, in *Turning Points in Religious Studies*, U. King (ed.), T & T Clark, Edinburgh, 1990.

'Pluralism: The Relationship of Theology to Religious Studies' in *Religious Pluralism and Unbelief: Studies Critical and Comparative*, Ian Hamnett (ed.), Routledge, London and New York, 1990, pp. 226–240, and in *What Should Methodists Teach?*, M. Douglas Meeks (ed.), Abingdon Press, Nashville, 1990, pp. 118–130.

'Politics and Religion in Southern Africa' in *Politics and Religion in the Modern World*, G. Moyser (ed.), Routledge, London, 1991, pp. 162–188.

'Catholic History from Vatican I to John Paul II' and 'The Key Texts' in *Modern Catholicism*, Adrian Hastings (ed.), SPCK, London/Oxford University Press, New York, 1991, pp. 1–13 and 56–67.

'The Christian-Chinese Encounter' in *All Under Heaven*, A. Hunter and D. Rimmington (eds.), J.H. Kok, Kampen, 1992, pp. 122–126.

'William Temple' in *The English Religious Tradition and the Genius of Anglicanism*, G. Rowell (ed.), Ikon, Wantage, 1992, pp. 211–226.

'All Change: The Presence of the Past in British Christianity' in *2020 Visions*, H. Willmer (ed.), SPCK, London, 1992, pp. 13–29.

'Were Women a Special Case?' in *Women and Missions: Past and Present*, F. Bowie, D. Kirkwood and S. Ardener (eds.), Berg, Providence/Oxford, 1993, pp. 109–125.

'The British Churches in the War and Post-War Reconstruction' in *God's Will in a Time of Crisis: A Colloquium Celebrating the 50th Anniversary of the Baillie Commission*, Andrew R. Morton (ed.), CTPI, University of Edinburgh, 1994, pp. 4–13.

'The Role of Leeds within English Religious History' in *Religion in Leeds*, Alistair Mason (ed.), Alan Sutton, Stroud, 1994, pp. 1–12.

'The Churches and Democracy: Reviewing a Relationship' in *The Christian Churches and the Democratisation of Africa*, Paul Gifford (ed.), E.J. Brill, Leiden, 1995, pp. 36–46.

'African Christianity since Independence: Fifteen Years on from *A History of African Christianity 1950–1975*' in *Christianity in Africa in the 1990s*, Christopher Fyfe and Andrew Walls (eds.), Centre of African Studies, University of Edinburgh, 1996, pp. 17–21.

'The Case for Retaining the Establishment' in *Church, State and Religious Minorities*, Tariq Modood (ed.), Policy Studies Institute, London, 1997, pp. 40–46.

Introduction and Part VIII: 'The Challenges of Modernity' in *Cantuar*, Edward Carpenter, Cassell, London, 1997, pp. xvii–xxviii and 516–560.

'Reconciliation and Bosnia' in *Open Hands: Reconciliation, Justice and Peace Work around the World*, in Barbara Butler (ed.), Kevin Mayhew Ltd., Bury St Edmunds, 1998, pp. 335–340.

'The Christianity of Pedro IV of the Kongo, "The Pacific" (1695–1718)' in *Christen und Gewürze: Konfrontation und Interaktion kolonialer und indigener Christentumsvarianten*, Klaus Koschorke (ed.), Vandenhoeck & Ruprecht, Göttingen, 1998, pp. 59–72.

'150–550' and 'Latin America' in Adrian Hastings (ed.), *A World History of Christianity*, Cassell, London/Eerdmans, Grand Rapids, 1999, pp. 25–65 and 328–368.

'Nationhood and the Nation-State: England and Germany' in *Religious Thinking and National Identity*, Hans-Dieter Metzger (ed.), Philo, Berlin and Vienna, 2000, pp. 17–37.

'Between Augustine and Columba' in *Christian Mission in Western Society: Precedents, Perspectives, Prospects*, Simon Barrow and Graeme Smith (eds.), Churches Together in Britain and Ireland, London, 2001, pp. 50–64.

'The Twentieth Century' in *Christianity: Two Thousand Years*, Richard Harries and Henry Mayr-Harting (eds.), Oxford University Press, Oxford, 2001, pp. 218–236.

'The British Empire and the Missionary Movement' in *Religion und Politik in Deutschland und Großbritannien/Religion and Politics in Britain and Germany* (Prince Albert Studies, vol. 19), Franz Bosbach (ed.), K.G. Saur, Munich, 2001.

'The Clash of Nationalism and Universalism within Twentieth-Century Missionary History' in *Missions, Nationalism and the End of Empire*, Brian Stanley (ed.), Curzon, London/Eerdmans, Grand Rapids, forthcoming 2002.

Articles in Journals

'Saint Benedict and the Eremitical Life', *Downside Review*, April 1950, pp. 191–211.

'The Missionary Vocation', *White Fathers*, June 1950, pp. 3–6.

'St Augustine: Model for our African Apostolate', *Lux*, 1954–5, pp. 4–8.

'Christ's Act of Existence', *Downside Review*, April 1955, pp. 139–159.

'Il Nationalismo in Africa Oggi', *Oltremare*, May and June 1955.

'Africa's Many Nationalisms', *Worldmission*, Fall 1955, Vol. 6, No. 3, pp. 343–354.

'The Prophet's Role in the Living Church', *Downside Review*, January 1956, pp. 38–47.

'Non-Catholic Baptism', *The Life of the Spirit*, April 1957, pp. 475–478.

'The Papacy and Rome's Civil Greatness', *Downside Review*, Autumn 1957, pp. 359–382.

'Home and Away: Towards a Theology of the Road', *The Month*, April 1958, pp. 222–231.

'Belloc's Letters', *The Dublin Review*, Summer 1958, pp. 169–174.

'The Salvation of Unbaptized Infants', *Downside Review*, Spring 1959, pp. 172–178.

'On General Councils', *Afer (African Ecclesiastical Review)*, April 1959, pp. 116–119.

'The Age for Confirmation', *Afer*, January 1960, pp. 43–48.

'Lay Missionaries', *The Old Palace*, No. 18, 1960, pp. 4–5.

'Morals and Worship', *Afer*, July 1960, pp. 188–192.

'Justice for Umbria: On a Walk in Central Italy', *The Month*, August 1960, pp. 106–110.

'The Teaching of the Catholic Faith and the Lay Apostolate', *Afer*, October 1961, pp. 285–293 (reprint of 'The Teaching of the Faith and the Lay Apostolate', *Proceedings, East African Lay Apostolate Meeting*).

'The Position of the Graduate in the Contemporary Church', *Afer*, January 1962, pp. 53–60; partly reprinted in *Search*, August 1962, pp. 131–136.

'Scripture and Tradition', *Afer*, April 1963, pp. 127–134.

'The Nature of the Church', *Afer*, October 1963, pp. 239–244.

'The Sacramentality of the Church', *Eastern Churches Quarterly* XVI, No. 3, 1964, pp. 219–225.

'The People of God', *Afer*, July 1964, pp. 207–213.

'The Church in Afro-Asia Today and Tomorrow', *Afer*, October 1964, pp. 287–298; reprinted as part of *The World Mission of the Church*.

'Ecumenism in Africa', published
(a) in *Teaching All Nations* (Manila), April 1965, pp. 188–195.
(b) in *Afer*, April 1965, pp. 113–120 ('Ecumenical Development in Africa').
(c) as a leaflet by the Africa Centre, London.
(d) in *Notes and Documents* (CIPA, Rome), September-October 1965, pp. 345–353.

'The Pattern of African Mission Work'
(a) published as a leaflet by the Africa Centre, London, 1965.

(b) partly republished in *Search*, February 1966, pp. 374–376.

(c) republished in *Afer*, October 1966, pp. 291–298.

'The Council's Central Achievement: The Constitution on the Church', *Afer*, July 1965, pp. 189–200.

'Missionary Thinking in the Context of Today', *New Blackfriars*, August 1965, pp. 629–639.

Editorial, *Afer*, January 1966, pp. 1–2.

'The Universality of Salvation', *The Clergy Review*, March 1966, pp. 171–184.

'Africa: The Second Revolution', *New Blackfriars*, March 1966, pp. 284–295.

'The Church in Africa', *The Dublin Review*, Spring 1966, pp. 34–47.

'The Ministry in Africa', *Afer*, April 1966, pp. 146–160.

'Christianity and African Cultures', *New Blackfriars*, December 1966, pp. 127–136.

'Ecumenical Reflections', *Afer*, April 1967, pp. 96–100; republished in Germany as 'Ökumene in Mission' in *Theologie der Gegenwart*, 1967, 3, pp. 135–138.

'Missionary Writing Today', *Afer*, April 1967, pp. 179–183.

'Fresh and New', *New Blackfriars*, June 1967, p. 492.

'A Missionary Correspondence' (with Eugene Hillman), *New Blackfriars*, August 1967, pp. 600–608.

'The Missionary Significance of "The Nations"', *Afer*, January 1968, pp. 61–64.

'Recent Missiology', *Afer*, 1969, 2, pp. 206–209.

'The Catholic Church in Tanzania', *Afer*, 1969, 2, pp. 125–30.

'The Theological Problem of Ministries in the Church', *Concilium*, March 1969, pp. 19–24.

'Renewal of the Liturgy in Africa', *Impact* (Lusaka), April 1969.

'From Mission to Church in Buganda', *Zeitschrift für Missionswissenschaft*, 1969, pp. 206–228.

'The Catholic Church in Uganda', *Afer*, 1969, 3, pp. 239–244.

'The Catholic Church in Zambia', *Afer*, 1969, 4, pp. 378–382.

'Independent Churches: Short Reading List', *Afer*, 1969, 4, pp. 417–419.

'The Catholic Church in East Africa', *Convergence* (English and French editions), 1969, 4, pp. 16–18.

'The Ministry in Eastern Africa', *Afer*, 1970, 1.

'We Need a Structural Revolution', *Afer*, 1970, 2, pp. 171–174.

'Intercommunion' (editorial), *One in Christ*, 1, 1971, pp. 14–27.

'The Church's Response to African Marriage', *Afer*, 1971, 3, pp. 193–203.

'Mission and Unity', *One in Christ*, 1, 1972, pp. 21–47; republished as 'Misión y Unidad', in *Misiones Extranjeras*, Madrid, May-June 1972, pp. 3–29.

'Should Church Reform Start from the Top or from Ground Level?', *Concilium*, March 1972, pp. 87–96.

'Celibacy in Africa', *Concilium*, Vol. 8, No. 8, October 1972, pp. 151–156.

'Anglican/Roman Catholic Relations Today and Growth in Intercommunion', *One in Christ*, 1, 1973, pp. 24–34.

'Ordinations and Seminarians Throughout Africa, 1959–71', *Afer*, 1973, 1, pp. 55–59.

'Africa, the Church and the Ministry', *Clergy Review*, January 1973, pp. 21–35, February 1973, pp. 115–129, March 1973, pp. 176–185. Reprinted as 'Restructuring the Ministry in Modern Africa', Bodija, Nigeria; translated into Spanish and published as 'Cuestionamiento y reestructuración de los ministerios en la iglesia a partir de las exigencias vitales de la iglesia africana', in *Misiones Extranjeras*, March-April 1973, pp. 7–41.

'A Report on Marriage', *New Blackfriars*, June 1973, pp. 253–260.

'Is There Room Today for Reciprocal Inter-Communion between Catholics and Anglicans?', *One in Christ*, 4, 1973, pp. 337–353.

'Christianity in Independent Africa', *African Affairs*, April 1974, pp. 229–232.

'Some Reflections upon the War in Mozambique', *African Affairs*, July 1974, pp. 263–276.

Editorial: 'International Consultation on Mixed Marriages, Dublin', *One in Christ*, 4, 1974, pp. 326–331.

'Christianity and Revolution', *African Affairs*, July 1975, pp. 347–361.

'The Question of Guilt in the Origin and Development of a Crisis', *Concilium*, April 1976.

'Ganda Catholic Spirituality', *Journal of Religion in Africa*, VIII.2, 1976, pp. 81–91.

'New Theological Light on Apartheid', *Crucible*, January-March 1977, pp. 16–19.

'Malta, Ten Years Later', *One in Christ*, 1, 1978, pp. 20–29.

'Celibacy', *New Blackfriars*, March 1978, pp. 104–111, reprinted in *Commonweal*, 13 October 1978, pp. 655–658.

'Celibacy: A Final Word', *New Blackfriars*, September 1978, pp. 402–408.

'Intercommunion' (Editorial), *One in Christ*, 4, 1978, pp. 312–317.

'A Theology of Law and Order', *Christian Action Journal*, Summer 1979, pp. 4–5, reprinted in *New Life*, August 1980, pp. 28–32.

'On the Reform of the Ministry', *Bulletin de Théologie Africaine* (Kinshasa), Vol. II, No. 3, January-July 1980, pp. 35–40.

'The Christian Churches and Liberation Movements in Southern Africa', *African Affairs*, July 1981, pp. 345–354.

'Clerical Celibacy: A Personal View', *Law and Justice*, No. 68/69, Hilary/Easter 1981, pp. 29–34.

'Theology and Praxis', *Aberdeen Divinity Bulletin*, No. 22, 1981, pp. 17–19.

'St Paul and Christian Unity', *One in Christ*, 3, 1981, pp. 243–248.

'The Papacy', *One in Christ*, 4, 1982, pp. 300–308.

'Opting for Vatican II Plus', *Journal of Theology for Southern Africa*, December 1982, pp. 25–28.

'Catholic and Protestant', *One in Christ*, 2, 1983, pp. 135–140.

'Origins of Priestly Celibacy', *The Heythrop Journal* XXIV, 1983, pp. 171–177.

'Hope and Optimism', *New Blackfriars*, October 1983, pp. 414–425.

'Mediums, Martyrs and Morals', *Zambezia* (University of Zimbabwe), Vol. 11, No. i, 1983, pp. 1–14.

'On African Theology', *Scottish Journal of Theology*, Vol. 37, 1984, pp. 359–374 (and translated as 'Sobre la teología africana' in *Selecciones de teología* (Barcelona), 1986, Vol. 25, pp. 303–307.

'25 Years of *Afer*. Memories and Hopes: 1. Beginnings', *Afer*, 26, February/April 1984, pp. 5–7.

'Mission, Church and State in Southern Africa: The First 150 Years', *Mission Studies* 2.1, 1985, pp. 22–32.

'"He Must Increase but I Must Decrease"', *New Blackfriars*, July/August 1985, pp. 312–316.

'Cities and Gods', *New Blackfriars*, September 1987, pp. 372–379.

'Fifty Years of Theology at Leeds', *University of Leeds Review*, Vol. 30, 1987/88, pp. 73–94.

'Where Does the Ecumenical Movement Stand Now?', *Anvil*, November 1987, pp. 2–4 and 10–12.

'On Both Sides', *The Franciscan*, Vol. XXX, No. 2, May 1988, pp. 91–93.

'On Persevering through the Dark Night', *CR* (the quarterly review of the Community of the Resurrection), Vol. 341, 1988, pp. 8–13.

'Your High Priest Melchisedek', *Missionalia* Vol. 18, No. 2, 1990, pp. 271–276.

'Western Christianity Confronts Other Cultures', *Studia Liturgica*, Vol. 20, No. 1, 1990, pp. 19–27.

'Church and State in Southern Africa', *African Affairs*, Vol. 91, No. 362, 1992, pp. 134–137.

'Church and State in a Pluralist Society', *Theology*, May/June 1992, pp. 165–176.

'My Pilgrimage in Mission', *International Bulletin of Missionary Research*, April 1992, pp. 60–64.

'Catholics and Protestants', *Interchurch Families*, Vol. 1, No. 1, 1993, pp. 4–7.

'Catholicism and Protestantism', *One in Christ*, 1, 1993, pp. 65–75.

'Henry VIII: Defender of the Faith or Just a Bloody Tyrant?', *Worcester College Record*, 1993, pp. 72–80.

'SOS Bosnia: 28 February 1994', *Theology*, July/August 1994, Vol. 97, No. 778, pp. 242–244.

'Theology and Contemporary Reality', *Milton Keynes and Malvern Papers*, May 1994, pp. 1–10.

'Is Passion Needed for Perception?', *University of Leeds Review*, Vol. 37, 1994–5, pp. 105–111.

'How to be Ecumenical in 1995', *Priests and People*, January 1995, Vol. 9, No. 1, pp. 3–6.

'Some Thoughts on Research Assessment Exercises', *Bulletin of the British Association for the Study of Religions*, No. 75, June 1995, pp. 6–9.

'The Contribution of St Benedict to European Civilisation', *Downside Review*, January 1996, pp. 56–69.

'Proclaiming the Gospel: Michael Ramsey and Oliver Tomkins', *One in Christ*, 1, 1996, pp. 3–21.

'The Diversities of Mission', *Missionalia*, April 1996, Vol. 24.1, pp. 3–16.

'Setting the Scene', *The Way* (special African issue), Vol. 37.3, July 1997, pp. 185–194.

'The Legacy of Pierre Jean de Menasce', *International Bulletin of Missionary Research*, Vol. 21.4, October 1997, pp. 168–172.

'From Africa to Oxford and Back: A Study of the Work of Professor Peter Hinchliff', *Theology*, November/December 1997, pp. 402–410.

'The Cancellation of International Debt', *New Blackfriars*, November

1997, Vol. 78, No. 921, pp. 459–463 (reprinted in the *Church Times*, 5 December 1997).

'The Church in England Today', *Priests and People*, Vol. 11, No. 12, December 1997, pp. 479–483.

'The Christianity of Pedro IV of the Kongo, "The Pacific" (1695–1718)', *Journal of Religion in Africa*, XXVIII.2, 1998, pp. 145–159 (also published as chapter in *Christen und Gewürze*, ed. K. Koschorke, see above).

'Special Peoples', *Nations and Nationalism*, Vol. 5(3), 1999, pp. 381–396.

'On Modernism' (Centenary Lecture of the Modern Churchpeople's Union, Lambeth Palace, 10 November 1998), *Modern Believing*, 40: 2, April 1999, pp. 5–15.

'Nationalism, Genocide and Justice', *Priests and People* Vol. 13, No. 7, July 1999, pp. 255–260 (shortened version of Las Casas lecture).

'African Christian Studies, 1967–1999: Reflections of an Editor', *Journal of Religion in Africa*, XXX.1, 2000, pp. 30–44.

'Cardinal Basil Hume', *Priests and People*, Vol. 14, No. 7, July 2000, pp. 255–259.

'Just War', *The Epworth Review*, 27.3, July 2000, pp. 47–52.

'The English Catholic Agenda, 1850–2000', *Priests and People*, Vol. 14, No. 10, October 2000, pp. 359–363.

'Constructing Nationhood: Between Ethnicity and Geography', *Australian Historical Association Bulletin*, No. 91, December 2000, pp. 47–59.

'Pre-Vatican II English Catholicism: The Case of Oliver Welch', *Downside Review*, Vol. 119, No. 414, January 2001, pp. 11–34.

'Christianity and Nationhood: Congruity or Antipathy', *Journal of Religious History*, October 2001.

'What is Christian Thought Today?', *Priests and People*, Vol. 15, No. 7, July 2001, pp. 270–273.

'Geoffrey Parrinder' (review article), *Journal of Religion in Africa*, XXXI.3, 2001.

Editorials (1–2 pp. each) in the *Journal of Religion in Africa*, between 1985 and December 1999.

Book Reviews

Looking for History in English Churches, M.D. Anderson, *Blackfriars*, September 1951, pp. 437–438.

In a Great Tradition: Tribute to Dame Laurentia McLachlan, Abbess of Stanbrook, by the Benedictines of Stanbrook, *The Tablet*, 22 September 1956.

Anglican Orders, A.A. Stephenson, *Anglican Orders and Defect of Intention*, F. Clark, *Downside Review*, Spring 1957, No. 240, pp. 171–5.

Holy Writ or Holy Church, George H. Tavard, *Catholicisme Romain et Protestantisme*, E. Chavaz, *Downside Review*, Summer 1960, pp. 221–224.

The Spirit and the Word, A.M. Allchin, *Eastern Churches Quarterly*, No. 4, 1964, pp. 345–347.

On Heresy, K. Rahner, *One in Christ*, 2, 1965, pp. 213–215.

The Church is a Communion, J. Hamer, *The Clergy Review*, February 1966, pp. 164–167.

Mission in the New Testament, Ferdinand Hahn, *New Blackfriars*, March 1966, pp. 333–334.

Schism and Renewal, David Barrett, *Target* (Nairobi), August 1968, p. 10.

The Church in Africa: Christian Mission in a Context of Change, William J. Wilson (ed.), *Zeitschrift für Missionswissenschaft und Religionswissenschaft*, February 1969, p. 179.

The Church Crossing Frontiers. Essays on the Nature of Mission, in Honour of Bengt Sundkler, P. Beyerhaus and C.F. Hallencreutz (eds.), *Zeitschrift für Missionswissenschaft und Religionswissenschaft*, 1971, 1, pp. 45–46.

Missionary Enterprise and Rivalry in Igboland 1857–1914, F.K. Ekechi, *The Month*, November 1972.

Does God Say Kill? An Investigation of the Justice of Current Fighting in Africa, John Eppstein, *The Tablet*, 25 November 1972.

Theological Battleground in Asia and Africa: The Issues Facing the Churches and the Efforts to Overcome Western Divisions, G.C. Oosthuizen, *The Tablet*, 9 December 1972.

Bells of Silence, Noel Crusz, *The Tablet*, 3 March 1973, pp. 205–206.

Cold Comfort Confronted, Guy and Molly Clutton-Brock, *Not Alone: A Story for the Future of Rhodesia*, Nan Partridge, *Zimbabwe Now*, S.E. Wilmer (ed.), *The Tablet*, 10 March 1973.

The Temptations of Religion, Charles Davis, *Angels and Dirt: An Enquiry into Theology and Prayer*, John Drury, *The Tablet*, 24 March 1973, p. 282.

Ambrose Reeves: A Biography, John S. Peart-Binns, *Encountering Darkness*, Gonville ffrench-Beytagh, *The Tablet*, 23 June 1973, pp. 587–588.

Theology of Mission, Aylward Shorter, *The Month*, June 1973, pp. 219–220.

The Polygamist, Ndabaningi Sithole, *The Tablet*, 20 October 1973.

African Traditional Religion: A Definition, E. Bolaji Idowu, *Marxist and Kimbanguist Mission: A Comparison*, W.J. Hollenweger, *Theology*, February 1974, pp. 98–99.

Ian Ramsey, Bishop of Durham—A Memoir, David L. Edwards, *Models for Divine Activity*, Ian T. Ramsey, *The Tablet*, 23 February 1974, p. 178.

Black Theology: The South African Voice, Basil Moore (ed.), *The Scope of African Theology*, Charles Nyamiti, *African Culture and the Christian Church*, Aylward Shorter, *The Tablet*, 23 March 1974.

The Ibo People and the Europeans: The Genesis of a Relationship—to 1906, Elizabeth Isichei, *Portuguese Settlement on the Zambezi*, M.D.D. Newitt, *The Tablet*, 11 May 1974, p. 449.

Outlook on a Century: South Africa 1870–1970, Francis Wilson and Dominique Perrot (eds.), *International Review of Mission*, July 1974, pp. 457–458.

The CIA and the Cult of Intelligence, Victor Marchetti and John D. Marks, *The Tablet*, 21 September 1974, pp. 913–914.

The Great Christian Centuries to Come: Essays in Honour of A.M. Ramsey, Christopher Martin (ed.), *The Tablet*, 11 January 1975.

After Polygamy was Made A Sin: The Social History of Christian Polygamy, John Cairncross, *The Tablet*, 18 January 1975, p. 57.

Portugal's African Wars, Arslan Humbaraci and Nicolo Muchnik, *The Last to Leave: Portuguese Colonialism in Africa*, Bruno da Ponte, *The Tablet*, 8 February 1975.

New Testament Christianity for Africa and the World: Essays in Honour of Harry Sawyerr, Mark E. Glasswell and Edward W. Fasholé-Luke (eds.), *Waterbuffalo Theology*, Kosuke Koyama, *The Tablet*, 22 February 1975, p. 177.

Inside the Company: CIA Diary, Philip Agee, *The Tablet*, 8 March 1975.

Rome and Canterbury Through Four Centuries, Bernard and Margaret Pawley, *The Tablet*, 17 May 1975, pp. 457–458.

The Fight for Zimbabwe: The Armed Conflict in Southern Rhodesia since UDI, Kees Maxey, *The Tablet*, 14 June 1975, pp. 553–554.

The Opening of the Nile Basin: Writings by Members of the Catholic Mission to Central Africa on the Geography and Ethnography of the Sudan, 1842–1881, Elias Toniolo and Richard Hill (eds.), *The Tablet*, 21 June 1975, p. 577.

Portugal's Fifty Years of Dictatorship, Antonio De Figueiredo, *The Tablet*, 15 November 1975, p. 1105.

Kimbangu: An African Prophet and his Church, Marie-Louise Martin, *The Tablet*, 22 November 1975, pp. 1132–1133.

Mozambique: Memoirs of a Revolution, John Paul, *New Blackfriars*, January 1976, pp. 46–47.

Ethiopia: The Fall of Haile Selassie's Empire, Colin Legum, *Southern Africa: The Secret Diplomacy of Détente: South Africa at the Crossroads*, Colin Legum, *The Tablet*, 13 March 1976, p. 260.

God in Africa, Malcolm J. McVeigh, *Concepts of God in Africa*, John S. Mbiti, *African Christian Theology*, Aylward Shorter, *The Tablet*, 3 April 1976, pp. 337–338.

The Coming of the Third Church, Walbert Bühlmann, *The Tablet*, 10 April 1976, pp. 369–370.

Polygamy Reconsidered, Eugene Hillman, *The Tablet*, 17 July 1976, pp. 689–690.

From Rhodesia to Zimbabwe, Lawrence Vambe, *The Tablet*, 21 August 1976, pp. 809–810.

Islam and the Confluence of Religion in Uganda, Noel King, Abdu Kasozi and Arye Oded, *Journal of Religion in Africa*, VIII.3, 1976, p. 227.

Quarantine Rhythms, Mudereri Kadhani, *The Tablet*, 13 November 1976, p. 1099.

Change and the Churches, David Perman, *The Tablet*, 20 August 1977, pp. 793–794.

Audacity to Believe, Sheila Cassidy, *The Tablet*, 29 October 1977, p. 1033.

Church and Revolution in Rwanda, Ian Linden, *The Tablet*, 18 February 1978, pp. 153–154.

The Shroud of Turin, Ian Wilson, *The Tablet*, 20 May 1978, pp. 485–486.

Christians and Marxists: The Mutual Challenge to Revolution, José Míguez Bonino, *Christians, Politics and Violent Revolution*, J.G. Davies, *The Clergy Review*, June 1978, Vol. LXIII, No. 6, pp. 238–239.

Black Evangelists: The Spread of Christianity in Uganda 1891–1914, M. Louise Pirouet, *The Tablet*, 12 August 1978, pp. 776–777.

The Heart of the Christian Faith, Donald Coggan, *The Tablet*, 25 November 1978.

Glory Under Your Feet, Michael Marshall, *The Tablet*, 13 January 1979, pp. 35–36.

The Year of the Three Popes, Peter Hebblethwaite, *The Tablet*, 20 January 1979, p. 81.

The Dynamics of Religion: Process and Movement in Christian Churches, Bruce Reed, *The Tablet*, 3 March 1979, pp. 209–210.

Christianity and the World Order, Edward Norman, *The Tablet*, 7 April 1979, pp. 343–344.

Mission Resumed, Michael Winter, *The Tablet*, 28 April 1979, pp. 404–405.

The End of an Era: Africa and the Missionary, Elliott Kendall, *Theology*, May 1979, pp. 226–228.

'Notes quotes', brief reviews of *Faith and Freedom: Towards a Theology of Liberation*, Schubert Ogden, *The Eucharist and Human Liberation*, Tissa

Balasuriya, *This is the Day: A Fresh Look at Christian Unity*, Michael Harper, *The Korsten Basketmakers*, Clive Dillon-Malone, *African Christian Spirituality*, Aylward Shorter, *The Open Secret*, Lesslie Newbigin, *The Tablet*, 21 July 1979, p. 704.

The Mombasa Rising against the Portuguese 1631; From Sworn Evidence, G.S.P. Freeman-Grenville (ed. and trans.), *Entirely for God: The Life of Michael Tansi*, Elizabeth Isichei, *The Tablet*, 17 January 1981, pp. 62–63.

African Socialism in Two Countries, Ahmed Mohiddin, *The Last Days of White Rhodesia*, Denis Hills, *The Struggle for Zimbabwe*, David Martin and Phyllis Johnson, *The Tablet*, 9 May 1981, pp. 454–455.

A Fifth Gospel: In Search of Black Christian Values, Joseph G. Healey, *Africa: The Case for an Auxiliary Priesthood*, Raymond Hickey, OSA, *Prophecy and Revolution*, Nathaniel I. Ndiokwere, *The Tablet*, 7 November 1981, pp. 1098–1099.

Guardians of the Land: Essays on Central African Territorial Cults, J.M. Schoffeleers (ed.), *Journal of Religion in Africa*, XIII.1, 1982, pp. 68–72.

Prophecy and Praxis, Robin Gill, *Marx—Money—Christ*, Oswald Hirmer, *The Gospel according to the Ghetto*, Canaan Banana, *The Tablet*, 24 April 1982, p. 405.

African Religions: A Symposium, Newell S. Booth (ed.), *Journal of Religion in Africa*, XIII.2, 1982, pp. 154–155.

Theology of Promise: The Dynamics of Self-Reliance, C.S. Banana, *Zambezia*, Vol. 10, No. ii, 1982, pp. 155–157.

The Testing of the Churches 1932–1982: A Symposium, Rupert Davies (ed.), *The Heythrop Journal*, Vol. XXVI, No. 4, 1985.

Caught in the Crossfire, Patricia Chater, *The Tablet*, 23 November 1985, pp. 1233–1234.

Windows on Origins, C. Landman and D.P. Whitelaw (eds.), *Views on Violence*, W. Vorster (ed.), *Journal of Religion in Africa*, XVI.1, 1986, p. 80.

Religion and Public Doctrine in Modern England, Maurice Cowling, *The Tablet*, 1986.

Theology on the Way to Emmaus, Nicholas Lash, *The Tablet*, 24 May 1986, pp. 538–539.

Whatever Happened to Vatican II?, Michael Winter, *New Blackfriars*, 1986.

Desire and Denial: Sexuality and Vocation—A Church in Crisis, Gordon Thomas, *The Tablet*, 6 December 1986, pp. 1314–1315.

Africa: The Gospel Belongs to Us. Problems and Prospects for an African Council, Valentino Salvoldi and Renato Kizito Sesana, *Priests and People*, Vol. 1, No. 1, April 1987, p. 35.

The Turn of the Tide: Christian Belief in Britain Today, Keith Ward, *The Tablet*, 1987.

After the Deluge: Essays Towards the Desecularisation of the Church, William Oddie (ed.), *Crucible*, July-September 1987, pp. 140–141.

The Futures of Christianity, David Edwards, *The Tablet*, 1987.

The Politics of Paradise: A Christian Approach to the Kingdom, Frank Field, *The Tablet*, 26 September 1987, pp. 1033–1034.

A Life of Bishop John A.T. Robinson, Scholar, Pastor, Prophet, Eric James, *The Guardian*, 16 October 1987.

The Unacceptable Face: The Modern Church in the Eyes of the Historian, John Kent, *New Blackfriars*, 1987.

Roman Catholics in England, Michael Hornsby Smith, *The Month*, November 1987, pp. 439–440.

Saints, Frank Longford, *The Guardian*, 11 December 1987.

Lovers of Discord: Twentieth Century Theological Controversies in England, Keith W. Clements, *Theology*, June 1988, pp. 329–331.

Theology and Society, Gregory Baum, *The Tablet*, 20 August 1988, p. 961.

A Reader in African Christian Theology, John Parratt, *Religious Studies*, 1988.

Bible and Theology in African Christianity, John Mbiti, *Common Ground: Christianity, African Religion and Philosophy*, Emmanuel Twesigye, *Variations in Christian Theology in Africa*, John Pobee and Carl Hallencreutz, (eds.), *The Origins and Development of African Theology*, Gwinyai Muzorewa, *Christ As Our Ancestor*, Charles Nyamiti, *Journal of Religion in Africa*, XVIII.2, 1988, pp. 196–197.

TheMATK in Between: Christian Healing and the Struggle for Spiritual Survival E. Milingo, *Theology in Africa*, Kwesi A. Dickson, *The Heythrop Journal*, Vol. XXIX, No. 4, pp. 492–494.

My Faith as an African, Jean-Marc Éla, *The Tablet*, 1989.

The Reception of Vatican II, Giuseppe Alberigo, Jean-Pierre Jossua and Joseph Komonchak (eds.), *The Tablet*, 1989.

A Catholic Sudan: Dream, Mission, Reality, Dorothea McEwan, *Journal of Religion in Africa*, XX.3, 1990, pp. 309–310.

Life and Work of Dr J.Th. Van der Kemp 1747–1811, Ido H. Enklaar; *John Philip (1775–1851): Missions, Race and Politics in South Africa*, Andrew Ross, *Journal of Religion in Africa*, XX.3, 1990, pp. 314–316.

A History of African Priests: Katigondo Major Seminary 1911–1986, J.M. Waliggo, *Journal of Religion in Africa*, XX.3, 1990, p. 318.

Michael Ramsey: A Life, Owen Chadwick, *Journal of Theological Studies*, Vol. 42.1, April 1991, pp. 421–423.

The Legion of Christ's Witnesses, Richard Shorten, *Journal of Religion in Africa*, XXI.1, 1991, p. 95.

Église et Histoire de l'Église en Afrique, Giuseppe Ruggieri, *Journal of Religion in Africa*, XXI.2, 1991, pp. 181–182.

Libermann, 1802–1852: Une pensée et une mystique missionnaires, Paul Coulon and Paule Brasseur, *Journal of Religion in Africa*, XXI.2, 1991, pp. 182–183.

Hedge of Wild Almonds: South Africa, the 'Pro-Boers' and the Quaker Conscience 1890–1910, Hope Hay Hewison, *Journal of Religion in Africa*, XXI.2, 1991, pp. 187–188.

Kwame Nkrumah and the Church in Ghana 1949–1966, John S. Pobee, *Journal of Religion in Africa*, XXI.2, 1991, pp. 188–189.

Church and State in Zimbabwe, Carl Hallencreutz and Ambrose Moyo (eds.), *Journal of Religion in Africa*, XXI.2, 1991, pp. 189–190.

A Bibliography of Lugbara Studies and Literature, A.T. Dalfovo, *Journal of Religion in Africa*, XXI.2, 1991, p. 192.

The Laity and the Growth of the Catholic Church in Nigeria, V.A. Nwosu, *Journal of Religion in Africa*, XXI.4, 1991, pp. 380–381.

Church, Conciliarity and Communion, L. Bermejo, *The Tablet*, 9 March 1991.

Église et pouvoir colonial au Soudan français: Administrateurs et missionnaires dans la Boucle Du Niger (1885–1945), Joseph-Roger de Benoist, *Journal of Religion in Africa*, XXII.2, 1992, pp. 189–192.

Black Christians and White Missionaries, Richard Gray, *The Tablet*, 18/25 April 1992.

The Community of the Resurrection: A Centenary History, Alan Wilkinson, *CR*, Epiphany 1993, No. 359, pp. 28–31.

The Community of the Resurrection: A Centenary History, Alan Wilkinson, *Journal of Theological Studies*, Vol. 44.1, April 1993, pp. 446–448.

A New Look at Christianity in Africa, Gerdien Verstraelen-Gilhuis, *Igbo Catholicism: The Onitsha Connection 1967–1984*, Ikenga Ozigboh, *Roman Catholicism in South Eastern Nigeria 1885–1931*, Ikenga Ozigboh; *The Honoured Crusade: Ralph Dodge's Theology of Liberation and Initiative for Social Change in Zimbabwe*, Dickson Mungazi, *Journal of Religion in Africa* XXIV.3, 1994, pp. 269–273.

The Idea of the University: A Reexamination, Jaroslav Pelikan, *Times Higher Education Supplement*, 18 September 1992, p. 22.

Undiscovered Ends: An Autobiography, Bruce Kent, *The Tablet*, 21 November 1992, pp. 1468 and 1470.

The Destruction of Yugoslavia: Tracking the Break-up 1980–92, Branka Magas, *The Tablet*, 27 March 1993, p. 405.

Cardinal Hume and the Changing Face of English Catholicism, Peter Stanford, *The Church under Thatcher*, Henry Clark, *New Statesman and Society*, 23 April 1993, pp. 37–38.

Blackwell Encyclopedia of Modern Christian Thought, Alister McGrath (ed.), *Times Higher Education Supplement*, 6 May 1994.

The Anatomy of the Catholic Church, Before and Since John Paul II, Gerard Noel and Peter Stanford, *The Tablet*, 1994.

Bosnia: A Short History, Noel Malcolm, *New Statesman and Society*, 25 March 1994.

Bosnia and Hercegovina: A Tradition Betrayed, Robert Donia and John Fine, *The Tablet*, 1994.

Christian Mission in the Twentieth Century, Timothy Yates, *Journal of Theological Studies*, April 1995, 46.1, pp. 413–415.

The Transformation of Anglicanism, William Sachs, *Journal of Theological Studies*, April 1995, 46.1, pp. 415–418.

Cardinal Lavigerie: Churchman, Prophet and Missionary, François Renault, *International Bulletin of Missionary Research*, April 1995, pp. 85–86.

The Church in the Nineties: Its Legacy, its Future, Pierre M. Hegy (ed.), *The Tablet*, 1995.

Balkan Odyssey, David Owen, *New Statesman & Society*, 8 December 1995, pp. 31–32.

Christianity in Africa: The Renewal of a Non-Western Religion, Kwame Bediako, *The Church Times*.

Vatican II Commence . . . Approches francophones, É. Foullioux (ed.), *Journal of Ecclesiastical History*, Vol. 47, No. 1, January 1996, pp. 204–206.

With No Peace to Keep . . . United Nations Peacekeeping and the War in the Former Yugoslavia, Ben Cohen and George Stamkoski (eds.), *The Tablet*, 17 February 1996, pp. 229–30.

Two Thousand Years of Christianity in Africa: An African History, 62–1992, John Baur, *International Bulletin of Missionary Research*, Vol. 20.3, July 1996, pp. 130–131.

A History of Christianity in Africa, from Antiquity to the Present, Elizabeth Isichei, *Modern Churchman*, 1996.

Interpellations et croissance de la foi: hommage au Professeur Abbé V. Mulago Gwa Cikala, Facultés Catholiques de Kinshasa, *Journal of Religion in Africa*, XXVII.1, 1997, pp. 98–99.

The Archives of the Congregation of the Immaculate Heart of Mary (CICM-SCHEUT) (1862–1967), 2 vols., D. Vanysacker, L. Van Rompaey, W. Bracke and B. Eggermont (eds.), *Journal of Ecclesiastical History*, Vol. 48.3, July 1997, p. 595.

History of Vatican II, Vol. I, *Announcing and Preparing Vatican Council II: Towards a New Era in Catholicism*, Giuseppe Alberigo and (for the

English version) Joseph A. Komonchak (eds.), *Journal of Ecclesiastical History*, Vol. 48, No. 3, July 1997, pp. 598–599.

Religion and Politics in East Africa: The Period Since Independence, Holger Bernt Hansen and Michael Twaddle (eds.), *Journal of African History*, 1997.

Christianity: The First Two Thousand Years, David Edwards, *The Tablet*, 20/27 December 1997, p. 1653.

The Bridge Betrayed: Religion and Genocide in Bosnia, Michael A. Sells, *The Heythrop Journal* 39.1, January 1998, pp. 92–94.

Taking Sides, Against Ethnic Cleansing in Bosnia, Workers Aid for Bosnia, *Bosnia Report*, June-July 1998, p. 9.

Fire and Water: Basic Issues in Asian Buddhism and Christianity, Aloysius Pieris, *The Tablet*, 30 May 1998, p. 705.

Dominican Gallery: Portrait of a Culture, Aidan Nicholls, *Priests and People*, August/September 1998, Vol. 12, Nos. 8 and 9, pp. 350–351.

Committed to Conflict: The Destruction of the Church in Rwanda, Laurent Mbanda, *The Tablet*, 3 September 1998, p. 1152.

Light to the Isles: A Study of Missionary Theology in Celtic and Early Anglo-Saxon Britain, Douglas Dales, *The Furrow*, November 1998, pp. 650–651.

Achille Ratti: Pape Pie XI. Actes du colloque organisé par l'École française de Rome (Rome, 15–18 mars 1989), Philippe Levillain (ed.), *Journal of Ecclesiastical History*, Vol. 50, No. 1, January 1999, pp. 176–177.

A History of the Popes, 1830–1914, Owen Chadwick, *Journal of Theological Studies*, April 1999, Vol. 50.1, pp. 408–411.

The Missionary Factor in Ethiopia, G. Haile, A. Lande and S. Rubenson (eds.), *Journal of African History*, Vol. 40, 1999, p. 486.

The Dominican Friars in Southern Africa: A Social History (1577–1990), Philippe Denis, *Journal of Religion in Africa*, XXIX.2, 1999, pp. 237–239.

The Churches in England from Elizabeth I to Elizabeth II, Vol. III *1833–1998*, Kenneth Hylson-Smith, *Modern Believing*, Vol. 40, 4, 1999.

In Search of Truth and Justice: Confrontations between Church and State in Malawi 1960–1994, Matthew Schoffeleers, *Journal of Religion in Africa*, XXIX.4, 1999, pp. 494–496.

The Worlock Archive, Clifford Longley, *The Tablet*, 11 December 1999, p. 1683.

Mary Douglas: An Intellectual Biography, Richard Fardon, *Journal of Contemporary Religion*, Vol. 15, No. 2, May 2000, pp. 282–283.

From Without the Flaminian Gate: 150 Years of Roman Catholicism in England and Wales 1850–2000, V.A. McClelland and M. Hodgetts (eds.), *Priests and People*, Vol. 14, No. 6, June 2000, pp. 249–251.

A History of the Church in Africa, Bengt Sundkler and Christopher Steed, *The Tablet*, 8 July 2000, p. 926.

The Dominican Friars in Southern Africa: A Social History (1577–1990), Philippe Denis, *Journal of Ecclesiastical History*, Vol. 51, No. 4, October 2000, p. 800.

Christianity: A Global History, David Chidester, *The Times Literary Supplement*, 17 November 2000, p. 28.

The Kongolese Saint Anthony: Dona Beatriz Kimpa Vita and the Antonian Movement, John Thornton, *Journal of Religion in Africa*, XXX.4, 2000, pp. 510–512.

Faith on the Frontier: A Life of J.H. Oldham, Keith Clements, *Journal of Religion in Africa*, XXXI.1, 2001, pp. 125–127.

The Holocaust: A Short History, Wolfgang Benz, *Church Times*, 5 January 2001, p. 15.

Cardinal Ratzinger: The Vatican's Enforcer of the Faith, John L. Allen Jr, *The Tablet*, 3 February 2001, pp. 153–154.

Lord Acton, Roland Hill, *Priests and People*, Vol. 15, No. 5, May 2001, pp. 208–209.

Papal Sin, Garry Wills, *Times Literary Supplement*, 22 June 2001, p. 31

A Century of Catholic Endeavour: Holy Ghost and Consolata Missions in Kenya, Lawrence M. Njoroge, *The Catholic Missionaries Within and Beyond the Politics of Exclusivity in Colonial Malawi, 1901–1945*, Stanislaus C. Muyebe, *Journal of Religion in Africa*, XXXI.3, 2001.

Articles in the Tablet

'Portugal, India and Goa II: A Roman View of the Problem', 11 December 1954, pp. 575–576.

'Reunion in South India: The Malankara Experience', 28 May 1955, p. 520.

'After Colonialism: Separation or Integration?', 20 August 1955, pp. 172–173.

'Albanian Fastness: Where the Curtain is Most Tightly Drawn', 17 December 1955, pp. 602–603.

'Catholics at Oxford: At Home and Not at Home', 26 January 1957, p. 82.

'Uganda Today. I: The Old Kingdoms', 28 November 1959, pp. 1028–1029.

'Uganda Today. II: The New Politicians', 5 December 1959, pp. 1054–1055.

'Another Issue in Equatorial Africa: Buganda's Claim to Survival', 23 April 1960, pp. 388–389.

'Uganda's Rival Loyalties: The Case for the Kabaka', 8 October 1960, pp. 908–909.

'An African Archbishop for Uganda: Building on the Foundations of Eighty Years', 11 February 1961, pp. 126–127.

'Uganda's Coming Elections: The Alternatives in a Time of Decision', 11 March 1961, pp. 221–222.

'The Future of Uganda: Keeping Religious Affiliations out of Politics', 16 September 1961, pp. 874–876.

'An Independent Uganda: Next Week's Lukiko Elections', 17 February 1962, pp. 149–151.

'The Independence of Uganda: Church and State Look to the Future', 6 October 1962, pp. 926–927.

'Uganda's Good Record: Constitutional and Progressive', 17 October 1964, pp. 1163–1164.

'An Encyclical from Pope Gregory II', 3 August 1968, p. 764.

'East Africa on the Move I: Nyerere's Tanzania', 1 August 1970, pp. 734–735.

'East Africa on the Move II: Growing Pains of Two Peoples', 8 August 1970, pp. 756–757.

'East Africa on the Move III: Mr Vorster's Neighbours', 15 August 1970, pp. 780–782.

'East Africa on the Move IV: The Writing on the Wall', 22 August 1970, pp. 805–807.

'After the Ugandan Coup', 10 July 1971, p. 663.

'Tanzania's Lonely Leader', 17 July 1971, p. 688.

'The Rhodesian Reality', 25 September 1971, pp. 923–924.

'South African Developments', 9 October 1971, pp. 972–973.

'South Africa 2: The Mounting Crisis', 16 October 1971, pp. 995–996.

'South Africa 3: The Uncertain Future', 23 October 1971, pp. 1021–1022.

'In the Margin' (Liturgical Reform, post-Vatican II), 9 September 1972, p. 863.

'In the Margin' (The Dangerous Ambitions of President Amin), 23 September 1972, p. 903.

'In the Margin' (Episcopal Appointment), 7 October 1972, p. 959.

'In the Margin' (Nigeria Revisited), 21 October 1972, p. 1011.

'In the Margin' (Marginal People), 4 November 1972, p. 1049.

'In the Margin' (Investment in South Africa), 18 November 1972, p. 1103.

'In the Margin' (Mixed Marriages), 2 December 1972, p. 1142.

'In the Margin' (Homelessness), 16 December 1972, p. 1207.

'In the Margin' (Christian Journalism in Africa), 6 January 1973, p. 9.

'In the Margin' (Dividing the Dioceses), 20 January 1973, p. 57.

'In the Margin' (Sharing Churches), 3 February 1973, p. 105.

'In the Margin' (Immigration), 17 February 1973, p. 153.

'In the Margin' (Reconciliation in Ireland), 3 March 1973, p. 201.

'In the Margin' (The Fourth World), 17 March 1973, p. 248.

'In the Margin' (Romanisation or Modernisation), 31 March 1973, p. 305.

'In the Margin' (Death Transfigured), 14 April 1973, p. 359.

'In the Margin' (*Scientia cordis*), 5 May 1973, p. 423.

'In the Margin' (The Church in Rhodesia), 19 May 1973, p. 472.

'In the Margin' (Seminary Renewal), 2 June 1973, p. 518.

'In the Margin' (Anglican Bishops), 16 June 1973, p. 566.

'In the Margin' (Intercommunion), 30 June 1973, p. 607.

'In the Margin' (Mission or Maintenance), 14 July 1973, p. 656.

'In the Margin' (Wiriyamu), 28 July 1973.

'In the Margin' (Why Mozambique?), 11 August 1973, p. 752.

'In the Margin' (Stanbrook Abbey), 25 August 1973, p. 805.

'In the Margin' (Wilfrid Scawen Blunt), 8 September 1973, p. 855.

'In the Margin' (Celibacy), 22 September 1973, p. 902.

'In the Margin' (*Virus Italiano*), 6 October 1973, p. 944.

'In the Margin' (The Future of the African Church), 20 October 1973, p. 992.

'In the Margin' (The Liberal Tradition), 3 November 1973, p. 1048.

'Africa's New Rulers, 10 November 1973, pp. 1055–1056.

'In the Margin' (Christianity in Post-Colonial Africa), 17 November 1973, p. 1088.

'An African Dictator' (a consideration of *General Amin*, by David Martin), 6 July 1974, pp. 644–645.

'A Church in Isolation—Portugal', 12 and 19 April 1975, 356–7.

'Angola's Dogs of War', 2 August 1975.

'Sermon on Portugal', 9 August 1975.

'Africa's Military Rulers', 1 November 1975.

'The Priesthood Today', 8 and 15 May, 1976.

'A Word to Anglicans', 13 November 1976.

A Statement on Communion of the Cup, 26 February 1977.

Sermon in Westminster Abbey, 7 January 1978.

African Christianity, extracts from, 12 May and 19 May 1979.

'The Zimbabwe I Know', 30 March 1985, pp. 328–332.

'Is there Room for Me?', 24 August 1985, pp. 875–878.

'An Idealist Steps Down' (on Julius Nyerere), 21/28 December 1985, pp. 1334–1336.

'The Prince of Peace', 22/29 December 1990, p. 1645.

'Henry VIII: Defender of the Faith, or Just a Bloody Tyrant', 29 June 1991 (also in the *Worcester College Record*, see above).

'Resist the Aggressors!' (Viewpoint), 29 August 1992.

On Bosnia, 10 October 1992.

'Give Bosnia a Chance', 16 January 1993.

'Croats and Muslims', 2 October 1993.

'A Prophet in Canterbury' (on William Temple), 22 October 1994, pp. 1342–1343.

'A Turning Point in Bosnia', 12 November 1994, pp. 1432–1435.

'Serbs Against Fascism', 6 May 1995.

'Countdown to a Bloodbath' (on Rwanda), 9 November 1996, pp. 1464–1467.

'The Butcher of the Balkans', 10 October 1998, pp. 1304 and 1306.

'Fighting for Peace', 3/10 April 1999, p. 462.

'What Will Become of Serbia?', 1 May 1999, pp. 580–581.

'This is Not a Just War', 5 June 1999.

'Where Have All the Catholics Gone?: 4, Meeting the Challenge', 14 August 1999, pp. 1102–1103.

'Beware Apocalypse', 8 January 2000, pp. 8–9.

'Sisters For All That', 21 October 2000, pp. 1410–1411.

'Good News from Uganda', 6 January 2001, pp. 6–7.

'Congo is Just Too Big', 27 January 2001, pp. 106–107.

'The Albanians: Rebels with a Cause', 31 March 2001, pp. 440–441.

Articles in Newspapers (excluding The Tablet*)*
and Minor Journals

'Christians can Conquer the Colour Bar', *The Catholic Worker*, Overseas Edition No. 2, December-January 1954–5.

'Social Problems in Buganda', *The Catholic Worker*, March-April 1955.

'"Go and Teach All Nations"', *The Catholic Worker*, Overseas Edition No. 11, September-October 1955.

'Comment on Current Affairs: Hungary and Suez', *The Catholic Worker*, January 1957.

'Simon of Cyrene', *Catholic Digest*, April 1958.

'Ecumenism among Christians', *Sharing*, June 1970.

'Vocations Explosion?', *Sharing*, June 1971.

'The Geographical Feat and the Missionary Enterprise', *USPG Network*, May 1973.

On Mozambique, *The Times*, 10 July 1973.

'The Three Inquiries: The Missionaries, the Bishops, and the Army' (on Wiriyamu), *The Times*, 2 August 1973.

On Mozambique, *The Observer*, 26 August 1973.

On Mozambique, *The Catholic Herald*, 14 December 1973.

'Portugal's Other Rebellion', *The Observer*, 21 April 1974.

'The Wind of Partition', *The Guardian*, 17 May 1974.

'Relaxed Vigour of African Christianity', *The Times*, 25 May 1974.

'Inter-Church Marriage as Stepping Stone to Christian Unity', *The Times*, 23 November 1974.

Interventions in 'Socialismo e Liberdade', *Jornal Novo*, Lisbon, 23 and 24 July 1975.

'Communion of the Cup', *The Catholic Herald*, 29 April 1977.

'Pope John Paul I,' *The Times*, 14 October 1978.

'The Case against Celibacy', *The Scotsman*, 6 June 1979.

'The Zimbabwe I Know', *Moto* (Harare), May 1985 (also published in *The Tablet*).

'Ecclesial-sclerosis', *The Catholic Herald*, 29 November 1985.

'Tackling the Bishop of Durham's Doubts', *Catholic Herald*, 13 June 1986.

'The Hurricane that Could Save Catholicism', *The Guardian*, 6 October 1986.

'Married Priests—A Wider Precedent', *The Catholic Herald*, 10 April 1987.

'The Primate and the Premier', *The Times*, 31 December 1990.

'Robert Runcie and Religious Leadership', *The Observer*, 3 February 1991.

'The Umpire Between Truths', *The Times Higher Education Supplement*, 7 September 1991.

'A City Siege that Challenges a Continent's Traditions' (on the Bosnian war), *The Scotsman*, 12 December 1992.

'Suitable Case for Intervention' (on the Bosnian war), *The Guardian*, 17 December 1992.

'A Crime that Puts the Church to Shame' (on the Bosnian war), *The Guardian*, 3 July 1993.

'The Role of Dr Owen', *Executive Intelligence Review*, 27 August 1993, pp. 36–7, and *Neue Solidarität*, 18 August 1993, p. 2.

'The Real Role of Unprofor', *The Guardian*, 2 November 1993.

'The Arms Embargo is Immoral', *Bosnia Report*, No. 4, February–March 1994.

'Bosnia, Coming Back from the Dead', *European Brief*, March/April 1994.

'On Bosnia, Washington Should Stop Deferring to London and Paris', *International Herald Tribune*, 29 November 1994 (with Norman Stone, Mark Almond, Noel Malcolm, Branka Magas).

'Time to Take Sides', *Christian Socialist*, No. 158, Autumn 1995.

'When It's Immoral *Not* to Trade Guns', *Focus on Ireland and the Wider World*, Issue 56, Summer 1997.

'Another Year Older and Deeper in Debt', *Church Times*, 5 December 1997 (reprinting of *New Blackfriars* article of November 1997).

'Responsibility for Srebrenica', *Bosnia Report*, 1 (New Series), Nov-Dec 1997.

'Authority Will Come with Unanimity' (on the 1998 Lambeth Conference), *Church Times*, 17 July 1998.

'This is War', *Catholic Post* (Diocese of Leeds), May 1999.

Obituaries

'In Memoriam: J. Kiwanuka', *Afer*, April 1966.
Oliver Green-Wilkinson, *The Times*, 11 September 1970.
Charles Runge, *The Tablet*, 1970.
David Knowles, *The Tablet*, 4 January 1975.
Martin Jarrett-Kerr, *The Guardian*, 27 November 1991.
Robert Liddell, *The Times*, 7 August 1992.
Christopher Gray, *The Guardian*, 15 August 1996.
Donald Nicholl, *The Independent*, 7 May 1997
Donald Nicholl, *The Tablet*, 10 May 1997.
Charles Davis, *The Independent*, 5 February 1999.
Julius Nyerere, *The Tablet*, 23 October 1999.

Constance Millington, *The Independent*, 4 February 2000.
Donald Coggan, *The Tablet*, 27 May 2000.
Robert Runcie, *The Tablet*, 15 July 2000.
Carl Fredrik Hallencreutz, *Journal of Religion in Africa*, XXXI.2, 2001.

Letters

On Indo-China, *The Tablet*, 21 August 1954.
On Goa, *The Catholic Herald*, 3 and 24 September, 1954.
On Goa, *The Tablet*, 15 January 1955.
On South Africa, *The Tablet*, 26 May and 16 June 1956.
On Suez, *The Catholic Herald*, 1956.
On Hungary, *The Catholic Herald*, 16 November 1956.
On Anglican Orders, *The Downside Review*, Summer 1957, pp. 199–201,
    January 1958, pp. 119–122.
On the Dialogue Mass, *The Tablet*, 6 April 1957.
On arms to South Africa, *The Times*, 1970.
On South Africa, *The Tablet*, 5 September 1970, p. 866.
On South Africa and the future, *The Tablet*, 6 November 1971,
    p. 1078.
On the Rhodesian settlement, *The Times*, 22 January 1972.
On Mozambique, *The Times*, 16 July 1973.
On Mozambique, *The Daily Telegraph*, 17 July 1973.
On Mozambique, *The Universe*, 3 August 1973.
On Mozambique, *The Times*, 9 August 1973.
On Mozambique, *The Guardian*, 9 August 1973.
On Mozambique, *The Catholic Herald*, 10 August 1973.
On Wiryamu, *The Daily Telegraph*, 23 August 1973.
On Wiriyamu, *The Tablet*, 2 March 1974.
On Portugal and Mozambique, *The Times*, 11 June 1974.
On Portugal and Mozambique, *The Tablet*, 29 June 1974.
On the Portuguese revolution, *The Times*, 29 May 1975.
On Marxism, *The Times*, 24 October 1975.
On Angola, *The Times*, 30 December 1975.
On black clergy in South Africa, *The Times*, 24 June 1976.
On the Tridentine mass, *The Times*, 12 August 1976.
On celibacy, *The Tablet*, 6 November 1976.
On reconciliation in Ulster, *The Times*, 12 January 1977.
On schools in Ulster, *The Times*, 29 June 1977.

On miles and kilometres, *The Times*, 4 January 1978.

On intercommunion, *The Times*, 6 February 1978.

On the Church, *The Tablet*, 22 April 1978.

On the Shroud of Turin, *The Tablet*, 20 May 1978.

On celibacy, *The Catholic Herald*, 14 April 1978.

On celibacy, *The Times*, 22 June 1978.

On the magisterium and contraception, *The Tablet*, 14 October 1978.

On priesthood, *The Tablet*, 20 January 1979.

On AH's marriage, *The Catholic Herald*, 22 June 1979.

On AH's marriage, *The Tablet*, 23 June 1979.

On Fermanagh and Tyrone, *The Times*, 20 April 1981.

On Mozambique (reply to Sir Patrick Wall), *The Catholic Herald*, 24 July 1987.

On the AUT pay dispute and the obligation to examine, *The Independent*, 21 March 1989.

On historic memories, *The Independent*, 23 June 1990.

Reply to review of *Modern Catholicism* by Aidan Nichols, *Priests and People*, Vol. 5, No. 6, June 1991, pp. 243–244.

On Ph.D. supervision and completion rates, *Times Higher Education Supplement*, 22 November 1991.

Reply to Cardinal Ratzinger, *The Tablet*, 23 November 1991.

On Serbian aggression, *The Times*, 27 November 1991.

On European inaction in Bosnia, *The Times*, 13 May 1992.

On sanctions on Serbia, *The Times*, 9 June 1992.

On the Bosnian airlift, *The Times*, 8 July 1992.

On the policy of appeasement in Bosnia, *The Independent*, 23 July 1992.

The world's response to Serbian aggression, *The Guardian*, 4 August 1992.

On a holocaust in Bosnia, *The Tablet*, 8 August 1992.

On assistance to Bosnia, *The Independent*, 8 August 1992.

On UN and EC betrayal of Bosnia, *The Guardian*, 19 September 1992.

On the library of the University of Sarajevo, *The Higher*, 2 October 1992.

On the destruction of Bosnia's identity, *The Guardian*, 10 October 1992.

On the siege of Sarajevo, *The Times*, 16 October 1992.

On the siege of Sarajevo, *The Times*, 31 October 1992 (with Saba Risaluddin, Michael Foot, Trevor Huddleston, Zaki Badawi, Hugo Gryn, Lord Hylton, Russell Johnston).

On Bosnia, *The Independent*, 2 December 1992.

On Bosnia, *The Catholic Herald* and *The Tablet*, 5 December 1992.

On Bosnia, *The Observer*, 17 January 1993.

On Bosnia, *The Tablet*, 13 February 1993.

On the United Nations in Bosnia, *The Guardian*, 20 February 1993.

On 'ethnic cleansing' in Bosnia, *The Guardian*, 22 April 1993.

On conflict and dialogue in Bosnia, *The Times*, 28 April 1993.

On crime and passion in Bosnia, *The Guardian*, 12 June 1993.

On Bosnia, *The Guardian*, 18 June 1993.

On military and political options for a Bosnian solution, *The Times*, 8 July 1993.

On the siege of Sarajevo and the survival of Bosnia, *The Guardian*, 26 July 1993.

On Bosnia, *The Tablet*, 31 July 1993.

On intervention in Bosnia, *The Independent*, 12 August 1993.

On the division of Bosnia, *The Guardian*, 21 August 1993.

On Serbia as aggressor, *Die Welt*, 31 August 1993.

On the injustice of proposals for Bosnia, *The Independent* and *The Guardian*, 31 August 1993 (with David Alton and nine others).

On Bosnia, *The Tablet*, 11 September 1993.

On Unprofor in Bosnia (reply to Douglas Hogg, 6.11.93), *The Guardian*, 9 November 1993.

On humanitarian aid to Bosnia, *The Guardian*, 25 November 1993.

On the siege of Sarajevo, *The Times*, 16 December 1993.

On responsibility of Mr Hurd, *The Guardian*, 28 December 1993.

On the Bosnian war, *The Guardian*, 22 January 1994.

On legality and the Bosnian war, *The Guardian*, 14 February 1994.

On the lessons of Goražde, *The Times*, 26 April 1994.

On understanding the Bosnian war, *Church Times*, 22 July 1994.

On the plot against Hitler, *The Tablet*, 30 July 1994.

On peace in the Balkans, *The Guardian*, 11 November 1994 (with David Alton, Michael Foot, Reginald Hibbert, Noel Malcolm, Norman Stone, Calum Macdonald, Malcolm Wicks).

On Douglas Hurd and aid for the Pergau dam, *The Times*, 16 November 1994.

On the Bosnian war and VE celebrations, *The Guardian*, 10 May 1995.

On Srebrenica, *The Guardian*, 15 July 1995.

On war crimes and the future of Bosnia, *Church Times*, 18 August 1995.

On planning peace for Bosnia, *The Independent*, 9 September 1995.

On the Serbs of northern Bosnia, *The Independent*, 20 September 1995.

On the Bosnian peace agreement, *The Independent*, 24 November 1995.

On Karadzic's regime in Bosnia, *The Independent*, 4 March 1996.

On elections in Bosnia, *The Guardian*, 11 September 1996.

On the Newman Bookshop (Oxford), *The Tablet*, 10 May 1997.

On Sinn Fein MPs and the oath of allegiance, *The Independent*, 19 May 1997.

On the Northern Ireland peace process, *The Independent*, 9 July 1997.

On arresting Bosnian war criminals, *The Times*, 22 August 1997.

On clerical celibacy, *The Independent*, 11 September 1997.

'Orangemen's Choice', *The Independent*, 13 July 1998.

On the early popes, *The Tablet*, 26 September 1998, and 17 October 1998.

On action over Kosovo, *The Times*, 6 October 1998.

On the House of Lords, *The Times*, 5 December 1998.

On priorities for Nato peace negotiators, *The Times*, 1 March 1999.

On Nato airstrikes on Kosovo, *The Times*, 23 March 1999.

On the war in Kosovo, *The Independent*, 1 April 1999.

'Mary as Priest', *The Tablet*, 29 January 2000, and 26 February 2000.

'Struggle for a School', *The Tablet*, 3 June 2000.

On Leonard Cheshire and Donald Nicholl, *The Tablet*, 22 July 2000.

On Sister Churches, *The Tablet*, 18 November 2000.

FOUR POEMS FROM ZAIRE
FOR ADRIAN HASTINGS

Donald Mackay

1. *Out of my Light*
(Bas-Zaire, 1981)

Into another ruined square I'd trail
Stanley-wise. Palms, forest leaves overhung
Tungwa, Kimpete, low eaves on houses,
Dogs and children with thin scabby faces,
children with big eyes, dusty skins wailing
'Mundele!', darting off, and then daring
a hand to touch at clothes, at my white arm.
In every town the smells, the heavy hung
smell of cassava soaking, rotting down,
chikwanga, fufu and a whiff of dung.
This was Africa, where to be pauper
or rich was minimal, measured out
in Chinese saucepans, cheap enamel ware;
the equal poor, with their measure of fear
of me entering like reason's saint.
Months over months, my over-mind darkened
and panicked. Europe vanished to a point
beyond the darkened door. Night was fearful
of movements in bedding sacks, in the air,
of holes in the corners. A little child
would have done better. He would have entered
happily the hand-made houses full of rats,
while I remained the emissary of glass,
cleanliness, to be seen through a window
of their devising, my quiet escape
behind white blinds.
   And yet ways still opened.
Thomas Nduma offered me a door
in through his prophecy. To me he said,

'You are a magi, sent here; you will pass
laden but empty into the stable.
Bend to the dirt, to rebirth. Seek and find.'
I should have bent, come in. I wasn't able.

2. *Mbanza Makuta*

A tree still stood,
A huge mahogany
Above a brushy wood

Was there, they said,
In Comber's time. We stood
Where once Makuta spread,

Where the roads met
And waited, the roads down
From where the River brought

The ivory
To this *mbanza*, city-state,
The richest ferrying

To Ambrizette.
We came to a village,
We got bored, we got wet

One afternoon
In the afternoon rains
Where there once was a town

And then walked on
Through the bewildered place
As Comber once had done.

3. *Kindoki, Kinsundi*

(for Tata Mpidisi,
d. 1985, 'empoisonné')

'It's bad for witches here.'
No sign
Of anybody anywhere,
Sandy-
Clean underfoot
And sin
He says it's atmosphere.
No saying
What it is I fear
But houses
Sitting with dark doors,
Spaces
Neat, not derelict.
He says
He saw the dog that looked
As we walked
Up over the hill lacked
A shadow.
He says that's how you know
After we're through, on tiptoe.

4. Human Geography

If you have seen a street after torrential rain
When the sun comes out and tarmac glistens
Steaming, and gutter-water heads for the drain,
Then you have seen the Congo, more or less,
Heading out of Malevu Pool in the long rush
Of its last three hundred miles to the sea.
I used to sit at first, there in Kinshasa
Trying again to tell myself to see
This flat, fattened mass of cubic water
As a wonder, the grandiloquent venture
Into the dark heart. When all that was there
Was a river with overly lush verdure,
The lost-causes of Belgian steamers, rusting,
And, right behind, Kinshasa's heart pulsating.

INDEX

Abeokuta, 129, 131–33, 138, 144, 148
Aberdeen, University of, 348–50
Abraham Church/Ethiopian Church/Topia Church, 245, 248
Acholi, 202–23
Achte, Fr Auguste, 67–68, 78–79, 82–83, 85–86
Aegidius, Brother, 104
AFER (African Ecclesiastical Review), 342–43
Africa Bureau, 338–39
African Assemblies of God, 242, 244–45
African Church (Malawi), 245, 248
African Church of St Francis, 114
African Inland Mission (AIM), 177, 185
African Greek Orthodox Church, 177
African National Congress, 101
Afrikania Movement (see also Damuah, Vincent), 5, 10, 12–13, 271–74, 277–93
Afrikania Voice (see also Damuah, Vincent), 278
Afrikan Renaissance Mission (ARM), 292–93
Agriculture, 45, 70, 97, 121–23, 167, 229
Aké: The Years of Childhood (Soyinka), 129, 131–33, 136–37
Akinyele, Bishop A.B., 131
Akurinu Churches (Independent Christian Churches) (see also *Dini ya Jesu Kristo*, Ethiopianism, Maranke, Masowe, Pentecostalism), 14, 159, 163, 178–79, 181–82, 192
Alcazar-el-Kabir, Battle of (1578), 27
Alcohol, 60, 90–91, 111–13, 124, 165, 175, 238–39, 246, 251, 257, 260, 304–05, 321, 326
Alexander I, Tsar, 46
All Africa Council of Churches, 353
Alvaro I, King of Kongo, 28
Alvaro II, King of Kongo, 31–33, 38
Ambassadors (to papacy), 3, 29–38

AMECEA (Association of the Members of Episcopal Conferences in Eastern Africa), 343
America, United States of, 6, 14, 16, 18–21, 43, 95, 96–97, 99, 138, 147, 154, 157, 185, 201, 241, 275–76, 298–99, 302–03, 307–10, 313–15, 319, 326, 329
American Methodist Episcopal Church (AMEC) (see also Methodists), 95, 119–26
Amin, President Idi, 5, 7, 199, 202–04, 209, 211–23, 357–58
Amissah, Archbishop John Kodwo, 274–75
Ana Afonso de Leão, Queen of Kongo, 25–26
Anaman, Revd J.B., 282
Ancestor Church, see Church of the Black Ancestors
Ancestor veneration, 8–9, 31, 100, 112, 121, 124, 126, 161–62, 190, 231, 250, 276, 289, 304
Anderson, Benedict, 127
Anglican Church of Kenya (ACK), 186
Anglican Roman Catholic Preparatory Commission, 343–44
Anglicanism (see also *Balokole*, Anglican Church of Kenya, Church of Uganda, Church Missionary Society, Society for the Propagation of the Gospel, Theology, UMCA, Westminster Abbey), 5–6, 11, 95–98, 109–114, 116, 125–26, 129, 148, 157, 163, 177, 182–85, 190, 199–223, 295, 345, 346–47
Angola, 27, 297
Anyuru, Abdulla, 221
Apostolic Churches, 238–42, 244–47
Apostolic Faith Church, 119–20, 238–41, 245, 260
Apostolic Faith Mission (AFM), 116, 240, 245, 298–301
Apostolics, see Maranke and Masowe
Arabic, 42–43, 48
Armando, 257–58
Asante-Antwi, Revd Dr S., 291

STUDIES OF RELIGION
IN AFRICA

SUPPLEMENTS TO THE JOURNAL OF RELIGION IN AFRICA

1. MOBLEY, H.W. *The Ghanaian's Image of the Missionary*. An Analysis of the Published Critiques of Christian Missionaries by Ghanaians, 1897-1965. 1970. ISBN 90 04 01185 4
2. POBEE, J.S. (ed.). *Religion in a Pluralistic Society*. Essays Presented to Professor C.G. Baëta in Celebration of his Retirement from the Service of the University of Ghana, September 1971, by Friends and Colleagues Scattered over the Globe. 1976. ISBN 90 04 04556 2
3. TASIE, G.O.M. *Christian Missionary Enterprise in the Niger Delta, 1864-1918*. 1978. ISBN 90 04 05243 7
4. REECK,D. *Deep Mende*. Religious Interactions in a Changing African Rural Society. 1978. ISBN 90 04 04769 7
5. BUTSELAAR, J. VAN. *Africains, missionnaires et colonialistes*. Les origines de l'Église Presbytérienne de Mozambique (Mission Suisse), 1880-1896. 1984. ISBN 90 04 07481 3
6. OMENKA, N.I. *The School in the Service of Evangelization*. The Catholic Educational Impact in Eastern Nigeria 1886-1950. 1989. ISBN 90 04 08932 3
7. JĘDREJ, M.C. & SHAW, R. (eds.). *Dreaming, Religion and Society in Africa*. 1992. ISBN 90 04 08936 5
8. GARVEY, B. *Bembaland Church*. Religious and Social Change in South Central Africa, 1891-1964. 1994. ISBN 90 04 09957 3
9. OOSTHUIZEN, G.C., KITSHOFF, M.C. & DUBE, S.W.D. (eds.). Afro-Christianity at the Grassroots. Its Dynamics and Strategies. Foreword by Archbishop Desmond Tutu. 1994. ISBN 90 04 10035 0
10. SHANK, D.A. *Prophet Harris, the 'Black Elijah' of West Africa*. Abridged by Jocelyn Murray. 1994. ISBN 90 04 09980 8
11. HINFELAAR, H.F. *Bemba-speaking Women of Zambia in a Century of Religious Change (1892-1992)*. 1994. ISBN 90 04 10149 7
12. GIFFORD, P. (ed.). *The Christian Churches and the Democratisation of Africa*. 1995. ISBN 90 04 10324 4
13. JĘDREJ, M.C. *Ingessana*. The Religious Institutions of a People of the Sudan-Ethiopia Borderland. 1995. ISBN 90 04 10361 9
14. FIEDLER, K. *Christianity and African Culture*. Conservative German Protestant Missionaries in Tanzania, 1900-1940. 1996. ISBN 90 04 10497 6

15. OBENG, P. *Asante Catholicims*. Religious and Cultural Reproduction Among the Akan of Ghana. 1996. ISBN 90 04 10631 6
16. FARGHER, B.L. *The Origins of the New Churches Movement in Southern Ethiopia, 1927-1944*. 1996. ISBN 90 04 10661 8
17. TAYLOR, W.H. *Mission te Educate*. A History of the Educational Work of the Scottish Presbyterian Mission in East Nigeria, 1846-1960. 1996. ISBN 90 04 10713 4
18. RUEL, M. *Belief, Ritual and the Securing of Life*. Reflexive Essays on a Bantu Religion. 1996. ISBN 90 04 10640 5
19. McKENZIE, P. *Hail Orisha!* A Phenomenology of a West African Religion in the Mid-Nineteenth Century. 1997.
ISBN 90 04 10942 0
20. MIDDLETON, K. *Ancestors, Power and History in Madagascar*. 1999.
ISBN 90 04 11289 8
21. LUDWIG, F. *Church and State in Tanzania*. Aspects of a Changing Relationship, 1961-1994. 1999. 90 04 11506 4
22. BURKE, J.F. *These Catholic Sisters are all* Mamas! Towards the Inculturation of the Sisterhood in Africa, an Ethnographic Study. 2001.
ISBN 90 04 11930 2
23. MAXWELL, D., with I. LAWRIE (eds.) *Christianity and the African Imagination*. Essays in Honour of Adrian Hastings. 2001.
ISBN 90 04 11668 0